THOMAS CRANE PUBLIC LIBRARY

QUINCY MASS

CITY APPROPRIATION

BLOOM'S PERIOD STUDIES

BLOOM'S PERIOD STUDIES

LITERATURE OF THE HOLOCAUST

Edited and with an introduction by
Harold Bloom
Sterling Professor of the Humanities
Yale University

CHELSEA HOUSE
PUBLISHERS
A Haights Cross Communications Company
Philadelphia

©2004 by Chelsea House Publishers, a subsidiary of
Haights Cross Communications.

A Haights Cross Communications ◀┬ Company

Introduction © 2004 by Harold Bloom.

All rights reserved. No part of this publication may be
reproduced or transmitted in any form or by any means
without the written permission of the publisher.

Printed and bound in the United States of America.
10 9 8 7 6 5 4 3 2 1

Library of Congress Cataloging-in-Publication Data
Literature of the Holocaust / edited and with an introduction by Harold Bloom.
    p. cm. — (Bloom's period studies)
Includes bibliographical references and index.
Contents: The Holocaust in the stories of Elie Wiesel / Thomas A. Idinopulos — The
problematics of Holocaust literature / Alvin H. Rosenfeld — Tragedy and the Holocaust /
Robert Skloot — Holocaust documentary fiction / James E. Young — Holocaust and
autobiography / Joseph Sungolowsky — The Holocaust / Deborah E. Lipstadt — Primo Levi
and the language of witness / Michael Tager — The utopian space of a nightmare / Barbara
Chiarello — The literature of Auschwitz / Lawrence L. Langer — Comedic distance in
Holocaust literature / Mark Cory — Public memory and its discontents / Geoffrey H.
Hartman — Two Holocaust voices / Lawrence L. Langer — The Holocaust and literary
studies / Jeffrey M. Peck — Rafael Seligmann's Rubinsteins Versteigerung / Ritchie Robertson
— Memorizing memory / Amy Hungerford.
   ISBN 0-7910-7677-6 (hc) — ISBN 0-7910-7985-6 (pbk.)
   1. Holocaust, Jewish (1939-1945), in literature. [1. Holocaust, Jewish (1939-1945), in
literature.] I. Bloom, Harold. II. Title. III. Series.
   PN56.H55L575 2003
   809'.93358—dc22

                                                              2003016888

Chelsea House Publishers
1974 Sproul Road, Suite 400
Broomall, PA 19008-0914

http://www.chelseahouse.com

Contributing Editor: Robertson Erskine
Cover designed by Keith Trego
Layout by EJB Publishing Services

Contents

Contents

Editor's Note

My Introduction meditates briefly upon what seems the impossibility of reading Holocaust literature from a merely aesthetic perspective.

Elie Wiesel, the most renowned of authors in this terrifying mode, is interpreted by Thomas A. Idinopulos as an heir of Hasidic wisdom, while Alvin H. Rosenfeld wonders if the influence of Camus and Sartre upon Wiesel was more inhibiting than ennobling.

For Robert Skloot, the literary form of stage tragedy seems an appropriate figuration for telling aspects of the Holocaust story, after which James E. Young invokes "documentary fiction" as a more appropriate form.

Autobiography, to Joseph Sungolowsky, seems still more the rightful genre, while Deborah E. Lipstadt tends to emphasize ghetto diaries.

The poignance of Primo Levi's mingled drive to bear witness and suicidal doubts as to such a possibility, are chronicled by Michael Tager, after which Barbara Chiarello, in a gallant effort of an essay, considers whether nightmare and Anne Frank's wistfulness can coexist.

Lawrence L. Langer makes a strong effort to summarize aspects of the literature of Auschwitz, while sardonic humor is studied as a distancing device by Mark Cory.

The major literary critic Geoffrey Hartman profoundly analyzes the strife between our "information sickness" and the humanity of personal memory.

Lawrence L. Langer returns by contrasting the autobiographical voice in Art Spiegelman to the "pure invention" of Cynthia Ozick, after which Jeffrey M. Peck investigates the interview as another literary resource in the study of the Holocaust.

Ritchie Robertson sees Rafael Seligman as a kind of Israeli-German-Jewish answer to Philip Roth, while Amy Hungerford concludes this volume by engaging Cathy Caruth's ongoing study of how trauma is transmitted.

HAROLD BLOOM

Introduction

I recall—some years back—rising up and abandoning a conference at the University of Indiana, when I heard a rabbi proclaim that the Holocaust was now permanently an aspect of "the Jewish religion." Whatever that religion was, is, or yet may be, the Holocaust is no part of it. In my own understanding, the Jewish religion is, in any case, not at all a question of believing that "something is so," unlike both Christianity and Islam. Judaism, of any authentic kind, entails trusting in the Covenant, and trust and belief are very different matters.

The most celebrated aesthetic remark about the Holocaust was Adorno's, who told us that after Auschwitz all poetry was barbaric. The distinguished American-Jewish poet Anthony Hecht once said to an equally eminent American-Jewish poet, Mark Strand, what could they do if Adorno was right, to which Strand replied: "After Auschwitz, we still eat lunch."

I confess that I do not know exactly what "Holocaust literature" is, and to avoid merely vulgar misunderstandings, I add that almost all of my own father's and mother's families were slaughtered by the Germans and their eager Polish, Ukrainian, Romanian, Hungarian, and other European helpers. If I remain skeptical about the literature of the Holocaust, my recalcitrance has to do with what is or is not possible to represent in imaginative literature. I doubt that a committee of Dante, Shakespeare, Milton, and Blake, despite their superhuman gifts, could be equal to such an endeavor.

The very rare achievements in this traumatic area would include the stunningly oblique poems of Paul Celan and the uncanny prophecies of Kafka, greatest of modern Jewish writers, in such fragments and stories as "The Hunter Gracchus," "A Country Doctor," "The Bucket Rider," and "In the Penal Colony."

Trauma, by its nature, has to be private. When it becomes public, then it threatens to join the dehumanizing "information sickness" against which Geoffrey Hartman eloquently warns us.

1

THOMAS A. IDINOPULOS

The Holocaust in the Stories
of Elie Wiesel

The stories, essays, and reportage of Elie Wiesel have been dominated to date by a single theme: the Holocaust. His writings are not, however, contributions to the historical and psychological study of the death camps seeking answers to the questions *How?* and *Why?* For Wiesel the destruction of six million men, women, and children, methodically and without passion, is a terrifying mystery before which one's reason is silenced. Facts can be discovered and explanations given, but the act of "making sense" is somehow incommensurable with the catastrophe.[1] The enormity of the evil, suggested in the very word—*holocaust*—forces Wiesel beyond explantions to judgments that one must call *theological*. For a fire lit by men with purpose of consuming men strikes at the very heart of creation; and it compels the survivor to ask not only whether God rules the universe but whether he deserves to rule. It is in a way Job's question that Wiesel raises in his stories, the question of divine justice or the morality of God; but he also raises the question at the heart of mediaeval Jewish mysticism, whether God truly defeated Satan in the primeval struggle—a question inescapable for one contemplating Job in the light of Auschwitz.[2]

Wiesel's childhood faith in the goodness and promise of God was forever shattered when as a young boy he was deported along with his family from their native Transylvania to Auschwitz. Arriving at Auschwitz Wiesel learned what Dostoevsky in his own time knew, that the sin against the child

From *Responses to Elie Wiesel*, ed. Harry James Cargas. © 1978 by Persea Books.

is the only unforgivable sin, for it indicts not only man but man's creator. Echoing Dostoevsky, he writes: "A Child who dies becomes the center of the universe: stars and meadows die with him." In one long train ride, Wiesel had been transported from the only world he had known, that of a young Jew growing up, devoutly studying Talmud by day, the Cabbala by night, to a new world which he describes in these stark lines:

> Never shall I forget that night, the first night in camp, which has turned my life into one long night, seven times cursed and seven times sealed. Never shall I forget that smoke. Never shall I forget the little faces of the children, whose bodies I saw turned into wreaths of smoke beneath a silent blue sky.

> Never shall I forget those flames which consumed my faith forever.

> Never shall I forget that nocturnal silence which deprived me, for all eternity, of the desire to live. Never shall I forget those moments which murdered my God and my soul and turned my dreams to dust. Never shall I forget these things, even if I am condemned to live as long as God himself. Never.[3]

The question of God is one strand in Wiesel's response to the Holocaust. Woven tightly with it is a second: the memory of the Holocaust, felt as an agonizing obligation on the part of the survivor. The hero of Wiesel's early stories is ashamed at having survived the dead. He yearns to crawl back into the grave. He cannot regard his life as any less absurd than the fire that turned into smoke his father, mother, and sister. He has survived, but it is a survival he can no more come to terms with than the wholly meaningless deaths visited on his family and the millions of others. His link with the past is found in the refrain, "Never shall I forget." He says of himself, "I was now just a messenger of the dead among the living."[4] This is Wiesel's own confession. In remembering the dead through his stories, Wiesel gives them honor; letting them speak again, he cheats the death factories of what would be their final victory, the silencing of each soul in the abstractness of the number *6,000,000*. "The act of writing," he says, "is for me often nothing more than the secret or conscious desire to carve words on a tombstone: to the memory of a town forever vanished, to the memory of a childhood in exile, to the memory of all those I loved and who, before I could tell them I loved them, went away."[5]

Wiesel begins to remember in his memoir, *Night*, when he tells the story of Sighet, his home town in Hungary, and recalls Moche the Beadle of the synagogue, and Kalman, the Hasid who initiated him in the mysteries of the Cabbala. What gives his writing its power is that the act of recollection is suffused with a sense of that deep mystery—how in one long night a small world of Jews, their lives and their history over centuries, could become transformed into a column of white smoke. It is the juxtaposition of the Holocaust with the sweetness of a child's memory of growing up that produces in *Night*, and in the stories that followed, a curious blend of beauty and suffering.

Story-telling is the medium of remembering for Wiesel. The meaning he discovers in the art of story-telling and its relation to his own life constitutes a third strand in his response to the Holocaust. In telling the story the dead are honored and the survivor can affirm his own life. The Hasidic saying which serves as prologue to his novel *The Gates of the Forest* could well be taken as prologue to Wiesel's whole authorship:

> When the great Rabbi Israel Baal Shem-Tov saw misfortune threatening the Jews it was his custom to go into a certain part of the forest to meditate. There he would light a fire, say a special prayer, and the miracle would be accomplished and the misfortune averted.

> Later, when his disciple, the celebrated Magid of Mezritch, had occasion, for the same reason, to intercede with heaven, he would go to the same place in the forest and say: "Master of the Universe, listen! I do not know how to light the fire, but I am still able to say the prayer," and again the miracle would be accomplished.

> Still later, Rabbi Moshe-Leib of Sasov, in order to save his people once more, would go into the forest and say: "I do not know how to light a fire, I do not know the prayer, but I know the place and this must be sufficient." It was sufficient and the miracle was accomplished.

> Then it fell to Rabbi Israel of Rizhyn to overcome misfortune. Sitting in his armchair, his head in his hands, he spoke to God: "I am unable to light the fire and I do not know the prayer; I cannot even find the place in the forest. All I can do is to tell the story, and this must be sufficient." And it was sufficient.

God made man because he loves stories.[6]

The evil of the Holocaust is impenetrable, but as a story-teller Wiesel can create a meaning where there was none before. And, as the Hasidic legend suggests, the art of the story is the telling of it. In telling his story, Wiesel is the artist who, to use Joseph Conrad's words, "speaks to our capacity for delight and wonder, to the sense of mystery surrounding our lives; to our sense of pity and beauty and pain."[7]

The alternative to art is madness. Madmen people Wiesel's stories, for it is in madness that one comes closest to perceiving the actual meaning of the Holocaust.[8] Wiesel suggests that there is a bond of madness which unites victims, survivors, and even executioners. In one story, after the Germans have machine-gunned all the Jews of a small village in the Carpathian mountains, the officer in charge discovers that one Jew has escaped the slaughter, that he is standing before his killers continuing to sing the song all the Jews were singing during the massacre. The officer tries unsuccessfully to kill this lone survivor; finally in desperation he falls to his knees before him, recognizing that in some fantastic way victim has become conqueror, and he says,

> You're humiliating me, you're taking your revenge. One day you'll regret it. You'll speak, but your words will fall on deaf ears. Some will laugh at you, others will try to redeem themselves through you. You'll try to reveal what should remain hidden, you'll try to incite people to learn from the past and rebel, but they will refuse to believe you. They will not listen to you. In the end you'll curse me for having spared you. You'll curse me because you'll possess the truth, you already do; but it's the truth of a madman.[9]

The question of God, the obligation to remember the past, and the importance of story-telling are intertwined in Wiesel's effort to create a meaning, a "legend" as he calls it, for all the people destroyed in the Holocaust. They are the motifs of all his stories, beginning with his memoir *Night*. However, in observing the succession of stories beginning with *Night*, one recognizes a development of sensibility in Wiesel's hero, a vision of escaping the nightmare of the past that becomes fully articulated in Wiesel's masterpiece, *The Gates of the Forest*.

Wiesel concludes his memoir with his liberation from Buchenwald. Looking at himself in the mirror for the first time since leaving the ghetto in

Hungary, he says, "From the depths of the mirror, a corpse gazed back to me. The look in his eyes, as they stared into mine, has never left me." Here Wiesel expresses his feeling of being haunted by the past, of belonging more to the dead than the living; it is the feeling that defines the central character in his stories *Dawn*, *The Accident*, and *The Town Beyond the Wall.*

Each of these stories has as its hero a survivor of the death camps who is struggling to discover in the past some meaning that will fulfill his obligation to the dead and thus justify his survival. In *Dawn* the hero, Elisha, has gone to Palestine after his release from a concentration camp to join an underground struggling to liberate Palestine from British control. Elisha learns that the death of his father in Buchenwald cannot be avenged when he is assigned the task of killing a British officer in reprisal for the execution of a Jewish agent. He recognizes that the ghost of the past cannot be exorcised by another death; rather, when he becomes an executioner, his dead reproach *him* for being a murder. The story ends when Elisha, confronted by the terrible ambiguity of living through his memories, realizes that he has found no way of overcoming the past.

It is in *The Town Beyond the Wall* that Wiesel expresses most deeply his feeling that memory has chained him to a ghost-filled past. Here the hero, now called Michael, has convinced himself that if he returns to his home town in Hungary and confronts the past, then somehow the ghost of the past will be exorcised. Michael both succeeds and fails in his mission. He returns to discover that a town which willingly emptied itself of all its Jews has erased the memory. No one there can remember the day in which the Jews were torn from their homes and deported by cattle car to their deaths. Where there is no memory there is no past, no pity, no sense of shame or of loss, no recognition of guilt. Michael eventually recognizes that the return to his home town is not a return to a past whose meaning he can recover. He sees that on the day that he, his family, and all the other Jews were rounded up in the synagogue and put on a train for Auschwitz, on that day the town of Szerencsevaros ceased to exist for Jews, just as Jews ceased to exist for the good citizens who continued to live out their lives in Szerencsevaros.

Though the journey to discover the meaning of the past has been a failure, it has made it possible to honor the memory of the dead, to repay a debt to the past. This occurs when Michael seeks out a man whom he remembers as watching at his window with indifference, each day for a week, the town's Jews being herded into the synagogue for deportation. Michael wants to look into this man's face, to talk to him, to understand how a man could remain indifferent to what he saw. The man is found, and Michael accuses him.

People of your kind scuttle along the margins of existence. Far from men, from their struggles, which you no doubt consider stupid and senseless. You tell yourself that it's the only way to survive, to keep your head above water. You're afraid of drowning, so you never embark. You huddle on the beach, at the edge of the sea you fear so much, even to its spray. Let the ships sail without you! Whatever their flag—Communist, Nazi, Tartar, what difference does it make? You tell yourself, "To link my life to other men's would be to diminish it, to set limits; so why do it?" You cling to your life. It's precious to you. You won't offer it to history or to country or to God. If living in peace means evolving in nothingness, you accept the nothingness. The Jews in the courtyard of the synagogue? Nothing. The shrieks of women gone mad in the cattle cars? Nothing. The silence of thirsty children? Nothing. All that's a game, you tell yourself. A movie! Fiction: seen and forgotten. I tell you, you're a machine for the fabrication of nothingness.

And he concludes:

The dead Jews, the women gone mad, the mute children—I'm their messenger. And I tell you they haven't forgotton you. Someday they'll come marching, trampling you, spitting in your face. And at their shouts of contempt you'll pray God to deafen you.[10]

Having spoken his accusation, Michael realizes that, to the extent it can be paid, he has paid his debt to the past. Honoring the memory of the dead, he has begun to earn the right to live. And for the first time in his stories Wiesel has his character speak as a healed man:

Suddenly I had no further desire to speak or listen. I was weary, as after a battle fought without conviction. I had come, I had seen, I had delivered the message; the wheel had come full circle. The act was consummated. Now I shall go. I shall return to the life they call normal. The past will have been exorcised. I'll live, I'll work, I'll love. I'll take a wife, I'll father a son, I'll fight to protect his future, his future happiness. The task is accomplished. No more concealed wrath, no more disguises. No more double life, lived on two levels. Now I am whole.[11]

The hero of *The Accident* is a journalist for an Israeli newspaper assigned to the United Nations. One day he is critically injured by an automobile when crossing Times Square with a young woman. Throughout his stay in the hospital he resists the efforts of his doctors to save him. Unlike Elisha, he seems to know that his only chance for life lies in putting an end to his suffering through accepting the love offered him by Kathleen, the young woman, and the friendship of Gyula, an Hungarian painter. But he is drawn to his suffering as a guilty man to his accuser. He cannot escape the past, because it is more real for him than anything in the present. The novel ends with the revelation that he might have avoided the accident but made no effort to do so.

Wiesel has said that the question which the Holocaust raises about man and his relation to God cannot be answered.[12] With the appearance of *The Gates of the Forest* one is persuaded that Wiesel has at least discovered ways to live with the question. The hero of the story, Gregor, is a boy of seventeen, hiding out from the Nazis after his family has been deported from their town in Transylvania. The story consists of four episodes, chronicling the period in which Gregor achieves self-discovery. In each of the episodes Gregor encounters persons who act to save his life; but more significantly, relationships of need, affection, friendship, comradeship, and love are formed with human beings—relationships that heal the wounds of the past, making it possible for him to live forward again.

Through Gregor, Wiesel expresses his belief that the past cannot and should not be forgotten. But the past is dangerous, for it can consume a person, destroying any chance of life. The effort must be made again and again to make out of memory a *witness* to the past, which is to bring the past into the present moment by exposing oneself to the actions, feelings, and thoughts of other human beings. Gregor comes to learn this beginning in the spring when he shares a cave with another young Jew who is also in hiding, and who has lost not only family and home, but strangely, also his name. Gregor gives his own Jewish name of Gavriel to his friend, for in the author's mind Gavriel has come to Gregor as an angelic messenger bringing news of the slaughter of Jews, but bringing as well the message of survival and the promise of new life. The giving of a name is in Wiesel's stories a symbol of human communion. Where *The Town Beyond the Wall* ends with this symbol, *The Gates of the Forest* begins with it. Gavriel fulfills his promise, for the sequence ends with Gavriel sacrificing himself to the police in order to effect the escape of Gregor.

Gavriel's friendship and courage have saved Gregor from the demons in the forest which lie in wait for innocent young Jewish boys. Here the forest is Wiesel's symbol for the experience of the Holocaust. Gavriel's act of freeing Gregor from this madness is paralleled throughout Wiesel's stories. In *The Accident* Gyula, the painter, seeks to free the survivor from the suffering which is driving him mad. Similarly Pedro in *The Town Beyond the Wall* liberates Michael as he struggles in the last scene of that story to unchain a young boy from the silence which is the symbol of his madness.

In the episode of summer, Gregor has taken refuge in the house of Maria, an old Christian woman who was once a servant in his father's house but now lives in her own village across the mountain border in Rumania. Maria knows that she can succeed in protecting Gregor only by concealing his identity as a Jew. She proposes that he pose as her nephew, the child of her sister who left the village some twenty years ago. To safeguard the deception Gregor must learn the rituals and beliefs of Christianity, but Maria is still anxious and persuades him to pose as a deaf-mute lest his voice and manner betray his real identity. Gregor willingly engages in the masquerade. He succeeds so brilliantly that in a short time the villagers regard him with that special affection reserved for those in whom one sees the working of God's hand. It seems that Gregor's "mother" had a reputation (in her youth) as the village whore; thus Gregor's "affliction" as a deaf-mute is interpreted by the superstitious villagers as God's punishment of the mother through the son. The villagers pour out their hearts and confess their inner secrets before this divinely stricken lad who, they believe, can neither speak nor hear.

The ruse is exposed when Gregor plays the part of Judas in the Easter passion play which the villagers perform. Gregor has been chosen for the part because he is so obviously innocent of any sin, bearing as he does the stigmata of his own mother's wickedness, so that he alone in the village has the inner security which frees him to take the role of the "Christ-killer." The irony that Wiesel has created is searing: the Jew-turned-Christian, in order now to remain alive, must pose before a Christian audience as the most detestable of all Jews.

The play is performed wretchedly before an indifferent audience. But when Judas finally makes his appearance on stage to confront Christ, new feeling seizes the peasants. Their boredom turns to hostility focused on the person of Christ's betrayer. "Judas! Traitor! ... Judas! You did it for money!" is heard in the audience. "You betrayed the Son of God! ... You killed the Savior!" In a few brief moments the figure of Judas, the Christ-killer, has obscured in their minds their beloved deaf-mute, Gregor. The script had called for a verbal denunciation of Judas, a clear vindication of the forces of righteousness; but the actors, sensing the possibility of a dramatic success where before there had been only tedium, heartily join the audience in a common attack on Judas. Now real blows are rained down on Gregor, and his face is quickly bloodied. Unknown to all, the Jew is now to suffer the real fate of the Jew. Wiesel describes Gregor's feelings as he accepts his punishment and then brings it suddenly to a halt.

> As the attack grew more violent Gregor discovered that he was stronger than they; they were suffering and he was not. The scene had the unreal, oppressive quality of a nightmare. The pain, there, on him, in him, an alien presence, was that of a nightmare. He felt the pain, but at the same time he knew that when he chose he could stop it....
>
> Gregor spread his legs in order to stand firm upon the stage and slowly, very slowly, he raised his right arm. The other actors, believing he had decided to defend himself, were ready to throw him down and trample him.
>
> One man in the audience picked up a chair and was going to use it. He had to act quickly to forestall him. Every second, every breath, every gesture counted. Time was pressing. A thousand veils were rent: the Prophets emerged from the past and the Messiah from the future. Quickly! Something had to happen. Gregor breathed deeply, and his voice rang out firmly as he spoke to the audience: "Men and women of this village, listen to me!"
>
> In their amazement they froze, incredulous, as if death had surprised them in the midst of battle. Projected out of time they were like wax figures, grotesque and idiotic, without destiny or soul, clay creatures, damned in the service of the devil. Their upraised arms hung in the air, their mouths were half open with tongues protruding and features swollen; the slightest breath would have knocked them over and returned them to dust. All breathing ceased. They were afraid of discovering themselves alive and responsible. The priest was bent over as if he were about to fall on his stomach; he seemed to have lost his eyelids. Then, their faces drained of hate gave way to animal fear. The silence was heavy with blood. Suddenly an old man recovered sufficiently to throw himself upon the floor and to cry out in terror, "Merciful God, have pity on us!"
>
> And he burst into sobs.

And another, imitating him, exclaimed, "Merciful God, forgive us our sins!"

And a third, "A miracle! A miracle, brothers! Pray to Our Lord to have pity on us, for we are miserable creatures."

"Yes, yes, yes! A miracle, a miracle before our eyes! Our dear Gregor is no longer dumb; he is speaking! Our own beloved Gregor! God had made him speak! Look and see for yourselves: God has accomplished a miracle before our eyes."[13]

A scene of macabre humor is now played out. The villagers are stunned by what they believe to be a miracle wrought by God before them. Gregor seizes the moment and compels his fellow villagers to confess fervently that they made a mistake, that their Gregor is not the hated Judas. He then commands them to ask forgiveness for their cruelty not from Christ but from Judas himself, for it was finally Judas, not Christ, whom they wronged. Even the priest is willing to admit that their guilt is before Judas not Christ. "Say after me," Gregor commands them, "'Judas is innocent and we humbly implore his forgiveness.'"

Then Gregor stuns them again. He announces his true identity. He is not the son of the village whore; not their precious deaf-mute. He is in fact a Jew from a village across the mountains who has been hiding from the killers of Jews. Now, Wiesel writes, Gregor

> was silent and there was a smile, not of triumph, but of pity on his face. The peasants opened their mouths wide in astonishment. This was the last thing that they had expected and it was too much for them. The priest collapsed onto his chair, and the villagers stared at the stage without comprehending. In all their minds there was a single thought: we are the victims of a Jew who holds us in his hands. If he goes on making these confessions, the earth will swallow us up.

> The old man who a few minutes before had called him a saint was the first to regain his composure. Brandishing his fists threateningly, he cried out, "Liar! Dirty Liar! You've deceived us, you've betrayed our trust, you've made fun of innocent people, and you shall pay for it!"[14]

Out of the traditional drama of Christ's suffering and death Wiesel has constructed a parable of the existence of the Jew ever since the death of Jesus.

History has reversed the roles. Judas, the Christ-killer, has become the victim; and Christ, in the form of Christian civilization, has become the Jew-killer. Since the death of Christ, the Jew is presented with the most degrading alternative: To survive he must renounce or conceal his identity as a Jew; to affirm his identity he must be prepared to suffer. Confronted always with this alternative the Jew could not help but feel "set apart." By the twisted ironies of history, it appears that the biblical writers really spoke the truth: The record of Jewish history shows that God did in fact choose his people; and that the Jew has paid in blood the price of his election.

Wiesel, like the theologian Richard L. Rubenstein,[15] recognizes that it is not in eschatology but rather in history that the Jew is to seek the basis of his unity with other Jews, living and dead. The solidarity of Jewish people is based on the simplest and most courageous of human cats: the communication of one Jew to another that he is a Jew, and thus shares his identity. In *Legends of Our Time* Wiesel tells the story of The Jew from Saragossa. On a holiday in Spain, in the famous city of the Basques, the narrator of this story engages a native to act as his guide. Upon discovering that the tourist is a Jew who knows the Hebrew language, the guide asks a special favor. Would he come to his room that evening and read to him the words on a treasured piece of paper that has been in his family for generations? The language is foreign to him, it may be Hebrew, but no one in his family that he can remember has ever been able to understand its meaning. That evening the tourist succeeds in deciphering to the Spaniard this testament of his ancestor, who, it turns out, was a Spanish Jew living in the time of the Exile.

> I, Moses, son of Abraham, forced to break all ties with my people and my faith, leave these lines to the children of my children, and theirs, in order that on the day when Israel will be able to walk again, its head high under the sun, without fear and without remorse, they will know where their roots lie. Written at Saragossa, this ninth day of the month of *Av*, in the year of punishment and exile.[16]

The Spaniard learns that he is a Jew, a descendant of the Marranos, those who disguised their identity five hundred years before to escape persecution and death in Spain. As the legend of Rabbi Israel of Rizhyn states, the telling of the story is sufficient to avoid disaster. The dead have succeeded in telling their story to the living. A Jew from the fifteenth century has brought to birth a Jew from the twentieth century.[17]

The Gates of the Forest moves through the fall, during which time Gregor is part of an underground resistance group of young Jews, and it concludes with a winter episode years later when, the war having ended, Gregor has emigrated to America. Gregor is now married to Clara, the sweetheart of a childhood friend, with whom he was reunited in the forest but who died at the hands of the Fascists. In this last episode Gregor has an exchange with a Hasidic Rabbi in which the fundamental question of his life is posed.

Gregor challenges the Rabbi to defend his belief in the righteousness of God in light of the slaughter of his people, Israel. The Rabbi, torn by the challenge, replies:

> So be it! ... He's guilty; do you think I don't know it? That I have no eyes to see, no ears to hear? That my heart doesn't revolt? That I have no desire to beat my head against the wall and shout like a madman, to give rein to my sorrow and disappointment? Yes, he is guilty. He has become the ally of evil, of death, of murder, but the problem is still not solved. I ask you a question and dare you answer: 'What is there left for us to do?'[18]

What indeed is there left to do? This is the question which Gregor must face if he is to live with his memories and not be robbed of life because of them. Gregor has lost faith in the God of Israel as young Elie Wiesel himself in the memoir *Night* confesses that he lost faith in the God of his childhood. But the Rabbi leads Gregor to the truth that if he is not to put his faith in the God of Israel then he must not deny faith in the community of Israel.

Wiesel seems to be saying that if there is meaning left in the God of the Jews, it must be found in Jewishness.[19] And, paradoxically, the road to Jewishness lies through community that is inextricably sacred and human. In the prayers of celebration, praise, and lamentation, the Jew *as Jew* responds most humanly to the mysteries of good and evil, and in that response heals the wounds inflicted on him by man in the sight of a helpless God. In a sense God died for Wiesel at Auschwitz, but if after Auschwitz the Jew is to affirm his identity through solidarity with other Jews, he must affirm God, the ground of solidarity. As the Jew cannot be Jew without God, so Wiesel, echoing the mystical teachings of the Cabbala, holds that God cannot be God without the Jew and all the other creatures of his creation. Wiesel speaks of this mutuality as the faith by which man liberates God from his own imprisonment. The life of one is incomplete without the other, though the story of their common existence is filled as much with strife as with love.

Referring to this bond, Wiesel writes in the epilogue to *The Town Beyond the Wall*:

> As the liberation of the one was bound to the liberation of the other, they renewed the ancient dialogue whose echoes come to us in the night, charged with hatred, with remorse, and most of all, with infinite yearning.

God remains guilty, but one must forgive God his sin if God and man are to continue to live again with each other; and for the Jew, there is no alternative.

The Rabbi knows this; Gregor will learn it. For in response to Gregor's indictment of God's immorality, the Rabbi asks, "Do you want me to stop praying and start shouting? Is that what you're after?" "Yes," whispered Gregor. And the Rabbi replies:

> "Who says that power comes from a shout, an outcry rather than from a prayer? From anger rather than compassion? Where do you find certainties when you claim to have denied them? The man who goes to death death is the brother of the man who goes to death fighting. A song on the lips is worth a dagger in the hand. I take this song and make it mine. Do you know what the song hides? A dagger, an outcry. Appearances have a depth of their own which has nothing to do with the depth. When you come to our celebrations you'll see how we dance and sing and rejoice. There is joy as well as fury in the *hasid's* dancing. It's his way of proclaiming, 'You don't want me to dance; too bad, I'll dance anyhow. You've taken away every reason for singing, but I shall sing, I shall sing of the deceit that walks by day and the truth that walks by night, yes, and of the silence of dusk as well. You didn't expect my joy, but here it is; yes, my joy will rise up; it will submerge you,' " [20]

Gregor does finally come to identify with a small group of Hasidic Jews in Brooklyn led by the rabbi, and he is drawn to the affirmation he recognizes in their celebration.

> The celebration was at its height. It seemed as if it would never come to an end. The *hasidim* were dancing, vertically, as if not moving from their place, but forcing the rhythm down into the earth. What did it matter if the walls gave way except to show

that no enclosure was large enough to contain their fervor? They sang; and the song gave them life and caused the sap to well up in them and bind them together. Ten times, fifty times, they repeated the same phrase, taken from the Psalms or some other portion of Scripture, and every time the fire would be renewed again with primordial passion: yes, once God and man were one, then their unity was broken; ever since they have sought each other, pursued each other, and before each other have proclaimed themselves invincible. As long as the song and dance go on, they are.[21]

Gregor has seen the truth of the Hasidic affirmation for his own life. The ghosts of Auschwitz and Buchenwald are as real as the corpses; but it is the ghosts alone that harm the living if the living allow them One cannot live the past. Gregor has learned this; Clara has not. She has married Gregor but she wishes to exist only the memory of her dead lover, Gregor's friend, Leib. She regards her suffering as faithfulness, and to share her suffering with another is faithlessness. But Gregor knows that if she does not share it, she will be possessed by the dead as he was himself possessed so very long. Resolving to continue struggling to win Clara back to a life with him and not with a dead man, he says to himself:

"Knowing then that all of us have our ghosts ... They come and go at will, breaking open doors, never shutting them tight; they bear different names. We mustn't let ourselves be seduced by their promises ... "Yes, Clara, they'll continue to haunt us, but we must fight them. It will be a bitter, austere, obstinate battle. The struggle to survive will begin here, in this room, where we are sitting. Whether or not the Messiah comes doesn't matter; we'll manage without him. It is because it is too late that we are commanded to hope. We shall be honest and humble and strong, and then he will come, he will come every day, thousands of times every day. He will have no face, because he will have a thousand faces. The Messiah isn't one man, Clara, he's all men. As long as there are men there will be a Messiah. One day you'll sing, and he will sing in you. Then for the last time, I'll want to cry. I shall cry. Without shame."[22]

It is with this humanistic vision of the meaninglessness of God without man, of God's dependence on man, that Wiesel's story draws to its close.

In the next moment Gregor recites the *Kaddish*, praying for the souls of his father and of his departed friend Leib, and praying too for the soul of God and for his own soul. In the sacred words of this prayer he senses for the first time the possibility of meaning. Wiesel writes:

> [Gregor] recited [the *Kaddish*] slowly, concentrating on every sentence, every word, every syllable of praise. His voice trembled, timid, like that of the orphan suddenly made aware of the relationship between death and eternity, between eternity and the word.[23]

Through Gregor, Wiesel expresses his acceptance of the Hasidic wisdom that men can survive the disasters of their lives through the experiences of other human beings, encountering meanings in whose depths one feels perhaps for the first time the presence of sacredness. In the recitation of the Kaddish, the traditional prayer for the dead, Wiesel finds it possible to live with the memory of his father's death at Buchenwald,[24] and he comes to know again that God *is*, and that it is possible to live without hating him.

But the prayer is inseparable from the story; after telling the story so many times, the wound has healed, memories which once haunted have now begun to nurture the living.

NOTES

1. "I cannot believe that an entire generation of fathers and sons could vanish into the abyss without creating; by their very disappearance, a mystery which exceeds and overwhelms us. I still do not understand what happened, or how, or why. All the words in all the mouths of the philosophers and psychologists are not worth the silent tears of that child and his mother, who live their own death twice. What can be done? In my calculations, all the figures always add up to the same number: six million." Elie Wiesel, *Legends of Our Time* (New York: Avon Books, 1970), pp. 222-223.

2. For a treatment of the influence of cabbalistic teachings on Wiesel see Byron L. Sherwin, "Elie Wiesel and Jewish Theology," *Judaism* (Winter, 1969), pp. 39-52. While it is plain from his stories that Wiesel doubts the power of God over evil, it is far from clear that he holds the "gnostic" belief that there is a second divine principle, a god-of-evil, as has been suggested by Seymour Cain in his article, "The Questions and Answers After Auschwitz," *Judaism*, (Summer, 1971), p. 274.

3. Elie Wiesel, *Night*, translated from the French by Stella Rodway (New York: Avon Books, 1970), p. 44.

4. Elie Wiesel, *The Accident*, translated from the French by Anne Borchardt (New York: Avon Books, 1962), p. 49.

5. Wiesel, *Legends of Our Time*, p. 26.

6. Elie Wiesel, *The Gates of the Forest*, translated from the French by Frances Frenage (New York: Avon Books, 1966).

7. Quoted by Gerald Green, *The Artists of Terezin* (New York, 1969), p. 159.

8. Moche the Beadle in *Night* witnesses the slaying of Jews by Nazis, returns to tell the story, and is taken as a madman by all the Jews of Sighet. Elsewhere Wiesel writes, "These days honest men can do only one thing: go mad! Spit on logic, intelligence, sacrosanct reason! That's what you have to do, that's the way to stay human, to keep your wholeness!" ... "God loves madmen. They're the only ones he allows near him." *The Town Beyond the Wall*, translated from the French by Stephen Barker (New York: Avon Books, 1964), pp. 20, 24.

9. Elie Wiesel, *A Beggar in Jerusalem*, translated from the French by Lily Edelman and the author (New York: Random House, 1970), p. 80.

10. Wiesel, *The Town Beyond The Wall*, pp. 172-173.

11. Ibid., p. 118.

12. *Legends of Our Time*, p. 222.

13. Wiesel, *The Gates of the Forest*, pp, 112, 113-114.

14. Ibid., p. 118.

15. Richard L. Rubenstein, *After Auschwitz* (Indianapolis, 1967).

16. Wiesel, *Legends of Our Time*, p. 97.

17. Thomas Lask has incisively observed that the use of history to create meaning for the contemporary event is a form which Wiesel has developed in his stories. "The written law and oral tradition support, explain and expand the 20th century event. Describing a Kol Nidre service in the camp for the Day of Atonement in *Legends of Our Time*, Wiesel recalls one legend that says that at that hour the dead rise from their graves and come to pray with the living. Looking about him in the barracks, he realizes that the legend is true, Auschwitz confirmed it." Thomas Lask, a review of *One Generation After* by Elie Wiesel, *The New York Times*, December 15, 1970.

18. Wiesel, *The Gates of the Forest*, p. 196.

19. It is the failure to recognize the centrality of Jewishness in Wiesel's stories that mars Maurice Friedman's analysis. The argument that Wiesel's hero is the "Job of Auschwitz" who "trusts and contends" with God has point, but it is overstated when Friedman interprets this motif according to the existentialist doctrine of moral responsibility before evil as expressed by Camus. The rebellion against the Absurd waged by Dr. Rieux, the hero of Camus' *The Plague*, is not parallel with Wiesel's struggles to learn to live with the memories of all those whom he knew and loved in the Jewish community in Sighet. Wiesel's "contention" with God occurs within an acutely Jewish sensibility where one can be angry with, pity, and even pray for God, but never reject God in favor of an ethical universal, rebellion against the absurd, as Rieux did. Maurice Friedman, "Elie Wiesel: The Job of Auschwitz," unpublished

paper delivered at the national meeting of the American Academy of Religion, New York, October, 1970.

20. Ibid.

21. Ibid., p. 187.

22. Ibid., p. 223.

23. Ibid.

24. Wiesel's account of his father's death in *Night* and *Legends of Our Time* conveys in its restraint, in its lack of physical horror, the depth of suffering of the son who witnessed and cannot cease remembering. It is not death per se which causes Wiesel suffering but the humiliation of those who died. This is perceptively noted by Thomas Lask (loc. Cit.): "There is surprisingly little physical horror in [Wiesel's] books. It is the mind that is outraged, the spirit that is degraded. When an emaciated father gives his bowl of soup to his starving son, when a naked mother covers her child's body with her own against the expected spray of bullets, pain and death pale before the suffering and humiliation in these events."

ALVIN H. ROSENFELD

The Problematics
of Holocaust Literature

Is there such a thing as Holocaust literature? By that I mean a literature that is more than topical, as, say, a literature of the sea or a literature of warfare might be considered merely topical. For if by Holocaust literature all we have in mind is a large but loosely arranged collection of novels, poems, essays, and plays about a *subject*, even one so enormous and unnerving as the Nazi genocide against the Jews, then our concerns, while interesting and legitimate enough, are not truly compelling. Topical studies of all kinds—of the family, of slavery, of the environment, of World War I or World War II— abound today, and while they can be individually engaging, their value does not and cannot transcend the limitations inherent in their definitions *as* topical literatures.

By contrast—and the contrast must be conceived of as being one of the first degree—Holocaust literature occupies another sphere of study, one that is not only topical in interest but that extends so far as to force us to contemplate what may be fundamental changes in our modes of perception and expression, our altered way of being-in-the-world. What needs to be stressed is this: the nature and magnitude of the Holocaust were such as to mark, almost certainly, the end of one era of consciousness and the beginning of another. And just as we designate and give validity to such concepts as "the Renaissance mind" and "romantic sensibility" and "the Victorian temper" to indicate earlier shifts in awareness and expression, so, too, should we begin

From *Confronting the Holocaust: The Impact of Elie Wiesel*, ed. Alvin H. Rosenfeld and Irving Greenberg. ©1978 by Indiana University Press.

to see that Holocaust literature is a striving to express a new order of consciousness, a recognizable shift in being. The human imagination after Auschwitz is simply not the same as it was before. Put another way, the addition to our vocabulary of the very word Auschwitz means that today we *know* things that before could not even be imagined. How we are to live with such knowledge is another matter, but there is no denying that possessed with it or by it, we are, in some basic ways, *different* from what we might have been before. Different because we have been compelled to occupy a realm of experience—acknowledge a realism—that previously was understood as that of private invention alone, a realm conceived of as being entirely separate from and of another kind than that which might ever cross with historical event. With the advent of Auschwitz, the necessary distance that once prevailed between even the most extreme imaginings and human occurrence closes. Following upon that closure, the eye opens to gaze unbelievingly on scenes of life-and-death, death-and-life, which the mind cannot rationally accept or the imagination take in and adequately record. Stunned by the awesomeness and pressure of event, the imagination comes to one of its periodic endings; undoubtedly, it also stands at the threshold of new and more difficult beginnings. Holocaust literature, situated at this point of threshold, is a chronicle of the human spirit's most turbulent strivings with an immense historical and metaphysical weight.

I use the term "human spirit" quite deliberately here, acknowledging in full the awkwardness and imprecision inherent in the term, because I cannot but conceive of Holocaust literature, when taken in its most encompassing definition, except as an attempt to retrieve some ongoing life—posit a future tense—for whatever it is of human definition that remains to us. The bodies—that is to say, the people—are gone and cannot be rescued back to life; neither can meaning in the old sense, nor absolute faith, nor old-fashioned humanism, nor even the senses intact; yet the writers we are concerned with have argued in their writings—by *writing*—that an articulate life must be preserved. Writing itself, as we know from such a strongly determined work as Chaim Kaplan's diary, could be an effective counterforce to nihilism, not so much an answer to death as an answer to barbarism, a last-ditch means of approximating and preserving the human in the face of a viciousness poised to destroy it. As a result, the vicious and the barbarous could win only partial victories, destroy the living but not altogether submerge life. What remains is less than what perished but more than that which wanted to conquer and prevail. We do have the books while the night has nothing but itself.

Given these considerations, what can we say about the attitude that denies the validity or even the possibility of a literature of the Holocaust? In one of its earliest and by now most famous formulations, that of the eminent critic T. W. Adorno, this position states that it is not only impossible but perhaps even immoral to attempt to write about the Holocaust.[1] Adorno had poetry specifically in mind, moreover—perhaps just a single poem, the "*Todesfuge*" of Paul Celan, which struck him as being incongruously, and perhaps even obscenely, lyrical. As it happens, this poem is one of the great documents of Holocaust literature, but to Adorno it was hopelessly out of touch with its subject, as, he surmised, all such literature seemed destined to be. That judgment is re-echoed by the German critic Reinhard Baumgart, who objects to Holocaust literature on the grounds that it imposes artificial meaning on mass suffering, and, "by removing some of the horror, commits a grave injustice against the victims."[2] The point has also been reaffirmed in a recent pronouncement of denunciation by Michael Wyschogrod:

> I firmly believe that art is not appropriate to the holocaust. Art takes the sting out of suffering.... It is therefore forbidden to make fiction of the holocaust.... Any attempt to transform the holocaust into art demeans the holocaust and must result in poor art.[3]

Those who would know and could best judge the truth of this assertion—the artists themselves—have on occasion spoken similarly, even if out of a different ground and for different reasons. Thus Elie Wiesel, whose writings perhaps more than any other's attest to the continuing possibility of Holocaust literature, has newly and pointedly spoke of its utter *impossibility:*

> One generation later, it can still be said and must now be affirmed: There is no such thing as a literature of the Holocaust, nor can there be. The very expression is a contradiction in terms. Auschwitz negates any form of literature, as it defies all systems, all doctrines.... A novel about Auschwitz is not a novel, or else it is not about Auschwitz. The very attempt to write such a novel is blasphemy....[4]

The fact that such a view is put before us by an Elie Wiesel—and only that fact—renders it understandable and respectable, even if not acceptable. We know, for a dozen books by Elie Wiesel alone have now told us, that the Holocaust demands speech even as it threatens to impose silence. The speech may be flawed, stuttering, and inadequate, as it must be given the sources out of which it originates, *but it is still speech*. Silence has not prevailed—to let it do so would be tantamount to granting Hitler one more posthumous victory—just as night has been refused its dominion. If it is a blasphemy, then, to attempt to write about the Holocaust, and an injustice against the victims, how much greater the injustice and more terrible the blasphemy to remain silent.

What really is involved here is the deep anguish and immense frustration of the writer who confronts a subject that belittles and threatens to overwhelm the resources of his language. The writer's position is, in this respect, analogous to that of the man of faith, who is likewise beset by frustration and anguish and, in just those moments when his spirit may yearn for the fullness of Presence, is forced to acknowledge the emptiness and silence of an imposed Absence. The life centers of the self—intelligence, imagination, assertiveness—undergo paralysis in such moments, which, if prolonged, have the almost autistic effect of a total detachment or the profoundest despair. If it is out of or about such negative and all but totally silencing experience that proclamations are made about the disappearance of God or, its close corollary, the collapse of language, then of course one is moved to sympathize. Yet it is simply not possible to sympathize by indulging in silence, for to do so is to court madness or death. At just those points where, through some abiding and still operative reflex of language, silence converts once more into words—even into words *about* silence—Holocaust literature is born. Its birth, a testament to more than silence, more than madness, more even than language itself, must be seen as a miracle of some sort, not only an overcoming of mute despair but an assertion and affirmation of faith.

Faith in what? In some cases, perhaps in nothing more than human tenacity, the sheer standing fast of life in the face of a brutal death; in other cases, faith in the will to reject a final and wicked obliteration; in still others, faith in the persistent and all but uncanny strength of character to search out and find new beginnings. Given these dimensions of its existence and power, Holocaust literature, with all its acknowledged difficulties and imperfections, can be seen as occupying not only a legitimate place in modern letters but a central place. Long after much else in contemporary literature is forgotten, future generations of readers will continue to answer—by their very presence *as* readers—the question that ends Chaim Kaplan's diary: "If my life ends— what will become of my diary?"[5] It will stand to the ages—and not by itself but with other accounts of what happened to man in the ghettos and camps of Europe—as a testament of our times.

If it is possible to reply to the view that would deny the existence or validity of Holocaust literature, it is much harder to know how to read confidently or assess adequately such literature. The problems are many and, in some cases, hardly manageable at all. For instance, one begins by recognizing that the diaries, notebooks, memoirs, sketches, stories, novels, essays, poems, and plays that comprise Holocaust literature have been written in virtually all the languages of Europe, including, of course, Yiddish and Hebrew, the specifically Jewish languages. Holocaust literature is, in short, an international literature, and it would be the rare scholar indeed who could command all the tools necessary to investigate it in its fullest sweep. Literary scholarship in this area is unusually demanding, for the linguistic and cross-cultural requirements that are wanted far exceed those normally called into play for literary studies. As a result, most scholars will have to limit themselves, of necessity, to only some of the material they might want to read and, in addition, will have to rely to an unusual degree on translation. Obviously these are handicaps, and while they need not be ultimately discouraging, they are limiting.

Then there is the question of knowing *how* to read, respond to, and comprehend the kinds of material that come before us. The stress here must fall on "kinds" because it is almost certain that we confront the works of survivors in markedly different ways than we do the works of those who perished, just as we assume still another reading stance for writings about the Holocaust by those who were not there. Knowing what we do know—but what the authors themselves could not when they wrote—about the ultimate fates of a Chaim Kaplan or an Emmanuel Ringelblum or a Moshe Flinker, we do not take up their books with the same expectations and read them with the same kinds of responses as we do, say, the books of a Primo Levi or an Alexander Donat or an Elie Wiesel. The difference is not reducible solely to the dimension of tragic irony implicit in the writings of the first group but absent from those of the second; nor is it just that we read, react to, and interpret the dead with a greater deference or solemnity than the living, for within the context of Holocaust literature the living often carry a knowledge of death more terrible in its intimacy than that ever recorded in the writings of the victims. Who, in fact, *are* the real victims here, the dead or those cursed back into life again, guilt-ridden and condemned by a fate that would not take them?

Is it not the case that the most lacerating writings often belong to those who survived, not perished in, the Holocaust? The concern here is with the problem of survivorship and with trying to determine the reader's role in Holocaust literature, a role that seems more difficult and anguished when confronting the living than the dead. When, for instance, we read the diary of young Moshe Finker or Ringelblum's notebooks, we inevitably "complete" the narrative by bringing to the text material that it itself does not contain; we do that almost by reflex, filling in and interpreting with knowledge gained through biographical or historical notes. That is a wrenching but still possible act for the sympathetic imagination to perform. Oddly enough, the fact that it is *we* who are asked to perform it, and not the authors themselves, makes reading them somewhat more bearable, somewhat more possible. When, however, the task of not only recording but also interpreting, judging, and ever again suffering through the agony falls to a living writer—as it clearly does in the works of Elie Wiesel—then we are no longer talking about acts of sympathetic imagination but about something else, something that we do not have a name for and hardly know how to grasp. The nightmare, in a word, is never-ending, and repeats itself over and over again.

It is not for nothing that the Holocaust seems to expel certain writers from its provenance after a single book, that they are, from this standpoint, one-book authors. Did the curse of obsessive recurrence lift from them (consider, for example, the writing careers of André Schwarz-Bart or Jerzy Kosinski) or merely change its terms? If they have found their way to new fictional territory, what was the purchase price for their release? Why can an Elie Wiesel ór a Ka-Tzetnik not pay it? These are problems—among other things, reader's problems—that we do not understand and have hardly even begun to take note of.

Here is a simple test: read Anne Frank's diary—one of the best-known but, as such things go, one of the "easiest" and most antiseptic works of Holocaust literature—and then read Ernst Schnabel's *Anne Frank: A Profile in Courage*,[6] which "completes" the work by supplying the details of the young girl's ending in Auschwitz and Bergen-Belsen. You will never again be able to rid your understanding of the original text of dimensions of terror, degradation, and despair *that it itself does not contain*. We need, but do not have, a suitable hermeneutics to explain that phenomenon and render it intelligible, just as we need, but do not have, a working theory of the miraculous to explain the mere existence of other texts. That certain books have come down to us at all is nothing short of astonishing, and we can never distance ourselves from an accompanying and transfiguring sense of awe as we encounter them. A manuscript written secretly and at the daily risk of life in the Warsaw ghetto, buried in milk tins or transmitted through the ghetto walls at the last moment, finally transmitted to *us*—such a manuscript begins to carry with it the aura of a holy text. Surely we do not take it in our hands and read it as we do those books that reach us through the normal channels of composition and publication. But how *do* we read it? At this point in the study of Holocaust literature, the question remains open-ended.

Other examples might be brought forth and additional problems raised, all with the aim of intentionally complicating our task. For if we do not make the effort to read Holocaust literature seriously, within the extraordinary precincts of its uncanny origins and problematic nature, we simply will never understand it. For instance, Emil Fackenheim not long ago suggested that eyewitness accounts of events may at times be less credible than studies made after the fact and by people at some distance from it. Although Fackenheim was incarcerated briefly at Sachsenhausen and thus was given first-hand knowledge of that camp, it was not until he read a study of Sachsenhausen years later, he admits, that he felt he truly understood what had taken place there and what he himself had experienced.[7]

The issue in this case is not analogous to the one that always obtains when a personal and perhaps "emotionally colored" account of experience is weighed against the "cooler" and more objective kinds of information gathered after the fact by the working historian. For, as Fackenheim came to understand only much later, a built-in feature of the Nazi camp system was deception of the victims, rendering accounts of the eyewitness in many cases less than reliable. The fictitious element of camp life—its pervasive irreality—was calculated to confuse and disarm the rational faculties, making the camp prisoners more pliable to their masters and hence more vulnerable to the diabolical system in which they were entrapped.

What does Fackenheim's case suggest about the relationship between proximity and authority in writings about the Holocaust? Normally we are willing to grant a greater validity to the accounts of those who were there, and to withhold it from—or grant it only reluctantly to—the writings of those who were not. Fackenheim's questions may bring us to revise these notions and to understand newly our measures not only of historical truth but of imaginative penetration and narrative effect as well. Within the contexts of Holocaust literature, in fact, the question of what constitutes *legitimacy* promises to become even more important as the years pass and direct access to events becomes impossible. But, as Fackenheim's statement already shows, even such direct access may not always reliably render up the truth.

And what about the truth of endings—writers' endings? Because Paul Celan and Tadeusz Borowski terminated their lives as they did, is it not the case that we are almost forced into a reader's stance vis-à-vis their stories and poems that we otherwise would not have and indeed do not want? Was suicide in each case an inevitable outcome of their work, a final and desperate conclusion to it, ultimately even a bitter evaluation of it? Was the self-destructive act of the man only and not of the writer? That such questions raise themselves at all means that we read these writers under a shadow of some kind—a different kind, incidentally, than the one that now hangs over the work of a Sylvia Plath or a John Berryman. (While their suicides also mediate between us and their books, one senses no historical determinism behind the personal anguish that must have led them to take their lives; the pressure to which they succumbed seems to have been biographically generated, its pain not larger than that of the single life.)

Kafka said that we are usually too easy on ourselves as readers, that we should choose books that ask more of us than we normally are willing to give. "We must have those books," he wrote, "which come upon us like ill-fortune, and distress us deeply, like the death of one we love better than ourselves, like suicide. A book must be an ice-axe to break the sea frozen inside us."[8] To make that formulation, Kafka must have been a great reader, as well as a great hungerer (in his case the two are really one), and yet, despite all his intense suffering and estrangement, he was spared the worst that the twentieth century was to bring upon writers such as Celan and Borowski. Had Kafka known them, could he still have spoken in the terms just cited above? When, in a writer's life, suicide becomes not a metaphor for something but the thing itself, we grow more cautious and defensive as readers and do not so readily welcome the kinds of hard blows that Kafka exhorts upon us. Better to read warily and keep the seas of empathy inside us safely frozen awhile longer.

By now the point should be clear: we lack a phenomenology of reading Holocaust literature, a series of maps that would guide us on our way as we picked up and variously tried to comprehend the writings of the victims, the survivors, the survivors-who-become-victims, and the kinds-of-survivors, those who were never there but know more than the outlines of the place. Until we devise such maps, our understanding of Holocaust literature will be only partial, well below that which belongs to full knowledge.

One conclusion to these questions is that we are yet to develop the kind of practical criticism that will allow us to read, interpret, and evaluate Holocaust literature with any precision or confidence.[9] Older criticisms of whatever orientation or variety—Freudian, Marxist, formalist, structuralist, or linguistic—will not do here for any number of reasons. The largest is that the conception of man, or world view, embodied in psychoanalysis or dialectical theory or theories of aesthetic autonomy had almost no place in the ghettos and camps, which were governed by forces of an altogether different and far less refined nature. As a result, it would seem a radical misapplication of method and intentions to search through literary accounts of Auschwitz or the Warsaw ghetto for covert Oedipal symbols, class struggle, revealing patterns of imagery and symbolism, mythic analogies, or deep grammatical structures. Auschwitz no more readily reduces to these considerations than death itself does.

Nor will it do to confine understanding within a framework of literary history that would tend to see Holocaust literature as part of the literature of warfare-in-general or even of World War II. There are novels eligible for such study, including certain novels by Jewish writers, such as Irwin Shaw's *The Young Lions*, Norman Mailer's *The Naked and the Dead*, or Herman Wouk's *The Caine Mutiny*. Each of these books will be of interest to students of the Second World War, but the interest will be the topical one that I referred to earlier and not that which belongs to our subject.

The distinction—a hard one that needs to be held firmly in mind—has an illuminating parallel within historical writings about the period. In a newly published history of the Second World War written by A. J. P. Taylor, for instance, I find a total of two pages out of two hundred and thirty-five devoted to the Holocaust, this despite the fact that the author concludes his four-paragraph summary by stating that "the memory of Oswiecim and the other murder camps will remain when all the other achievements of the Nazi Empire are forgotten."[10] Given that view—a correct one—it seems shocking at first that Taylor would mention the Holocaust only, as it were, in passing. And yet he is not entirely wrong to do so, for to do otherwise would be to see the war against the Jews as an integral part of World War II. More and more it seems that it was not, neither in intention, nor in kind, nor in outcome. The war against the Jews may have occupied some of the same dimensions of time and space as World War II, but it was not fought as a logical part of that war, nor can the literature it generated be compared to or profitably studied with the topical literature of the Second World War. Holocaust literature is simply and complexly something else, as the cataclysm that triggered it was something else, and not part of the general storm that swept over Europe four decades ago.

In referring to such extreme cases we tend to use the language of weather, but the analogy with earthquakes and storms will finally not hold; nor will most other analogies. That precisely is part of the problem. It supports the view that we must make distinctions between the literature of the Holocaust and the literature of general warfare, including that of World War II. This is not to belittle those books that belong to this other literature or to suggest that the Great Wars of our century did not pose their own problems for writers. Clearly they did. The First World War in particular came with an enormous jolt and hardly presented itself to the grasping intelligence in neatly formed and easily apprehensible ways. Hemingway wrote that among the casualties of that war were "the words 'sacred,' 'glorious,' and 'sacrifice' and the expression 'in vain,'" that these were words he "could not stand to hear," and that "finally only the names of places had dignity." Hemingway's loss was huge, the collapse of a whole idealistic code that once sustained life by giving it a measure of purpose and honor. In reading his fiction of the Great War, it does not take much to realize that Hemingway was saying farewell to far more than arms.

To what, though, was the young Elie Wiesel saying farewell when, in an often quoted and by now famous passage from *Night*, he wrote that he will never forget the flames that turned the bodies of children "into wreaths of smoke beneath a silent blue sky," the flames that consumed his faith forever?[11] What was his loss when, in turning the pages of an album of Holocaust photographs, he made this monstrous discovery:

> At every page, in front of every image, I stop to catch my breath. And I tell myself: This is the end, they have reached the last limit; what follows can only be less horrible; surely it is impossible to invent suffering more naked, cruelty more refined. Moments later I admit my error: I underestimated the assassin's ingenuity. The progression into the inhuman transcends the exploration of the human. Evil, more than good, suggests infinity.[12]

For that plunge to the bottom of a final knowledge, that fall into a wicked and savage clarity, we simply have no analogy, except perhaps to hell—a possibility that we shall have occasion to pursue a little later. For now, though, I think we must accept as a given the proposition that the Holocaust was something new in the world, without likeness or kind, a truth that was set forth years ago in a forceful and memorable poem by Uri Zvi Greenberg:

> Are there other analogies to this, our disaster that came to us
>   at their hands?
> There are no other analogies (all words are shades of shadow)—
> Therein lies the horrifying phrase: No other analogies!
> For every cruel torture that man may yet do to man in a
>   Gentile country—
> He who comes to compare will state: He was tortured like a
>   Jew.
> Every fright, every terror, every loneliness, every chagrin,

Every murmuring, weeping in the world
He who compares will say: This analogy is of the Jewish kind.[13]

There have been attempts to find analogies—with Job, with the destruction of the Second Temple, with the *Akeda*, with the concepts of *Kiddush ha-Shem* or the Thirty-Six Righteous Men who uphold the world— and, to the extent that such allusions and antecedents have allowed certain writers at least a partial grasp of the tragedy, it would seem that we must qualify the notion that the Holocaust was altogether without parallels. On closer examination, however, it becomes clear in almost all cases that the gains in perspective are only temporary and provisional, for what inevitably emerges in Holocaust literature is that such analogies are introduced only to reveal their inadequacy, and they are in turn either refuted or rejected as being unworkable. Schwartz-Bart, for instance, ultimately shows us the *exhaustion* of the tradition of the *Lamed Vov* rather than its continuing usefulness, just as Elie Wiesel will time and again adopt the stance of a Job only to find that it will not serve. In the end he will have to stand alone, rooted in the solitary ground that became his the moment he was struck by the isolating knowledge that "the Holocaust defies reference, analogy."[14] It must have been this realization more than any other that led Wiesel to remark that "by its nature, the Holocaust defies literature,"[15] an incapacitating insight that a writer *as* writer simply cannot tolerate and that this writer has been struggling against in book after book, sometimes winning his way through, at other times all but succumbing.

As Wiesel's case shows, the implications of a literature without antecedents or analogy are frightening in the extreme, for our whole conception of literature insists on recognizing its traditional base, and, as such, affirms that writing grows as much from within as from without. A poem or a novel, that is to say, is not a new and wholly undetermined thing— a sudden and unprecedented appearance in the world—but bears some necessary relationship to other poems and novels that have gone before and, in some sense, have sired it. While every good piece of writing must be, in its way, an original act of creation, all literature is formed as much from reactions to an antecedent literature as from more direct or unmediated reactions to life. A poem descends from other poems, a novel from other novels, a play from other plays. Whether we know it or not, we read and understand literature exactly in this way, with implicit reference to and analogy with prior texts. Indeed, we could not begin to read at all, nor could writers write, if that were not so. Our whole fund of literacy, in short, comes into play in reading.

Yet when we confront those texts that are our concern here, we sooner or later find ourselves without the expected and necessary moorings in a familiar literary landscape, and, as a result, it is sometimes hardly possible to know how to proceed. Lost in a place whose dimensions we cannot easily recognize, let alone acknowledge as our own, we strive for orientation through intimacy with the common and familiar things of the world, but grasp only fog. The object in our hands looks like a book but seems to have turned into something else.

Some contrasting examples from past literature can be instructive here. Even a casual reader of Edgar Allan Poe or Franz Kafka, for instance, knows that a literature of terror and radical estrangement is not exclusively a product of the post–World War II decades. Read Poe's "The Pit and the Pendulum" or Kafka's "In the Penal Colony" and you will have all the terror you might want. Poe, in particular, relished macabre sensations and "the exquisite terror of the soul," and was gifted at finding precise literary correlatives for them. That is why to this day the best of his stories possess the power to "thrill" and "haunt" us with simulations of extreme psychic torment. It was his subject, and he went about developing it with all the props and atmospherics of the Gothic romance or early symbolist fiction—a whole catalogue of literary horrors that will please and stimulate the imagination with fright. Yet at no time in reading Poe do we ever come to believe that the fantasy world we are invited to enter—his "dream kingdom"—is the "real" world, the phenomenal world of our day-to-day existence. We know that Poe is inventing, that at his best he is a gifted inventor, that his literary inventions possess a stark psychological power and can grip us, at times, mightily. In short, we pretty well know how to read him.

Kafka is a deeper and more complicated writer, one who is still far enough ahead of us to render his works less accessible to full and confident understanding. In his case, we may recognize affinities with an antecedent literature of the grotesque or absurd, but to read him in these terms does not carry us very far, just as it finally will not do to reduce his more enigmatic parables and stories to the critical categories of symbolism or expressionism or surrealism. While Kafka seems to embody elements of all of these, he simultaneously transcends them, so that in the end he is only what we have come to call, inadequately and at the risk of tautology, "Kafkaesque." Let us admit that we have not yet entirely caught up with him and, as a result, he is a far more dangerous writer for us than Poe.

Nevertheless, even in Kafka's case—as, say, in "In the Penal Colony" or "The Metamorphosis"—we are never led to abandon altogether our hold on a normative, stabilizing sense of things, on the saving power of the mundane.

We may be released by his fiction into a universe of absurd and frightening proportions, but it is a highly *composed* universe, and while few would welcome a prolonged residence there, it is not a totally alien place. Kafka possessed the power, in fact, to domesticate us rather easily to his strange but familiar world, and we can cross back and forth between it and what we perhaps too comfortably call "reality" without paying an ultimate price in credulity. In its depictions of a mechanized or technological terror, of a reigning injustice, of brutal and systematic and causeless punishment, of an accepted guilt and passivity before annihilation, "In the Penal Colony" is an uncanny prefiguration of Holocaust literature, a premonitory text. Nevertheless, in reading it we are still a step or two away from a direct knowledge of *history* as Holocaust, and no reader of the novella would confuse the infernal torture machine that is its elaborate centerpiece with the actual machinery of Auschwitz or Treblinka, just as no reader of "The Metamorphosis" would accept Gregor Samsa's transformation into a giant insect as a change that could ever actually overtake him. We accept these intricate literary devices as complex acts of initiation—a series of bridges that we must cross to enter the Kafkaesque world—and once we acknowledge them as such, we are usually content to let the stories take over and develop in their own terms. Since we do not read Kafka within predominantly realistic or naturalistic frameworks, credulity is not unduly strained by these inventions, which we recognize as the components of a profoundly disturbing but nevertheless fictional universe.

What happens, though, when we enter *l'univers concentrationnaire* and come upon the kind of metamorphosis cited earlier, one in which living children are suddenly tranformed into wreaths of smoke? What is our interpretive frame of reference for *that*? One finds nothing like it in Poe or Kafka or any other literary precursor I know, including the Marquis de Sade. Since it is altogether too disorienting to acknowledge such writing as a piece of realism, one perhaps tries initially to shift the terms into the language of dreams—of some inverted symbolism or dark allegory. Yet these are evasive gestures, strategies of defense, and ultimately they must be abandoned in order to perform a reluctant and all but impossible act—*reading*—which in this case means acknowledging a truth that we do not want to be true. How, after all, can we accept a realism more extreme than any surrealism yet invented? It is one thing to grant Kafka the artistic liberty he needs to write "The Metamorphosis," changing a man into a bug, but it is something else again entirely—and altogether too much for rational belief—when Elie Wiesel writes of children being metamorphosed into smoke. Yet that is what is presented to us in *Night*, presented moreover in such a way as to permit us to read it on one level only—the literal one—the level of plainly declared, unencumbered truth. This, we are told, is what happened. It has no symbolic dimensions, carries no allegorical weight, possesses no apparent or covert meaning. Do not think about it in terms of Ovid or Poe or Kafka, for the mythical or metaphorical aspects of their writings do not come into play here; nor does anything else you have ever read before. Know only one thing—the truth of what happened—which sounds like this:

> Not far from us, flames were leaping up from a ditch, gigantic flames. They were burning something. A lorry drew up at the pit and delivered its load—little children. Babies! Yes, I saw it—saw it with my own eyes ... those children in the flames.[16]

Has there ever before been a literature more dispiriting and forlorn, more scandalous than this? Who would not erase it at once from memory? Yet we must stay with these words, or with others like them, in an effort to determine one of the distinguishing characteristics of Holocaust literature.

In order to do that, I turn briefly from prose to poetry and offer two short poems. The first was written in the nineteenth century by Henry David Thoreau; the second, written closer to our own day, is by the Yiddish poet Jacob Glatstein. The poems carry the same title: "Smoke." Here is Thoreau's:

> Light-winged Smoke, Icarian bird,
> Melting thy pinions in thy upward flight,
> Lark without song, and messenger of dawn,
> Circling above the hamlets as thy nest;
> Or else, departing dream, and shadowy form
> Of midnight vision, gathering up thy skirts;
> By night star-veiling, and by day
> Darkening the light and blotting out the sun;
> Go thou my incense upward from this hearth,
> And ask the gods to pardon this clear flame.

Among the first observations one makes about this poem is that, in writing it, Thoreau had little interest in smoke *as* smoke but rather was attracted to it as the base for his transfiguring imagination, which loved to dissolve phenomena into fanciful patterns of thought. The poem, that is to say, employs its central figure in a clearly metaphorical sense, likening the smoke to other things—to birds, to the mythical Icarus, to dreams and clouds, finally to incense. Through this series of delicate imagistic changes, the poem develops the author's sense of the fugitive and transient quality of life. It is a finely wrought if uncomplicated poem, one that holds closely to classical patterns of poetic rhetoric, and therefore presents no particular problems to interpretation.

Compare it to Glatstein's "Smoke" (in the original Yiddish title, "*Roikh*"), which I quote now in an English translation:

From the crematory flue
A Jew aspires to the Holy One.
And when the smoke of him is gone,
His wife and children filter through.

Above us, in the height of sky,
Saintly billows weep and wait.
God, wherever you may be,
There all of us are also not.[17]

This, too, is a fine poem, but what is it saying? In the opening lines it describes a Jew ascending to his God through a chimney, followed soon after by his wife and children passing upward in the same way. The poem says that they do so by turning into smoke; moreover, it says so with a certain jauntiness of rhythm—the hippety-hop of nursery school jingles—and the playfulness of rhyme. Is it a children's poem of some kind? It is not inconceivable that a reader who chances upon this poem a hundred years from now might ask such questions, for there are elements here that call them forth. They do so, however, only to disabuse us rather quickly of our innocence, for before very long we will see that the sprightliness of rhythm and rhyme serves as a trap, the apparent lightheartedness only a lure to draw us forward into the poem's deadly center.

In searching to locate this center, we are soon brought to see that the entire poem is predicated upon the author's certain knowledge that we will recognize and be able to name the crime that resides behind or before words, in the silence that the poem was written to break. The unspoken but unmistakable ground of this poem, that is to say, is the Holocaust—our impoverished term for the cruelty that overtook the Jew and turned him into smoke.

Now we have just looked at a poem about smoke and recognized that it served as a source of considerable metaphorical richness and variety. Thoreau changed the smoke into birds and clouds and religious incense, into a whole flock of wafting and melting and dissolving images. Glatstein, far from doing that, does the opposite: he changes the Jew into smoke. Worse yet—and at this point the poem turns into something else, something new in the history of poetry—he does so in a way that has *nothing at all to do with metaphor* a disabling fact that he forces upon us from the start. To read this poem at all, we must disown the figurative use of language, then, and interpret literally: the Jew has become smoke, and a similar fate will overtake his wife and children. Thereafter Glatstein will add a religious dimension to his poem, at which point we recognize play of another kind, that of Jewish speculative theology. The poem ends, in fact, on a note of theological paradox: the destroyed Jews will become absent company for an Absent God. Their "aspiration," or ascent, however, must not be understood in the first place in terms of paradox or fantasy or anything else that would detract from the brutal literalness of their end. For an exact parallel to their fate, remind yourselves of that casual but unforgettable moment in Hochhuth's *The Deputy* when the Doctor remarks, quite matter-of-factly, that "On Tuesday I piped the sister of Sigmund Freud up the chimney."[18]

It is all too strange but, at the same time, it is powerfully affecting. The poem, as we come to realize, is an assertion about a negation, a *double* negation: that of man and that of God, Both in this poem *are not*. Is there also a triple negation implied, the third loss being that of poetry itself? For what kind of poetry can we have that eschews the metaphorical use of language? The answer to this question compels us to recognize one of the deepest and most distinguishing characteristics of Holocaust literature and to state what may be one of its abiding laws: *there are no metaphors for Auschwitz, just as Auschwitz is not a metaphor for anything else*. Why is that the case? Because the flames were real flames, the ashes only ashes, the smoke always and only smoke. If one wants "meaning" out of that, it can only be this: at Auschwitz humanity incinerated its own heart.[19] Otherwise the burnings do not lend themselves to metaphor, simile, or symbol—to likeness or association with anything else. They can only "be" or "mean" what they in fact were: the death of the Jews.

The only knowledge we are left with, then, is this: in our own day, annihilation overleapt the bounds of metaphor and was *enacted* on earth. Is it possible to make poetry out of that? Insofar as it is a poem that has led us to this question, the answer, clearly, must be yes. Poetry—in this instance, a something about nothing, an assertion about a negation—survives to remind us of all that has been destroyed. And also to remind us of what has not been destroyed, for while it is true that Holocaust literature is nothing if not language in a condition of severe diminishment and decline, it is still capable of articulating powerful truths—if none other, then those that reflect life in its diminishment and decline. We have lost so much, but not yet the power to register what it is that has been taken from us.

Surely that is one of the major functions of Holocaust literature, to register and record the enormity of human loss. "For me," as Elie Wiesel once stated, "writing is a *matzeva* an invisible tombstone, erected to the memory of the dead unburied."[20] There is no denying the nobility of that conception of art nor the importance of its execution. Yet a tombstone is not a literary genre, and part of Wiesel's problem as a writer, as of all writers of the Holocaust, is to discover the literary forms most appropriate to representing the extremities of dehumanization and heroism that together begin to define what the Holocaust was.

In this connection, we must begin by recognizing that even before the advent of a literature of the Holocaust, the major literary genres were in a weakened state of flux and great uncertainty. Holocaust literature, which places its own heavy burdens on literary forms of all kinds, arrived, in fact, at a time when considerable doubt was already being raised about the ongoing viability of the narrative, dramatic, and lyrical modes. While it is not possible here to rehearse adequately the troubled state of modern fiction, drama, and poetry, it can be stated that a large part of the trouble derives from an increasingly felt imbalance between what the world daily offers us as raw data and the mind's ability to make sense of it through its own conceptual and inventive capacities. This imbalance reached its most extreme point in Nazism's campaign of terror and destruction against the Jews. In the ghettos and camps of Europe "reality" underwent so radical a distortion as to disarm and render no longer trustworthy the normal cognitive and expressive powers. As a result, reason seemed to give way to madness, as language did time and again to silence. When those thresholds dissolve, literature—a product of the composed mind and senses—is reduced to screams and whimpers: *it decomposes*. And there is no escaping the fact that, in part, Holocaust literature is a literature of decomposition. "No, this is not life!" runs the familiar refrain in Chaim Kaplan's diary. Although Kaplan had lived in Warsaw for forty years and must have come to know it well, the city's transformation under Nazi rule into a place of madness and slaughter disoriented him almost totally. "At times," he wrote, "it seems to me that I am in an alien land, entirely unknown to me." At other times his sense of displacement exceeded anything even resembling the terrestrial, so that it appeared "the ghetto was suspended over nothingness."[21]

That strain of irreality runs throughout Holocaust literature and continually undermines it. "Today at this very moment as I sit writing at a table, I am not convinced that these things really happened."[22] The confession in this instance is Primo Levi's, but it speaks a common truth, one known to all writers of the Holocaust and one as well that quite obviously subverts the writer's enterprise. For what literary means—what mere words—could possibly compete with the extravagant inventiveness of Nazism? In that time when day was ruled over by the twisted sun of the swastika and night by the dominant black of the Death's Head, life itself became a kind of macabre theatre. Nazism was far more than that, of course, was nothing less than an unrestrained plague of steel and flame, but it also worked in more subtle ways, preparing its ultimate terror by intermediary steps of manipulative distortion and deception. In this respect it might legitimately be grasped within the terms of literary fabrication, terms that a Joseph Goebbels or a Leni Riefenstahl was intimate with. Moreover, it is not difficult to locate the imaginative sources of this aspect of its genius. George Steiner pointed to them quite specifically and also quite accurately, I think, when he argued that Nazism was a literal staging of hell on earth, a perception confirmed by virtually all writers of Holocaust literature.[23] Hell as a prototype of the ghettos and death camps—that, it seems, was Christianity's distinctive contribution to the Final Solution, although one would hope to understand it as a Christianity turned against itself, in rebellion against itself and its own deepest principles.

In this paradigm of ethical and religious subversion, we may be able to discover a literary paradigm as well, one that is constant enough in Holocaust literature to constitute another of its governing laws. To grasp it, we must understand the revisionary and essentially antithetical nature of so much of Holocaust writing, which not only mimics and parodies but finally refutes and rejects its direct literary antecedents. The *Bildungsroman*, as Lawrence Langer has demonstrated, is one of these.[24] In such a book as *Night*, the traditional pattern of successfully initiating a young boy into social life and his own maturity is altogether reversed. Primo Levi's *Survival in Auschwitz*, which chronicles the devolution of a man, is a more complicated instance of the same thing. In both cases one sees not only the reversal of a familiar literary pattern but also a repudiation of the philosophical basis on which it rests. Wiesel defined that for us precisely when he concluded that "at Auschwitz, not only man died, but also the idea of man."[25] With the crumbling of that idea, all narrative forms that posit the reality of *persons*— rational, educable, morally responsible beings—are undermined and perhaps even invalidated. Yet such personal narratives of the Holocaust as the two just mentioned necessarily depend upon the traditional means of memoir, autobiography, and *Bildungsroman*, even though the stories they relate rewind the progress of growth *backwards*—from life toward death. I do not know that Wiesel and Levi consciously chose to counterpose their terrifying accounts of dehumanization against forms that are essentially civilized and humane, but the effects of such a jarring contrast are unmistakable and strongly felt in their books.

In the case of Paul Celan, it is clear that an attitude of repudiation was not only consciously held but specifically developed as a technique for writing post-Holocaust poetry. The evidence, as Jerry Glenn has shown,[26] is everywhere—in the ironically destructive allusions to the Songs of Songs and Goethe's Faust in *"Todesfuge"*; in the radical undoing of Hölderlin's famous hymn "Patmos" in *"Tenebrae"*; in the denial of the Genesis account of God's creation of man in *"Psalm"*. In each of these cases (and many similar ones could be brought forward), Celan employs a technique of literary subversion that the German critic Götz Wienold has called a "Widerruf."[27] We have no precise English equivalent for the term—"repudiation" comes closest—but it is not difficult to explain through an illustrating example.

Consider, for instance, this line from Chaim Kaplan's diary: "The enemy of Israel neither sleeps nor slumbers."[28] Kaplan wrote that, almost certainly, not out of a mood of blasphemy but as an expression of genuine religious despair. It appears in his pages in an entry dated "October 12, 1940/End of Yom Kippur, 5701." On that very day the edict to establish the ghetto went into effect. The year before, at the end of Yom Kippur 5700, Kaplan noted in his diary that "on the Day of Atonement the enemy displayed even greater might than usual," employing its artillery to destroy and kill at random. In the intervening year the bombardments only got worse, and it became clear to Kaplan that Warsaw Jewry was to face complete destruction. "Is this the way the Almighty looks after His dear ones?" he asks. "Has Israel no God?" He could not admit that, so on Yom Kippur 5701 he gathered with his fellow Jews, "like Marranos in the fifteenth century," to pray secretly and illegally for God's forgiveness and mercy. What Jewish Warsaw received, however, was not the protection of the Guardian of Israel but the ghetto edict, which then and there effectively sealed the fate of hundreds of thousands of Polish Jews. Kaplan's profound shock at this reversal registers in that terrible line—"The enemy of Israel neither sleeps nor slumbers"—a few words only but enough to show a whole sustaining faith come crashing down. The entry for "October 24, 1940/ The night of Simhat Torah, 5701" brings the matter to its bitter conclusion: "But he who sits in Heaven laughs."[29]

In Kaplan's case, it would make no sense to identify such expressions of forlornness and raw pain as examples of "technique," if by that we imply a conscious literary method. Kaplan, a highly literate Jew, composed his diary in Hebrew and quite naturally thought in a language pervaded by biblical and Talmudic passages. These influences never drop from his prose, but, as he witnessed the level of Nazi barbarism rise in the ghetto, they undergo inversion, substitution, and reversals. In brief, they are demoralized, destabilized, subverted. Writing under this kind of pressure becomes countercommentary.

Celan, uneducated to Talmud but a sophisticated modern poet, adopted these changes deliberately and developed them technically in his poems. The Yiddish poet Jacob Glatstein frequently did the same. I suspect that André Schwarz-Bart worked somewhat similarly in writing *The Last of the Just*, a novel that should be understood, I believe, not only as an exhaustion of the Jewish tradition of the *Lamed-Vov* but of the Christian traditions of the saint's life and the *imitatio Christi* as well. In *The Painted Bird Jerzy* Kosinski will appropriate some of the language of the New Testament and Christian liturgy only to undermine it and invalidate its claims to permanent religious truth. Rolf Hochhuth will do the same in his highly charged and controversial play, which, among other things, offers itself as a contemporary rewriting of the lives of the popes.

The common element in all these examples is the employment of the literary text as refutation and repudiation, a denial not only of an antecedent literary assertion but also of its implicit premises and explicit affirmations. If the camps had lasted longer, Primo Levi speculated, "a new, harsh language would have been born,"[30] an argot sufficiently wasted in spirit and befouled by crime to express the demolition of man that took place in the Holocaust universe. Such a new language in fact did begin to emerge, but in the main Holocaust literature relies for its expression on the received languages and the established literary forms. It does so, however, in the profoundly revisionary way that we have been noticing, turning earlier literary models against themselves and, in the process, overturning the reigning conceptions of man and his world that speak in and through the major writings of our literary traditions.

In part, the result is a literature of dystopia, a winding down of human actions and expectations, a severe record of life "on the bottom." Recording as it does the unprecedented fate of innocent people sealed into the living hell of boxcars, penned into filth and terror by ghetto walls and electrified barbed wires, how could it be anything but constricted, despairing, and dystopic?

And yet, for the greater part it *is* otherwise, for while Holocaust literature offers no new affirmations, the very fact that it exists is proof that its writers have not opted for the ultimate negation: *silence*. The struggle into words may appear an impossibility to some and a madness to others, but the story will be told, again and again and again, even if there is little confidence that it will be listened to and heeded.

What kind of story is it? Who is its rightful teller? And how much should we trust him? Among other questions about the nature of Holocaust literature, these three are particularly pressing. For if we do not recognize the story for what it is, or the storyteller for who he is, it becomes impossible to give credence to his tale.

The first of these questions is best answered by another question—this one, posed by Primo Levi: "Our stories, ... all different and all full of a tragic, disturbing necessity, ... are they not themselves stories of a new Bible?"[31] I think we must agree that they are, that Holocaust literature at its heart of hearts is revelatory in some new way, although of what we do not yet know. We must acknowledge, however, that it returns us to biblical revelation in newly compelling and urgently critical ways, which force us to rethink all received truths about God and man and world under the pressure of history's worst crime.

There is something preposterous and even obscene about the notion of gross evil being inspiring, yet more than anything else, it is this crime, simultaneously searing and illuminating, that has inflicted the writer's vocation on the novelists and poets of the Holocaust. That it *is* an infliction is no longer open to doubt, for all survivors of this catastrophe who venture to write about it confess a disfiguration or impairment of one kind or another—a lapse in vision, a muteness of voice, other vaguer disturbances of the sensorium. Think of how badly mutilated Ernie Levy is, how some of Celan's poems break down into stammering, how pervasive the fear of blinding is in Kosinski's writings, how often Elie Wiesel's survivors seem to be struck dumb. For a summarizing example, think most of all of that frightening line in one of Nelly Sachs's late poems—the most costly *ars poetica* I know—"This can be put on paper only / with one eye ripped out."[32] No one touched by the Holocaust is ever whole again—that much this literature makes clear.

Yet that is not the whole truth, for while crime is impairing, it is also powerfully vivifying, exposing the world as never before in all its most frightful detail. The Holocaust has worked on its authors in a double way, then, simultaneously disabling them and enlarging their vision. If you would know the type, think of Bellow's Artur Sammler, whose left eye, crushed by the blow of a gun butt, "distinguished only light and shade," but whose right eye, "dark-bright," was full of the keenest observations.[33] Sammler, I believe, is our prototype of the Holocaust writer, a man so wounded by his past as to suffer a detached and admittedly distorted sense of the present but also so thoroughly chastened by experience as to see with an almost prophetic exactness, farther and deeper than ordinary insight allows. *Holocaust writers, in short, are one-eyed seers, men possessed of a double knowledge: cursed into knowing how perverse the human being can be to create such barbarism and blessed by knowing how strong he can be to survive it.*

How, though, can we put our trust in one-eyed seers, men of impaired and only partial vision? How can we not trust them, for they are the prophets of our time—maimed into truth by the crack of the gun butt. To see with them may indeed mean to risk seeing under the handicap of a shattered vision, but to foreswear what they have seen is to court blindness altogether.

If all Holocaust writers are in some sense one-eyed seers, what is the extent and what are the forms of impairment in the writings of Elie Wiesel? And how well does he cope with it? The first of these questions is answered readily enough: virtually all of Wiesel's writings are shadowed by silence and madness, the twin terrors of a childhood experience so monstrous as to be hardly accessible to language or to reason. Read almost anywhere in the succession of books from *Night* to *Zalmen* and you will find words struggling to express a pain that, the author insistently believes, may best be indicated by acts of deliberate silence. Yet speechlessness does not give us a dozen books—*writing* does—and Wiesel is a prolific, even a driven, writer. How, then, does one reconcile this extreme tension between the claims of silence and the claims of the word? That is one of the most persistent and least resolved questions that one asks in reading through the canon of this author's work.

As to madness, it is a fearsome thing, although some readers have preferred to see elements of sanctity in it and to interpret it in "positive" terms, as a necessary part of some kind of religious mystique. Wiesel himself has encouraged this kind of thinking by reiterating a theme of "holy madness" in many of his books. Consider, for instance, how Zalmen pushes the rabbi to the limits of his spiritual and imaginative powers—"Be mad, Rabbi, be mad!" he urges, for "one has to be mad today to believe in God and man."[34] We try to understand the experience that moves Wiesel in that direction, and to understand as well the urgency behind it, but nonetheless it is wiser to distrust the impulse to have imagination go mad. For most, it is far better to resist rather than provoke such feelings.

As outsiders, though, we have to acknowledge that Wiesel must follow his own compulsions, wherever they might lead him. Is it not the case, however, that in *Zalmen* they lead him to contemplate the end of his strength as a writer? For this is, among other things, a play about the futility of gesture, the emptiness of language, the uselessness of Jewish protest. Ultimately, and in the most highly personal terms, it is also a play in which Wiesel reflects despairingly on his whole career as one of futile gesture, impotent and empty words, an unlistened to and unheeded story.[35] Hence the madness that haunts so much of his writing, which increasingly has become the compelling *subject* of that writing.

Yet just as there are no literary forms that encompass silence, there are none that accommodate madness. There is a kind of prose that approximates hallucination, and Wiesel has written in it, at times with great success. He has also taken frequent recourse to parables, paradoxes, riddles, dreams, and reverie—once more, apparently, in an attempt to discover some adequate form to express the extreme *gnosis* that stands at the heart of his vision. The aim seems to be to descend deeper into madness, there to confront and even perhaps to heal the fearful madness of God himself. Such a prospect takes the breath away; it also reduces words to what they were at Babel. Does the rabbi in *Zalmen* not state the case revealingly for the author himself when he cries, in utter frustration, "My strength is gone. Sentences tear apart inside me. Words are drained of meaning, they fly away, disperse and fall on me like enemies. They strangle me."[36] There is nothing liberating or illuminating about that kind of wildness, which, if too long encouraged, carries us beyond literature into a silence that has nothing holy or otherwise "positive" about it. It is a side to Wiesel's writing that badly needs to be tamed or transcended. To plunge further into it, though, is to enter a madness from which there is no assured return. It is, in fact, to join the Kotzker rebbe behind a locked and never-to-be-opened door.[37]

These, we might say, are the maimings that Wiesel has suffered as a writer. There is no question but that he is aware of them, is alert to their dangers, and has taken steps to defend against and grow beyond them. One such step is to adopt a style of discursive prose that permits a far greater control of ideas than is possible in the trancelike prose-poetry of some of his fiction. Wiesel has written with great sensitivity and a notable persuasiveness in the essay form, which seems on occasion the most appropriate for some of the problems he addresses. Actually, he has been laboring to create a literary form situated somewhere *between* fiction and the essay, a kind of writing that will allow him to utilize the dramatic elements of dialogue and character, which we normally associate with fiction, together with the more rational elements of discourse and coherent argument, which belong more typically to exposition. He has already achieved some memorable successes in this mixed mode—as many of the pieces in *Legends of Our Time* and *One*

Generation After show—and one expects that he will go on to refine and further develop a significant strain of his writing along these lines.

His turn to Midrash, or neo-Midrash, represents another movement away from silence and madness, and one which twice now in recent years has shown itself to be especially fruitful. Both *Souls on Fire* and *Messengers of God* are strong books—works of original commentary and synoptic insight—that demonstrate an ability to exercise imagination and intellect without driving either mad. In giving us these portraits and legends, it is clear that Wiesel has returned to one of the specifically Jewish sources of his literary and spiritual sensibility, and one expects that this rediscovery of a native strain will be sustaining and not quickly played out.

Fiction, though—and, more than anything else, Wiesel has been seen as a fiction writer—presents problems that are not so easily solved. A fiction writer responds in the first place to the texture of experience—to *this* particular place, and how it looked and smelled and sounded; to *these* particular people, and how they dressed and talked and ran about; to specific seasons of the year, and their special fruitfulness or desolateness; to a landscape seen once and never forgotten, against which a life played itself out in a way that had an inevitability and a consequence all its own. Sighet, Wiesel's particular place, was torn away from him too violently and too soon, one imagines, for it to return in his fiction in this closely felt and completely rounded way. It does return, to be sure, but more as *idea* than as place; perhaps it would be more accurate to say that he returns in idea to *it*, but to it as it existed for him in potential, not as densely lived and concretely realized fact. This loss of surfaces is, to a novelist, a deprivation that no amount of ideas can make up for. And while Wiesel has worked admirably to relocate himself in the town of his birth, to resettle its streets and repopulate its houses, one feels that his is a homecoming that will remain forever incomplete and unfulfilled.

As it must be unfulfilled, given the fate of Sighet and of the young boy hurled so brutally out of that place into a realm of unreality. What exists between the two—between home and hell—is a space that fiction is hard put to occupy. Ideas can flow into that kind of existential vacuum, but the senses cannot. As a result, in most of his books *nothing palpable comes to replace place*. Wiesel's fiction, rich in reflection, meditation, and the accents of a sustained spiritual striving, does not shape itself easily around a phenomenal world. *Things* are lacking, and it is through things that a novelist makes his progress into thought. After *Night*, though, the pattern in Wiesel's writings largely seems to run the other way: thought *precedes* and is looking to find its way back into things. But for the most part this is a searching without finding, a return to a place that is no longer there; hence the abstract, somewhat disembodied quality of experience in much of the fiction, its frequent disconnections, and its heavy reliance on a world made up of words alone. Wiesel's French masters—especially Camus and Sartre—seem to have been able to manage better in that mode, but they were writing by and large about a merely theoretical or philosophical *Angst* an anguish and fear several steps removed from the pit of flames that the young Elie Wiesel almost was forced into at Auschwitz. For that tragically Jewish experience, French thought and French literary forms seem inadequate. Whether there *is* an adequate fictional form for it at all is a question that still remains to be answered. It would seem that Wiesel is at a stage in his career where he is striving to reach an accommodation between what the French writers taught him fiction might be able to do and what his Jewish masters tell him must be done. In this respect, the recent turn to Midrash seems especially promising.

NOTES

1. T.W. Adorno, "Engagement," in *Noten zur Literatur III* (Frankfurt am Main: Suhrkamp Verlag, 1965), pp. 109–35.

2. Reinhard Baumgart, "Unmenschlichkeit beschreiben," in *Literatur für Zeitgenossen: Essays* (Frankfurt am Main: Suhrkamp Verlag, 1966), pp. 12–36.

3. Michael Wyschogrod, "Some Theological Reflections on the Holocaust," *Response* 25 (Spring 1975), 68.

4. Elie Wiesel, "For Some Measure of Humility," *Sh' ma* 5/100 (October 31, 1975), 314.

5. Abraham I. Katsh, ed., *The Warsaw Diary of Chaim Kaplan* (New York: Collier Books, 1973), p. 400.

6. Ernst Schnabel, *Anne Frank: A Portrait in Courage* (New York: Harbace Paperback Library, 1958).

7. Emil Fackenheim, "Sachsenhausen 1938: Groundwork for Auschwitz," *Midstream* XXI (April 1975), 27–31.

8. See George Steiner, *Language and Silence* (New York: Atheneum, 1967), p. 67.

9. Two critical studies are in print: Irving Halperin's *Messengers from the Dead* (Philadelphia: The Westminster Press, 1970) and Lawrence Langer's *The Holocaust and the Literary Imagination* (New Haven: Yale University Press, 1976).

10. A. J. P. Taylor, *The Second World War* (New York: G. P. Putnam's Sons, 1975), p. 149. By distinguishing "the war against the Jews" from the Second World War, I do not want to imply, of course, any approval of avoidance of the Holocaust in texts on the war period. My intention is quite the opposite: to see the Holocaust for what it was so as to afford it a greater emphasis in historical writings.

11. Elie Wiesel, *Night* (New York: Avon, 1969), p. 44.

12. Wiesel, "Snapshots," in *One Generation After* (New York: Random House, 1970), pp. 46–47.

13. Uri Zvi Greenberg, "We Were Not Likened to Dogs among the Gentiles," in Ruth Finer Mintz, *Modern Hebrew Poetry* (Berkeley: University of California Press, 1968), p. 126.

14. Wiesel, "The Death of My Father," in *Legends of Our Time* (New York: Holt, Rinehart and Winston, 1968), p. 7.

15. "One Generation After," in *One Generation After*, p. 10.

16. *Night*, p. 42.

17. Jacob Glatstein, "Smoke," in I. Howe and E. Greenberg, *A Treasury of Yiddish Poetry* (New York: Holt, Rinehart and Winston, 1969), p. 331; the translation is by Chana Faerstein. Reprinted by permission.

18. Rolf Hochhuth, *The Deputy* (New York: Grove Press, Inc., 1964), p. 72.

19. "A Plea for the Dead," in *Legends of Our Time*, p. 190.

20. "My Teachers," in *Legends of Our Time*, p. 8.

21. *The Warsaw Diary of Chaim Kaplan*, pp. 27, 34, 377.

22. Primo Levi, *Survival in Auschwitz* (New York: Collier Books, 1973), p. 94.

23. George Steiner, *In Bluebeard's Castle* (New Haven: Yale University Press, 1971), pp. 53–56. The landscape of hell is referred to repeatedly throughout the literature; the moral conditions that obtain, however, are altogether absent. My interest here is only in the endless tortures of the place, not at all in the ethical system that governs it in Christian religious writings.

24. *The Holocaust and the Literary Imagination*, pp. 82, 84.

25. "A Plea for the Dead," in *Legends of Our Time*, p. 190.

26. Jerry Glenn, *Paul Celan* (New York: Twayne Publishers, Inc., 1973).

27. Götz Wienold, "Paul Celan's Hölderlin-Widerruf," *Poetica* 2 (1968), 216–28.

28. *The Warsaw Diary of Chaim Kaplan*, p. 208.

29. Ibid., pp. 36, 209, 207, 213. As conditions in the ghetto changed, Kaplan vacillated between moments of religious despair and moments of faith; the attitude illustrated by the quotation cited in these passages, while prevalent, was not constant.

30. *Survival in Auschwitz*, p. 113.

31. Ibid., p. 59.

32. Nelly Sachs, *The Seeker and Other Poems* (New York: Farrar, Straus and Giroux, 1970), p. 387; the translation is by Michael Hamburger.

33. Saul Bellow, *Mr. Sammler's Planet* (New York: Viking, 1970), p. 4.

34. Wiesel, *Zalmen, or the Madness of God* (New York: Random House, 1974), p. 79.

35. Ibid., p. 169: "Poor hero, poor dreamer. You have lost.... How could you have been so naive? Did you really—really—believe that your gesture would shake the

earth? Mankind has other worries.... Life goes on. And those who don't suffer refuse to hear about suffering—and particularly about Jewish suffering."

36. Ibid., p. 96.

37. Scholars have excavated several layers of madness in the writings of Elie Wiesel, but the one that I am stressing here—the nonmystical layer—has gone virtually ignored. Yet it is precisely madness in the common or clinical sense that requires attention. Wiesel himself has indicated its presence all along, as in this passage from *The Accident* (New York: Hill and Wang, 1962), p. 104: "We cannot forget. The images are there in front of our eyes. Even if our eyes were no longer there, the images would remain. I think if I were able to forget I would hate myself. Our stay there planted time bombs within us. From time to time one of them explodes.... One of these bombs ... will undoubtedly bring about madness."

ROBERT SKLOOT

Tragedy and the Holocaust

And yet, first of all, I should like to slaughter one or two men, just to
throw off the concentration camp mentality, the effects of continual
subservience, the effects of helplessly watching others being beaten and
murdered, the effects of all this horror. I suspect, though, that I will be
marked for life. I do not know whether we shall survive, but I like to
think that one day we shall have the courage to tell the world the whole
truth and call it by its proper name.

—Tadeusz Borowski
"Auschwitz, Our Home (A Letter)"

I

Artists and their critics live with the hard and humbling truth that their
writing keeps raising the same questions that have been asked for centuries.
They also live with the harder truth that despite passion and concern, the
answers to significant moral and aesthetic questions remain elusive. What *has*
changed over the course of much time, especially the accelerated time of the
last half-century, is the awareness of a greater urgency to these questions and
a greater burden we carry to them. The issue of tragedy, of its nature and
possibility, and of how it is related to the Holocaust is the two-edged
problem I would like to discuss.

From *The Darkness We Carry: The Drama of the Holocaust*. © 1988 by The Board of Regents of
the University of Wisconsin System.

In the considerable debate over the relationship of Holocaust literature to tragedy, much attention has focused on the characteristics that distinguish tragedy from other theatrical forms, i.e., comedy and tragicomedy. But before that problem can be addressed, it is necessary to decide where to search for the characteristics that contribute to what can be called tragic in drama: in the play's elements ("the tragic character" or "the tragic action"), in the audience ("the tragic response"), or in the playwright ("the tragic vision"). Since Aristotle, these have been the places where the confirmation of the tragic experience can be found.

The kinds of plays that comprise the theatre of the Holocaust usually describe the lives of Jews who succumbed to or survived Nazi persecution. Their stories have both a historical and a fictional dimension. That these victims of violence possess distinguishing characteristics—of their conditions or of their actions—that permit them to represent us, or at least most of us, seems to me indisputable. And because all serious drama seeks its effects through identification with stage characters and emblematic settings, it is possible that the Jewish character in the Holocaust context may represent all people, Jew and non-Jew, in the description of universal human conditions.

There is, of course, much debate over whether tragedy can be written at all in the twentieth century, and the dramatized Holocaust experience that reaches for the tragic condition adds to the debate. At various times over the last several generations, the impossibility of writing tragedy has been credited to a host of disparate (often contradictory) causes, including nineteenth-century theories of determinism, Freudian psychology, political democracy, rejection of classical artistic forms, twentieth-century theories of existential meaninglessness, and Christian salvation. Yet tragedy, or at least the *idea* of tragedy, réfuses to die despite the eloquent refutations of numerous critics, among whom George Steiner is one.

Steiner, a prolific and wide-ranging commentator on culture in general and European literatures in particular, has written with extraordinary insight into the issues raised by the Holocaust and its literary manifestations. He was among the earliest critics whose expansive preoccupations with the Holocaust included an anxious personal statement for the future of the Jewish people combined with a professional concern for the implications of genocide on dramatic form. Among Steiner's earliest important works was *The Death of Tragedy* (1961), a book that surveys the history of Western literature with the objective of charting the demise of the tragic possibility in literary creation. Curiously, *The Death of Tragedy* begins with a brief discussion of the relationship between "the Judaic sense of the world" and tragedy, a relationship Steiner describes as one of alienation, but one he rarely attends to again in the course of his book. He writes: "The Judaic spirit is vehement in its conviction that the order of the universe and of man's estate is accessible to reason."[1]

Steiner believes that tragedy can flourish only alongside a conviction of the world's essential irrationality, a perspective on life that was unavailable to the Jews from their earliest days as a people because of the rational bias of their culture. He argues that as Western society became increasingly drawn to the rational, a shift that culminated in the nineteenth century and the Age of Reason, Western art became less tragic. At the conclusion of his book, he implies that tragedy becomes possible again when cultures become *less* rational in behavior and belief. In a later essay, "A Kind of Survivor" (1964), Steiner surveys the eternal status of Jews as the scapegoat of the world's other religions and calls this permanent condition of persecution "a condition almost beyond rational understanding."[2] Acknowledging his Jewishness, he is able to describe himself as "a kind of survivor" despite his geographical distance from the Holocaust in Europe.

By accepting the historical, *inevitable* fact of the Jews' persecution across centuries, and by focusing his attention on the irrational terminus of irrational behavior, the Holocaust, Steiner edges closer to relocating the true tragic material for contemporary literary and dramatic expression in the murder of six million Jews between 1939 and 1945. In the *failure* of rationality in the enlightened center of Europe, he comes to see the crucial, paradoxical event of modern times.

> Why did humanistic traditions and models of conduct prove so fragile a barrier against political bestiality? In fact, were they a barrier, or is it more realistic to perceive in humanistic culture express solicitations of authoritarian rule and cruelty?[3]

At the same time that Steiner discovers terror, confusion, and identity, he also discovers in the Holocaust a countervailing positive force that produces a restored aesthetic opportunity; tragedy, purchased at the price of one-third of his people, may be a kind of perverse reward of their destruction. This conclusion poses the possibility of reawakened tragedy and a reawakening cultural heritage as the result of an abominable historical event. (I sense that this recognition created serious psychological discomfort for Steiner, which can be seen in his response to the criticism of his 1982 novella *The Portage to San Cristobal of A.H.* and the play adapted from it by Christopher Hampton the following year. I discuss the play and its reception in chapter 4.)

Steiner thus locates in his heritage and in recent history the material that can produce, in the right hands, the tragic vision. Based on a millennial vocation for suffering that, arriving at the Holocaust, con tinues to elude understanding despite the most thorough of cultural investigations, Steiner's personal journey seems to have returned him to the tragic mystery after a lifelong search. While struggling to make sense of the most irrational event in modern history, applying a deeply rational energy to it, he finds only warning, frustration, and fear. Yet, if traditional tragedy flourished in an ancient world characterized by ignorance, faith, turbulence, suffering, and death, then the Holocaust, from the perspective of artists and critics, replicates those same conditions, enabling (if it were desired) the rediscovery of the idea of the tragic. Simply, in the record of humiliations endured through time and across continents, in the mad hatred against Jews, may be found the organizing experience of tragedy.

Drawing himself back into the history of his people, Steiner has given a new legitimacy and a new context to his historical-aesthetic investigations. At the same time, he appears to admit the failure of his search to produce results that are fully understandable, not to say consoling. In Richmond Hathorn's terms, he has perceived in his life both objective dilemmas and subjective confusions, turning to criticism and then to art to relax the grip of his discomfort. In Jewish myth and history he has found material endlessly provocative and mysterious which pressures him to "acknowledge that the existence of ... ignorance is itself inevitable."[4] The conclusion also seems inevitable: the dramatizing of the irrational loss of human life in an unfathomable universe, which began in ancient Greece, continues in the work of contemporary playwrights challenged by the Holocaust's conditions of suffering and mystery.

There is, as has been pointed out by commentators on the Holocaust, a double danger in rediscovering one's heritage in the attempted destruction of it.[5] First, of lesser interest, is that the rediscovery may result in living negatively, i.e., of wanting to frustrate your enemies as a way to maintain your own continuance. Of greater importance is that it can blind the individual to the positive, life-affirming, and beautiful aspects of one's culture and history. In the context of the Holocaust, this second problem can be minimized by playwrights who, while acknowledging the magnitude of the destruction, revert to the older, traditional artistic forms to convey a more positive design and significance in the world. Further, if Steiner's long struggle can be seen as a model critical and personal journey, his assertion of a renewed tragic possibility in effect neutralizes the following specific objections of three critics who maintain that Holocaust material is unavailable for tragic theatrical presentation:

1.   Stephen Spender's assessment, derived from his study of Holocaust poetry, that "the anonymous victim is, in the Western tradition, no subject for tragedy;"[6]

2.   Terrence Des Pres's belief, derived from his important study of life in concentration camps, that the "tragic hero finds in death a victory.... He is proof of spirit's contempt for the flesh, and death itself becomes a confirmation of the greatness. There is much to be admired in such a stance, but not in the time of plague;"[7]

3.   Lawrence Langer's assertion that "man's fate in the death camps can never be 'celebrated' through the traditional forms of tragic experience."[8]

In the face of the intractable demands of dramatic presentation, including the need to identify emotionally with characters portrayed on stage as dynamic individuals by live performers, Holocaust material confronts playwrights with a situation that appears to *restrict* the creation of tragic images and experiences in at least four ways: the anonymity of the victims' death (untragic characters), the seeming meaninglessness of their suffering (untragic vision), the circumscribed nature of the actions available to the protagonists (untragic action), and the unavailability of certain emotional options to the audience (untragic response). Can playwrights overcome these obstacles and provide moving and meaningful portrayals of characters caught acting in their destructive history?

Playwrights who respond affirmatively are likely to believe that traditional tragedy provides an appropriate form for the story they have to tell. Some have continued to fashion characters and plays faithful to classical tragic models (of which *Oedipus the King* is one paradigm) by describing protagonists whose heroic stature is confirmed by their choosing actions that are then shown to determine their fate. In other words, some playwrights continue to create characters who possess the individual autonomy to influence their future and who behave in ways that affirm universal values amid their personal and terminal distress. The clearest examples (but not the only ones) of this type of character are found in plays written about historical figures: Janusz Korczak, Hannah Senesh, or Anne Frank—characters who defy group identity and anonymous death and who contradict the restrictive conditions of helplessness and futility to achieve a personal triumph that accompanies their destruction.[9]

Understandably, the sharpest refutation of the "sense" of these plays is historical and cultural in nature. First, the totality of the Holocaust overwhelms (or negates) the small, occasional examples of resistance or integrity. Second, the larger artistic problem of postwar writing, which Wylie Sypher has called the "loss of the self," also impinges on the tragic form by locating, in a more general sense, the diminishment of the human figure by technology. Sypher writes:

> We have already reached the crux of our problem: Is it possible, while the individual is vanishing behind the functionary throughout the technological world, to have any sort of humanism that does not depend on the older notions of the self, the independent self that is outdated or at least victimized by the operations of power on its present scale? Any such humanism must come to terms with our sense of anonymity of the self, must therefore get beyond any romantic notion of selfhood.[10]

In the light of the historical concreteness of Hitler's "final solution to the Jewish question" (a product of the Nazis' technical mastery) and the cultural decline of the autonomous citizen, it can be argued that humanity is literally *and* metaphorically shrunken, making any positive image less tenable and harder to accept in the modern world. Anonymity seems to attach itself to life *and* death in the Holocaust. In addition, because of "the privileged position of the Holocaust reader" as "'collaborative'" witness to the events recounted,[11] the loss of self involves a moral as well as a historical and cultural dimension.[12]

Nonetheless, if a belief in the efficacy of traditional forms can be sustained, or a fear of anonymous, meaningless life and death rejected (*which amounts to the same thing*), it is possible that "positive" plays about the Holocaust can be accepted on their own terms and judged for their honesty and effectiveness. Above all, the need these plays fill in the lives of audiences and playwrights must be acknowledged.

> ... an essential part of our conviction that an experience [in the theatre] is momentous derives from what we take to be the import of the play.

> ... if part of this conviction derives from what the play means, another part derives from the mere fact *that* it means.

Meaningfulness is itself momentous for human beings, as they discover, *a contrario*, whenever life has no meaning for them. All art serves as a lifeboat to rescue us from the ocean of meaninglessness—an extraordinary service to perform at any time and more than ever when religion and philosophy prove less and less able to perform it. To be thus rescued is to rediscover our personal dignity, through which alone we can discover dignity in others, dignity in human life as such.[13]

This traditional belief in art and its ethical function cannot attract all artists, but it has exercised a considerable influence on a number of playwrights who have taken up the Holocaust theme. Their objective is more than the creation of a "momentary stay against confusion" (in Robert Frost's phrase), but it certainly encompasses that. It involves a formal program or strategy for dealing with the terror and mystery of human experience in a Holocaust or post-Holocaust world. Taken to an unwholesome extreme, these plays may define a sentimental or delusionary picture of the world devoid of any sense of historical catastrophe, as Lawrence Langer has pointed out.[14] But, when playwrights sincerely adhere to this belief as a genuine aesthetic (and thus moral) option, audiences witness images of a world whose values can confront meaningless, terrible existence with the implication that, in special cases at least, victory is in some small way possible. And, according to traditional tragedy, the individuals who do challenge the forces of catastrophic fate *are* unique, like us and different from us at the same time. Whether or not this strategy is irresponsible and childish or necessary and courageous, we do not seem wholly able to dispense with the hopeful and heroic aspects of tragedy. And although sorely tempted, neither can most artists *totally* sacrifice their intuitive, natural use of some life-affirming action, even in the presence of concentration camps. Robert J. Lifton identifies this condition, which helps to explain (but for some, not excuse) the reluctance to jettison traditional dramatic forms:

A Western world would [fail] if it sought to cope with a massive death immersion by totally abandoning the emotional and literary heritage of tragedy. While tragedy posits a heroic struggle against death-linked destiny ..., [it is] a means of reasserting a connection, integrity, and movement necessary for symbolic integrity ... [15]

II

As a theatrical character, the figure of Janusz Korczak has come to represent the qualities of integrity, responsibility, and courage that enhance the image of the Holocaust's victims, who so often are pictured as compromising, passive, and helpless. In his decision to shield the children in his care from the worst horrors of their deportation—and in his determination to adhere to a philosophy of respect, responsibility, and love for people of all ages despite penalty of terrible death—he has been embraced by numerous playwrights as a forceful, positive counterweight to the denial of meaning and the anonymity of death so often stressed in the recounting of the Holocaust experience. In the same historical experience where others find nihilism and unredeemed suffering, these playwrights (with varying degrees of success and assurance) discover evidence of heroism and humane possibility. All retain the sense of extraordinary loss (seen in the deaths of Korczak and the children he cared for), but they refuse to relinquish the positive image without which their vision of the moral world would totally collapse. Thus, they reject outright the notion of circumscribing human action to the degree that it denies the tragic vision, as Walter Kerr has shown:

> There is only one development chilling enough to have done the job [of killing off tragedy]. Man would have had to press beyond the business of analyzing his freedom to act, beyond watching himself in a mirror as he debated whether or not he might responsibly use his freedom to act. He would have had to come to disbelieve in his freedom to act. He would have had to deny freedom itself in order to kill tragedy.[16]

Erwin Sylvanus's play *Dr. Korczak and the Children* (see chapter 5) is perhaps the best-known play on the life of Korczak, winning the Leo Baeck Prize in 1958; more recent plays by Tamara Karren (*Who Was That Man?*) and Gabriel Emanuel (*Children of the Night*) are not as dramatically skilled. But of all the Korczak plays, it is Michael Brady's *Korczak's Children* that deserves more attention than it has received, for it possesses considerable theatrical power and can shed much light on the possibilities for one kind of a tragic retelling of the Holocaust experience.[17]

Korczak's Children focuses on Korczak's efforts to save his orphanage and provide for its children, but Brady broadens the action to include a fuller discussion of the historical and cultural context in which Korczak lived and worked. The play begins with the orphanage children performing a little play

about Poland's King Casimir, who, despite counsel to the contrary, is
determined to protect Poland's Jewish population. Outside in the Warsaw
street, a Polish mob is threatening them all with violence; inside, the children
are starving. There is both charm and irony in this little playlet for, in 1942,
there was no one to protect the Jews, and their condition was truly desperate.
For the rest of the play, Korczak, with little success and diminishing hope,
will attempt to extract from potential benefactors some assistance for the
children in his care.

A secondary figure in the play is Emmanuel Ringelblum. Ringelblum
was the noted historian of the Warsaw Ghetto, whose determination to
collect the written materials of its daily life helped to preserve for later
generations the primary evidence of awful existence. Here, Ringelblum has
tutored the same three children who acted in the "King Casimir" story to
learn enough about the Catholic religion so they might pass as non-Jews
outside the ghetto walls. On "the other side," they can smuggle food or
weapons, kill German soldiers, or, if the ghetto is liquidated, escape into the
surrounding Polish territory and fight for their survival. "You called them
your magnificent children," says Ringelblum to Korczak,

> I agree. You've taught them loyalty, belief in an ideal world,
> sacrifice for the good of the group. If the Gestapo close off this
> street and I have twenty minutes to pull Hanna and Moski and
> Mendel into the sewer, will they come if they see the orphanage
> about to be evacuated? You must cut the cord, Janusz.
>
> (act 1, scene 1)

In the play, it is important that Korczak and Ringelblum are *not* enemies,
although they do confront their terrible dilemma with differing responses.
Still, they clearly respect each other, and Korczak orders the three children
to prepare for evacuating the orphanage in accordance with the training that
Ringelblum has provided for them.

In succeeding scenes, Korczak is tormented by the Nazis and, at the
conclusion of act 1, asks advice of his assistant Stefania Wilczynska: should
he begin instructing the children in Jewish heritage and prayer? He has
resisted this sort of indoctrination in the belief that young people must not
be coerced in matters of religion. But, in desperation, it is clear that Korczak
realizes that something spiritual is absent in his much-abused life, and that
his starving children also need more sustenance than they are receiving.
Reduced to tears, Korczak, wearing a prayer shawl, expresses his frustration
and despair in a "talk with God."

In act 2, the deportation order is conveyed by a young German soldier who, many years before the war, had himself been cared for in Korczak's orphanage. Later, the scene shifts to a dream sequence in the country a week before the outbreak of the war; we see the children and their elders enjoying a picnic on church land, whose use they have humbly requested. The little vacation is intended, Ringelblum and Korczak recognize, as "a Chekhovian moment of peacefulness" before the breaking storm. (Chekhov os Korczak's favorite author.) In the "dream," the children march "to the sun" and escape, but in reality (as prefigured earlier in the boy Hirsz's dream) death awaits them all. The final words we hear are the voice of a "neutral" narrator describing the destruction of the ghetto and the heroic finish to Korczak's life. The concluding image is of Korczak, alone onstage, crushing the suicide pills he had kept for himself, and making his single statement: "If my presence will save even one child one second of terror, my life will be well lost."

It is Brady's intention to present a tragic Korczak, founder of his own "Children's Republic," doomed to death by his Nazi antagonists. He attempts no "message" for us, but instead offers a perspective on the Holocaust that, because of its particular positive imagery, conveys a sense of renewal and possibility. This is especially true because the burden of the loss falls on the small shoulders of the children, all of whom perished, but whose lives are preserved in the continual retelling of Korczak's story. (The play's title refers to them, but the play's action, moral and physical, centers on Korczak.) Instilled with Korczak's humane teaching about the respect and love due them and all people, they carry a legacy of hope despite the terrible fate that befell them. For Brady, it seems, the mystery of goodness is even greater than the mystery of evil, and it is with the former that his sympathies clearly lie.

The enormous question of why the Nazis murdered six million Jews (including one and a half million children) will certainly continue for the foreseeable future, and historians and others will emphasize economic, historical, political, cultural, and psychological or other reasons for the "final solution." But, remembering Steiner, the strongest argument for maintaining the sense of tragic mystery is that *no rational investigation* completely explains the Holocaust—not the fears and beliefs of the obsessed German leadership, not the dislocations following the First World War, not the vague but powerful psychological and cultural needs of an acquiescing population, not the agony of the Nazis' victims. In these plays, the heroic figure assumes a tragic stature that, *validated by history*, guides the audience's attention to images of moral repair in a violent world that is out of ethical control. Thus, while the Holocaust as an all-encompassing historical event remains in large degree intellectually impenetrable, in its smaller aspects or details playwrights discern a meaningful rescue of humane possibility. From an aesthetic point of view the danger to this strategy is the same as in any tragic writing: making too explicit or too easy the restoration of a moral order. "How much darkness must we acknowledge before we will be able to confess that the Holocaust story cannot be told in terms of heroic dignity, moral courage, and the triumph of the human spirit in adversity?" asks Lawrence Langer.[18] No answer is possible or necessary for playwrights who reject the question, refusing to be separated from a traditional tragic perspective. Taking refuge in those older forms, they aim to succeed in the kind of aesthetic—and moral—victory described by Richard Sewell:

> There has been suffering and disaster, ultimate and irredeemable loss, and there is a promise of more to come. But all who have been involved have been witness to new revelations about human existence, the evil of evil and the goodness of good. They are more "ready." The same old paradoxes and ambiguities remain, but for the moment they are transcended in the higher vision.[19]

III

But by highlighting the heroism of Korczak or Hannah Senesh or Anne Frank, playwrights may be seen as departing from traditional tragic form in another way: by eliminating the protagonist's culpability in his or her own destruction. An impetuous Senesh (the young Jew who parachuted behind Nazi lines and was captured and executed in 1944) or an occasionally intemperate Korczak are only feeble attempts to "humanize" them and show a flaw in an otherwise perfect character. In part this is because, in searching the Holocaust for dramatic material, the impermissible premise is the one that asserts that Jews brought their destruction on themselves. Thus, the aspect of a protagonist's guilt traditionally associated with the tragic form is exceedingly difficult to sustain.

In responding to this aesthetic problem, playwrights have resorted to two additional but differing approaches that allow for continued adherence to moral images and tragic form concerning the creation of stage characters.

1. They have subsumed the individual figures into a larger portrait where differences among characters are rejected in favor of the universality of the group protagonist.

2. They have provided around the protagonist a range of characters who reveal different and often contradictory responses to oppression, so that some individual Jews *do* contribute to the mechanism of death that has trapped them.

Each of these approaches requires a philosophical decision concerning where to locate the source of evil in human beings. The first strategy stresses the human capacity for goodness and sees evil "out there," that is, in a contaminated, threatening world determined to destroy any evidence of righteousness. The second strategy locates the source of evil *in* people, and finds in human weakness permission to settle upon the Holocaust's victims an otherwise unavailable tragic guiltiness. (This condition is validated less by history and more by an understanding of human psychology that sees people behaving naturally in their own self-interest in times of great personal threat.)

The classical tragic model for the first type of play is *The Trojan Women*. Euripides, in his play about the destruction of a city and a whole people, gathers his suffering multitudes for a final, if futile, spasm of resistance to genocide. *The Trojan Women*, in fact, is even bleaker in outlook than most tragedies, classical or modern, because it concludes with the destruction of the last male in Troy, the boy Astyanax. The Greeks throw him from the city's walls, and his death signals the end of a proud and great nation; at the play's conclusion, the abused women survivors are led away to be the spoils of war for their enemies.

The lament of *The Trojan Women*, joined into a single voice of suffering, embodies a powerful condemnation of war and those who carry out war. For our purposes, it becomes important as a tragic model for modern playwrights who treat the Holocaust theme and who seek to stress the monumentality of the terror in the last moments of victims who were, and who remain, essentially innocent. In a way, these playwrights make a virtue out of anonymity. The twenty-two women prisoners who are incarcerated in Auschwitz at the beginning of Charlotte Delbo's *Who Will Carry The Word?* are in a situation similar to their Trojan ancestors. Slowly decreased by murder and suicide in the course of Delbo's play, their situation is postexilic, that is, after the deportation. In the closing moments, only two women remain alive to direct at the audience (and by implication all people who have not suffered as they have) the "word" they are charged with carrying. They speak, but with Cassandra-like misgivings. They fear that the concentration camp experiences are too gruesome and appalling to be believed. "Why should you believe those stories of ghosts," asks Francoise, "ghosts who came back and who are not able to explain how?"[20]

Delbo's interest is in the fate of non-Jewish political victims of the Nazis, but her theme concerns how small groups of survivors affect the mass of uncaring, uncomprehending, larger groups of postwar citizens. It is a problem that continues to confront all survivors as the Holocaust moves further from us in time. Delbo's skill in presenting the group's story accumulates power as it shows their numbers decreasing. She asserts the qualities of innocence, courage, and compassionate cooperation, the last quality appearing here and elsewhere in Holocaust drama as especially feminine. She laments the destruction of those precious values to the point where succeeding generations—precisely because of this loss—cannot believe, let alone accept, the reality of history.

Liliane Atlan, in *Monsieur Fugue or Earth Sick*, also stresses the innocence and purity lost to the world at the hands of the Nazis.[21] Among the factors influencing the writing of the play is the Korczak story, to which Atlan directly refers in an epigraph appended to the printed text. The play itself describes the last journey of a group of four children, "almost animals if it were not for their mad eyes," who have survived in the sewers "after the total destruction of a ghetto." The play begins and ends with an image of fire, first of the ghetto burning in the distance, and later at the edge of the pit used to incinerate the corpses of the Nazis' victims.

Accompanied by an innocent German soldier, Grol (also known as Monsieur Fugue), a "sweet and simple [and] very disturbing" deserter from the Nazi ideology of death, the four children ride to their destruction through a fog-filled night (*"nacht und nebel"*) on the back of a truck. The action mostly consists of the children's fantasies of a different, although no happier, life, which are "acted out" by the five innocents. They assume the identities of various characters from their past and their imagined, foreclosed, future, and they play the roles of various animals and objects, one of which is a large doll that "carries" the soul of one of the deceased friends of the children. At the play's conclusion, under the supervision of their murderers, the children, who have become "very old," walk to their fiery death in "The Valley of Bones" (a biblical allusion that Sylvanus, in his Korczak play, used with less irony and greater optimism as a prophecy of resurrection).

Monsieur Fugue is a heartbreaking play, surreal in its conception and poetic in its language. Its evocative power comes from its relentless image of childhood defiled in the Nazi land of fog and flame. The innocence and purity of all children—qualities only occasionally seen here, since the four

young people begin the play possessed by a frightening savagery—are what
Atlan laments for. Her victims, including the childlike Monsieur Fugue, are
memorable not as individuals (they often exchange identities) but as a group.
Their death, like the Trojan boy's, is meant to represent the irreparable loss
to all people whose very continuance as recognizably human creatures is
rendered impossible by the deadly effects of Nazi ideology taken to its
inevitable extreme. "That, that's not just," concludes Raissa about the world
before she hobbles to her death. "That's dirt. I don't understand why God
does dirt to children. I'm not good for anything anymore."

George Tabori, in *The Cannibals*,[22] adjusts the strategy for the group
portrait only slightly, but with important ramifications. His play, as I
described in the previous chapter, is set in a concentration camp barracks
where a group of starving prisoners (not all Jewish) are forced to confront a
hideous moral choice: accept their dead comrade's flesh as food and live, or
reject cannibalism and be immediately killed. The "choice" is forced upon
them by the Nazi "Angel of Death," SS Shreckinger, who makes his
ultimatum only moments after the prisoners *as a group* have decided *not* to
eat human flesh. Although we have watched the prisoners retell stories of
previous moral lapses and criminal behavior, by finally rejecting the human
meal—as all except two of the prisoners do—they seem to have regained
some sort of positive image of human behavior despite their abominably
degraded circumstances. The two "survivors," Heltai and Hirschler, serve as
narrators of the grim story and appear as unhappy and lonely individuals;
their comrades in the reenactment of the story are the surviving sons of their
dead "fathers." Those who go to their deaths, now joined together by an
extraordinary renewal of moral purpose, actually seem to regain some
measure of recognizable humanity.

In rejecting cannibalism, the majority of Tabori's characters establish a
bond between them which has the effect of restoring a kind of damaged
innocence and irreducable humanity, the crucial characteristics of the group
protagonist. Shreckinger torments them with the accusation that "there is a
Fuehrer in the asshole of the best of us," but except for Heltai and Hirschler,
the charge is disproved. As with Atlan's *Monsieur Fugue*, and to a lesser
extent, with Delbo's *Who Will Carry the Word?*, an extraordinary,
phantasmagorical setting seems to focus our attention on the human figure
in its fragility and vulnerability while at the same time emotionally conveying
the texture of the terrifying violence responsible for the destruction of
individual identity. The individual is subsumed into a group protagonist who
confronts an external evil and maintains (or reclaims) a stature of innocence
by finding courage and a reflected dignity in the companionship of peers, a

fidelity to goodness, and a yearning for freedom. The destruction of the group protagonist in the plays, either by attrition or by sudden, multiple termination, creates a moving image of suffering and resistance whereby anonymity is simultaneously created and transcended by desperate positive behavior, which, though unavailing to survival, validates for audiences a moral option available to *all* people even in the worst of times.

Resort 76, by Shimon Wincelberg,[23] in its description of a wide range of character and action, is the best example of a play that combines the two kinds of dramatic strategies discussed earlier. Unwilling to discard the image of a tragic hero, Wincelberg crowds around his protagonist Blaustain a group of characters who challenge his battered innocence, take advantage of his generosity, and distract him from his personal search for a moral basis for his own life. The play is strongest in its depiction of a variety of character types, less satisfying in the methods it uses to achieve a conclusion with a positive statement about ghetto life in the Holocaust. In fact, Wincelberg, in setting all the action of his play in the Lodz Ghetto *prior* to its destruction, mitigates somewhat the sense of catastrophe that pervades most Holocaust drama. His objective is to leave us with the strongest possible image of humane behavior under abominable circumstances.

Blaustain is faced with a series of moral dilemmas that require urgent resolution because of the time limits established in the story and because the other characters of the ghetto factory he heads demand his counsel in solving their problems. In a position of some responsibility, his trials are everybody's. As noted in chapter 1, in the course of the play, Blaustain must decide whether to give up his position and flee the ghetto for the forests to join the armed resistance; whether the child his pregnant wife is carrying should be born; whether to hide a cat entrusted to him by other ghetto residents.

Blaustain makes the "right," i.e., moral, decisions, affirming life on all counts. In the process, Wincelberg somewhat diminishes the sense of tragedy the play conveys because the pressure of death is alleviated through the continuance of the ghetto environment, and because of the obvious dependency on melodramatic (structural) artifice. At the same time, Wincelberg does acknowledge the presence of death, as Schnur, the teacher, is taken away by the Nazis, and Krause, the German "outsider" among them dies by his own hand. Nonetheless, *Resort 76* undermines the dramatic inevitability associated with the life of a tragic protagonist or group. With less at stake than Brady's Korczak, Wincelberg (a genuinely compassionate witness) guides his protagonist back into a group that, at the play's conclusion, is purged of moral confusions and ambiguities that baffle the more tragic protagonists of other Holocaust dramas whose dilemmas have no simple solutions.

The play's weakness is perhaps its partaking of the several formal options of this kind of Holocaust drama without clearly committing itself to one of them. In a final assessment, Wincelberg's group portrait of solidarity amid suffering is less demanding than that of Delbo's women or Atlan's children because it exchanges the pressures of imminent and complete destruction for a more deliberately positive picture of victims under something slightly less than maximum penalty. With the tragic context somewhat diminished, the kind of emotional effect *Resort 76* finally achieves is a worthy mixture of sadness and hopefulness, secured by human tenacity in the face of intermittent violence, and perhaps touched by an air of unreality when we remember the actual fate of the Lodz Ghetto.

The second type of tragic Holocaust drama is based on the playwright's acceptance of evil *inside* of all of us, even the Holocaust's victims. From the historical perspective, the assignment of mass ethical failure to the Jews is irrelevant and irresponsible, simply because there is little evidence for attributing the responsibility for the Jews' destruction to themselves. But from a theatrical perspective, this approach assumes crucial importance, for neglecting this aspect of negative human behavior would eliminate useful *dramatic* choices and, to a lesser extent, would reject the occasional evidence that *some* Jews, like so many others at that time in Europe, behaved badly. Here playwrights focus on the most volatile of all Holocaust themes: Jewish collaboration with the Nazis.

The material discussing Jews cooperating with the Germans to buy either time or favors is ample, and is best consulted in the prodigious scholarship of Holocaust historians.[24] Their investigations explore the work of the *Judenrat*, the Jewish administrative councils that were established to organize and oversee the daily lives of the ghettoized Jewish communities of Europe. The Nazis first appointed and then exploited these groups for their own purposes, although ostensibly they served to make dealing between the two communities less difficult and more efficient. Depending on the city in question or the period of the war, the influence of the *Judenrat* over Jews under its control varied greatly, but the councils were always subservient to the Germans and directly controlled by them. In certain cities, members of the *Judenrat* acted honorably by organizing resistance in numerous, often secret ways while seeming to assist the Nazis. Some were murdered by the Germans for no apparent reason (the irrationality factor again), some chose to take their own lives. In some cities, individual members of the Jewish councils openly collaborated with the Nazis, seeking and obtaining special favors for their families or friends. Members and leaders of the Jewish police forces in the ghettos were gripped by a particularly untenable dilemma from a moral perspective, since they were the most obvious and most capable force for asserting the Germans' will and carrying it out while appearing as the group best able to resist the Nazi mandate.

Playwrights have taken up the sensitive issue of collaboration, creating protagonists whose behavior seems to challenge the possibility of positive images of a kind discussed earlier in plays by Sylvanus, Brady, Wincelberg, or Delbo. They shrink the volitional area of moral action to a space no longer admitting of the "heroic," although most still are reluctant to sacrifice everything to a vision of total foulness. This approach to character and action involves its own kind of risk, and playwrights of these "plays of collaboration" have been accused of betrayal of the victims, nihilism, and even of anti-Semitism. As purveyors of unflattering images of Jews, the authors have usually held to a belief in the ambiguity of moral action that inevitably results in the destruction of all idealized portrayals of character. For theatre audiences, characters who reveal both self-interest *and* moral aspiration create a mixture of dislike and sympathy; in the most extreme cases, where characters have wholly negative personalities, we usually respond with contempt for their actions and rejection of their motives despite a playwright's attempts to have us accept them as also part of the human community.

The character of Mordechai Chaim Rumkowski, protagonist of Harold and Edith Lieberman's *Throne of Straw*,[25] has received much attention for being an apparently negative portrayal of an exceedingly complicated figure. Based on the actual figure of Rumkowski, the head of the Lodz *Judenrat* during the five years that Polish ghetto existed, the central character is a man caught in the trap of collaboration with the enemy, and the playwrights explore the implications of his dilemma. There is evidence that Rumkowski was a ruthless and self-serving tyrant, both petty and cruel, perhaps even mad by the end of his life. But his significance for the Liebermans and for us is that he never loses (in the play, at least) his sense of moral aspiration.

Indisputably, Rumkowski's position was an impossible one. Believing he could make Jewish labor essential to the German war effort, he enthusiastically participated in every plan that would allow the ghetto factories to continue producing, thereby rescuing "his" workers from death. Squeezed between the Nazi chief civilian administrator, Hans Biebow, and the demands of his own suffering people, he experienced a torment in making the required decisions that was surely genuine. In September 1942, he was ordered to arrange the deportation for extermination of the sick, the old, and anyone under the age of ten; this incident provides one of the most terrible moments in the play (act 2, scene 5). His immediate response is to engage the skills he has used more or less successfully in the past with Biebow, the "Jewish" skills of bargaining and negotiating, for which his Nazi boss both appreciates and despises him. But Biebow refuses to change the order (he also has *his* orders, of course), and, in the next scene, one of the two orphan boys is brutally taken away. Thus, in the most graphic way, the question of collaboration with evil is starkly present. Behind it, death lurks everywhere. Eventually, everyone, including Chairman Rumkowski, the Great Collaborator himself, is claimed by it.

To Rumkowski's historical character clings a shameful judgment reserved for those who betray their own people. His character, both historical and theatrical, also exhibits a powerful connection to Jewish folklore and history, and this provides him with an elevated stature not uncommon in traditional tragic characters. In addition, the Liebermans are insistent that Rumkowski's type of personality is a peculiar fixture in European Jewish culture: vain and power-seeking to hide a lack of intellectual confidence, shrewd and opportunistic yet capable of easy charm and great generosity. Nowhere is the archetype more clearly revealed than in the scene with Biebow. First, Rumkowski tries bargaining for a lower deportation age for the children, as Abraham argued with God over the number of righteous to be found in Sodom and Gomorrah, which would enable those cities to be saved. When rebuffed, Rumkowski shows his own deep concern for a positive place in a long, tragic chronicle of Jewish history. "[The children] are my life. And our future. If I do that [agree to the terms of the order], my name would breed maggots. There wouldn't be a single soul who'd say *kaddish* [the prayer for the dead] for me." Later, alone, Rumkowski expresses his feelings directly toward heaven. The stage directions read: "*He looks up, rises and paces back and forth in the following dialog with God. This is not a form of madness—but is part of a long tradition of Jews talking and arguing with Jehovah.*" In addition, Rumkowski's dilemma and his resolution of it are directly related to the teachings of the medieval Jewish philosopher, Maimonides, whose well-known advice on the subject of betrayal and collaboration is quoted in the play and rejected by the Chairman. In these attachments to Jewish history, the Liebermans have created a strong-willed protagonist of a stature and complexity which compares favorably with recognizable tragic protagonists of previous centuries.

Several scenes and two years later, with his power and his will nearly broken, Rumkowski is taunted by Jews he had earlier protected, including his wife, Miriam, and his vicious Chief of Police, Rabinowitz. The small resistance to the final liquidation of the ghetto is neutralized by the Germans with Rumkowski's help (the Liebermans use actual speeches of the Chairman and Biebow at this point in the play), and the final remnant of Lodz's Jewish population is deported for extermination. But the playwrights skillfully direct our attention to the moral implications Rumkowski's dilemma has for the audience concerning the issues of collaboration and complicity. They have dramatized part of the life of a controversial historical figure, and they have continued the controversy in making his actions morally ambiguous and his story theatrically compelling.

The complexity of the human personality, which can draw a person either to goodness or evil in times of extreme stress, is the real subject of this kind of Holocaust drama. Reflecting a tragic conception, the playwrights see their protagonists as gravely flawed, but not without a kind of perverse greatness. In *Throne*, however, they argue not for reclamation of his low reputation, but for an awareness of the confused textures of the human personality, which may issue forth at extreme moments in action that possesses ambiguous dimensions. As a result, they counsel moderation in any posthumous judgment we render. Surrounded by a range of characters who behave either horribly (Gabriel, Rabinowitz) or well (Israel, Miriam), Rumkowski shares with others (Ada, David) a mixture of good and evil that eludes understanding and simple judgment. At the end, the Liebermans force the audience away from an emotional commitment for the suffering victims of the Holocaust through several objectifying (Brechtian) staging devices, but they ungrudgingly accord a measure of respect to a man who, while involved with grievous crimes and responsible for terrible suffering, was always mindful of the moral imperatives of life. Thus, with an astonishing eloquence, he is given time to plead his own tragic case, one not without merit in an ethically shrunken universe.

> First ask yourself where are the other ghettos? Why is it that only mine survives? Because I understood that when the end is good, everything is good. I won't deny that I had to do terrible things. To give away my poor pigeons. But for every hundred I saved a hundred. I stood as a watchman before the door of death and snatched them from the furnace one by one. *And I am not ashamed.*
>
> (act 2, scene 8)

The life of Jacob Gens, chief of the Vilna Ghetto in Lithuania, was no easier than Rumkowski's in Lodz, but there is some reason to believe that, because of his intelligence and military background, he bore his trial somewhat better, although with no happier result. His career as head of his ghetto was filled with the same moral dilemmas as Rumkowski's, and he too ended up as an ignominious failure. Joshua Sobol's *Ghetto*,[26] like the Liebermans' *Throne*, attempts to tell Gens's story with fairness and sympathy, using similar structural and staging devices. By forcefully dramatizing Gens's career, often using song, dance, extraordinary visual symbolism, and play-within-the-play devices, Sobol is successful in evoking the sense of tragedy often lacking in Holocaust drama.

Ghetto begins in the Tel Aviv apartment of Srulik, a one-armed survivor of the Vilna Ghetto who was the leader of its resident theatre company. Addressing an invisible interviewer, Srulik reflects back on his life, forty years earlier, when his profession allowed him and his troupe certain privileges (including their lives) at the order of Gens. In fact, Gens's attitude toward theatre and all cultural activity in general is both benign and pragmatic: he sees it as a way to raise the morale of the depressed and frightened ghetto inhabitants as well as a way to save more Jews by giving them work. The theatre company actors (and others) assume various additional identities, and they "perform" for the Germans (and, of course, for "us"), thereby lending moments of startling theatricality to a play heavy with ethical speculation.

Gens has two antagonists: Kruk, the ghetto librarian, and Kittel, the corrupt, jazz-loving Nazi, both actual figures in Vilna's history. Although Sobol wants to emphasize the conflict between Gens and Kruk, for theatrical reasons he often returns to Gens *versus* Kittel. There is an additional conflict developed between Kruk and an anti-Semitic German academician, Dr. Paul, who is portrayed by the same actor playing Kittel. But it is Gens who carries the ethical burden of *Ghetto*, and the tragic burden as well.

Sobol's Gens, like the Liebermans' Rumkowski, suffers from the anguish of his impossible position as unquestioned (though not un-challenged) leader of the ghetto. Also like Rumkowski, his life was characterized by the harshness of his authority, the slow compromise of his principles, and the quickness of his wits. Although the moods of despair and hope that seized the ghetto could be frequently reversed by the manipulation of the economic, social, or nutritional conditions he controlled, in truth the political space Gens operated in was exceedingly small. The ghetto he sought to protect through strict adherence to German directives, ameliorated by his own imaginative policies in favor of the young and strong, was doomed by incremental slaughter. In fact, the Vilna Ghetto existed for only a little more than two years (Lodz lasted five), and Gens's death (he was shot by the Gestapo) preceded the ghetto's total liquidation by only a few days. Sobol takes up the ethical issues presented by the act of collaboration and finds in Gens's short, intensely lived career an essentially tragic experience.

Kruk's position in *Ghetto* is that of nay-sayer. He is Gens's mirror image: an idealistic, individualistic, withdrawn intellectual who in the play is frequently accompanied by the sound of a typewriter as he narrates or dictates his diary (actually published in Yiddish in 1961). In their first confrontation, Kruk accuses Gens of trying to appear virtuous when he is really a self-aggrandizing, autocratic traitor. Gens, clearly conscious of his uncertain reputation, responds: "History has yet to judge which of us gave more at this hour of crisis in the history of the Jewish people: you or me!" (act 1, scene 8). Gens's personal sense of his historical place awards him a considerable stature, and, at the same time, lends to his actions a wider, more universal resonance. Later in the play, he is defiant in declaring his objection to Kruk's partiality to satirical-political theatre rather than morale-raising entertainment.

> Not that kind of theater, not the kind that pours salt in our wounds and incites people to rebel.... Is this the time for provocation? Theater—by all means. But make people happy. The population here needs to be calm, disciplined, industrious.... Objectively speaking, you are traitors! ... If there's anyone with a genuine national sentiment in this ghetto, it's me! If there's a real Jewish patriot and nationalist here, it's me!   (act 3, scene 1)

Of course, there is a self-serving point to Gens's anger, too: a more passive population will reduce the threat to his authority.

Still, Sobol retains for Gens a large measure of sympathy while Gens struggles with his antagonists to justify his eminently worthwhile goal: to keep alive as many Jews as possible until the certain defeat of the Germans. His actions, sentencing some Jews to death while bargaining to keep others alive, are simultaneously laudable and contemptible. His drunken concluding speech (Gens's actual words) in act 2, where he "*seems to be responding to the voice of Kruk,*" is shattering in its logic, terrifying in its eloquence.

> Many of you consider me a traitor and many of you are wondering what I'm still doing here, among innocent and immaculate souls like yourselves.... I, Gens, give orders to blow up hideaways that you prepared, and I, Gens, try to figure out ways of protecting Jews from death. I do the reckoning of Jewish blood, not of Jewish dignity. If the Germans ask me for one

thousand Jews, I give them what they want because if we don't do it ourselves, the Germans will come and take the people by force. And then they wouldn't take one thousand, but thousands. Thousands. You with your sanctimonious morality. You don't deign to touch the filth. And if you do survive, you'll be able to say: we came out of it with a clear conscience, while I, Jacob Gens, if I have the good fortune of getting out of this alive, I'll be covered in slime, my hands will be dripping with blood. Nevertheless, I'd be prepared to stand trial, to submit to Jewish justice. I would get up and say: whatever I did was meant to save as many Jews as I could, to lead them to freedom. In order for some of them to be spared I had no choice but to lead others to their death with my very own hands. And in order to spare some Jews their clear conscience I had no choice but to plunge into the filth, leaving my own conscience behind.[27]   (act 2, scene 4)

Gens is surrounded by people who span the full range of the Jewish response to oppression. Dessler and Mushkat (Jewish police), Weiskopf (Jewish profiteer), and several Jewish gangster-murderers represent the negative extreme; Hayya (an actress and singer) and Srulik (ventriloquist and puppeteer), the positive. Gens is defined by the moral position he takes between them, and thus he is often a picture of melancholy confusion (as Kittel notes) whose torment is genuine and whose dilemma is insoluble. Only when *Ghetto* takes up the more philosophical, subsidiary theme of the nature of the Jewish soul does its theatrical power diminish somewhat. (Sobol deals with that theme more forcefully in his companion play written around the same time, *Soul of a Jew*.) Nonetheless, for its audacious theatricality and scenic effects (the dominant visual image is a ten-foot-high pile of clothing at stage center representing Jewish occupations, Jewish enslavement, Jewish accommodation, and Jewish destruction), for its provocative intellectual debate of crucial moral issues, and especially for its gripping image of an aspiring, guilty, doomed protagonist, *Ghetto* makes a significant claim to finding true tragedy in the Holocaust experience.

IV

What then can be said of the tragic "response" of audiences in the presence of these plays? There are many paradoxes associated with tragedy in the theatre, not the least of which is our attraction to seeing other people suffer in the expectation that some profit (catharsis? insight?) will be derived. Receiving and assimilating the knowledge of six million dead depends on the ability of the playwright to portray historical reality and at the same time to force from us a deep emotional response that touches upon our own sense of survival. In modern times, romantic postures and optimistic creeds have been inferior to portrayals of terrible dilemmas and ambiguous truths in human history and behavior. Nonetheless, despite the irreparable, catastrophic result of the Holocaust, despair is rarely total, in part because some *did* survive the genocidal frenzy, and in part because these playwrights cannot accept unmitigated negation. (An exception may be several of the contemporary German playwrights I discuss in chapter 5.)

When the traditional tragic protagonists concluded their painful careers, they were touched by discovery; through them audiences received an illumination that diminished (slightly? temporarily?) the dark components (ignorance? evil?) of human existence. Writers of tragedy have always had to calibrate this balance of gain amid loss with extreme care. Making audiences accept themselves, if only for the span of a theatrical performance, as the living legacy of the Holocaust presents enormous challenges for the playwright who must cope with the contraction in the freedom to maneuver demanded by history. But the mysteries at the heart of human existence that tragedy has always tried to convey have never disappeared, and neither has the attempt to write tragedy in the theatre. Lawrence Langer, writing about how, in images of the concentration camps, "affirmation *includes* negation,"[28] was inevitably writing about the opposite condition: these plays call out for us to realize that negation also includes affirmation.

NOTES

1. George Steiner, *The Death of Tragedy* (New York: Knopf, 1961), p. 4.

2. George Steiner, "A Kind of Survivor," in *Language and Silence: Essays on Language, Literature, and the Inhuman* (New York: Atheneum, 1967), p. 141.

3. George Steiner, "A Season In Hell," in *In Bluebeard's Castle: Some Notes Toward the Redefinition of Culture* (New Haven: Yale University Press, 1971), p. 30.

4. Richmond Y. Hathorn, *Tragedy, Myth and Mystery* (Bloomington: Indiana University Press, 1962), p. 30.

5. See for example, Robert Alter, "Deformations of the Holocaust," *Commentary* (February 1981): 48-54.

6. Stephen Spender, Introduction to *Selected Poems of Abba Kovner and Nellie Sachs* (Harmondsworth, England: Penguin Books, 1971), p. 7.

7. Terrence Des Pres, *The Survivor* (New York: Oxford University Press, 1976), pp. 9-10.

8. Lawrence L. Langer, *Versions of Survival: The Holocaust and the Human Spirit* (Albany: State University of New York Press, 1982), p. 21.

9. There are, of course, many plays that focus on the actions of heroic Christians such as Raoul Wallenberg, Maximillian Kolbe, or (in Hochhuth's *The Deputy*) Kurt Gerstein, but they are not the subject of my interest here.

10. Wylie Sypher, *Loss of the Self in Modern Literature and Art* (New York: Vintage Books, 1962), p. 14.

11. Sidra DeKoven Ezrahi, *By Words Alone: The Holocaust in Literature* (Chicago: University of Chicago Press, 1980), pp. 8, 9.

12. "Because we, the readers, know what happened after their [the play wrights'] last line was written, the tragic spirit of the text is implicit and we are obliged to complete the tale ... We must remember that we are posterity, the future generation to whom this testimony was addressed under penalty of death." Ellen S. Fine, "Surviving Voice: Literature of the Holocaust," in *Perspectives on the Holocaust*, ed. Randolph L. Braham (Boston: Kluwer-Nijoff, 1983), p. 110.

13. Eric Bentley, *The Life of the Drama* (New York: Atheneum, 1967), p. 147.

14. See Lawrence L. Langer, "The Americanization of the Holocaust on Stage and Screen," in *From Hester Street to Hollywood*, ed. Sarah Blacher Cohen (Bloomington: Indiana University Press, 1983), pp. 213-230.

15. Robert J. Lifton, *Death in Life* (New York: Random House, 1967), p. 475.

16. Walter Kerr, *Tragedy and Comedy* (New York: Simon and Schuster, 1967), pp. 271-72.

17. Michael K. Brady, *Korczak's Children*, in manuscript version, available from the author. The play premiered at Boston College in 1983.

18. Langer, "The Americanization of the Holocaust," p. 214. James Rosenberg has written:

> The real problem for American playwrights and directors and actors has been, not that they have refused to learn the lessons of the master, in a technical sense, but that they have been unwilling to pay the price of the lesson in tears and suffering and humiliation.

The history of the American nation has been one of avoidance of experience—particularly any painful or upsetting experience. But this, needless to say, is a dangerously immature attitude, and out of it no very profound or useful insights can be expected to develop.

"European Influences" in *American Theatre*, ed. J. R. Brown and B. Harris (London: Edward Arnold, 1967), p. 64.

19. Richard B. Sewell, "The Tragic Form," in *Tragedy: Modern Essays in Criticism* (Englewood Cliffs, N.J.: Prentice-Hall, 1963), pp. 128-29.

20. Charlotte Delbo, *Who Will Carry the Word?* in *The Theatre of the Holocaust*, ed. Robert Skloot (Madison: University of Wisconsin Press, 1982), p. 325.

21. Liliane Atlan, *Monsieur Fugue ou le mal de terre* (Paris: Éditions du Seuil, 1967). The play is available in English translation by Marguerite Feitlowitz from the Penkevill Publishing Co., Greenwood, Fla., 32443.

22. In Skloot, *The Theatre of the Holocaust*, pp. 197-265.

23. Ibid., pp. 39-112.

24. See Isaiah Trunk's *Judenrat: The Jewish Councils in Eastern Europe Under Nazi Occupation* (New York: Macmillan, 1972) and Raul Hilberg's newly revised *The Destruction of the European Jews* (New York: Holmes and Meier, 1985), 3 vols.

25. In Skloot, *The Theatre of the Holocaust*, pp. 113-196.

26. Joshua Sobol, *Ghetto*, trans. Miriam Shlesinger (Tel Aviv: Institute for the Translation of Hebrew Literature, 1986). The play premiered in 1984. Much of the historical material about Gens is found in Leonard Tushnet's book, *The Pavement of Hell* (New York: St. Martin's Press, 1972), which describes the parallel careers of three ghetto leaders: Gens (Vilna), Rumkowski (Lodz) and Adam Czerniakow (Warsaw). Four specific incidents in Sobol's play are also narrated in Tushnet's account. Interviews with resistance fighters from the ghetto in Josh Waletzky's excellent 1987 film *The Partisans of Vilna* present a sympathetic picture of Gen's leadership.

27. See Tushnet, *Pavement*, pp. 169-70, where some of this speech is to be found word for word. In the foreword to the book, Tushnet writes: "Tragedy in art gives understanding of man's strivings and failings as well as catharsis. We know what will happen to Oedipus and yet we follow the play with mounting terror as the inexcusable workings of his destiny unfold. We try to comprehend what strengths and weaknesses brought him to his blind end. Putting aside all prejudice, we should seek to understand why Rumkowski, Czerniakow, and Gens did what they did" (p. xi).

28. Langer, *Versions*, p.128.

JAMES E. YOUNG

Holocaust Documentary Fiction: Novelist as Eyewitness

Imagination and memory are but one thing, which for divers considerations hath divers names.

—Thomas Hobbes

There is no fiction or nonfiction as we commonly understand the distinction: there is only narrative.

—E. L. Doctorow

That is what the survivors are afraid of, the tricks of art.

—Arnold Wesker

I

The impulse in Holocaust writers to insist on a documentary link between their texts and the events inspiring them has not been limited to diarists and memoirists: it extends to the novelists and playwrights of the Holocaust as well. Where the diarists and memoirists have struggled to preserve or reconstruct the eyewitness authority displaced by their narrative, however, the "docu-novelists" and "docu-dramatists" of the Holocaust work as hard at manufacturing their own testimonial authority as part of their fictional discourse. In many cases, their reasons for reinforcing the factual authority

From *Writing and Rewriting the Holocaust: Narrative and the Consequences of Interpretation.* © 1988 by James E. Young.

in narrative are similar: all of these writers seem to fear that the rhetoricity of their literary medium inadvertently confers a fictiveness onto events themselves. But in many other cases, the novelists' reasons for fabricating an eyewitness authority in their fiction stem more from traditional aesthetic and dramatic than from documentary interests. In addition to exploring the ways in which documentary authority is constructed within Holocaust fiction, this chapter will look at how testimony is adopted rhetorically as a narrative strategy in this fiction.

On the one hand, it is difficult to argue with the spirit of Hana Wirth-Nesher's suggestion that "While all narratives are imaginative reconstructions, when it comes to those of mass suffering, we should be particularly vigilant about honoring the line between fact and fiction."[1] On the other hand, it may be just as difficult to delineate this border between fact and fiction in the first place; for as long as facts are presented to us in fictionalizing media and fiction is presented as fact, the categories themselves remain all too fuzzily defined. If there is a line between fact and fiction, it may by necessity be a winding border that tends to bind these two categories as much as it separates them, allowing each side to dissolve occasionally into the other.

In an article about William Styron's *Sophie's Choice*, Arnold Wesker also wants to know both "Where we [are] dealing with fact and where with fiction" and "Why, in this novel more than any other, do I want to know?"[2] Even though she is not referring specifically to Styron's novel, Barbara Foley answers this question in part, in reference to a semifictional character in another of the "docu-novels," Gerald Green's *Holocaust*:

> By claiming for Dorf a status halfway between history and myth ... and by grafting this hybrid creature onto a fictive tale that purports to encompass the enormity of the Holocaust in a single tale of victimization and villainy—Green at once reduces agony to the status of melodrama and distorts the locus of historical responsibility. *Holocaust* is not a fraudulent work simply because it aspires to make history accessible in a popular format ... ; it is fraudulent because it both proposes a shallow resolution and catharsis and performs a frivolous reshuffling of historical facts.[3]

That is, the problem with this and other "documentary fictions" of the Holocaust is that by mixing actual events with completely fictional characters, a writer simultaneously relieves himself of an obligation to historical accuracy (invoking poetic license), even as he imbues his fiction with the historical authority of real events. By inviting this ambiguity, the author of documentary fiction would thus move the reader with the pathos created in the rhetoric of historically authentic characters, even as he suggests the possibility that both his events and those in the world are fictional.

Several other questions arise at this point: First, why is the writer of Holocaust fiction so forcefully compelled to assert the factual basis underlying his work? That is, why is it so important for novelists like D. M. Thomas, Jean-Francois Steiner, Gerald Green, and Anatoli Kuznetsov (among others) to establish an authoritative link between their fictions and the Holocaust experiences they represent? Second, to what extent do such claims to historical authority serve this literature's dramatic interests and to what extent its supposed documentary interests? And how does the perception of authority in the Holocaust novel affect the way readers approach and respond to Holocaust fiction? That is, can Holocaust documentary fiction ever really document events, or will it always fictionalize them?

Having explored already the process of making witness in the diaries and memoirs, we now turn to the ways authentic testimony is incorporated into the fictional text by novelists and used as a figure and literary device in Holocaust fiction. In this context, we will examine the rhetorical trope of eyewitness in Holocaust fiction and some of the narrative methods by which it is generated. For even as many novelists would claim on ethical grounds that they have had no "right" to imagine such suffering and must therefore rely on actual witnesses' voices, I find that these claims may in themselves also be part of their novelistic discourse. Whether a writer is attempting to retain an eyewitness authority in his diary or memoir or to fabricate it altogether in his documentary novel, testimony continues to function as the preeminent rhetorical trope underlying the very possibility of a "documentary narrative."

II

This question of "documentary authority" in Holocaust fiction was brought into particularly sharp relief in the pages of the *Times Literary Supplement*, when letter writer D. A. Kenrick called readers' attention to the rather pronounced debt D. M. Thomas's novel *The White Hotel* owed to Anatoli Kuznetsov's "document in the form of a novel," *Babi Yar*.[4] As Kenrick and other indignant letter-writers pointed out, Thomas has not merely

paraphrased Kuznetsov, but has actually quoted directly from the text of
Kuznetsov's work, in what seems to be an attempt to infuse the most violent
scenes in his Holocaust fiction with what he perceives to be their
"documentary authority." The following are passages from both novels, the
first from *Babi Yar*:

> It began to grow dark.
>
> Suddenly an open car drove up, carrying a tall, well-knit,
> elegant officer carrying a riding crop.... His [Russian] interpreter
> stood at his side.
>
> "Who are these?" he asked a *Polizei* through his interpreter.
> There were about 50 people sitting on the hillock now.
>
> "These are our people [Ukrainians]," replied the *Polizei*. "We
> weren't sure whether to release them."
>
> "Shoot them! Shoot them right away!" stormed the officer. "If
> just one of them gets away and spreads the story, not a single Jew
> will come here tomorrow."
>
> ... "Get going! Move! Get up!" shouted the *Polizei*. They
> staggered to their feet as though drunk. It was already late, and
> this was perhaps why nothing was done to undress this group.
> Instead, they were led through the passage in the sand wall just as
> they were.
>
> ... Coming through the passage, they emerged on the brow of
> a deep sand quarry with almost sheer walls. All were herded to
> the left, single file, along a very narrow ledge.
>
> The wall rose on the left, and the quarry fell away on the right.
> The ledge, evidently cut specially for the executions, was so
> narrow that the victims instinctively leaned against the sand wall
> so as not to fall in.
>
> Dina glanced down and grew dizzy. The quarry was fearfully
> deep. Below lay a sea of bloody bodies. She caught sight of light
> machine guns strung out on the opposite side of the quarry, and
> also of German soldiers. They had lit a campfire and seemed to
> be cooking something.
>
> When the file of victims had occupied the ledge, one of the
> Germans moved away from the fire, took his place at a machine
> gun and began shooting.[5]

And then from *The White Hotel*, where Thomas's omniscient narrator
describes his heroine's fate at Babi Yar:

... it started to get dark.

Suddenly an open car drew up and in it was a tall, well-built, smartly turned-out officer with a riding crop in his hand. At his side was a Russian prisoner.

"Who are these?" the officer asked the policeman, through the interpreter: pointing to the hillock, where there were about fifty people sitting by this time.

"They are our people, Ukrainians. They were seeing people off; they ought to be let out."

Lisa heard the officer shout: "Shoot the lot at once! If even one of them gets out of here and starts talking in the city, not a single Jew will turn up tomorrow."

... "Come on then! Let's go! Get yourselves up!" the policeman shouted. The people stood up as if they were drunk.... Maybe because it was already late the Germans did not bother to undress this group, but led them through the gap in their clothes.

... They went through the gap and came out into a sand quarry with sides practically overhanging. It was already half dark, and she could not see the quarry properly. One after the other, they were hurried on to the left, along a very narrow ledge.

On their left was the side of the quarry, to the right a deep drop; the ledge had apparently been specially cut out for the purposes of the execution, and it was so narrow that as they went along it people instinctively leaned towards the wall of sandstone, so as not to fall in.

... Lisa looked down and her head swam, she seemed so high up. Beneath her was a sea of bodies covered in blood. On the other side of the quarry she could just see the machine guns and a few soldiers. The German soldiers had lit a bonfire and it looked as though they were making coffee on it.

... A German finished his coffee and strolled to a machine gun ... [6]

Kenrick notes that many such resemblances might be found and then follows by alleging not plagiarism but rather a more subtle failing on Thomas's part. "It can be argued," Kenrick writes, "that Mr. Thomas has made moving use of the Babi Yar material. But should the author of a fiction choose as his proper subject events which are not only outside his own experience but also, evidently, beyond his own resources of imaginative re-creation?"

Kenrick neglects to mention, however, that Kuznetsov's own novel was also based upon the verbatim transcription of yet another testimonial source. By relying upon the remembrances of the Babi Yar survivor, Dina Pronicheva, as the basis for his narrative, Kuznetsov may also have been "beyond his own resources of imagination." Because he was not a victim and was too young to remember the surrounding details properly—i.e., with appropriate meaning—he has deferred to an actual survivor's testimony and to the authority it carries. If anything, Thomas and Kuznetsov thus seem to share similar motivations in their narrative technique, both believing that in some areas of their own fiction they have neither the right nor the requisite experience to reimagine such suffering.

In his reply to Kenrick, however, Thomas reminds readers that he had, in fact, declared his indebtedness to *Babi Yar* both in the book's acknowledgments and in many interviews. And then, after noting that since his account of Babi Yar is three times the length of Dina Pronicheva's testimony in Kuznetsov's novel and "equally spare in style," he goes on to offer his own critical interpretation—*qua* justification—of this passage:

> This section is where my heroine, Lisa Erdman, changes from being Lisa an individual to Lisa in history—an anonymous victim. It is this transition, reflected in style as well as content, which has moved and disturbed many readers. From individual self-expression she moves to the common fate. From the infinitely varied world of narrative fiction we move to a world in which fiction is not only severely constrained but irrelevant.
>
> At the outset of Part V, the narrative voice is still largely authorial (though affected by Pronicheva's tone) because there is still room for fiction; Lisa is still a person. But gradually her individuality is taken from her on that road to the ravine; and gradually the only appropriate voice becomes the voice which is like a recording camera: the voice of one who was there. It would have been perfectly easy for me to have avoided the possibility of such attacks as Kenrick's, through some spurious "imaginative re-creation"; but it would have been wrong. The witness's testimony was the truthful voice of the narrative at that point: "It started to get dark," etc. This is how it was—for all the victims. It could not be altered. The time for imagination was before; and, in my novel, after. Imagination, at the point quoted by Kenrick, is exhausted in the effort to take in the unimaginable which happened.[7]

In fact, Thomas even tried to make this point clear in the text of the novel itself, when his narrator explicitly attributes the authority for Lisa's experiences to Dina Pronicheva's testimony. As part of his fictional narrative, the author thus informs the reader that "Dina [Pronicheva] survived to be the only witness, the sole authority for what Lisa [i.e., Thomas's fictional heroine] saw and felt," adding, "Nor can the living ever speak for the dead" (p. 251).

Several issues pertinent to the question of literary testimony and authority emerge in this exchange. In noting that the most stunning passages of *The White Hotel* depend for their power on "the moving use" Thomas has made of the *Babi Yar* material, Kenrick suggests that the order of Thomas's fiction has been less "historical" than aesthetic, intended to excite the emotions and merely to move the reader. Sensitive to this charge and to the implication that he has used an authentic resource merely to heighten the horror in his account in order to exploit it further at the aesthetic level, Thomas answers that it is precisely because he was not there that he must constrain his fiction, that there are some events one has no right to imagine. The only legitimate voice, he implies, is the authentic, genuine voice of one who was there, who is empirically—not imaginatively—linked to these experiences.

At the same time, however, Thomas concedes somewhat ingenuously that he has affected an "equally spare style" because the "only appropriate voice becomes that voice which is like a recording camera: the voice of one who was there." But here he loses track, it seems, of whose voice is whose. For is the "appropriate voice" here that of Dina, the eyewitness, or is it the more figurative "voice" of his eyewitness style? If it is a voice that is like a recording camera, it is a style; if it is the literal voice of a person who was there, it is Dina's. For Thomas, however, this voice is both a style *and* Dina's actual voice, for Thomas has appropriated Dina's voice *as a style*, a rhetorical move by which he would impute to his fiction the authority of testimony without the authenticity of actual testimony.

Seemingly torn between presenting Babi Yar as a fictional construct and simultaneously asserting that Babi Yar was not a fiction, Thomas has thus labored to create the authority of an authentic witness within the realm of his text. To do otherwise, he suggests, "through 'spurious re-creation.'" would be to violate the factual integrity of real events, which are now "unimaginable" (i.e., not to be imagined) because they happened. The supreme irony in all of this, of course, is that by invoking Dina Pronicheva's testimony for his authority, Thomas is actually relying on Kuznetsov's own novelistic reconstruction of her account. Kuznetsov's declarations of his work's explicit factuality notwithstanding, Thomas is ultimately invoking a secondhand rendering of a third party's memory, which had been massively censored in the Russian, then rewritten (i.e., "uncensored") by Kuznetsov on his immigration to the West, and then translated: hardly the stuff of "authentic" or unmediated testimony. The point here is that no matter how strenuously Thomas defends his debt to Kuznetsov, as a fiction writer, even one so beholden to certain horrific facts, he is still a maker of illusions, which in this case become all the more persuasive because he imputes to them a testimonial authority. In fact, by so dutifully acknowledging both his debt to Kuznetsov and Lisa's debt to Dina, thereby establishing an apparent link between his text and a past fact, Thomas may be reinforcing the illusion of factual authority precisely in order to absolve himself of responsibility for making such an illusion.

The further irony here is that Thomas is ultimately at no more ethical risk than Kuznetsov himself; in fact, Kuznetsov has gone to much greater lengths than Thomas to reinforce his own rhetoric of fact. In his preface to *Babi Yar*, Kuznetsov frames all that follows with: "The word 'documentary' in the subtitle of this novel means that I am presenting only authenticated facts and documents and that here you will find not the slightest literary invention—that is, not 'how it might have happened' or 'how it should have been'" (p. xv). He invokes Aristotle's distinction between history and poetry precisely to disclaim all poetic license, to distinguish between poetry and history in order to deny anything but historical quality to his narrative. "The result," he has said in an interview, "is not a novel in the conventional sense, but a photographically accurate picture of actual events."[8] As did Thomas, Kuznetsov would also invoke the most persuasive of all documentary representations—the photograph—as a figure for his narrative.

Though the sense of eyewitness is fabricated here, rather than retained as it is in the diaries and memoirs, this quality of witness in testimony thus functions as the operative trope underpinning the factual authority generated in "documentary literature." In this context, we might note further that Thomas's invocation of the "recording camera" as a stylistic model even has a quite literal, if unintentional, dimension as well. For although he has not acknowledged any other authentic sources, Thomas seems in several instances to have based many of his most "graphic" descriptions not just on Dina Pronicheva's novelized testimony, but also on the witness of several well-known photographs of the Riga massacres of Jews by the SS *Einsatzgruppen*, taken in December 1941 by the SS.[9] In this way, photographs become his surrogate experiences of events, which then function both as his own "eyewitness" memory of events and as the source of further authority in his narrative when the readers' own memory of these images is awakened by Thomas's recollection of them. In effect, however, by recalling in narrative the photographs of the SS, Thomas has ironically depended for his testimonial authority on the *Nazis*' "witness" of their deeds; that is, part of the factual authority in Thomas's "victim-based" narrative may ultimately be deriving not just from the testimony of the victims but from that of the photographs taken by the killers themselves.

As Barthes, Sontag, and many others have demonstrated, however, photographs are as constructed and as mediated as any other kind of representation.[10] In fact, as a figure for documentary narrative, the photograph may even be more appropriate than the documentary writers imagined: for the photograph operates rhetorically on precisely the same assumption at work in documentary narrative. That is, as a seeming trace or fragment of its referent that appeals to the eye for its proof, the photograph is able to invoke the authority of its empirical link to events, which in turn seems to reinforce the sense of its own unmediated factuality. As a metonymical trope of witness, the photograph persuades the viewer of its testimonial and factual authority in ways that are unavailable to narrative. One of the reasons that narrative and photographs are so convincing together is that they seem to represent a combination of pure object and commentary on the object, each seeming to complete the other by reinforcing a sense of contrasting functions.

As Terrence Des Pres distinguished between the survivors' testimony and his own commentary in *The Survivor*, Kuznetsov creates a distinction between authentic documents in his work and his own voice. By including "A Chapter of Documents" and several short sections entitled "The Author's Voice," Kuznetsov attempts to create an intertext, in which a hierarchy of speakers' authority is generated. In another example of this tendency, the prize-winning novel *Efraim's Book* ("part diary, part documentary, part interior history," according to the jacket cover), the author Alfred Andersch incorporates into his text courtroom testimony from the Treblinka and Auschwitz trials in Germany in 1965 even as he suggests that such testimony may be phenomenologically unincorporable:

> ... But there was no explanation for Auschwitz. *On at least one occasion SS-Man Küttner, known as Kiewe, flung a baby into the air and Franz killed it with two shots.* No one has been able to explain Auschwitz. *We saw an enormous fire and men were throwing things into it. I saw a man who was holding something that moved its head. I said: 'For the love of God, Marusha, he's throwing a live dog into it.'*

But my companion said: 'That's not a dog, it's a baby.' I am suspicious
of anyone who tries to explain Auschwitz.[11]

By citing the source of these lines in a prefatory note and setting them off in
italics within the text itself, Andersch disclaims both authorship and
authority for them, and in so doing suggests to the reader that the
ontological status of these lines differs fundamentally from that of the
surrounding "fictional" text. Because these things actually happened,
Andersch (like Thomas and Kuznetsov) would claim not to re-create them
imaginatively, thereby keeping "facts" separate from "fiction" and absolving
himself of responsibility for imagining—and thereby re-perpetrating
somehow—the most violent scenes in his novel.

Where Andersch separates testimony from fiction in order to privilege
it over his surrounding fiction, others seem to make the distinction in order
to privilege the surrounding text as well. And where Thomas would indicate
this distinction in relatively subtle ways (in his speaker's asides and in
frontispiece acknowledgments), other novelists assert the difference much
more graphically. By separating "documents" from his own narrative in *Babi
Yar*, Kuznetsov simultaneously heightens the distinction between reimagined
narrative and authentic documents, even as he allows his narrative to draw its
authority from the documents he cites. As do photographs and narrative in
photojournalistic media, each kind of representation seems to demand and to
fulfill the other, providing either the necessary photographic proof or
narrative meaning that comes in captions.

Though Kuznetsov's *Babi Yar* is probably the most celebrated work of
Holocaust "documentary fiction" (it was also one of the first to call itself a
"documentary novel"), there are dozens of others no less insistent on their
documentary authority. Among them, we might note that in the preface to
Pierre Juliue's *Block 26: Sabotage at Buchenwald*, Joseph Kessel assures the
reader that "nothing of the work derives of fiction, and that everything is
true, even so to speak, the commas."[12] But, as we find in so many other
"documentary novels," the facts of this revolt are necessarily shaped, edited,
and explained by both the writer's and his witnesses' linguistic, cultural, and
religious perceptions of them. In this vein, Ezrahi has shown us that even
though Jean-Francois Steiner insists repeatedly on the absolute facticity of
his documentary novel based on the revolt at Treblinka, the story he writes
is ultimately so couched in biblical language and archetypes as to render all
of its participants either Jewish martyrs or heroes—a presentation that
conflicts markedly with other accounts of the same revolt.[13] As commentary
on the events at Treblinka and as representation of how survivors of the

revolt have apprehended their experiences, this novel succeeds. But, as Ezrahi observes, even though "this fiction is grounded in reality, it is sustained more by the spiritual authority of authentic testimony than by accurate documentary" (p. 25). That is, it becomes the illusion of documentary authority generated by authentic eyewitnesses that sustains the putative factuality of these texts and, by extension, the power of this fiction.

In a further twist recalling the cases of Thomas and Kuznetsov, the discrepancies between events as they are represented in Steiner's *Treblinka* and as narrated by Vasili Grossman in his version take on an irony of their own. As Thomas drew upon Kuznetsov, and Kuznetsov upon Pronicheva, Steiner seems to have relied heavily on Vasili Grossman's *L'Enfer de Treblinka* for his witness—even though Grossman himself came to Treblinka as a Soviet journalist after the camp was destroyed. Unlike the other authors, however, Steiner does not make direct attribution to Grossman's work. Instead, he acknowledges that three books on Treblinka exist, one of which (*The Hell of Treblinka*) "is by a war correspondent in the Soviet army who interviewed the first witnesses."[14]

In a related case, Cythia Haft notes that the historian Vidal Nacquet discovered that another novel, *Et la terre sera pure*, by Sylvain Reiner, lifted passages directly from Miklos Nyiszli's *Medecin a Auschwitz (Auschwitz: A Doctor's Eye-witness Account)*, without making any acknowledgment.[15] In the cases of both Reiner and Steiner, where full acknowledgments of source material were not made, the writers seem to have assumed that these other works retained a witness quality their narrative could not have—but which, even if it went uncited, might still infuse the surrounding text with the authority of witness.

By interweaving into fictional narrative the words of actual witnesses, perhaps written at the time, these novelists would thus create the texture of fact, suffusing the surrounding text with the privilege and authority of witness. At a crucial place near the end of *Treblinka*, Steiner thus goes directly to Yankel Wiernek's memoir, not only trusting the eyewitness to tell the story better but, by seeming to yield to the authority of an actual eyewitness, hoping to incorporate this same authority into his text. As Thomas and Kuznetsov have done, Steiner now distinguishes between his mere reconstruction and an authentic witness's memoir—now quoted verbatim— precisely to lend testimonial authority to his own surrounding narrative. And as so often happens in Holocaust fiction, the interpolation comes at a particularly dramatic moment, partly to heighten the drama, and, it seems, to shore up the authoritative integrity of the text at its most vulnerable moment: "Everything seems threatened. Only one man can still save the situation: Wiernik. Let us listen to his testimony" (p. 289). As part of the transition from his words to Wiernek's, Steiner turns to both present tense and first person at this moment and indents the testimony, setting it apart from his own. It is, in fact, first-rate storytelling, precisely because it is purportedly verified now by the witness to events just when we needed his authority most.

The interspersing of authentic witness with less authentic finds its place as a narrative technique in all kinds of Holocaust documentary literature, especially in the memoirs. Even the most authentic memoirs, like Leon W. Wells's *The Death Brigade*, often incorporate the witness of diary: the narrative written within events would now suffuse that written after events with an even more privileged authority. As photographs are used to authenticate and to increase the authority in actual witness accounts like Erich Kulka's *Escape from Auschwitz* or Filip Müller's *Eyewitness Auschwitz*, Leon Wells incorporates fragments of his diary into his own memoir precisely at the moment when the killing process begins.[16]

From invoking the "spiritual authority of authentic testimony," however, it is only a short step to fabricating it altogether within a text, whether it is called "fictional" or "nonfictional." Alvin Rosenfeld has noted in this regard that two other writers—John Hersey and Leon Uris—have, as part of their fictions, actually created their own documentary sources. In the editor's prologue to Hersey's *The Wall*, based on Emmanuel Ringelblum's *Notes from the Warsaw Ghetto*, the author exclaims of his own novel, "What a wonder of documentation!" and then goes on to tell the reader that the narrator, Levinson, "was too scrupulous to imagine *anything*," though Rosenfeld reminds us that the writer has actually had to imagine *everything*.[17] Rosenfeld also suggests that if documentary evidence is the aim, the reader might prefer to turn directly to the "actual historical testimonies we do have." But this is to imply that the primary difference between fabricated and "actual" testimony is a matter of actual documentary evidence—when, in fact, neither may actually be evidence but only the persuasively constructed illusion of evidence. Where the nonfiction account attempts to retrieve its authentic connection to events in order to reinforce its documentary authority, fiction necessarily fabricates its link to events in order to reinforce its documentary authority. The difference between fictional and nonfictional "documentary narratives" of the Holocaust may not be between degrees of actual evidential authority, but between the ontological sources of this sense of authority: one is retrieved and one is constructed wholly within the text as part of the text's fiction. As it was for the diaries and memoirs, the operative trope underpinning the documentary character of Holocaust "documentary fiction" is thus the rhetorical principle of testimony, not its actuality.

III

At the end of his study of "literary non-fiction," Ronald Weber concludes that "The first task of the writer of literary non-fiction is always *to convince the reader that his work is adequate as history*."[18] That is, the aim is not to write factual history but merely to persuade the reader that it is factual. If Holocaust documentary fiction depends upon the concept of testimony as a rhetorical trope only in order to provide an "unusually compelling experience for the reader," however, then these writers' narrative methods remain a matter of style. For documentary narratives are in this view compelling as "reading experience" precisely because they claim to be so much more than mere "reading experience."

In a way, the literary documentarist draws on the same sort of ambiguity between factual and fictional narrative that the novelist has always generated. Indeed, much of the force of novelistic discourse seems to derive precisely from the ambiguity its dual claims of fact and fiction stimulate in the reader, as Lennard Davis has noted in his study on the origins of the English novel. "Novels are framed works (even if they seem unframed)," he writes, "whose attitude toward fact and fiction is constitutively ambivalent."[19] By sustaining, encouraging, and even exacerbating what Davis calls the "constitutive ambivalence" toward fact and fiction, a writer like Daniel Defoe ("the journalist *par excellence* of the early eighteenth century") might therefore exemplify the novelist, at least partly because he claimed disingenuously to be a journalist. Where Cervantes drew attention to the fabulative nature of his work and, indeed, both celebrated and marked the confusion of mind that results from mistaking "real" for imaginary worlds, Defoe seems to have delighted in causing just this confusion of mind in the reader. "The process of reading a Defoean novel," Davis remarks, "is that the reader is asked first to believe that the novel is real, and then to understand that the reality of the novel is bogus. In effect, suspension of disbelief is itself suspended" (p. 23).

There is a sense in which part of novelistic discourse becomes not only a matter of "factual fiction," but really an attempt to generate fictional facts. When Defoe "places himself outside of the novel—into the prestructure—by the gesture of authorial disavowal," as Davis observes (p. 17), we might note further that this act remains only a gesture, a sleight of authorial hand by which he would appear to be outside of the narrative he has actually created. Contrary to Davis's contention that these writers are somehow "forced into the position of claiming to be the editor to some found document" (p. 35), we need to recognize this claim as part of the overall fiction of the writer's work. And just as earlier novelists dissembled, veiling their authorial presence to create the illusion of the text's autonomy, contemporary documentary novelists now conflate their narratives with rhetorically factual materials like photographs, newspaper articles, and eyewitness testimony in order to lend them a certain factual authority.

As fundamental to the nature of the novel as this ambiguity might be, however, without keeping in mind the distinction between the novelist's claims to fact and the actual fabulative character of his narrative, the reader risks a certain phenomenological beguilement at the hands of the novelist— and now at the hands of the "documentary novelist"—and not collusion with the novelist, as Davis suggests. By allowing himself to be moved to the willing suspension of disbelief by the documentary novel's contrived historical authority, the reader risks becoming ensnared in the allencompassing fiction of the discourse itself, mistaking the historical *force* of this discourse for the historical facts it purports to document.

That the reader responds to a work differently when he believes that it is "true" and has actually happened than he does when he believes the work is only "fiction" is a principal part of a documentary fiction's phenomenology; as such, the emotional experience of such an illusion becomes the aim of the writer. If the stimulation of emotional response is the "unique power" in realistic fiction and the "creation of such feelings in the reader [is] the fiction's highest achievement" (p. 16), as Thomas Wolfe might have it, then to read documentary fiction for its factual content would be to mistake the writer's literary means (i.e., apparent factuality) for the ends to which they are employed (i.e., emotional response). Like Weber, Wolfe acknowledges that the greatest advantage of this hybrid narrative is the *sense* that what it represents was real, not that it was real. In this literature, the facts (such as they are) thus remain subordinate to the effect they have on the reader.

In the case of Holocaust documentary narrative, this "rhetoric of fact" is invoked toward a number of different ends; and among them, it seems, is also an emotional response to the "sense of the real," a reinforcement of a work's supposed factuality, and the establishment of the authentic link between writer, text, and events. The purpose for documentary authority in the works of writers like Thomas, Kuznetsov, Steiner, and Andersch thus begins to assume critical importance. If this "rhetoric of fact" is intended to provide an unusually compelling reading experience, merely to move the reader, then Adorno's objections to "Holocaust art" retain a certain validity. For in this case, the authors would indeed be wringing pleasure from the naked pain of the victims. If, on the other hand, these works only want to refrain from conferring an essential fictionality on actual historical events, then we might take into account both the legitimate impulse to document events *and* the manner in which "real past events" are inevitably fictionalized by any narrative that gives them form. Insofar as it works to authenticate—and thereby naturalize—its particular interpretation of events, documentary narrative might even be considered an expressly ideological mode of discourse in both its means and its ends—a proposition that is explored at length in the next section on documentary drama, ideology, and the rhetoric of fact.

NOTES

1. Hana Wirth-Nesher, "The Ethics of Narration in D.M. Thomas's *The White Hotel*," *The Journal of Narrative Technique* 15, no. 1 (Winter 1985): 17.

2. Arnold Wesker, "Art Between Truth and Fiction: Thoughts on William Styron's Novel," *Encounter* (January 1980): 52.

3. Barbara Foley, "Fact, Fiction, Fascism: Testimony and Mimesis in Holocaust Narratives," *Comparative Literature* 34, no. 4 (Fall 1982): 337.

4. "The White Hotel," *Times Literary Supplement*, 26 March 1982.

5. Anatoli Kuznetsov, *Babi Yar: A Documentary Novel* (New York: The Dial Press, 1967), pp. 74-75.

6. D.M. Thomas, *The White Hotel* (New York: The Viking Press, 1981), pp. 246-47.

7. "The White Hotel," *Times Literary Supplement*, 2 April 1982, p. 24.

8. "The Memories," *New York Times Book Review*, 9 April 1967, p. 45. Also quoted in Ezrahi, *By Words Alone*, p. 31.

9. Cf. the descriptions on p. 243 of *The White Hotel* and photographs of massacres in Lijepaja, Latvia, and Sniadowa, Poland, in Gerhard Schoenberner, *The Yellow Star* (New York, London, and Toronto: Bantam Books, 1969), pp. 92-97.

10. See Roland Barthes, *Camera Lucida: Reflections on Photography* (New York: Hill and Wang, 1981), and *Image-Music-Text* (New York: Hill and Wang, 1977), pp. 15-51.
Susan Sontag, *On Photography* (New York: Farrar, Straus, and Giroux, 1973); it is worth noting here that Sontag writes specifically of Holocaust photographs she saw when she was twelve years old that "Nothing I had seen—in photographs or in real life—ever cut me as sharply, deeply, instantaneously," suggesting the sheer "power" of referential evidence in the photograph.

Also see Joel Snyder and Neil Walsh Allen, "Photography, Vision, and Representation," *Critical Inquiry*, Autumn 1975, p. 145; John Berger, *About Looking* (New York: Pantheon Press, 1980); and Kendall L. Walton, "Transparent Pictures: On the Nature of Photographic Realism," *Critical Inquiry* 11, no. 2 (December 1984): 246-77.

11. Alfred Andersch, *Efraim's Book* (New York: Viking Penguin, 1984), p. 143.

12. Pierre Julitte, *Block 26: Sabotage at Buchenwald* (New York: Doubleday, 1971), p. xi. Also quoted in Ezrahi, *By Words Alone*, p. 25, as part of an excellent discussion of "Documentation as Art."

13. Ezrahi suggests we compare Steiner's account, for example, with Yankel Wiernik's diary, *A Year in Treblinka*, and Vasili Grossman's *L'Enfer de Treblinka (By Words Alone, p. 32)*.

14. Jean-Francois Steiner, *Treblinka* (New York: New American Library, 1979), p. 304. In the afterword to the original French edition, Steiner's reference is exactly the same ("*L'Enfer de Treblinka*, par un correspondant de guerre de l'armée soviétique qui interrogea les premiers témoins"). *Treblinka* (Paris: Librairie Artheme Fayand, 1966), p. 394.

15. In her study, *The Theme of Nazi Concentration Camps in French Literature* (The Hague and Paris: Mouton and Company, 1973), Cynthia Haft cites Steiner's and Reiner's as instances of dishonest fiction, "part of a trend which we abhor," and notes that after legal proceedings, Reiner reedited his book to include acknowledgments where they were due (p. 191).

16. Leon W. Wells, *The Death Brigade* (New York: Holocaust Library, 1978), p. 133. See, among many other excellent memoirs, Erich Kulka, *Escape from Auschwitz* (South Hadley, Mass.: Bergin and Garvey Publishers, Inc., 1986), and Filip Müller, *Eyewitness Auschwitz: Three Years in the Gas Chambers* (New York: Stein and Day, 1979).

17. Alvin H. Rosenfeld, *A Double Dying: Reflections on Holocaust Literature* (Bloomington and London: Indiana University Press, 1980), p. 66. John Hersey, *The Wall* (New York: Knopf, 1950). Leon Uris, *Mila 18* (New York: Doubleday, 1961).

18. Ronald Weber, *The Literature of Fact* (Athens: Ohio University Press, 1980), p. 163 (emphasis mine).

19. Lennard Davis, *Factual Fictions: The Origins of the English Novel* (New York: Columbia University Press, 1983), pp. 212-13.

JOSEPH SUNGOLOWSKY

Holocaust and Autobiography:
Wiesel, Friedländer, Pisar

Autobiography is usually defined as a retrospective narrative written about one's life, in the first person and in prose. Such writing has appeared with increasing frequency in Western literature since the beginning of the nineteenth century. As a result of the events of World War II, it gained considerable significance in France, as can be seen in the works of authors such as André Malraux and Simone de Beauvoir. In view of the proliferation of autobiography, the recent studies by the critics Philippe Lejeune and Georges May have attempted to examine its characteristics and determine to what extent it could represent a literary genre.

The history of the destruction of European Jewry by the Nazis has relied heavily upon the accounts written by survivors, which will probably remain a prime source of information concerning the magnitude of the catastrophe. Autobiography written as a result of experiences lived during the Holocaust is therefore an integral part of its literature. Since such literature cannot be linked to any of the norms of literary art, it has been termed a literature of "atrocity" or "decomposition." Holocaust autobiography inherits, therefore, the problematic aspect of both autobiography and the literature of the Holocaust. In the light of the above-mentioned studies on autobiography and on the basis of *Night* (1958) by Elie Wiesel, *When Memory Comes* (1978) by Saul Friedländer, and *Of Blood and Hope* (1979) and *La Ressource humaine* (1983) by Samuel Pisar, we shall

From *Reflections of the Holocaust in Art and Literature*, ed. Randolph L. Braham. © 1990 by Randolph L. Braham.

examine who writes Holocaust autobiography, why and how it is written, and what is the substance of such writing.

I

Autobiography is generally written in midlife by an author who has achieved fame thanks to previous works which have been recognized for their value, or by an individual who has played a significant role in public life. Saul Friedländer was 46 years old when *When Memory Comes* was published. At that time, he had gained an international reputation as a historian of Nazism. Samuel Pisar was 50 when he wrote *Of Blood and Hope*. He is also the author of *Coexistence and Commerce* (1970), an impressive political and economic treatise advocating trade relations between East and West, especially as a means to ease the Cold War. He, too, has achieved recognition as a political scientist, as an advisor to governments, and as an international lawyer.

Writing autobiography at an earlier age or as a first book is considered an exception.[1] Elie Wiesel's *Night* is such an exception. He recounts how fortuitous his career as a writer was in its beginnings, especially considering that he might not have survived the concentration camps at all. Upon his liberation, he vowed not to speak of his experience for at least ten years. It was the French novelist Francois Mauriac who persuaded him to tell his story, and Wiesel adds that at the time Mauriac was as well-known as he was obscure.[2] Thus, at the age of 28, Wiesel published his autobiographical narrative concerning his experience in the concentration camps, first in Yiddish under the title *Un die velt hot geshvigen*, subsequently in French under the title *La Nuit*. In 1976, Wiesel stated that *Night* could have remained his one and only book;[3] indeed, when he began to write fiction, the French critic Rene Lalou wondered how Wiesel could have undertaken to write anything else after *Night*.[4] Clearly, at the time Wiesel published *Night*, he lacked the fame as an author of previous works usually expected of an autobiography, as indicated by Philippe Lejeune and Georges May.[5]

An autobiography is deemed authentic when there is identity between the name of the author appearing on the title page and the narrator of the story.[6] In *Night*, Wiesel relates that during a rollcall in Auschwitz, he heard a man crying out: "Who among you is Wiesel from Sighet?" He turned out to be relative that had been deported from Antwerp. Subsequently, Wiesel is called by his first name "Eliezer" by that relative, by Juliek, a fellow-inmate, and by his father.[7] Friedländer refers to his name several times in the course of his narrative. He recalls how difficult it was for him to get accustomed to his new first-name "Paul-Henri" given to him in the Catholic boarding school in France, as he was called "Pavel" or "Pawlicek," the diminutive given to him by his family. He names himself again when he recalls his stay, in 1950, with an uncle who directed an institution for mentally ill children. One of them tried to communicate with him during a fit, and all he could say was "Herr Friedländer." (Friedländer sees in this incident an example of the unlocking of the inner world which he experienced himself when he began to write his book.)

Pisar names himself throughout *Of Blood and Hope*. Upon returning to Auschwitz as a member of a delegation to a commemorative ceremony, he describes himself as follows: "a reincarnated Samuel Pisar clothed simply in his respectable attire of international lawyer, scholar, American citizen had to step into the light and avow once more that once, not so long ago, he had crawled in the pain, the filth and the degradation of the factories of death."[8] Later on, he quotes Solzhenitsyn commenting upon his views on coexistence between East and West: "Pisar is one of the few to see clearly."[9]

Autobiography is considered genuine when the author states, either in the text itself or in connection with it, that his intent has indeed been autobiographical. Lejeune calls such a statement an "autobiographical pact"—an agreement between author and reader according to which the reader is assured that he is reading the truth.[10]

Upon the publication of his book, Friedländer told an interviewer that he wrote it as a result of an "inner necessity," and he discussed its main themes: his childhood, his life as a youngster in a Catholic boarding school after he was separated from his parents during the war, his discovery of Zionism and his views on Israel where he lives.[11] In the preface to the French edition of his book, Pisar explains that in order to write it he had to revive from within the depths of his self the tragic episodes of his life which represent such a sharp contrast with his "reincarnation" as a brilliant public figure.[12] Pisar's subsequent book intitled *La Ressource humaine* is of a similar intent. It opens as follows: "I sleep with eyes half-closed. I have done so for the last forty years. Even since I entered the precincts of Auschwitz."[13] Wiesel's autobiographical pact was established twenty years after the publication of *Night*, when he told an interviewer: "*Night*, my first narrative, was an autobiographical story, a kind of testimony of one witness speaking of his own life, his own death."[14]

II

Autobiography is written in order to come to terms with oneself.[15] Recapturing the past is, therefore, the most common preoccupation of the autobiographer. This motivation is repeatedly stressed by Saul Friedländer whose childhood was shattered by the events of the war. Recounting his suicide attempt after he was separated from his parents, he wonders whether he is the same person or even the same Jew "if there were such a thing as a collective Jew."[16] When he tries to seek out a former schoolmate 35 years later, he suspects that this impulse is dictated by the "need for synthesis ... that no longer excludes anything."[17] Therefore, in order to recapture the past, his sole recourse is to write, for "writing retraces the contours of the past ..., it does at least preserve a presence."[18] In measuring the distance between past and present, Friedländer realizes that he has retained a reticence toward people, a tendency to passivity, moral preoccupations and self-examination inculcated to him by the "taboos" of his former Catholic education.[19]

In searching for himself, the autobiographer may indulge in narcissism and conceit.[20] Pisar hardly avoids these temptations. Self-glorification is a pervasive theme in both of his autobiographical books. He dwells extensively upon his close relationships with world celebrities, on his brilliance as a political scientist whose advice is sought by statesmen, on his participation in international conferences where he is eagerly listened to, on his talent at handling the affairs of renowned movie stars. However, such vanity seems deliberate, for Pisar never fails to stress the contrast between his present success and his former condition as a concentration camp inmate. He often recalls "the young boy with a shaven head, pale skin tightly drawn over his face, and an almost broken body."[21] In La Ressource humaine, he writes: "I carry the immense privilege of a double experience. That of a sub-human thrown in the deepest hell of the century and that of an individual treasured by the great and productive cultures of this planet that are still free."[22]

Autobiography is written as a testimony, especially when the author has lived a particular moment of history that must not be forgotten.[23] Such was Elie Wiesel's intent when he wrote Night. For him, "Auschwitz was a unique phenomenon, a unique event, like the revelation at Sinai."[24] Had it not been for the war, he would not have become a storyteller but would have written on philosophy, the Bible, and the Talmud. He recalls that as he looked at himself in the mirror after his liberation, he realized how much he had changed and decided that someone had to write about that change. Although he had vowed to remain silent for ten years, he had absorbed "the obsession to tell the tale." He states: "I knew that anyone who remained alive had to become a story-teller, a messenger, had to speak up."[25]

Autobiography may also be written to educate. The autobiographer wishes his reader to learn from his experience.[26] In the preface to the French edition of *Blood and Hope*, Pisar writes that he did not mean to write a narrative describing the atrocities of the Holocaust or an abstract ideological work on the subject, but: "to forget those four hellish years spent in the most loathsome trashcan of history."[27] For him, the danger of a thermonuclear war is a mere repetition of the former madness. He writes, therefore, to educate the youth of today. "They need to arm themselves against the tragedies, the hypocrisies, the false gods of history."[28] In *La Ressource humaine*, Pisar further explores the means by which a third world war can be avoided. The autobiographical element is present in it again, and with the same educational intent. He relates that while he was about to enter the gas chamber, he escaped from the line, seized a brush and pail, and began scrubbing the floor of the waiting room much to the liking of the guards. He is convinced, therefore, that the world possesses likewise the resources to avoid a nuclear war.[29]

III

No matter how sincere or truthful the autobiographer intends to be, he must face the technical and literary problems related to the writing. Such problems are even more acute in the case of Holocaust autobiography. Before they write autobiography, authors will make sure that a reasonable amount of time has elapsed between the events they wish to relate and the actual writing. Such "distanciation" ensures orderliness to the narrative. In the case of Holocaust autobiography, the waiting period is not only technical but also emotional. Elie Wiesel states that he feared being unable to live up to the past, "of saying the wrong things, of saying too much or too little." He therefore decided to wait ten years before writing.[30] Friedländer stated that he had unsuccessfully attempted to write his account fifteen years earlier.[31] Pisar waited about 35 years before he decided to write.

With the best faith or memory in the world, it is impossible to re-create in writing a reality long gone by.[32] In this respect, Holocaust autobiographers are even more frustrated. They constantly suspect that whatever the form and content of their narrative, they have not succeeded in conveying the past adequately. Wiesel feels that, while *Night* is the center of his work, "what happened during that night ... will not be revealed."[33] In the midst of writing, Friedländer feels "deeply discouraged." He writes: "I will never be able to express what I want to say; these lines, often clumsy, are very far removed, I know, from my memories, and even my memories retrieve only sparse fragments of my parents' existence, of their world, of the time when I was a child." At the conclusion of his book, he is still wondering whether he has succeeded "in setting down even so much as a tiny part of what [he] wanted to express."[34] However, since they represent an attempt to recapture whatever is retained of the past, such memories, as fragmented as they may be, remain invaluable. As put by Leon Wieseltier, they are "all the more illuminating, because memory is the consciousness of things and events that have not yet disappeared completely into knowledge."[35]

No matter how truthful the autobiographer tries to be, he cannot avoid having recourse to fictional or literary devices. Indeed, autobiography is necessarily linked to related literary genres such as the novel, the theater, the diary, or the chronicle.[36] Thus, despite Theodore W. Adorno's contention that it is barbaric to write literature after Auschwitz, the Holocaust writer or autobiographer must engage in a "writing experience" if he wishes to express himself.

The terse language of Wiesel's *Night* is occasionally broken by harrowing scenes such as that of Madame Shachter gone mad in the cattle car or by dialogues such as those that take place between himself and his erstwhile master Moshe-the-Beadle or with his dying father. Fantasy is present when he depicts his native Sighet as "an open tomb" after its Jews have been rounded up. He uses irony when he recalls that a fellow inmate has faith in Hitler because he has kept all his promises to the Jewish people. Images express the author's feelings. Gallows set up in the assembly place in preparation of a hanging appear to him as "three black crows," and the violin of a fellow inmate who has died after playing a Beethoven concerto lies beside him like "a strange overwhelming little corpse." The grotesque best portrays his fellow inmates, "Poor mountebanks, wider than they were tall, more dead than alive; poor clowns, their ghost like faces emerging from piles of prison clothes! Buffoons!"[37]

While Friedländer and Pisar are not writers in the artistic sense of the word, they cannot avoid resorting to literary devices. On page 78 of *When Memory Comes*, Friedländer writes in a footnote: "All the names associated with my stay in Montlucon, the Indre and Sweden are fictitious," clearly a technique widely used by discretion-conscious autobiographers and by authors of autobiographical novels.[38] The universe of the concentration camp has imprinted on Pisar's mind indelible images and myths. Upon visiting the naval base at Norfolk, Virginia, he is impressed by the latest inventions in warfare such as the nuclear aircraft carriers. The white star which adorns one of them reminds him of the same emblem on the American tank that liberated him. Witnessing the array of these formidable weapons meant to be used in a third world war, he cannot help but seeing in them a "nuclear gas chamber."[39]

According to Georges May, reproducing letters and evoking historical episodes and personalities enliven autobiography and enhance its authenticity.[40] Friedländer reproduces correspondence related to his childhood in France. There are letters written by his mother to the guardian to whose care she entrusted him, by his father to the director of the Catholic school authorizing her to baptize the child; and he reproduces the last letter written by both parents from the train that took them to the death camp. There are letters written by himself after the Liberation to his new guardians inquiring about the fate of his parents and eventually informing them that he would not return home since he had decided to leave for the newly born State of Israel. Retracing the stages of his ascent from a subhuman survivor to his present position, Pisar rarely misses an opportunity to name the celebrities with whom he associated. As a student in Australia, he took walks with Prime Minister Menzies. At Harvard, Ralph Nader and Zaki Yamani were his classmates. During a ceremony in Auschwitz, he stood next to Giscard d'Estaing of France and Gierek of Poland. At the World Gathering of Holocaust Survivors, he stood next to Begin. *Of Blood and Hope* includes a centerfold where he is pictured with Kissinger, Arthur Rubinstein, etc. Mitterand agrees with his views on coexistence between East and West. He is the lawyer of Richard Burton, Ava Gardner, and Catherine Deneuve.

IV

While autobiography may choose to embrace a greater or smaller part of one's life, Holocaust autobiography will essentially deal with the period marked by the events of the Nazi genocide. Just as any autobiography related to a troubled historical period acquires an added significance,[41] so does Holocaust autobiography exert a unique fascination upon the reader because of its central motive.

Like many autobiographers who try to resurrect their happy past, Wiesel, Pisar, and Friedländer dwell upon their childhood as they recall their native towns, their families, and their early schooling shortly before the outbreak of the war. Wiesel and Pisar are sons of educated fathers who were actively involved in Jewish communal affairs. While Friedländer's father had not retained much from his early Jewish education, he was not indifferent to his origins. At the age of 12, Wiesel was eager to study the Kabbalah with his enigmatic teacher Moshe-the-Beadle in his native Sighet. Pisar's native city, Bialystok, is a "vibrant center of Jewish cultural life," where socialism and Zionism mingle and vie with the study of Torah. As he studies for his Bar Mitzvah, which takes place in the ghetto, he realizes that the persecutions which beset the Jewish people throughout its history had forged its very identity. For Friedländer the child, his native Prague is a city of legends, especially that of the Golem, the robot built by the sixteenth-century Rabbi Loewe to protect the endangered Jews of the city. While attending the English school in that city, Friedländer becomes aware of his Jewishness as he is invited to leave catechism classes and told to attend instead Jewish religious instruction.

These evocations of childhood are all the more dramatic as they abruptly came to an end. As he completes the recollection of his early childhood, Friedländer writes: "I hesitate somehow to leave this calm and, when all is said and done, happy period of my life."[42] What follows in the writings of all three authors are scenes of departures. When Wiesel's family must join the roundup of Jews in Sighet, he sees his father weeping for the first time. Looking at his little sister, Tzipora, he notices that "the bundle on her back was too heavy for her."[43] On the eve of the family's departure from Prague, Friedländer is ceremoniously given a ring by his father so that he may not forget his native city. What is concealed from him is that they are fleeing the Nazis. Before leaving the house for the ghetto of Bialystok, Pisar's father gathers his family in the drawing-room, lights a big fire in the fireplace, throws in it the most cherished mementoes of the family and states: "We are living our last moments in our home. We don't know when we will return. We don't know who will move in here after we are gone."[44]

As painful as it may be to both author and reader, these autobiographical writings attempt to come to grips with the hard reality of the concentrationary universe. If *Night* has become a classic, it is because it remains one of the most concise and factual eyewitness accounts of the horrors. Wiesel goes into such details as the early disbelief of the victims ("The yellow star? Oh! well, what of it?" says his own father), the anguish of those who have been marked by death by Mengele in the course of a selection and Wiesel's own joy at having escaped it, the careless trampling of inmates by their own comrades in the course of the agonizing death marches.

The opening pages of Pisar's *Of Blood and Hope* are dedicated to a rather detailed account of his life in the concentration camps. Among the numerous descriptions of his experiences is a shattering portrait of a dying inmate, called "Musulman" in concentration camp terminology. Such an individual who had succeeded in escaping many a selection, once given that label by his own fellow-inmates, "was left feeling he had exhausted his last reserves of strength and hope," and would drop lifeless while no one cared.[45] However, most of his experiences as a former inmate are related in the light of his activities as a political or economic advisor. When he addresses a session of the Bundestag in Bonn, he finds irony in the fact that his previous dialogue with the Germans was a one sided: "caps off, caps on!" coming from his guards.[46] He feels that it is utterly dangerous to subject economy to a nondemocratic regime. Under Nazism, such an alliance led to the I. G. Farben phenomenon which treated human beings as "an expandable raw material ... from which all vital force was first extracted, was then treated with Zyklon B gas so that it could yield its secondary products: gold teeth and fillings for the Reichsbank, hair for the mattresses, grease for the soap and skin for the lampshades."[47] The struggle for inalienable human rights must go on. In the concentration camps, many died with the conviction that no one would ever learn of their utter suffering, while today violations of human rights anywhere are swiftly publicized to the world at large.[48]

Unlike Wiesel and Pisar, Friedländer did not experience concentration-camp life. Yet, the Holocaust remains a central theme of his book. He relates how he narrowly escaped a transport of children rounded up by the French police as a result of an agreement between the Vichy government and the Nazis. As for other typical aspects of the Holocaust, one might say that he attempts to live them vicariously. As an adult, he visits the village on the French-Swiss border where his parents were kept from crossing into Switzerland, handed over to the French police, and returned to a concentration camp in France while awaiting deportation. Upon the anniversary of the Warsaw ghetto uprising, he meditates about a story told by a survivor concerning a boy begging for a piece of bread in the ghetto and dying before he could reach the piece thrown to him by the narrator from his window. Eight years before the release of *Shoah*, the film by Claude Lanzman, Friedländer relates the detailed testimony concerning the destruction of the Jews at Treblinka given by a former SS guard to Lanzman.[49] He writes that he must leave the room when he hears a former SS officer telling about the burning of villages in Russia where he served. He is appalled when Admiral Donitz, Hitler's successor, tells him that he knew nothing of the extermination of the Jews, and when he does research in Germany, he feels the urge to pack up and leave. Yet, Friedländer admits that he is unable to fathom the reality of Belzec and Maidanek. He writes: "The veil between the events and me had not been rent. I had lived on the edges of the catastrophe ... and despite all my efforts, I remained in my own eyes not so much a victim as a spectator."[50]

V

"Autobiography," writes Georges May, "is capable of absorbing the most diverse material, to assimilate it and to change it into autobiography."[51] Inasmuch as Holocaust autobiography deals with the events of one of the greatest upheavals of the twentieth century and the most traumatic destruction of the Jewish people, it is natural that autobiographers reflect upon the impact of those events on their personality, on the destiny of the Jewish people and on the post-Holocaust world.

Confession is an essential ingredient of autobiography. Its degree of sincerity remains the sole prerogative of the autobiographer who can choose to shield himself behind his own writing. In Wiesel's *Night*, the frankness of his confession serves as a testimony to the extent of the dehumanization he has reached as a result of his concentration-camp life. While he has been separated forever from his mother and sister upon arrival in Auschwitz, he has managed to stay with his father. Both have miraculously escaped selection for death on several occasions. Yet, the survival instinct has overtaken him in the face of his dying father. When a guard tells him that in the camp "there are no fathers, no brothers, no friends," he thinks in his innermost heart that the guard is right but does not dare admit it. When he wakes up the next morning (less than four months before the Liberation) to find his father dead, he thinks "something like—free at last."[52] Henceforth, Wiesel's life is devoid of meaning. *Night* concludes with the episode of the author looking at himself in the mirror. He writes: "a corpse gazed at me. The look in his eyes as they stared into mine has never left me."[53] As indicated by Ellen Fine, the shift from the first to the third person in that sentence points to the "fragmented self,"[54] and, as indicated by Wiesel himself, that sight was to determine his career as a "writer-witness."[55]

Friedländer informs us of the psychological effects the separation from his parents has had on his childhood. An immediate result of it is his attempted suicide followed by nightmarish fits of fever during which he is vainly looking for his mother in rolling trains. "Passing by the hospital where his father lay sick, he wonders, "if one of the glass doors wouldn't suddenly open and [my] mother or father lean out over the edge of the terrace to signal discreetly to [me]."[56] Without news from his parents, he becomes very devout, worshipping especially the Virgin Mary for he rediscovered in her "something of the presence of a mother."[57] When he does not see his parents return after the Liberation, anxiety overtakes him, and he describes in detail its physiological and psychological effects."[58] To this day, the adult remains unsettled by his past. He writes: "In my heart of hearts, I still feel a strange attraction, mingled with profound repulsion, for this phase of my childhood."[59]

The Holocaust causes all three writers to question God's ways. One of the main themes of *Night* is Wiesel's shattered faith. When he recalls his arrival in Auschwitz, he writes the now famous words: "Never shall I forget those flames which consumed my faith forever."[60] He subsequently doubts God's justice,[61] argues with God on RoshHashanah,[62] eats on Yom Kippur as an act of defiance against God, and feels that God Himself is hanging on the gallows when he witnesses the hanging of a child.[63] In fact, the "Trial of God"[64] obsesses Wiesel throughout his work. Without being specifically preoccupied with metaphysics in their account, both Friedländer and Pisar seem nevertheless to take God to task. In the last letter written to his guardian, Friedländer's parents express the wish that God may repay and bless her, which prompts the author's comment: "What God was meant?"[65] Upon being separated forever from his mother and sister, Pisar, too, raises his fist to heaven "in a blasphemous cry towards the Almighty."[66]

Many inmates were able to survive by means of "spiritual resistance"— by clinging to an ideal which would keep them from being destroyed against all odds. For Pisar, such an ideal was friendship in the camps with Ben, a childhood friend, and with Nico, "a resourceful older ally in the daily struggle against death."[67] Having escaped death on several occasions, it is they that he seeks out and it is with them that he is ultimately reunited until they were liberated. For Pisar, this lasting friendship not only meant that they had endured the Holocaust together but also proved that "man can overcome, if he has the courage not to despair."[68]

Having reasonably distanced themselves from the events of the Holocaust before they engaged into autobiographical writing, Friedländer and Pisar are able to put their experience in perspective and, therefore, reflect upon Jewish destiny and identity and express views on the post-Holocaust world.

If, as a child, Friedländer is fascinated by the legend of the Golem or by the sacrifice of Isaac, to the adult, the former symbolizes Jewish "perpetual restlessness"[69] and the latter Jewish obedience to "some mysterious destiny."[70] Upon discovering Zionism after the war, he becomes convinced that a state is needed so that the Jewish people may never again go to the slaughter like sheep.[71] Recalling that his father had waited to become a refugee in France to tell him the Hannukah story, he realizes that his father had rediscovered a "permanent and lasting" feeling of kinship to the community only as a result of the crisis.[73] He himself observes sincere Jewish prayer while living with a religious guardian after the war,[74] experiences a genuine feeling of Jewishness upon discovering Hasidism in the books of Martin Buber,[75] and, on the occasion of Yom Kippur 1977, he states that one can hardly define the Jewish people without the Jewish religion.[76] As an Israeli, Friedländer would like to see his country at peace. He wonders, therefore, whether Israel fails "to accept compromise at the proper moment."[77] He acknowledges, however, that the Jewish people has always been engaged in an "endless quest" which is symbolic of that pursued by mankind as a whole.[78] Therefore, Friedländer surmises that Israel is not likely to alter the course of Jewish history.[79]

Pisar views Jewish destiny and the post-Holocaust world solely with the eyes of a survivor. He concludes the account of a family trip to Masada, the historic symbol of Jewish resistance, with the words "No more Auschwitz, no more Masada."[80] The existence of the State of Israel and the freedom of Soviet Jews are causes that are very close to his heart. The sight of Israeli soldiers praying at the Wailing Wall they had just conquered during the Six-Day War convinces him that "the trains headed for Treblinka, Maidanek and Auschwitz had finally reached their destination."[81] He is indignant at the UN resolution which equates Zionism with racism. It causes him to question his own survival and to realize that perhaps "there was no way to escape from the mentality of the ghettos and the camps after all."[82] Therefore, Israel must remain the ultimate "haven for survivors," especially in the light of recent attacks upon Jews in Europe, which show that the Jew remains prime target.[83] He is heartened by the fact that a Jewish community continues to exist in the Soviet Union sixty five years after the revolution. As a member of an American delegation to a conference on *détente* that took place in Kiev in 1971, he daringly confronts the Russians with their persistant anti-Semitic policy. Introducing himself as a survivor, he criticizes them for requiring that the word JEW be inscribed on the identity cards of Soviet Jews and for failing to recognize Babi Yar as the burial place of thousands of Jews killed by the Nazis.[84] Nevertheless, Pisar remains unequivocally committed to the idea of peaceful coexistence, which is the underlying idea of his autobiographical writings. When he is reminded that, as a survivor, he ought to advocate a militant attitude toward the Russians, he replies that firmness and open mindedness in dealing with them are not incompatible.[85]

Meant as a stark narrative of the events and despite the ten-year period that preceded its writing, Wiesel's *Night* is devoid of reflections extraneous to his experiences in the concentration camps. He has stated that, except for *Night*, his other works are not autobiographical, although he occasionally brings into them "autobiographical data and moods."[86] Yet, Wiesel has emphasized the importance of *Night* as the foundation of his subsequent works. He states: "*Night*, my first narrative, was an autobiographical story, a kind of testimony of one witness speaking of his own life, his own death. All kinds of options were available: suicide, madness, killing, political action, hate, friendship. I note all these options: faith, rejection of faith, blasphemy, atheism, denial, rejection of man, despair, and in each book I explore one aspect. In *Dawn*, I explore the political action; in *The Accident*, suicide; in *The Town Beyond the Wall*, madness; in *The Gates of the Forest,*, faith and friendship; in *A Beggar in Jerusalem*, history, the return. All the stories are one story except that I build them in concentric circles. The center is the same and is in *Night*."[87] Such a position illustrates Philippe Lejeune's concept of "autobiographical space."[88] Indeed, according to Lejeune, it is not always possible to derive the total image of a writer solely on the basis of a work explicitly declared to be autobiographical. Such an image is to be sought rather in the totality of his work which cannot fail to contain autobiographical data. Reflections on Jewish destiny and identity and on the post-Holocaust world are surely the very essence of Wiesel's writings whether they take the form of fiction, tales, plays, or essays.

Autobiography does not necessarily encompass a whole life. Many autobiographers choose to write about a part of it which they deem significant enough to reflect a profound if not crucial human experience. The Holocaust illustrates this aspect of autobiographical writing. As recognized authors in their respective fields, Wiesel, Friedländer, and Pisar feel a compelling need at one point or another in their lives to tell of their experiences. Whether they write to settle the past, to testify or to educate, they mobilize a variety of devices and themes available to the autobiographer who seeks to share his experiences with the reader. As the Holocaust continues to be represented in an ever-growing multiplicity of forms, autobiography remains a fascinating means to express it. It is noteworthy, therefore, that the Holocaust autobiographer encounters consciously or not many of the problems faced by any autobiographer. However, in the case of the Holocaust autobiographer, such problems become even more crucial because of the nature of the material he is dealing with. Autobiography universalizes one's life. In the hands of the writers examined in this study, Holocaust autobiography not only serves as an invaluable testimony of events that must never be forgotten, but also strengthens the feeling of all those who wish to identify with the victims of the greatest crime that ever took place amidst modern civilization.

NOTES

1. Georges May, *L'Autobiographie*. Paris: Presses Universitaires de France, 1979, pp. 33-39.

2. Elie Wiesel, *A Jew Today*. New York: Random House, 1978, pp. 14-19.

3. *Harry James Cargas in Conversation with Elie Wiesel*. New York: Paulist Press, 1976, p. 88.

4. Quoted by Wladimir Rabi, "Elie Wiesel: Un homme, une oeuvre, un public." *Esprit*, Sept. 1980, p. 81.

5. Philippe Lejeune, *Le Pacte autobiographique*. Paris: Editions du Seuil, 1975, p. 23; May, pp. 31-32.

6. Lejeune, p. 26.

7. I disagree with Ted L. Estess who sees a discrepancy between "Eliezer" the story-teller and "Elie" the author, which he interprets as a device of "distanciation" between the character and the author who is unable to fully retell the horror he has witnessed. See Ted L. Estess, *Elie Wiesel*, New York: Ungar, 1980, pp., 17-18. One should bear in mind that the original edition in Yiddish carries the first name "Eliezer" on its title page. Furthermore, Wiesel has unequivocally stressed the symbolic importance of his full Hebrew name "Eliezer ben Chlomo." See Cargas, p. 52.

8. Samuel Pisar, *Of Blood and Hope*. Boston, Toronto: Little, Brown & Co., 1979, p. 18.

9. *Ibid.*, p. 64.

10. Philippe Lejeune, *L'Autobiographie en France*. Paris: Armand Colin, 1971, p. 23.

11. Jacques Sabbath, "Israël á coeur ouvert," *L'Arche*, Nov. 1978, p. 35.

12. Samuel Pisar, *Le Sang et l'espoir*, Paris: Laffont, 1979, pp. 12-13. (Translations from that work are my own.)

13. Samuel Pisar, *La Ressource humaine*. Paris: Jean-Claude Lattes, 1983, p. 15. (Translations from that work are my own.)

14. Cargas, p. 86.

15. Lejeune, *L'Autobiographie*, p. 19; May, p. 55.

16. Saul Friedländer, *When Memory Comes*. New York: Avon Books, 1980, p. 100.

17. *Ibid.*, p. 114.

18. *Ibid.*, p. 135.

19. *Ibid.*, p. 164.

20. May, p. 160.

21. Pisar, *Of Blood and Hope*, p. 188.

22. Pisar, *La Ressource humaine*, p. 351.

23. May, p. 43.

24. Cargas, p. 8.

25. *Ibid.*, p. 87.

26. Lejeune, *L'Autobiographie*, p. 82.

27. Pisar, *Le Sang et l'espoir*, p. 20.

28. Pisar, *Of Blood and Hope*, p. 23.

29. Pisar, *La Ressource humaine*, pp. 47-49.

30. Cargas, p. 87.

31. Sabbath, p. 35.

32. May, p. 82.

33. Cargas, p. 86.

34. Friedländer, pp. 134, 182.

35. "Between Paris and Jerusalem," *New York Review of Books* Oct. 25, 1979, p. 3.

36. Lejeune, *L'Autobiographie*, p. 28; May, pp. 113-116.

37. Elie Wiesel, *Night*. New York: Avon Books, 1969, p. 94. For a literary evaluation of *Night*, see Lawrence L. Langer, *The Holocaust and the Literary Imagination*. New Haven & London: Yale University Press, 1975, pp. 75-89; Ted L. Estess, *Elie Wiesel*, pp. 17-32.

38. Lejeune, *L'Autobiographie*, p. 83; May, p. 194.

39. Pisar, *La Ressource humaine*, pp. 216-217.

40. May, pp. 133-135.

41. *Ibid.*, p. 103.

42. Friedländer, p. 15.

43. Wiesel, *Night*, p. 29.

44. Pisar, *Of Blood and Hope*, p. 35.

45. *Ibid.*, p. 75.

46. *Ibid.*, p. 230.

47. *Ibid.*, p. 248.

48. Pisar, *La Ressource humaine*, p. 333.

49. Friedländer, pp. 116-117. See the testimony of Franz Suchomel in Claude Lanzman, *Shoah*. New York: Pantheon Books, 1985. In a letter to this writer, Saul Friedländer has confirmed his reporting of this testimony prior to the release of the film.

50. Friedländer, p. 155.

51. May, pp. 200-201.

52. Wiesel, *Night*, pp. 122-124. For a thorough and moving analysis of the father-son relationship in *Night*, See Ellen S. Fine, *Legacy of Night: The Literary Universe of Elie Wiesel*. Albany: State University Press, 1982, pp. 18-26.

53. Wiesel, *Night*, p. 127.

54. Fine, p. 25.

55. Cargas, p. 88.

56. Friedländer, p. 118.

57. *Ibid.*, p. 122.

58. *Ibid.*, pp. 132-133.

59. *Ibid.*, p. 140.

60. Wiesel, *Night*, p. 44.

61. *Ibid.*, p. 55

62. *Ibid.*, p. 79.

63. *Ibid.*, p. 76.

64. Such is indeed the title of one of Wiesel's plays.

65. Friedländer, p. 90.

66. Pisar, *Of Blood and Hope*, p. 43.

67. *Ibid.*, p. 69.

68. *Ibid.*, p. 297.

69. Friedländer, p. 19.

70. *Ibid.*, p. 29

71. *Ibid.*, p. 161.

72. *Ibid.*, p. 96.

73. *Ibid.*, p. 69.

74. *Ibid.*, p. 149.

75. *Ibid.*, pp. 103-104.

76. *Ibid.*, p. 123

77. *Ibid.*, p. 182-183.

78. *Ibid.*, p. 83.

79. Leon Wieseltier's review of *When Memory Comes* (above, note 35) ascribes to the work political overtones which seem exaggerated to this writer.

80. Pisar, *Le Sang et l'espoir*, p. 303.

81. Pisar, of *Blood and Hope*, p.54. Wiesel also writes on the same occasion: "Thus, by inviting hallucination and then rejecting it, I plunge into it and find friends, parents and neighbors, all the dead of the town, all the dead towns of the cemetery that was Europe. Here they are, at the timeless twilight hour, pilgrims all, invading

the Temple of which they are both fiery foundation and guardians.... For they have no tombs to hold them back, no cemeteries to bind them to the earth." A *Beggar in Jerusalem*. New York: Random House, 1970, p. 201.

82. Pisar, *Of Blood and Hope*, p. 288.

83. Pisar, *La Ressource humaine*, pp. 249, 242.

84. Pisar, *Of Blood and Hope*, pp. 205-209.

85. Pisar, *La Ressource humaine*, p. 201.

86. Cargas, p. 62.

87. *Ibid.*, p. 86.

88. Lejeune, *Le Pacte autobiographique*, p. 173.

DEBORAH E. LIPSTADT

The Holocaust

No area of Jewish studies has experienced as significant a spurt of interest in recent years among scholars, students, and the population at large—Jewish and non-Jewish—as the Holocaust. The most cursory examination of any bibliography on topics in Jewish history and literature will quickly reveal that for close to twenty-five years after the end of World War II books on and interest in the Holocaust was minimal. Even the Eichmann trial did not arouse much interest on the part of historians or readers. Hannah Arendt's *Eichmann in Jerusalem* (Penguin, 1977), which addressed the question of the banality of evil, prompted some discussion among American intellectuals but it did not penetrate the fog or break the silence which seemed to surround this topic. Survivors rarely spoke about what happened to them and no one seemed interested enough to ask. With the exception of Yad Vashem in Jerusalem and a number of other museums in Israel, there were virtually no museums, research centers, memorials, or courses on the topic. Textbooks and curricula in Jewish and non-Jewish schools studiously avoided this subject.

Today, as is obvious to all, the situation has changed dramatically. The United States Holocaust Memorial Council recently published a list of over one hundred Holocaust memorial organizations in the United States and Canada. And that list is far from complete. On over one thousand different American campuses courses on the Holocaust are offered.

From *The Shocken Guide to Jewish Books*, ed. Barry W. Holtz. © 1992 by Shocken Books.

The growth of interest in this topic evolved in the late 1960s. The Six-Day War and the rise in ethnicity in America contributed to it. A post-Holocaust generation of "baby boomers," were then on college campuses and in the process of revolting against the "establishment." They used the Holocaust as a means of differentiating between themselves and their parents' quiescent generation. During the 1970s the Holocaust was increasingly made part of the Jewish communal agenda. As the survivors achieved both the age and the material security to feel at ease in America, they began to support the building of museums and memorials.

In the late 1970s NBC's miniseries, "Holocaust," while trivializing the event in many respects, also generated interest in the topic. Now the Holocaust was something worthy of prime time. Also by the late 1970s books, articles, memoirs, novels, and psychological, sociological, and philosophical studies began to appear in incredible numbers. The growth of interest was staggering. It is probably safe to say that no other limited era in history—twelve years—has had as many volumes devoted to it as has the Holocaust.

Consequently, those who are anxious to probe this material face both a rich selection from which to choose and a challenge. The proliferation of material has been so intense that the uninitiated reader can easily be overwhelmed.

The reader's excursion into this topic is further complicated by the fact that the Holocaust is not one but a series of stories, each focusing on a different set of characters who can be broadly subsumed under the headings: perpetrators, victims, and bystanders. But within each group there are a variety of actors each of whom played dramatically different roles. The perpetrators include high-ranking Nazis who conceived of this horrendous act as well as bureaucrats who sat in railway offices devising the schedules for the trains which carried victims eastward; SS guards who volunteered for service in places such as Auschwitz and Treblinka as well as government clerks who registered Jewish property and stamped a "J" in Jewish passports; and members of the Einsatzgruppen who shot millions of Jews on the Russian front and those who in 1933 devised the regulations which legally excluded Jews from jobs as judges, teachers, and lawyers. Each contributed in a different degree and fashion to this event we have come to call the Holocaust.

The victims are an equally diverse group and any discussion of their behavior must take those different attributes and experiences into consideration. They were old and young, rich and poor, highly assimilated and extremely traditional Jews. There were those who lived in countries where Jews were barely distinguishable from the majority population and those who lived in virtual isolation from their non-Jewish neighbors. There were those who fought and those who did not; those who tried to escape and those who followed orders; and those who maintained their religious faith and those who lost it.

The bystanders include individuals, groups, and institutions with vastly different characteristics. The most notable difference was between those who had the actual power to rescue, e.g., the American and British governments, and those who only had the power of persuasion to try to convince others to act, e.g., world Jewry. There were bystanders who witnessed what was happening in front of their eyes and those who heard about it from afar. There were those who hid Jews and those who stood idly by. Particular attention has been focused on those bystander institutions such as the International Red Cross and the Vatican whose response to this tragedy was at odds with their own moral mandate.

Where does one begin? How should one make sense of this material? One way may be to isolate some of the most frequently asked and perplexing questions about this event. These queries can be grouped into a number of broad categories.

Uniqueness—Was the Holocaust unique? Was Hitler any worse than myriad other reprehensible historical figures including Stalin and Pol Pot? Other than their use of modern means of destruction—gas chambers—are the crimes of the Nazis fundamentally different from other genocidal outrages, such as the Armenian massacres? How do they differ from other acts of anti-Semitism? If the Crusaders or Chmielnicki had had the "benefit" of twentieth-century technology, would their actions have been the equivalent of the Final Solution?

Resistance—How did the Jews respond? Is there any truth to the charge that they went "like sheep to the slaughter"? How do we define resistance? Do resisters include only those who physically resisted or can we adopt a broader definition of resistance without diluting its meaning? Why did some non-Jews resist Nazi orders and hide Jews while others turned them in?

Knowledge—Who knew what and when did they know it? Was the existence of Auschwitz and the other death camps a secret until the end of the war? Were Jews aware of the true meaning of "relocation" and "resettlement" in the East? When people, both victims and bystanders, say they did not know, was their ignorance a result of a lack of information or an inability to make the leap of the imagination necessary to grasp the implications of what they were hearing? If so much information was available—as it was—during the war, why do so many people claim to have been so utterly shocked by what they saw once the war was over?

World Response—How did the rest of the world respond? What did the Allies *do* and what *could* they have done to prevent the Holocaust from happening? Was there military action that they could have taken which would have stopped the killings?

How did Jewish communities, particularly those in Allied lands, respond? What *could* they have done? Were they indifferent to the suffering of their fellow Jews or are post-Holocaust generations applying a contemporary standard of action to previous generations? Did they have the political clout to effect any real changes in Allied policy?

There are also an array of questions regarding the post-Holocaust era. Some are theological, while others are psychological and sociological. How can one reconcile a compassionate and just God with the Holocaust? Is religious faith possible after the Holocaust? What about the survivors, how did they fare? How were they able to resume their lives? What about their children: What impact has this event had on them? Why were so many perpetrators able to elude punishment? Finally, how has the Jewish community incorporated the Holocaust into the contemporary communal agenda? Is there such a thing as "too" much emphasis on this topic or are such fears without basis?

The books discussed in the following pages were chosen because they address themselves to these questions to one degree or another. We begin our excursion through this field with two caveats. There are many works on the Holocaust which are not included here. Many will peruse this essay and notice that volumes they admire are missing. This is probably the result of the limits of space and the need to select books which will be of interest to the non-specialized reader. It is certainly not a reflection on the intrinsic value of a particular book.

The second caveat is that there is no one mandated entry point into this complex field. Some will choose to begin with a memoir, such as Elie Wiesel's *Night* (Bantam, 1982) or Primo Levi's *Survival in Auschwitz* (Collier/Macmillan, 1988), while others may choose a more straightforward historical overview. The order in which I present these books tends to adhere to a historical unfolding of events. Some readers will choose to follow this order, while others will create their own sequence.

Given the complexity of this topic a comprehensive history of the Holocaust is extremely important. This is particularly so because many people have been exposed to disparate parts of this history but have never really grasped how the various pieces fit together. What connection is there between the

Versailles Treaty and the rise of Nazism? What relationship, for instance, is there between the course of the war on the Russian front and the pace of the killings?

The best known of any of these overviews is Lucy Dawidowicz's *The War Against the Jews: 1933–1945* (Free Press, 1986). It generated a great deal of attention partly because it appeared just when interest in the Holocaust was growing. Well written and of a manageable length, it will probably not overwhelm the reader. The major shortcoming of the book is that it fails to address certain crucial topics. There is virtually no attention paid to the fate of Jews in Western Europe. More importantly, there is little description of how the death camps functioned and what life and death were like in them. The book places an unduly heavy emphasis on ghetto life, particularly in the Warsaw ghetto. Dawidowicz, who had a long commitment to the Jewish Labor Bund and Yiddishist movement, focuses on the role the Bundists played while virtually ignoring the contributions of other organizations, including the Zionists. Dawidowicz, anxious to demonstrate that the Jews did not meekly submit to their fate, devotes a significant portion of the book to the important cultural and social organizations that existed in the ghetto. In so doing she makes an important point about the role of spiritual resistance but she inadvertently makes the ghetto sometimes sound like a Jewish cultural center rather than the inferno it was. Nonetheless the book is valuable and a good place to gain a general overview of the event.

A less compellingly written but more comprehensive portrait is provided by Yehuda Bauer in *A History of the Holocaust* (Franklin Watts, 1982). One of the strengths of the book is that it devotes a significant amount of space to the history of emancipation, anti-Semitism, and Weimar Germany. Consequently the reader is helped to understand that the Holocaust did not spring *de novo* but had its roots in European history. Bauer's discussion of life in the ghettoes as well as that of the death camps is far more complete than Dawidowicz's and he includes a number of maps which allow the reader to place the event in a geographic context.

Readers who wish to broaden their grasp of the geographic context in which the Holocaust occurred would be well advised to peruse Martin Gilbert's *The Macmillan Atlas of the Holocaust* (Da Capo Press, 1984). With over three hundred maps it serves as an important reference tool which helps place the Holocaust in the broader picture of World War II.

The most recent and most comprehensive of any of these volumes is Leni Yahil's *The Holocaust: The Fate of European Jewry, 1941–45* (Oxford University Press, 1990). Because of its comprehensive nature it will probably eventually become the text of choice in classes and seminars on the

Holocaust. In contrast to Raul Hilberg's classic three-volume work, *The Destruction of the European Jews*, rev. ed. (Holmes & Meier, 1985), Yahil is not attempting to break new ground in this book but to synthesize much of what has already been written. It addresses many of the questions that have been raised by scholars during the past forty-five years. Her audience is the non-specialist who is interested in more than a cursory overview. Hilberg's *magnum opus* may be too dense a work for the general reader. Moreover, its focus is on the German bureaucracy which carried out the Final Solution and not on the victims or any of the ancillary issues.

Among the questions that often arise in the course of an exploration of this topic are: How did the nation which was considered to be the seat of culture and intellectual accomplishment, the home of Beethoven and Schiller, become the place where the most odious event in human history was launched? How were Hitler and his Nazi followers able to win control of the nation? What were the German public's reactions to Nazi ideology in general and Nazi anti-Semitism in particular? Did they enthusiastically go along with all aspects of his preaching? Was this something forced on them?

One of the studies that helps us begin to answer this question is William Sheridan Allen's *The Nazi Seizure of Power: The Experience of a Single German Town*, 1930-1935 (Franklin Watts, 1984). Using a wide variety of sources including archival material, town records, and personal interviews, Allen traces the Nazi rise to power in one small town. Allen believes that Hitler was able to seize power in the spring of 1933 because the Nazis had been successful with the base population, those at the "lower" socioeconomic rungs. While an in-depth study of one particular town may not be representative of all of Germany, Allen's work does allow the reader to understand in a detailed fashion how one group of people responded to the Nazis.

To fully understand how the Nazi leadership managed to cement its hold over the population at large it is instructive to read some of the materials that were distributed to the German population. A good selection of these can be found in *Nazi Culture: Intellectual Cultural and Social Life in the Third Reich* (Schocken Books, 1981), which is edited by one of the leading scholars on the topic, George L. Mosse. Included are a prayer written for children, selections from a novel by Goebbels, and Hitler's argument that women were not worthy of equal status with men. Every aspect of German life—culture, economy, recreation, religion, and, of course, politics—was totally regulated. This collection helps illustrate that point.

Even as one probes the reactions of "ordinary" Germans, some readers will wish to examine the background of the man who was Nazism's central figure. Alan Bullock's *Hitler, A Study in Tyranny* (Harper & Row, 1990, abr. ed.) and Joachim Fest's *Hitler* (Vintage Books, 1975) are both solid and interesting studies. Neither work focuses in any measure on Hitler's anti-Semitism or how that portion of his ideology that resulted in the Final Solution was shaped. While this omission weakens the ultimate value of these books, it is instructive in and of itself, in that it demonstrates how much—if not most—of the world treats Nazism in general and Nazi anti-Semitism in particular. Most curricula dealing with World War II and the vast majority of studies of Nazi Germany treat the Holocaust as an addendum to the main story. It is seen as an important but *isolated* event. These works fail to recognize the degree to which anti-Semitism was ingrained into all aspects of Nazi ideology.

Another important insight into Nazism and its success in permeating every aspect of society is contained in Robert Jay Lifton's *Nazi Doctors: Medical Killings and the Psychology of Genocide* (Basic Books, 1988). Lifton, a medical doctor, asks a question that has disturbed him on both a personal and scholarly level: how were doctors—whose professional identity is, at least in theory, rooted in the responsibility to heal—able to allow themselves to participate in the Final Solution? A significant number of doctors, Mengele best known among them, played an intimate role in the running of the death and concentration camps. They were also the ones who carried out the pre-war euthanasia program against Germans who were mentally ill. Understanding how they were so easily able to participate in this endeavor sheds light on how German society in general responded to the Nazis. These questions lead to queries which are applicable to the German population at large and not just to the doctors.

One of the most remarkable endeavors in documenting the history of the Holocaust is Claude Lanzmann's film, *Shoah*. Because of its length and its intensity it was often difficult to fully grasp all the nuances contained therein. Consequently the book, *Shoah: An Oral History of the Holocaust* (Pantheon Books, 1987), which contains the text of the film, is useful. Of particular interest in relation to understanding the nature of Nazi Germany are the interviews with two high-ranking officials. One was assistant to the commissioner in charge of the Warsaw Ghetto and the other was part of the chain of command at Treblinka. Using a degree of subterfuge to get them to reveal themselves, Lanzmann demonstrates how lacking in remorse either of them are. These interviews are also useful because they constitute a wonderful response to those who are perverse enough to try to deny that the

Holocaust occurred. Here are two people who played intimate roles in it. They were there and they do not deny it; how can anyone else do so?

We turn now to one of the more complex aspects of this topic: the response of the Jewish community. Every teacher who has broached this topic has been asked, How did Jews respond to this terrible persecution? It is one of the most difficult queries to answer, in part because of the great diversity of human nature and the myriad of different situations in which Jews found themselves.

One of the most efficacious ways of getting at this question is through the use of diaries. Though diaries have a limited focus and do not encompass the experiences of a broad array of individuals and communities, probing the response of one individual or community in depth is illuminating and has an immediacy missing from more general studies.

The diaries kept in the various ghettoes both by the Jewish leadership as well as by individuals reveal a tremendous amount about the way life was organized in these settings and how desperate were the attempts made to retain a semblance of normalcy. *The Warsaw Diary of Adam Czerniakow* (Stein and Day, 1982) allows the reader to follow the evolution of the ghetto. Czerniakow was the head of the Jewish Council of Warsaw. He oversaw the transfer of the Jews to the ghetto and the running of the ghetto from its establishment until the summer of 1942 when he was instructed by the Nazis to prepare lists of Jews for deportation. Instead of complying with their instructions, he committed suicide. Though parts of Czerniakow's diary are somewhat tedious and composed of many mundane details, as would be the case with any diary kept by a mayor of a city, the overall impact is quite powerful.

There are other important diaries which chronicle the Warsaw ghetto including *The Warsaw Diary of Chaim A. Kaplan* (Collier, 1973) and Emmanuel Ringelblum's *Notes from the Warsaw Ghetto* (Schocken Books, 1974). Ringelblum was trained as a social historian and his diary reflects his understanding of the importance of presenting as full and detailed a portrait of ghetto life as possible. The story of the resistance and the ghetto uprising is contained in Vladka Meed's *On Both Sides of the Wall: Memoirs of the Warsaw Ghetto* (Holocaust Library, 1979). Meed joined the underground in 1942 and thanks to her Aryan appearance was able to smuggle Jews out and weapons into the ghetto.

There are a number of compelling novels about the Warsaw ghetto including John Hersey's *The Wall* (Vintage Books, 1988), which is based on

Ringelblum's experiences, and Leon Uris's *Mila* 18 (Bantam, 1983), which tells the story of the uprising itself. Though they take a measure of license with the facts, many readers, particularly younger ones, find such novels a valuable introduction to the topic.

The *Chronicle of the Lodz Ghetto, 1941–1944* (Yale University Press, 1987), which was edited by Lucjan Dobroszycki who survived the Lodz ghetto, tells the history of this unique ghetto. The ghetto was run by Mordecai Chaim Rumkowski who long after his death remains a controversial figure. Some despised him for his autocratic and self-aggrandizing behavior. He ran the ghetto with an iron fist and often included on deportation lists anyone who was critical of him. He had his own personal police force and lived in relative luxury. His dictatorial style has been captured in Leslie Epstein's novel *King of the Jews* (Summit Books, 1989). Others point out that because he made the ghetto economically profitable for the Nazis, it was not liquidated until the summer of 1944, long after most other ghettoes had been destroyed. More Jews survived in Lodz than in any other ghetto. That Rumkowski, a despicable character, was able to preserve the lives of so many Jews for so long illustrates some of the terrible moral dilemmas which faced individuals in leadership positions during this period. See also *Lodz Ghetto*, edited by Alan Adelson and Robert Lapides (Viking, 1989).

A diary of a different sort is Janusz Korczak's *Ghetto Diary* (Holocaust Library, 1978). It is a record of the struggle of a prominent doctor and child psychologist to protect and educate the children in his care. Korczak, well known for his work with children, tried to maintain a semblance of normalcy inside the ghetto orphanage. His gentleness and humanity provide a striking counterpoint to the Nazis' brutality. A fuller portrait of Korczak is contained in Betty Jean Lifton's biography *The King of Children* (Schocken Books, 1989). Ultimately he chose to go to his death at Treblinka with the children in his orphanage rather than take advantage of the opportunity to save himself. One of the most memorable portraits of this period is the description of Korczak leading the children to the *Umschlagplatz*, the place where people boarded the trains to be deported to the death camps. If resistance can be found in dignity, then Korczak was the ultimate resistance fighter. He may not have lifted a physical hand against the Nazis but his behavior was the ultimate contrast to theirs.

A portrait of an entirely different ghetto experience is contained in *The Terezin Requiem* (Avon Books, 1978) by Josef Bor. It is the story of the young orchestra conductor Raphael Schachter, who decides to conduct Verdi's Requiem with the camp orchestra and the five-hundred-voice choir. This is a fictionalized account of a performance which actually did take place and which was attended by high-ranking Nazi officials. Bor, himself a survivor of Terezin, has written a remarkable tribute to the human spirit in which he offers important insights into this strange camp which was used by the Nazis as a showcase to convince the Red Cross that the Jews were being well treated. It is one of the earliest works I read on the Holocaust and it has remained with me for many years. A companion volume, in a manner of speaking, contains the drawings and poems of the children of Terezin, *I Never Saw Another Butterfly* (Schocken Books, 1978). Pain, hope, bewilderment, and childlike faith permeate every page.

Jews in ghettoes and Jews in hiding had remarkably different physical and emotional experiences. A diary that describes the latter is *Young Moshe's Diary* (New York: Board of Jewish Education, 1965) by Moshe Flinker. Flinker, a native of Holland, hides with his family in Brussels until they are eventually caught and deported to Auschwitz where he and parents perished. The diary is among the most moving and compelling works to emerge from the Holocaust. Written by a teenager, it contains his struggles with profound theological problems: how does one who believes deeply in a just and merciful God make sense of the horror of the Holocaust? Well aware of what is happening to his fellow Jews, he expresses intense love for the Jewish people. His love is as strong as his conflict over the relative comfort in which he lives while his fellow Jews suffer: "Something devours my heart—a vast yearning to participate with my brothers in all that is happening to them." This diary is an extraordinary contrast with the other teenage diary which has captivated so much of the world's attention, *Anne Frank: The Diary of a Young Girl* (Pocket Books, 1985). Anne Frank had the vaguest sense of her Jewish identity; Flinker's heart and soul was bond up with his people. One can only marvel at what a Moshe Flinker would have contributed to his people had he been granted more than his fifteen years.

Two other personal memoirs, written not during the war but subsequent to it, also tell the story of children who were hidden during the Holocaust. Saul Friedlander's *When Memory Comes* (Avon Books, 1980) is the story of Friedlander's experience as a young boy in a highly assimilated Czech family which manages to escape to France. When his parents realize that they will soon be caught by the Nazis they leave him with a Catholic family. He is so taken with his Catholic education that in 1946 at the age of fourteen he decides to enter a Jesuit seminary in order to prepare for the priesthood. It is only when a priest says to him, "Didn't your parents die at Auschwitz?" that he comes to learn the full extent of the tragedy which had befallen him and his people. Friedlander intertwines this memoir with a diary he keeps many years later in Jerusalem.

The third memoir of a family in hiding written from the child's perspective is Nechama Tec's *Dry Tears: The Story of a Lost Childhood* (Oxford University Press, 1984). Tec and her family were hidden by Polish non-Jews who repeatedly risked their own lives to protect their guests. But this kindness coexisted with other, less positive sentiments. The elderly grandmother admitted to the young Tec that she opposed hiding Jews. "I would not harm a Jew," she said, "but I see no point in going out of my way to help one. Besides, it is outright stupid to risk Christian blood for Jewish blood. No amount of money could pay for that." But she tells the young Tec, "You and your family are not like Jews. If they wanted to send you away now, I would not let them."

When Tec's family leaves at the end of the war their saviours ask them not to reveal their true identity to the people of the town. (The Polish family obviously knew the mind-set of their neighbors. They lived in Kielce, the site of a pogrom in 1946. It was this final act of horror that prompted many Jews to conclude that there was no future for them in Poland and decide to leave.) The Polish rescuers expressed no sense of gratification at having participated in the rescue and survival of Tec's family. They were just anxious for them to leave.

An anthology of personal memoirs is contained in *Witnesses to the Holocaust: An Oral History* (Twayne Publishers, 1989). Edited by Rhoda Lewin, it contains the numerous personal recollections of survivors of concentration camps as well as survivors who were not in camps. It also contains the recollections of American liberators of the camps. They were the first witnesses from the West to come upon the victims of Nazi terror and their recollections form an important part of this story.

For those who do not have the personal memories of a Moshe Flinker, Saul Friedlander, or the countless others, these memoirs impart knowledge in a fashion that touches the heart even as it expands the mind.

The entire issue of Christians who rescued Jews is a relatively new area of research. It is axiomatic to observe that in virtually no area of the study of the Holocaust is there much "good news." There is little—if anything—that leaves one with a sense of hope or faith in the actions of humanity. This is particularly problematic because the Holocaust has become such a linchpin of contemporary Jewish identity.

The one area of the Holocaust which runs counter to this message of "everybody hates the Jews" is the story of those who risked their own lives and those of their family to aid Jews. It has been an arena of study which has been neglected for too long. When it was discussed it was usually in a purely anecdotal fashion and in terms of a few well-known cases, but even these stories were told in sketchy detail. In the *Encyclopaedia Judaica* more than a page is devoted to the story of the Frank family. But as Professor Nechama Tec observes in her highly readable *When Light Pierced the Darkness* (Oxford University Press, 1987), the only mention of those who risked their lives trying to save Anne and her family reads: "From July 9, 1942 until August 4, 1944 the Frank family remained in their hiding place, kept alive by friendly Gentiles. An act of betrayal resulted in their discovery by the German police." No names. No biographical details. No explanation of why they did what they did. Other works on Anne Frank compounded this omission. One of the ways of rectifying this lacuna is by reading Miep Gies's *Anne Frank Remembered* (Touchstone, 1988). It is essentially the other half or the "flip side" of the Frank family story, told from a perspective of looking into the attic from the outside.

Study of the action of the rescuers gives the lie to the oft-repeated claim "there was nothing anyone could do to help these hapless people." There was something some could do to help and many, far more than we thought, did.

There are a growing number of works which document the behavior of the rescuers. In addition to those already mentioned, there is Philip Hallie's study of Le Chambon, *Lest Innocent Blood Be Shed* (Harper & Row, 1980). Le Chambon was a Huguenot village in France which saved thousands of Jews. A cinematic parallel to Hallie's study is Pierre Sauvage's documentary film *Weapons of the Spirit*. Sauvage was a young child in Le Chambon; consequently his attempt to discover why the people of Le Chambon did what they did takes the form of a personal quest.

The Courage to Care (New York University Press, 1986), edited by Carol Rittner and Sondra Myers, contains the personal reflections of those who engaged in rescuing Jews. One is repeatedly struck by their matter-of-fact attitude and modesty about what they did. "We still don't think what we did in the war was a big deal.... We don't like to be called heroes," observed one man who hid thirty-six people in Holland. There were other acts of heroism which did not entail hiding Jews but which put those who performed them at equal risk. Walter Laqueur and Richard Breitman's *Breaking the Silence* (Simon & Schuster, 1986) tells the story of Eduard Schulte, one of Germany's top industrialists, who was responsible for transmitting the news in the summer of 1942 regarding the Nazi plans for genocide. His information resulted in the famous telegram sent by the World Jewish Congress representative in Geneva, Gerhart Riegner, informing Jewish leaders in Britain and America that "all Jews in countries occupied or controlled [by] German ... after deportation and concentration in East [will] be exterminated at one blow."

A very readable novel which tells the remarkable story of Oskar Schindler, a German industrialist who saved thousands of Jews by giving them work in his factory, is Thomas Keneally's *Schindler's List* (Penguin, 1983). It is based on interviews the author conducted with the people Schindler saved. Siegfried Jagendorf's memoir, *Jagendorf's Foundry*, edited by Aron Hirt-Manheimer (Harper Collins, 1991) tells the extraordinary story of a Romanian Jew who started an ironworks labor force that saved 15,000 deportees.

What made these people do what they did? Is there anything that would enable us to predict such behavior? And given contemporary levels of moral behavior, is there any way that we can use what we know about them to inculcate such values in young people—or older ones as well—today? Can we use their example to teach goodness? These were normal people and not unique "do-gooders." Many are convinced that what they did was unextraordinary. They made a habit of virtue. We can do no less.

A place where there was no virtue was Auschwitz and the other death camps. The miracle of survival there remains one of the incomprehensible aspects of this topic. Primo Levi's *Survival in Auschwitz: The Nazi Assault on Humanity* (Collier/Macmillan, 1988) is a powerful and dispassionate account of how some inmates who were lucky enough not to be sent to the gas chambers or to die of disease were able to survive. It is a short but compelling account. Another powerful memoir of life in a camp is *The Holocaust Kingdom* (Holocaust Library, 1963) by Alexander Donat. Elie Wiesel's *Night* (mentioned earlier) remains one of the most riveting essays about the world of the death camps. Many people begin their excursion into this field with this book.

For those who are interested in how the concentration camps functioned and in the nature of the SS, which was responsible for them, Eugen Kogon's *The Theory and Practice of Hell: The German Concentration Camps and the System Behind Them* (Berkley Publishing Group, 1984) provides important insights. Much of this material is contained in Yahil and the other general histories. There are also many novels which try to capture the horrors of this existence. One of the most powerful is Tadeusz Borowski's *This Way for the Gas, Ladies and Gentlemen* (Penguin, 1976). Borowski, who survived the camps, reflects on the ability of human beings to endure the unendurable.

André Schwarz-Bart's novel, *The Last of the Just* (Atheneum, 1973), stands out as one of the masterful works on this topic. It chronicles the story of a young boy from the rise of the Nazis to his death at Auschwitz. The

book is based on the Jewish legend of the thirty-six unknown righteous
people who persist throughout Jewish history.

The horror of the transit camps and the ability of some of those held
there to focus their energies not only on their own survival but on the
survival of others as well is contained in *An Interrupted Life: The Diaries of
Etty Hillesum* (Pocket Books, 1985). Hillesum, a well-to-do and highly
assimilated Dutch Jew, was well aware of the fate that awaited her and the
other inmates of the camp. Still, she maintained an indomitable spirit in the
face of this frightful future. This is a poignant and powerful book.

The ability of people to survive the camps for even limited periods of
time is something that continues to boggle the imagination. Terrence Des
Près's *The Survivor; An Anatomy of Life in the Death Camps* (Oxford University
Press, 1976) addresses "not the fact that so many died, but ... the fact that
some survived."

One of the too frequently ignored aspects of the Holocaust is Jewish
physical resistance. While most Jews did not have the opportunity or ability
to physically resist the Nazis, a significant number, given the terrible
circumstances that faced them, did. The history of resistance is told in Yisrael
Gutman's *Fighter Among the Ruins: The Story of Jewish Heroism During World
War II* (B'nai B'rith, 1988) and in Yuri Suhl's edited volume *They Fought Back*
(Schocken Books, 1975). Gutman explores both the varied forms of Jewish
resistance as well as the question of why wasn't there more resistance.

One of the most dramatic attempts to revolt in a death camp occurred at
Treblinka. Jean-François Steiner's novel *Treblinka* (Mentor, 1968) is a
dramatic and compelling account of this important story. See also Samuel
Willenberg's memoir, *Surviving Treblinka* (Basil Blackwell, 1989). Books such
as these demonstrate that while the Warsaw ghetto uprising may be the best
known instance of Jewish resistance, it does not stand alone.

Anthologies are helpful in providing a broad overview to various aspects
of the Holocaust. One of the earliest anthologies to appear was *Out of the
Whirlwind* (Schocken Books, 1976). Prepared for both the general reader and
classroom use, it is a useful compilation of fiction and nonfiction material
dealing with a range of questions and issues. Another important anthology
which contains over sixty excerpts by victims and eyewitnesses is Jacob
Glatstein's *Anthology of Holocaust Literature* (Atheneum, 1972).

One of the questions which seems to haunt the post-Holocaust generation,
particularly those who live in "Allied" countries is what was known, when
was it known, and what was and was not done? Specific interest is

concentrated on the United States because it is difficult—particularly for Americans—to reconcile the mythic idea of a country which proclaimed itself the home of those seeking liberty and freedom from persecution with the fact that the same country barred its gates to those desperately in need of refuge during the 1930s and 1940s.

Allied officials were more concerned about the fact that they would have to aid Jews rather than that Jews were being killed. At times they actually worked to frustrate and prevent rescue. Disbelief, indifference, anti-Semitism, and political expediency all served to hamper rescue efforts.

One of the first works on this topic was Arthur Morse's *While Six Million Died: A Chronicle of American Apathy* (Overlook Press, 1985). It remains one of the most riveting. Morse argues that the State Department was home to numerous anti-Semites, a number of whom had a direct hand in thwarting American rescue efforts. David Wyman's first work on this topic, *Paper Walls: America and the Refugee Crisis, 1938–1941* (Pantheon Books, 1985), graphically demonstrates how American anti-Semitism in both official and popular circles helped to keep Jewish refugees out of this country. Wyman's second volume, *The Abandonment of the Jews: America and the Holocaust, 1941–1945* (Pantheon Books, 1986), earned the distinction of being one of the few—if not only—historical works on this topic to be on the *New York Times* best-seller list. Wyman is relentless in his condemnations of Roosevelt and the entire administration for their response to the persecution of the Jews. His meticulous research is very impressive.

One of the great areas of interest is what did the bystanders know about Final Solution? How much information was available to them? Walter Laqueur's *The Terrible Secret: Suppression of the Truth about Hitler's "Final Solution"* (Little, Brown, 1980), demonstrates that within a short time after the Nazis decided to annihilate the Jews, the Allies knew about it. In a forceful fashion he illustrates that not only the Allies but the Vatican and the International Red Cross all had the information regarding the annihilation of the Jews.

Bernard Wasserstein's *Britain and the Jews of Europe, 1939–1945* (Oxford University Press, 1988) reveals that at times British officials were more heartless than their American counterparts. They preferred to see a boat filled with Jews escaping persecution sink off the coast of Turkey rather than allow them to be rescued. Had the Jews been allowed to escape and enter Palestine, British officials worried, it would have the "deplorable effect" of "encouraging" other Jews to try to escape.

My work on the American press coverage of the entire period, *Beyond Belief: The American Press and the Coming of the Holocaust, 1933–1945* (Free

Press, 1986), an analysis of the way in which four hundred American newspapers covered this topic, is at its heart an attempt to deal with the issue of information and knowledge, particularly in relation to public opinion. Unless we know what people knew and how they learned of it, we will never be able to fully determine the role of public opinion in formulating American policy. The press generally followed the government's lead and treated the news in a way that made it entirely "missable" or "dismissable." The shortcomings in press coverage, even after the news was verified and confirmed by the Allies, are legion. The gap between information and knowledge is striking. Even when the press had the information, it was often buried in inside pages where it could easily be missed. There is of course no guarantee that if the press had covered this in a more forthright fashion, American rescue policy would have been different. However, one can still ask, did the press fulfill its obligation to inform readers of events?

One of the most potent areas of interest is the behavior of the American Jewish community, which continued to maintain its faith in Franklin D. Roosevelt even while his record on rescue was dismal. Wyman is convinced that had American Jews been more forceful, there might have been a change in government policy. Other authors dissent. Richard Breitman and Alan Kraut's *American Refugee Policy and European Jewry 1933–1945* (Indiana University Press, 1988) argues that American Jews used all the means available to them—private pleas, mass public protest, and political pressure—to try to open America's gates to European Jews. They argue that American Jews were not, as some have contended, "docile" or paralyzed by fear of domestic anti-Semitism. Both those Jews who believed open protest was the most efficacious response and those who believed in quiet backdoor diplomacy "worked tirelessly to command the attention of the hydra-headed government bureaucracy in Washington." Jews were terribly frustrated by their inability to convince the Allies to act.

Haskel Lookstein's *Were We Our Brother's Keepers: The Public Response of American Jews to the Holocaust 1938–1944* (Vintage Books, 1988) condemns American Jewry. The Holocaust may have been "unstoppable" by American Jews, but, he argues, that it should also have been "unbearable." And it was not. Lookstein bases his work on the major newspapers and journals published in the Jewish community. He does not probe the activities of various Jewish organizations beyond what was published in these papers and magazines. Consequently there are many things we still do not know about American Jews' response.

Another Jewish community whose response has been scrutinized is Palestinian Jewry in Dina Porat's *The Blue and Yellow Stars of David: The*

Zionist Leadership in Palestine and the Holocaust, 1939–1945 (Harvard University Press, 1990). She demonstrates how leaders of the Jewish community in Palestine spent a great portion of their energies engaged in party squabbling rather than in rescue efforts. But the other part of the problem was that the Jewish community had little leverage with the British and yet had nowhere else to turn. They were caught in a bind between killers who were intent on murdering European Jews and British leaders who feared they might be saved. The British supported the dispatch of young Palestinian Jews to Hungary (including Hannah Senesh), to engage in what they knew would be futile attempts at rescue because, Porat argues, Britain would succeed in "removing from Palestine a number of active and resourceful Jews," especially since "the chances of many of them returning in the future to give trouble in Palestine are slight." If these were your only allies, how much hope was there for rescue?

There is an array of significant postwar questions. The Allied failure to prosecute Nazi war criminals is a fairly recent area of research. In the United States the FBI, CIA, and Departments of State and Defense all helped known war criminals escape from Europe. American officials "sanitized" the files of over four hundred German and Austrian scientists so that their war crimes would be hidden. Among them were Wernher von Braun and Arthur Rudolph, both of whom played a crucial role in America's space program and who during the war worked at Nordhausen where thousands of slave laborers died. This entire sordid saga has been documented in Tom Bower's *The Paperclip Conspiracy: The Hunt for Nazi Scientists* (Little, Brown, 1988).

Allan A. Ryan, Jr.'s *Quiet Neighbors: Prosecuting Nazi War Criminals in America* (Harcourt Brace Jovanovich, 1984) is written from personal experience. Ryan was director of the United States Office of Special Investigation at a time when revelations about the American role in the postwar harboring of approximately ten thousand Nazi war criminals were made and prosecution begun.

How the postwar world engages in remembrance is analyzed in a compelling fashion by journalist Judith Miller's *One By One By One: Facing the Holocaust* (Simon & Schuster, 1990). Miller examines how six different countries engage in remembering the Holocaust. She places special emphasis on how American Jews incorporate remembering into their communal agenda. It is a significant contribution to this topic.

For many people the Holocaust presents fundamental questions about faith in a just and merciful God. How can one believe in the face of such horror? Theologians have struggled and continue to struggle with this question. Two extremes are represented by the writings of Emil Fackenheim and Richard Rubenstein. In *After Auschwitz* (Bobbs-Merrill, 1966) Rubenstein offers one of the most radical theological reflections in reaction to the Holocaust. He questions whether it is possible to maintain any faith in an all-powerful God in a post-Holocaust world. Fackenheim's *God's Presence in History* (Harper & Row, 1972) is a response to Rubenstein. Fackenheim argues that the Holocaust as an epoch-making event mandates a 614th commandment, "Thou shall not hand Hitler a posthumous victory," that is, by ceasing to be Jews. A selection of essays which explore a variety of responses is contained in John K. Roth and Michael Berenbaum's *Holocaust: Religious and Philosophical Implications* (Paragon House, 1989).

The question of guilt, responsibility, and forgiveness is creatively addressed in Simon Wiesenthal's *Sunflower* (Schocken Books, 1976). The first section of the book is a novella of a young German soldier who, from his hospital bed, asks forgiveness of a Jew for the atrocities he has committed. The Jew's response is silence. This story is followed by a symposium of responses by theologians, philosophers, and religious leaders. They were asked by Wiesenthal to respond to the following question: Should the Jew have responded? Should he have forgiven the soldier? Did he have the right to do so? Is there any way the soldier can absolve himself of the guilt for the atrocities he performed? This is an accessible volume which addresses some of the important post-Holocaust questions.

The experience of the survivors and of their children is a fitting place to end this excursion. They are the living reminders of an event about which millions of words have been written and yet which still remains largely beyond comprehension. Helen Epstein's *Children of the Holocaust* (Penguin Books, 1988), which started out as a *New York Times Magazine* cover story, opened a virtual floodgate of emotions for thousands of children of survivors who suddenly discovered that they shared certain legacies. Their childhood experiences had been different from others and continued to be so. Though other books have subsequently been published on this topic, Epstein's remains one of the more riveting. An anthology of survivors' voices is contained in Dorothy Rabinowitz's *New Lives: Survivors of the Holocaust in America* (Alfred A. Knopf, 1976). In addition to describing their experiences during the Holocaust, they discuss their experiences in rebuilding their lives in America. This book demonstrates that even after surviving the horrors of the Nazis, they faced many additional obstacles.

I conclude this essay knowing that I have only scratched the surface of a topic which has had and continues to have overwhelming historical implications. Readers may choose to "detour" from one particular path in order to conduct their own investigation into this whirlwind. I hope that this essay will provide some important guideposts for the reader. The books I have suggested will not answer all the readers' questions. While they answer some questions, they will serve more as catalysts for others, for even after the most often asked questions are answered, the Holocaust can never be fully explained. And this is how it should be.

MICHAEL TAGER

Primo Levi and the Language
of Witness

Like many Holocaust survivors writing about their experiences, Primo Levi expresses both the urge to bear witness, and doubt about whether he can use language to communicate his experience adequately.[1] To enhance his memory, he began making notes while still in Auschwitz, even though he could not keep them because any writing by a prisoner was considered espionage. Recalling his life just after his return to Italy, Levi compares himself to Coleridge's Ancient Mariner who waylaid guests on the way to the wedding feast to tell them of his misfortunes, because Levi behaved similarly, telling his story to everyone and anyone who would listen. Indeed, his last two books about Auschwitz, published thirty-five and forty years after his release, take the same verse from *The Ancient Mariner* as their epigraph:

> Since then, at an uncertain hour,
> That agony returns,
> And till my ghastly tale is told,
> This heart within me burns.

Near the end of his life, his memory of his year in Auschwitz, remained "much sharper and more detailed than anything before or since,"[2] and he could not bear to let remembered details fade away. Part of his compulsion to write about Auschwitz reflected an attempt to cope psychologically with

From *Criticism* 34, no. 2 (Spring 1993). © 1993 by Wayne State University Press.

the injury done to him, to somehow "become a man again ... neither a martyr, nor debased, nor a saint."[3] But upon his release in 1945 he sensed that "nothing could ever happen good and pure enough to rub out our past, and that the scars of the outrage would remain with us forever,"[4] and his repeated return to this subject matter supports his later conclusion that his injury "cannot be healed"[5] by the passage of time. Levi's own suicide in 1987 more than forty years after his liberation perhaps shows the ongoing nature of the psychic wound inflicted upon him.[6] Surveying videotaped interviews of concentration camp survivors, Lawrence Langer argues that using words like "liberation" in connection with the Holocaust can be misleading because they "entice us into a kind of verbal enchantment that too easily dispels the miasma of the death camp ordeal and its residual malodors."[7]

Misgivings accompany Levi's continuing drive to remember and discuss: could he convincingly recount what happened? In Auschwitz, he had dreams in which he would tell his story and people would turn away, refusing to listen or believe him. He admits that words like "hunger," "fear," "pain," "cold," fail to convey the intensity of those feelings at Auschwitz, and that only a "new, harsh language" could describe them.[8] Words developed in normal life did not seem applicable to Auschwitz; Langer describes how one survivor, who when first trying to tell others what had happened to her family in the camp, "remembers thinking that 'My family were killed' was totally inadequate, because 'killed,' she says, was a word used for 'ordinary' forms of dying."[9] Neither did the word "gassed" seem satisfactory to communicate the enormity of the event, and she was driven toward silence despite her desire to speak. So much of what happened was incredible, and not comparable to anything Levi previously experienced or imagined, that he states simply in one passage, "no one can boast of understanding the Germans"[10] (SA 126). Entry into the death camp began with a journey of many days in a sealed boxcar that deposited him in an unknown location, leaving him spatially disoriented. His shock deepened upon arrival as he was further stripped of control over his destiny and even his basic bodily functions. Intense and unpredictable violence undermined his sense of connection between the present and the past and future. The problem of intelligibly describing such a profoundly disorienting experience, and finding language to bear witness to events he found incredible, and that many people did want to listen to, informs much of Levi's work. In his survey of Holocaust literature, Alvin Rosenfeld finds this a common dilemma. He notes that camp inmates witnessed cruelty, deprivation, and terror on a scale that "so far surpassed anything previously known as to make writing about it a next-to-impossible task," and that "all memoirists have known this sense of radical self-estrangement, which handicaps any thinking and writing about the Holocaust, but which their books themselves are written to break."[11]

Because the overwhelming majority of Jews sent to Auschwitz perished, Levi also questions whether his exceptional status as a survivor qualifies him to discuss the true nature of the concentration camp. In his first memoir he uses the metaphor of "the drowned and the saved" to describe the prisoners, of whom the drowned "form the backbone of the camp ... continually renewed and always identical" (SA, 82), whereas the paths to salvation were very few, difficult and improbable. In Levi's own case an unlikely combination of factors helped him survive: he arrived relatively late in January of 1944, his knowledge of chemistry and German secured him a job inside a laboratory for several months, and a prisoner in another labor camp for non-Jewish Italian workers befriended him and smuggled him an extra ration of food every day for six months. In his last memoir he revisits the troubling issue of the validity of his witness. He writes that

> I must repeat: we, the survivors, are not the true witnesses ... We survivors are not only an exiguous but also an anomalous minority: we are those who by their prevarications or abilities or good luck did not touch bottom. Those who did so, those who saw the Gorgon, have not returned to tell about it or have returned mute, but they are ... the complete witnesses, the ones whose deposition would have a general significance. They are the rule, we are the exception" (DS, 83-84).

Testimony about the death camps comes from witnesses who by definition "never fathomed them to the bottom" (DS, 17) because they survived. Even if he could find words to convey the horror of his experiences, his witness still might misrepresent what "really" happened.

Levi's struggle to develop a style suitable to his material helps explain his fascination with language itself, both as a creator and' reflection of our identities and politics. He explores the etymology of words, the use of metaphors and colloquial expressions, the construction of euphemisms, and the link between words and power. Linguistic patterns disclose political concepts and relationships that enable him better to understand his experiences. Sensitivity to such patterns also helps him construct a powerful language for his witness. Through bearing witness he seeks to commemorate the victims of the Holocaust, find some present peace, and increase awareness of what happened to deter future genocides. Above all he wants his testimony to put on trial the countless people who participated in or assented to the slaughter, and then returned to their normal lives after the war. Though no justice can ever right the wrongs inflicted, his witness demands his readers judge the perpetrators, and consider how the manipulation of language fit into the system of extermination.

LANGUAGE AND IDENTITY

In the first chapter of *The Periodic Table*, Levi sketches the history of his Sephardic Jewish ancestors beginning with their arrival in the Italian Piedmont around 1500. Exiled from Spain, he surmises that they traveled through Provence because of certain typical surnames based on towns like Foix, Cavaillon, Millau, and Lunel. The names thus embed a history of exile and movement through Europe. He also recalls an Uncle Bonaparte, a common name among the Piedmontese Jews that memorialized their first "ephemeral emancipation" (PT 6) granted by Napoleon. Their names not only reflect their geographical travels, but record landmark events in the life of the community. Such names contribute to their distinctive identity. He recognizes that an important initial step in the Nazi effort to destroy him involved the erasure of his name. At the Fossoli detention camp, he heard Nazi officers use the German word for "pieces" to refer to the Jewish prisoners[12] (SA 12). In Auschwitz, he recalls an officer reproaching a rookie Kapo for using the word "Mann" (men) instead of the prescribed word "Haftlinge" (prisoners) when reporting the number of his work squad present at roll-call (DS 92). The most direct attempt to dehumanize him by suppressing his name came through the constant use of his camp number, which was inscribed permanently onto him. He calls getting the number his "real, true initiation" to Auschwitz, and describes its significance in a short stark paragraph: "Haftling: I have learned I am a Haftling. My number is 174517; we have been baptized, we will carry the tattoo on our left arm until we die" (SA 23). The ironic use of the word "baptized," with its implication of giving someone a new name and spiritual identity, shows how the Nazis inverted the naming process in preparation for annihilation. Numbers were tattooed on arms and sewn on jackets, pants, and coats, creating a symbolic equivalence between people and pieces of cloth. Just as cattle were branded and eventually slaughtered, the tattoo signified a descent from a human to an animal status (DS 119). Prisoners recognized each others' nationalities and length of stay inside the camp through their numbers, which partly determined how they behaved toward each other. Replacing names with numbers furthered the breakdown of prisoners' individuality and will to resist, as well as reinforcing the Nazi mentality of considering Jews less than human.

Aside from names, language functions more generally to structure identity. In his travels under the Red Army's authority after the liberation of Auschwitz, he met two Russian Jewish girls who told him and his fellow Italian camp survivors that "you do not speak Yiddish; so you can not be Jews" (R 99). Jewish identity in Russia and Eastern Europe revolved around its distinctive language, whereas the Sephardic Jews of Italy and Western Europe did not use Yiddish (before coming to Auschwitz, Levi only vaguely knew of its existence). Even after he recited a Hebrew prayer for them, they could not understand what differentiated him from the Gentile Italian prisoners who spoke the same language, wore the same clothes, and had the same faces as Levi. He had already experienced this isolation at Auschwitz, where Yiddish was the de facto second language of the inmates, and many of them disliked and distrusted the Italian Jews who could not speak it. And in fact without a distinctive language, strong religious convictions, or a tradition of virulent anti-semitism in Italy comparable to that of Eastern Europe, Levi's family had gone far toward assimilating into Italian life. Prior to the passage of the Fascist racial laws in 1938, he remembers that he considered his origins a "small anomaly, like having a crooked nose or freckles; a Jew is somebody who at Christmas does not have a tree, who should not eat salami but eats it all the same, who has learned a bit of Hebrew at thirteen and then has forgotten it" (PT 35–36). One of the only uplifting moments at Auschwitz occurred when he recited the poetry of Dante for a fellow prisoner—his language and patrimony were Italian, and only secondarily Jewish.[13] His memoir *Survival in Auschwitz* contains few references to religion or Judaism.

And yet Levi's ancestors did develop a distinctive vocabulary composed of Hebrew roots with Piedmontese endings and inflections that for several hundred years both reflected and reinforced their separate identity. By the twentieth century this jargon of a few hundred words and expressions, never spoken by more than a few thousand people, began to disappear. Because of its small scope, he acknowledges that its historical interest is meager, but he claims that "its human interest is great, as are all languages on the frontier and in transition" (PT 8–9). "On the frontier and in transition" describes not only the language, but the ambiguous status of the Jews in Italian history.[14] He believes that this jargon contributed to his family's traditional tendency to withdraw from others, and, therefore, titles the sketch of his ancestors "Argon," an inert gas that does not interfere in any chemical reaction, nor combine with any other element. Throughout the essay he moves easily from discussions of the language's words to stories of his aunts and uncles and cousins who spoke it. Though a good-natured, skeptical language with a comic aspect due to the unlikely combination of Piedmontese dialect and Hebrew, he argues that its "humiliated roots" become apparent in the kind of words it lacks, such as "sun," "man," or "city," compared to the words it contains, such as "night," "to hide," "money," "prison," "to steal," "to hang," and "dream," the last of which was used in the phrase "in a dream," and always understood to mean its contrary (PT 9). He explains that "even a hasty examination points to its dissimulative and underground function, a crafty language meant to be employed when speaking about goyim in the presence of goyim," which represented a defensive reaction against the "regime of restriction and oppression" imposed on the Jews (PT 8). As anti-semitic restrictions gradually lifted, the original purpose of the language also dissipated. It embodied the hierarchical status relations between Jews and Gentiles at a certain historical moment. Some phrases, notably from the cloth trade that Piedmont Jews specialized in, eventually crossed over into common usage as people lost track of their Hebrew roots. Such words signaled a Jewish presence even after they moved on to other trades. All languages contain metaphors and images "whose origin is being lost, together with the art from which they are drawn" (PT, 150), so that language conserves earlier attitudes and activities. He recounts how during his father's boyhood, other children would mock his father ("without malice") by gathering the corners of their jackets into their fists to resemble donkey's ears and chanting "pig's ear, donkey's ear, give 'em to the Jew that's here" (PT 5) without knowing the meaning of their gesture or chant, which originated in a sacrilegious parody of the greeting pious Jews exchanged in temple by showing each other the hems of their prayer shawls. The chant's language preserved a residual anti-semitism after people abandoned its real substance. His book *The Periodic Table* thus considers a range of anti-semitisms, from the relatively benign and half-conscious, to the most murderous and systematic. Levi's analysis of language helps him to understand the formation of the Jewish community in the Piedmont, how anti-semitism shaped the identity of his ancestors, and how its declining significance in Italy shaped his own identity.

Inside Auschwitz a specialized jargon also developed. The word "fressen," normally only used to apply to the way animals eat, was used instead of "essen," the human way of eating (SA 68–69). The expression for "go away" came from "abhauen," which in proper German means to cut, or chop off (DS 99). The phrase for "never" in camp slang was "Morgen früh," or "tomorrow morning" (SA 121). The word "Muselmann," or Muslim, referred to a worn out prisoner ready to die from exhaustion and starvation, and likely to be "selected" to go from the labor camps to the gas chambers and ovens at Birkenau (DS 98). Rather than the freely chosen and sometimes comical jargon of his ancestors, the camp slang was largely imposed by the German overseers and reflected their contempt for the Jewish identity of their prisoners. The words embody the camp's violent and degraded conditions, and even reflect the distorted sense of time produced by the pervasiveness and imminence of death.[15] Levi writes of a post-war business meeting with some representatives of Bayer (one of the companies that comprised the chemical conglomerate I.G. Farben; Levi worked at Farben's slave-labor Buna plant in Auschwitz) where he used some of the harsh, degraded German camp jargon he learned at Auschwitz, and watched them react with astonishment because his words "belonged to a linguistic register different from that in which our preceding conversation had been conducted and is certainly not taught in 'foreign language' courses" (DS 99). The camp vocabulary was intimately related to his identity as a Jew in Auschwitz. By employing it outside its original context, he not only revealed who he was, but confronted the Bayer employees with the horror that their firm helped create. He states that "later on I realized also that my pronunciation is coarse, but I deliberately have not tried to make it more genteel; for the same reason, I have never had the tattoo removed from my left arm" (DS 99). Concentration camp German, just as the Piedmontese-Hebrew dialect, contains much information about the people who spoke it, so he does not want it to be completely forgotten.

LANGUAGE AND POLITICS

Primo Levi was three years old when the Fascists took power in 1922. He recalls that his youthful disgust with Fascism stemmed not only from the regime's actions, but also from its overblown rhetoric, which he characterizes as a collection of dogmas, unproved affirmations, and imperatives (PT 42). In high school and college he became enamored with science, particularly chemistry, because it appeared the antithesis of Fascist rhetoric. Instead of dogmas, propositions were experimentally tested and verified. Instead of grandiose claims to superiority, chemists used clear and concise language based on the elements in Mendeleev's periodic table that scientists universally understood. Science seemed to offer a much surer way to understanding how the world really worked than did the "truths" of fascist ideology. He saw in it an uncontaminated refuge from official political discourse.

But scientific activity, like all others, felt the impact of Fascist ideology. Though none of his fellow chemistry students made hostile statements or gestures to him after the passage of the 1938 racial laws, they all belonged to the Fascist student organization, and Levi recalls an unspoken tension in his contact with most of them. The praise and high grades he received in college he believes resulted not only from his hard work, but also from his professors' desire to express their vague anti-Fascism. Yet when it came time to do his senior thesis, every professor but one refused to work with him for fear of violating the racial laws and getting in trouble with the government. After graduating in 1941, his first job as a chemist came in a lab attached to a mine controlled by the military, a job that depended on a passively anti-fascist lieutenant's willingness to ignore the laws requiring racial separation. Levi recalls enjoying the chemical analysis and the challenge of finding ways to obtain more nickel from the rock, but acknowledges that "I was not thinking that if the method of extraction I had caught sight of could have found industrial application, the nickel produced would have entirely ended up in Fascist Italy's and Hitler Germany's armor plate and artillery shells" (PT 77). Science inevitably became entwined with the prevailing political order, and he gradually abandoned his hope that it could remain uncorrupted. An incident from his work at a Swiss laboratory in Milan in 1942 showed to him a disturbing intermingling of political and scientific discourse. The director ordered him to pursue the proposals of German scientist named Kerrn, but after studying them, he concluded that Kerrn's work was a combination of biochemistry and witchcraft. He writes that

> It was a strange book: it would be hard to think of its being written and published in any other place than the Third Reich. The author was not without a certain ability, but every one of his pages gave off the arrogance of someone who knows that his statements will not be disputed. He wrote, indeed harangued, like a possessed prophet, as though the metabolism of glucose, in the diabetic and the healthy person, had been revealed to him by Jehovah on Sinai or, rather, by Wotan on Valhalla. (PT 119)

The results that Kerrn predicted theoretically could not be reproduced in the lab. By censoring scientific debate, and investing power in certain politically approved individuals and theories, the Nazis undermined the self-regulating checks that protect science from error. Scientists participated in this process either due to self-interest or coercion. But even if scientific progress suffered, the ability to control discourse was essential to the survival of totalitarian regimes. Levi writes that

> in countries and epochs in which communication is impeded, soon all other liberties wither; discussion dies by inanition, ignorance of the opinion of others becomes rampant, imposed opinions triumph. The well-known example of this is the crazy genetics preached in the USSR by Lysenko, which in the absence of discussion (his opponents were exiled to Siberia) compromised the harvests for twenty years. Intolerance is inclined to censorship, and censorship promotes ignorance of the arguments of others and thus intolerance itself: a rigid, vicious circle that is hard to break. (DS 103–104)

Levi's temporary retreat into science ironically had the depoliticizing effect that Fascist censorship aimed at. Through its control of public discourse, the regime created a "white, anesthetized limbo" (PT 37) that isolated people and inhibited political organization. Censorship reinforced Levi's own attempt to ignore the rumors of the fate of the Jews under Nazi occupation so he could continue to live a "normal" life. In the early 1940s his family lacked the money and initiative to escape and besides, he experienced no overt anti-semitism in the Piedmont (even though the racial laws forbade Jews from higher education, the University of Turin apparently did not strictly enforce them, because Levi graduated in 1941 apparently without incident). This self-censorship, or discounting of whatever disquieting news slipped past the official Fascist censors, limited him to a very passive resistance against the regime. It blocked him from the knowledge that Turin, and his own Turinese Jewish community, had been a center of anti-Fascism. He writes that by 1941

> The seed of active struggle had not survived down to us, it had been stifled a few years before with the final sweep of the scythe, which had relegated to prison, house arrest, exile, or silence the last Turinese protagonists and witnesses—Einaudi, Ginzburg, Monti, Vittorio Foa, Zini, Carlo Levi. These names said nothing to us, we knew hardly anything about them—the Fascism around us did not have opponents. We had to begin from scratch, "invent" our anti-Fascism, create it from the germ, from the roots, from our roots. (PT 51)

Only late in 1942, when the war began to turn against the Axis powers, does he recall that people silenced for twenty years began to emerge and openly advocate and organize opposition. They supplied the missing language of resistance for youths like Levi who grew up knowing no other regime than Mussolini's: "They talked to us about unknowns: Gramsci, Salvemini, Gobetti, the Roselli brothers—who were they? So there actually existed a second history, a history parallel to the one the *liceo* had administered to us from on high? In those convulsed months we tried in vain to reconstruct, to repopulate the historic blank of the last twenty years, but those new characters remained "heroes," like Garibaldi and Nazario Sauro, they did not have thickness or human substance" (PT 130). Political action presumes free speech and communication, which the regime had long stifled. This reopened dialogue helped create more political space, and allowed people to build on a lost tradition of activism. After the collapse of Fascism in 1943, and the subsequent German invasion, occupation, and establishment of the puppet Salo Republic in Italy, Levi joined a partisan band associated with the resistance movement Liberty and Justice. His group was betrayed and captured in December, and by January of 1944, he was deported to Auschwitz.

Fascist censorship extended beyond political discussion to the language itself through a campaign to remove non-Italian phrases from usage. When a prospective employer told Levi in 1942 to meet him for a job interview at the "Hotel Suisse," not the "Albergo Svizzera" as according to the Fascist language rules, it revealed something of the employer's political perspective. His willingness to stick to the original foreign French words suggested he would ignore the racial laws and hire a Jew, officially considered a foreigner in Fascist Italy. The Nazis also tried to purify German of foreign expressions. Levi notes that German scientists "rushed to rename bronchitis as "air-pipes inflammation," the duodenum as "twelve-finger intestine," and pyruvic acid as "burn-grapes acid" (DS 98). The effort to purify language parallels the drive to eliminate dissent or political impurities, and in the case of the Nazis, to exterminate impure races threatening to contaminate the Aryan race.[16] Levi writes that "it is an obvious observation that where violence is inflicted on man it is also inflicted on language" (DS, 97). German words changed meanings and made dissent more difficult to express; the nationalistic overtones assumed by the adjective "volkisch," and the change from a negative to a positive connotation for the adjective "fanatisch" are cited by Levi as examples of the close interaction between language and Nazi politics. Philosopher Berel Lang explains that the Nazi regime intended to subordinate language itself to political authority, if only in order to demonstrate that this common medium of exchange, which often appears in the guise of nature itself, also will not escape political domination. The Nazis would not only contrive a language *of* domination, but they intended to demonstrate that language itself was subject to political authority. The means by which the theme of domination is given a linguistic form are designed in such a way as to leave an audience no option except submission to the spoken or written words that address it.[17]

Levi recalls his shock when one of the Buna lab technicians once said the word "please" to him, because this violated the code governing relations between Germans and Jews;[18] like the Italian employer who used the forbidden name "Hotel Suisse," it expressed an attitude antithetical to the regime's ideology. Given the degradation of language under the Nazis and Fascists, not surprisingly two of the most positively depicted figures in Levi's memoirs, Sandro Delmastro (PT 37–49) and Lorenzo Perrone (MR 149–160), are quiet men notable for deeds rather than rhetoric, almost as if their verbal concision helped insulate them from official bombast and dogma, and maintain their humanity and capacity for altruism.

Levi's revulsion with the grandiose rhetoric, euphemisms, and dehumanizing categories of Fascist and Nazi language left him with a life-long determination to write clearly and concisely. When composing his first book on Auschwitz he remembers feeling exalted "to search and find, or create, the right word, that is commensurate, concise, and strong; to dredge up events from my memory and describe them with the greatest rigor and the least clutter" (PT 153). Cynthia Ozick suggests that his style not only reflects a reaction against the barbarism he encountered, but an attempt to manage the rage he felt through adherence to "a picture of how a civilized man ought to conduct himself when he is documenting savagery."[19] Other critics suggest that Levi's measured tone of objective witness might reflect his passage through Auschwitz unaccompanied by any members of his immediate family, whereas many survivors experienced the annihilation of their entire families in the camps, and his return after the war to his intact home and family in Turin, whereas many survivors had nothing or no one to return to; these distinctive circumstances might have enabled him to develop a more dispassionate tone than was possible for other memoirists of the Holocaust[20] Levi attributes his writing style partly to his scientific training, which stresses objective observation, detached analysis, and the "mental habit of concreteness and concision" (OPT, 187). Gabriel Motola notes that

Levi's scientific outlook contributes to the emotional power of *Survival in Auschwitz*, where his simple, restrained prose style contrasts with, and highlights the horrible events that it describes.[21] Much of his vocabulary and many of his metaphors come from chemistry, most obviously in *The Periodic Table*, where each chapter title is an element that corresponds to and illuminates the event or person focused on in the chapter. Chemical terms dealing with the transformation of matter like "distill," "purify," "crystallize," and "filter" appear frequently in his work.

Undoubtedly this scientific training influenced his use of language. But his choice of style also has a political dimension. George Orwell in his essay "Politics and the English Language" recognized how abuses of language make it easier for regimes to justify the unjustifiable ("make lies sound truthful and murder respectable"), which tends to corrupt language further.[22] Writers like Hannah Arendt have observed that the extensive Nazi "language rules" (itself a euphemism for "lies") contributed to the efficiency of their bureaucracy of murder, or to what they termed the "final solution."[23] Lang acknowledges that alterations in language are neither necessary nor sufficient causes to explain genocidal actions, but argues that "the violence done to language in the genocide ... provides a distinctive representation of what the intention to exterminate the Jews required of its perpetrators in the way of will and of artifice; it discloses how deeply set the design of genocide was and how fully developed a world view it became."[24] Orwell recommends that all political writing follow a simple clear style that avoids the passive voice, cliches, and euphemisms so that stupid or murderous thoughts become immediately apparent as such. Levi remembers vividly the slogan "Arbeit Macht Frei" (work gives freedom) illuminated above the front gate through which he entered the Monowitz camp at Auschwitz. Since Monowitz was a slave labor camp where Jews were either worked to death, or eventually sent to be exterminated at Birkenau, the mocking absurdity of cliches like "Arbeit Macht Frei" perhaps impelled him toward a clear declarative style. In one of his later essays he responds to a young writer seeking advice by stating that "I have an acute need for clarity and rationality, and I think that the majority of readers feel the same way. A clear text is not perforce elementary; it can be read at several levels, but the lowest level, in my opinion, should be accessible to a broad public."[25]

This perspective shaped not only his own writing, but his literary taste. It accounts for his objections to the poetry of Paul Celan, a survivor who escaped the Nazi deportations of the Jews of Bukovina by going into hiding, but who was sent to do forced labor in a Rumanian camp for most of the war. The deliberate obscurity of Celan's later work creates an "atrocious chaos" and a "darkness" that "grows from page to page until the last inarticulate babble consternates like the rattle of a dying man" (OPT 173). The language frustrates the reader from understanding the later poems and in that sense "defrauds" the reader of something that should have been communicated. Levi explains further that "if his is a message, it gets lost in the 'background noise': it is not a communication, it is not a language, or at most it is a dark and truncated language precisely like that of a person who is about to die and is alone, as we all will be at the point of death. But since we the living are not alone, we must not write as if we were alone. As long as we live we have a responsibility: we must answer for what we write, word by word, and make sure that every word reaches the target" (OPT 173–74). He does not accept that a disorderly or surreal style is necessary to describe disorder.[26] Speaking in a language others do not understand enables speakers to assert their superiority over nonspeakers; Levi cannot forget how the guards and Kapos in Auschwitz savagely took advantage of many of the prisoners' inability to speak German to intimidate and humiliate them. He attributes his own survival partly to his rudimentary knowledge of German learned in college and from other prisoners, which enabled him to assimilate the rules of Auschwitz with fewer beatings. More generally he claims that foreign or incomprehensible languages have helped maintain the dominance of churchmen and colonial governors throughout history. Although he respects Celan's dense, hermetic poems as "tragic and noble," he argues that their style should not be imitated or propagated. Ironically for someone with an acute need for clarity and rationality, Levi translated Kafka's novel *The Trial* into Italian. He finds that Kafka's enigmatic parables anticipate symbolically much of what he witnessed at Auschwitz. Kafka's ability to create a world of suffering characters condemned by an inscrutable tribunal both dazzles and repels him. Despite his admiration, he admits that he has little literary affinity for Kafka, who writes in a way "totally unavailable" to him. His attraction to Kafka may stem from his recognition that Kafka developed a prose style, even if very different from his own, designed to comprehend evil on a grand scale, the same literary challenge facing Levi. He explains further that "In my writing, for good or evil, knowingly or not, I've always strived to pass from darkness into the light, as ... a filtering pump which sucks up turbid water and expels it decanted: possibly sterile. Kafka forges his path in the opposite direction: he endlessly unravels the hallucinations that he draws from incredibly profound layers, and he never filters them."[27]

Levi's strong attraction to clear comprehensible language to ensure communication and understanding reflects his contrary experience in Auschwitz where violence replaced language as the standard for human interaction. The beatings started when the Germans loaded the Italian Jews onto the train for deportation. The blows served no purpose, and Levi recalls his amazement that the Germans beat them without provocation and seemingly without anger. In the initial "selection" at Auschwitz, he describes how a man named Renzo "stayed an instant too long to say goodbye to Francesca, his fiancée, and with a single blow they knocked him to the ground. It was their everyday duty" (SA 15). After several days in the locked freight car without food or water, and not receiving any water on his arrival at Auschwitz, Levi recalls opening a window to break off an icicle to satisfy his thirst. A guard roughly snatched it away and shoved him back inside. Levi asked in his poor German why, and the guard replied "Hier ist kein warum" [there is no why here] (SA 25). Disputes, infractions, misunderstandings among the prisoners received the same violent response. The Kapos also knew that pain serves to stimulate a last reserve of energy, so that when performing hard physical labor, he recalls that prisoners were beaten not only from sheer cruelty, but to keep them from dropping under the weight of their burden, as one might beat tired draft animals (SA 60). People communicate with other people, but the Germans did not consider the Jews real people. He observes that to get a horse to stop or turn does not require a detailed explanation, which the horse would not understand anyway, and that pulling the reins, jabbing the spurs, or cracking the whip, might serve equally well as a shouted command (DS 91). Language would imply a certain equality between speakers, whereas violence implies the superiority of the striker over the victim. It eliminates argument and persuasion. At concentration camps like Mauthausen, the rubber truncheon was called "der Dolmetcher, the interpreter: the one who made himself understood to everybody" (DS 92). In the "daily language" of punches and slaps, Levi recalls that the prisoners learned to recognize nuances in the violence, and could distinguish between blows designed as "nonverbal communication," and those intended to inflict pain, which often ended in death. He recounts an incident where a German Kapo named Eddy caught him writing a letter home against the camp rules, and

> slammed me to the ground with a violent slap. But there: as I write this sentence today, and as I am in the act of typing the word "slap," I realize that I am lying, or at least transmitting biased emotions and information to the reader. Eddy was not a brute; he did not mean to punish me or make me suffer. A slap inflicted in the camp had a very different significance from what it might have here among us in today's here and now. Precisely: it

had a meaning; it was simply another way of expressing oneself. In that context it meant roughly "Watch out, you've really made a big mistake this time, you're endangering your life, maybe without realizing it, and you're endangering mine as well." But between Eddy, a German thief and juggler, and me, a young, inexperienced Italian, flustered and confused, such a speech would have been useless, not understood (if nothing else because of language problems), out of tune, and much too roundabout. (MR, 31)

To transmute experiences of such pervasive, intense violence back into language became the challenge of his witness.

LANGUAGE AND WITNESS

Levi captures the language-destroying nature of camp life in his story of his post-liberation meeting with a mute, dying child in the Soviet hospital at Auschwitz. Other survivors called the child "Hurbinek" because the name resembled the sound of his inarticulate cries. Levi supposes Hurbinek's muteness resulted simply from no one having taught him to speak, but his account makes clear that he considers the child symbolic of the traumatizing effect of the tremendous violence of the concentration camp, which threatens to render everyone who experienced it mute or despairing of articulating what happened. He sees an anguished judgement in the child's intense stare, and feels obligated to speak that judgement, and to memorialize the child in prose so that he does not vanish from the earth without leaving a trace, like so many of the Holocaust's victims. His last description of Hurbinek sounds almost like a eulogy said for the child's family, none of whom survived to hear it. He writes that "Hurbinek, who was three years old and perhaps had been born in Auschwitz and had never seen a tree; Hurbinek, who had fought like a man, to the last breath, to gain his entry into the world of men, from which a bestial power had excluded him; Hurbinek, the nameless, whose tiny forearm—even his—bore the tattoo of Auschwitz; Hurbinek died in the first days of March 1945, free but not redeemed. Nothing remains of him: he bears witness through these words of mine" (R 12). In his essay on his student friend Sandro Delmastro, a partisan killed by a Fascist guard in 1944, he recognizes the inadequacy of his literary portraits to recreate the complexities of actual individuals by writing "I know that it is a hopeless task to dress a man in words, make him live again on the printed page, especially a man like Sandro" (PT 49). But even flawed depictions of Hurbinek or Sandro compel the reader to witness what happened to them and to judge the people who murdered them. He explains that he consciously employs a simple, understated style to strengthen the force of his testimony:

> when describing the tragic world of Auschwitz, I have deliberately assumed the calm, sober language of the witness, neither the lamenting tones of the victim, nor the irate voice of someone who seeks revenge. I thought that my account would be all the more credible and useful the more it appeared objective and the less it sounded overly emotional; only in this way does a witness in matters of justice perform his task, which is that of preparing the ground for the judge. The judges are my readers. (R 196)

Levi's chapter on the chemical examination he received a few months after his arrival at Auschwitz exemplifies his method. In this strange, almost surreal scene, a German chemist named Dr. Pannwitz questioned him to determine the extent of his scientific knowledge, and whether he should work inside the laboratory of the large Farben synthetic rubber ("Buna") plant. I. G. Farben was then the largest chemical conglomerate in the world, and it ultimately invested more than 700 million marks in plants at Auschwitz where it contracted with the SS for a supply of slave labor. The company provided the prisoners in the Monowitz camp with a starvation ration that normally only sustained them for about three months.[28] At the examination Pannwitz made no acknowledgement of Levi's emaciated, exhausted, unwashed condition, and proceeded to question him in German about chemistry, showing particular interest in Levi's senior thesis on the measurement of dielectrical constants. Levi describes the beginning of their meeting with objective, detached language: "Pannwitz is tall, thin, blond; he has eyes, hair and nose as all Germans ought to have them, and sits formidably behind a complicated writing-table. I, Haftling 174517, stand in his office, which is a real office, shining, clean and ordered, and I feel that I would leave a dirty stain whatever I touched" (SA 96). In this brief passage he suggests the great gulf that the Nazi dehumanization process created: the German is identified by name, is seated, and possesses a writing table and an office, whereas the Jew is identified by number, stands, and possesses nothing. The passage's direct, unemotional tone lends credence to Pannwitz's almost unbelievable lack of human empathy, and highlights the bizarre juxtaposition of an academic conversation about chemistry with the routine nonverbal brutality of life in the camp. At the end of the chapter Levi describes how a Kapo named Alex, who escorted him back to work from the examination, grabbed a grease covered cable to keep his balance, and then wiped his hand clean on Levi's shirt as if Levi did not exist. Having calmly accumulated the details to recreate the scene, he concludes the chapter by writing "he would be amazed, the poor brute Alex, if someone told him that today, on the basis of this action, I judge him and Pannwitz and the innumerable others like him, big and small, in Auschwitz and everywhere" (SA 98). Because he does not explicitly state the content of his own judgement, he forces the reader to judge based on the evidence he has presented.

A demand for justice underlies Levi's witness. By recreating the violence of the concentration camp in language, he places it in a political realm where it can be discussed, analyzed, and judged. He explains that personally he can not use violence or "return the blow," not due to religious or philosophical convictions, but simply from an "intrinsic incapacity" and because "trading punches is an experience I do not have, as far back as I can go in memory" (DS 136). He attributes his lack of success as a partisan to this deficiency in his character. However imperfectly it functions, he must rely on the legal system to mete out punishment. His witness therefore can influence public opinion, which shapes the law and its enforcement. And because relatively few camp functionaries ever received formal trials, his writings challenge a wider audience of readers to render judgement.

Naturally, the German audience became particularly important to him. When he found out in 1959 that a German publisher had acquired the translation rights for *Survival in Auschwitz*, he "felt overwhelmed by the violent and new emotion of having won a battle" (DS 168). Although he had many different reasons for writing the book, he states that "its true recipients, those against whom the book was aimed like a gun were they, the Germans. Now the gun was loaded" (DS 168). Despite his rejection of physical violence, his metaphors suggest he considers his witness a weapon in the struggle for justice.

The penultimate chapters in *The Periodic Table* and *The Drowned and the Saved* both discuss letters from German readers of his translated account of Auschwitz. The German responses allow him to assess the effect of his witness on those who assented, or whose parents assented, to the destruction of the Jews. He describes his accidental encounter with one of the German chemists he knew at Auschwitz, who still worked for a German company formerly part of I.G. Farben which supplied some defective resin to the

Italian factory Levi worked at. In the correspondence to resolve this problem, Dr. Müller (a common German name equivalent to the English name Miller) repeatedly misspelled "naphthenate" as "naptenate," and Levi recognized the characteristic error of the Buna lab chemist who habitually said "beta-Naptylamin" instead of the correct "beta-Naphthylamin" (PT 213). This small linguistic detail marked him almost like a fingerprint, and from it Levi identified Dr. Müller, who in turn remembered Levi from the Buna lab. After sending him a copy of the German edition of *Survival in Auschwitz*, Müller wrote back requesting a personal meeting "useful both to myself and to you, and necessary for the purpose of overcoming that terrible past" (PT 217). Fearing what might happen at such a meeting, and that he could never adequately express himself in such a setting, Levi decided that "it was best for me to stick to writing" (PT 218). He responded in a letter by asking whether Müller "accepted the judgments" of his book, why he thought Farben so readily utilized slave labor, and what he knew of the extermination camps within Auschwitz. Müller replied in a long letter that Levi spends nearly three pages summarizing. In it he blamed Auschwitz on general flaws in mankind, attributed his membership in the SA (Storm Troopers) to his being "dragged initially along by the general enthusiasm for Hitler's regime," defended Farben's Monowitz camp as intended to protect the Jews, denied any knowledge of the gas chambers at Auschwitz, emphasized the personal favors he did Levi in the lab, and perceived in his book "an overcoming of Judaism, a fulfillment of the Christian precept to love one's enemies, and a testimony of faith in Man" (PT 219, 221). Levi credits Müller with at least having a conscience, because the letters and attempt to establish direct contact suggest to him that Müller could not quite settle his accounts with the past. However his evasion of personal responsibility, and ridiculous explanation of Farben's past, indicated he had not understood the significance of Levi's witness. Levi concludes that

> in his first letter he had spoken of "overcoming the past," "Bewältigung der Vergangenheit": I later found out that this is a stereotyped phrase, a euphemism in today's Germany, where it is universally understood as "redemption from Nazism"; but the root word that it contains also appears in the words that express "domination," "violence," and "rape," and I believe that translating the expression "distortion of the past" or "violence done to the past" would not stray very far from its profound meaning. (PT 222)

Nazi rhetoric like "Arbeit Macht Frei" obscured or euphemistically described reality, but here the language unmasks a truth deeper than its speaker's intended meaning. Some of the German letters quoted in his later book *The Drowned and the Saved* give greater cause for optimism about the impact of his witness, but he expresses a general frustration that forty years later, few people anywhere seem interested in his testimony. The Müllers of the world worked and prospered at the same companies that helped run the concentration camps almost as if nothing had happened. Ozick writes that one of the "single most terrible"[29] sentences ever written on the issue of "overcoming the past" comes in the Preface to *The Drowned and the Saved* where Levi observes that "the crematoria ovens themselves were designed, built, assembled, and tested by a German company, Topf of Wiesbaden (it was still in operation in 1975, building crematoria for civilian use, and had not considered the advisability of changing its name)" (DS, 16). The moral obtuseness displayed by companies like Topf or individuals like Dr. Müller found more public outlet in the 1980s in the writings of conservative revisionist German historians of the Second World War, and in the governing coalition's "normalization" campaign designed to remove any lingering stigma from the Nazi era so that [West] Germany could rejoin fully the community of nations, which culminated in the invitation given to Ronald Reagan to speak at Bitburg cemetery in 1985.[30]

Levi's witness attempts to combat the deliberate amnesia of Holocaust participants like Müller, and the waning historical awareness of succeeding generations. He manages to reconstruct through words a place he compares to Babel: "the confusion of languages is a fundamental component of the manner of living here: one is surrounded by a perpetual Babel, in which everyone shouts orders and threats in languages never heard before, and woe betide whoever fails to grasp the meaning. No one has time here, no one has patience, no one listens to you; we recent arrivals instinctively collect in the corners, against the walls, afraid of being beaten" (SA 33). Suppressing language's normal function to create and express meaning rapidly dehumanized the prisoners at Auschwitz. And to depict with language a situation where language faltered presents difficulties. He extends the Babel metaphor by linking the linguistic confusion of the camp to its horrible moral chaos: "The Carbide Tower, which rises in the middle of Buna and whose top is rarely visible in the fog, was built by us. Its bricks were called Ziegel, briques, tegula, cegli, kamenny, mattoni, téglak, and they were cemented by hate; hate and discord, like the Tower of Babel, and it is this that we call it:- Babelturm, Bobelturm; and in it we hate the insane dream of grandeur of our masters, their contempt for God and men, for us men" (SA

66). Though Levi was and remained an unbeliever, the Biblical metaphor helps suggest the epic scale of the suffering and evil present. Babel in the camp resulted not only from the multiplicity of languages spoken by the inmates, but from the attempt to negate language through violence. The diverse linguistically-based identities of the inmates were destroyed, and replaced by one identity based on race (as the Nazis understood it) that signified a sub-human status. Levi observes that paradoxically Auschwitz was both noisy and silent, a barrage of sounds that communicated nothing, "a hubbub of people without names or faces drowned in a continuous, deafening background noise from which, however, the human word did not surface. A black and white film, with sound but not a talkie" (DS 93–94). His witness confronts the linguistic nihilism unleashed by the Nazis that he believes facilitated their crimes. By moving this very dark episode toward the light he performs an important public service, and despite his own uncertainty about the impact of his witness, he compellingly describes what one observer of the liberation of the concentration camp at Belsen called "beyond the imagination of mankind."[31]

NOTES

1. George Steiner claims that "the world of Auschwitz lies outside speech as it lies outside reason" in *Language and Silence* (New York: Atheneum, 1967), 123. Lawerence Langer observes that the volume of Holocaust literature contradicts the first half of Steiner's claim, but the truth of the second half creates serious difficulties for writers trying to assimilate the reality of the concentration camps into their work. See Lawrence Langer, *The Holocaust and the Literary Imagination* (New Haven: Yale University Press, 1975), 15. Alvin Rosenfeld finds this simultaneous urge to speech and pull toward silence common in Holocaust literature. He explains that "what is really involved here is the deep anguish and immense frustration of the writer who confronts a subject that belittles and threatens to overwhelm the resources of his language ... reality underwent so radical a distortion as to disarm and render no longer trustworthy the normal cognitive and expressive powers. As a result, reason seemed to give way to madness, as language did time and again to silence." See Alvin Rosenfeld, *A Double Dying: Reflections on Holocaust Literature* (Bloomington: Indiana University Press, 1980), 14, 28.

2. Risa Sodi, "An Interview With Primo Levi," *Partisan Review* 54.3 (Summer 1987), 356.

3. Primo Levi, *The Periodic Table*, trans. Raymond Rosenthal (N.Y: Schocken Books, 1984), 151. The book was first published in Italy in 1975. All further references will appear as (PT) in the text.

4. Primo Levi, *The Reawakening*, trans. Stuart Woolf (N.Y: Collier Books, 1987), 2. The book was first published in 1963 as *La tregua (The Truce)*. All further references will appear as (R) in the text.

5. Primo Levi, *The Drowned and the Saved* (N.Y: Vintage Books, 1989), 24. All further references will appear as (DS) in the text.

6. There remains some controversy surrounding Levi's death, but most seem to concur with the idea of suicide. For two essays that interpret his suicide in the light of his last published Holocaust memoir, see Cynthia Ozick, "Primo Levi's Suicide Note" in *Metaphor and Memory* (N.Y: Alfred Knopf, 1989), 34–48, and Alexander Stille, "Forward" in Jean Amery, *At the Mind's Limits* (N.Y: Schocken Books, 1990), vii–xvi.

7. Lawrence Langer, *Holocaust Testimonies* (New Haven: Yale University Press, 1991), 171. Neither of Levi's accounts of his liberation from Auschwitz in his first two memoirs describe feelings of joyful celebration. In a passage cited by Langer to suggest how the concentration camp experience distanced the term "liberation" from its normal meaning of freedom, Levi explains that "for most [liberation] occurred against a tragic background of destruction, slaughter, and suffering. Just as they felt they were again becoming men, that is responsible, the sorrows of men returned: the sorrow of the dispersed or lost family; the universal suffering all around; their own exhaustion, which seemed definitive, past cure; the problems of a life to begin all over again amid the rubble, often alone. Not pleasure the son of misery,' but misery the son of misery. Leaving pain behind was a delight for only a few fortunate beings, or only for a few instants, or for very simple souls; almost always it coincided with a phase of anguish" (DS, 70–71). In his book *Holocaust Testimonies*, Langer develops concepts like "anguished memory" and "humiliated memory" to explain the continued suffering of survivors long after their release.

8. Primo Levi, *Survival in Auschwitz*, trans. Stuart Woolf (New York: Collier, 1961), 112–13. The book was first published in 1947 as *Se questo è un huomo* (*If This Is A Man*). All further references will appear as (SA) in the text.

9. Langer, *Holocaust Testimonies*, 61.

10. The sense of "incredibility" recurs in Holocaust memoirs and diaries. Even to as powerful a chronicler as Elie Wiesel, it seems ultimately incomprehensible; in 1967 he stated about Auschwitz that "I do not believe it. The event seems unreal, as if it occurred on a different planet." Elie Wiesel, "Jewish Values in the Post-Holocaust Future," *Judaism* 16.3 (Summer 1967): 285, cited in Langer, 78.

11. Rosenfeld, 55. Langer finds this same dilemma present in oral testimonies by Holocaust survivors, about which he writes that "the anxiety of futility lurks beneath the surface of many of these narratives" (*Holocaust Testimonies*, xiii).

12. This usage was apparently widespread because Eugen Kogon reports that when trainloads of deportees arrived, camp guards often asked each other "Wie viele Stücke" (How many "pieces")? Kogon cited in Rosenfeld, 137.

13. In an interview Levi observes that in Italy he is known as a writer who is occasionally Jewish, whereas in America he is known and marketed as a Jewish writer. Though he "gladly accepts" the label of "Jewish writer," it does not fully reflect his own self-conception (Sodi, 355).

14. For an overview of that history, see H. Stuart Hughes, *Prisoners of Hope: The Silver Age of the Italian Jews, 1924–1974* (Cambridge: Harvard University Press,

1983), 1–28, and Susan Zuccotti, *The Italians and the Holocaust* (N.Y: Basic Books, 1987), 12–27.

15. For further discussion of camp vocabulary, see Sidra Ezrahi, *By Words Alone: The Holocaust in Literature* (Chicago: University of Chicago Press, 1980), 10–11.

16. For a discussion of "Nazi-Deutsch" see Rosenfeld, 129–42, and Henry Friedlander, "The Manipulation of Language" in Henry Friedlander and Sybil Milton, eds., *The Holocaust: Ideology, Bureaucracy, and Genocide* (Millwood, N.Y: Kraus International Publications, 1980), 103–13.

17. Berel Lang, "Language and Genocide" in *Act and Idea in the Nazi Genocide* (Chicago: University of Chicago Press, 1990), 97–98.

18. Primo Levi, *Moments of Reprieve*, trans. Ruth Feldman (N.Y: Schocken Books, 1986), 90. All further references will appear as (MR) in the text.

19. Ozick, 47. She argues that Levi's suicide might reflect the futility of such a defense mechanism.

20. Stille, xii-xiii.

21. Gabriel Motola, "Primo Levi: The Language of the Scientist," *The Literary Review* 34.2 (Winter 1991): 204. Ozick observes similarly that Levi's prose style represents a "psychological oxymoron: the well-mannered cicerone of hell, mortal horror in a decorous voice" (40). Fernanda Eberstadt concurs that Levi's style incorporates "precision, economy, subtlety, a dry and rueful wit, an intimate understanding of the dramatic potential of understatement, and a certain frigidity of manner which combines effectively with the explosiveness of his subject matter," but she attributes this not to his scientific training but rather to his secular, skeptical temperament and his "classical Mediterranean education" ("Reading Primo Levi," *Commentary* 80 [October 1985]: 43). Discussing his first book in an interview with Philip Roth, Levi pointed to still another source of influence: "my model (or, if you prefer, my style) was that of the 'weekly report' commonly used in factories: it must be precise, concise, and written in a language comprehensible to everybody in the industrial hierarchy" (Philip Roth, "A Man Saved By His Skills," *The New York Times Book Review* [October 12, 1986]: 41). Levi worked in the same Turinese paint factory for nearly thirty years, both as a research chemist, and for thirteen years as the plant's general manager. He retired in 1977 to write full time.

22. George Orwell, "Politics and the English Language" in *A Collection of Essays by George Orwell* (N.Y: Harcourt Brace Jovanovich, 1946), 171.

23. Hannah Arendt, *Eichmann in Jerusalem* (Harmondsworth: Penguin Books, 1963), 48–55, 85–86, 105–109. See Lang's illuminating analysis of the phrase "Endlösung" ("final solution"), which the Nazis' adopted at the Wannsee Conference in January 1942 as the standard usage for referring to the extermination of the Jews, in "Language and Genocide," 85–92.

24. Lang, 81–82.

25. Primo Levi, *Other People's Trades*, trans. Raymond Rosenthal (N.Y: Summit Books, 1989), 221. All further references will appear as (OPT) in the text. Ezrahi notes that similar concerns about the Nazi debasement of language and its political effects drove some post-war German writers toward the clear vigorous prose style

Levi sought: "for some German writers the memory of symbols and abstractions used to forge national unity and camouflage heinous crimes is a warning against inflated rhetoric" (45). See also Ann Mason, "Nazism and Postwar German Literary Style," *Contemporary Literature* 17.1 (Winter, 1976): 63–83.

26. Langer argues to the contrary that "in duplicating [the Holocaust's] contradictions without providing an opportunity for "ordering" one's reactions or assembling them into a meaningful pattern, Celan has invented a poetic form singularly appropriate for the substance of his vision" (*The Holocaust and the Literary Imagination*, 12). Rosenfeld observes that autobiographical writings by Holocaust survivors display a range of styles including opposites like Levi and Celan: "in an effort to recall their experiences faithfully and without any adornment, some memoirists have aimed for strict narrative realism; others, believing that these same experiences were almost otherworldly in their strangeness and brutality, have tried to simulate them in a prose that is itself wrenched and estranging" (54).

27. Primo Levi, *The Mirror Maker*, trans. Raymond Rosenthal (N.Y: Schocken Books, 1989), 106–107.

28. For a more detailed discussion of I.G. Farben and the many other large German companies that used slave labor from the concentration camps, see Raul Hilberg, *The Destruction of the European Jews* (Chicago: Quadrangle Books, 1961), 586–60, Richard Rubenstein, *The Cunning of History: The Holocaust and the American Future* (N.Y: Harper Colophon Books, 1975), 36–67, Richard Borkin, *The Crime and Punishment of I.G. Farben* (N.Y: The Free Press, 1978), and John Roth, "Holocaust Business: Some Reflections on Arbeit Macht Frei," *Annals* 450 (July 1980): 68–82.

29. Ozick, 42.

30. For a critique of conservative revisionist historians like Michael Sturmer, Andreas Hillgruber, and Ernest Nolte (perhaps the most extreme claims were made in 1986 by Nolte, who argued that the Nazi death camps adopted procedures already developed in Stalin's Gulag, and were motivated by Hitler's fear that the Germans themselves would become victims of Stalin's "Asiatic" onslaught), see Jurgen Habermas, *The New Conservatism: Cultural Criticism and the Historians' Debate*, trans. Shierry Nicholsen (Cambridge: MIT Press, 1989), 212–28. On the controversy engendered by the conservative historians and Habermas's attack upon them, see Charles Maier, *The Unmasterable Past: History, Holocaust, and German National Identity* (Cambridge: Harvard University Press, 1988), 9–65, and Judith Miller, *One, By One, By One: Facing the Holocaust* (N.Y: Simon And Schuster, 1990), 32–51. On the controversy surrounding Reagan's visit to Bitburg, see Geoffrey Hartman, ed., *Bitburg in Moral and Political Perspective* (Bloomington: Indiana University Press, 1986).

31. Cited in Ezrahi, 3.

BARBARA CHIARELLO

The Utopian Space of a Nightmare:
*The Diary of Anne Frank**

Defining a Holocaust text as utopian literature verges on the impossible. How can works depicting imaginary better wolds emerge from people forced to live in a Nazi-created Hell? How could Jews—the prime objectives of Hitler's Final Solution—contemplate the ideal? How could a person depict good, too-good-to-be-true, while coping with evil, too-evil-to-comprehend? Yet detailing a utopia while being threatened by an ever-encroaching dystopia may mean spiritual survival to a victim of the Holocaust's fury.

Circumstances forced Anne Frank to reject More's historical definition of utopia as a place too good to be true. In *Socialism: The Active Utopia*, Zygmunt Bauman acknowledged the importance of circumstances when he wrote "... utopian ideals ... are shaped ... under the double pressure of the galvanizing feeling of deprivation and the chastening squeeze of omnipresent and stubborn realities" (14). Anne had to create a utopia—"the expression of the desire for a better way of being and living" (Levitas 8)—or perish in despair. Other Holocaust victims chose despair. Charlotte Salomon, a Jewish painter born in Berlin, fled to France in 1939 at the age of 22. One of her works was captioned, "I cannot bear this life, I cannot bear these times" (Steenmeyer 10). But when Nazism pushed 13-year-old Anne out of her customary world into a new one, she used her diary to both depict an imaginary place and to prove the possibility of positive changes in the present. Anne acknowledges the compensatory utopian intention of her diary

From *Utopian Studies* 5, no.1 (1994). © 1994 by the Society for Utopian Studies.

in her first sentence, which precedes the first officially dated entry, "I hope you will be a great support and comfort to me" (177).

Evaluating *The Diary of Anne Frank* for inclusion in utopian literature would be easier if the academic community clearly defined utopia. But "working definitions range from the refusal of any definition at all," Levitas writes, "through definitions in terms of form, form and content, function, function and form" (7). As she argues for a broad definition, she unintentionally seems to welcome Anne's diary to the field.

The "emphasis has changed from the presentation of finished perfection to a more open exploration in which the construction of the individual, and thus the question of another way of being, has become the central issue" (7). *The Diary of Anne Frank* is clearly a "construction of the individual" that addresses :the question of another way of being."

Another obstacle this work must overcome to be accepted as utopian literature also serves as its unique strength: the diary form. Custom often limits utopian expression to book-length fiction, but the form Anne chose gave her work the authority, credibility, immediacy and a straight-forward, non-didactic tone unique to this genre. Anne could have expressed her message of hope in various other forms—indeed, she did write several essays and short stories while in hiding that were first published in part under the title *Tales From the House Behind*. But the diary form also fulfills another of Levitas' assertions: "the pursuit of a better way of being ... may mean the pursuance of spiritual or psychological states" (191-2).

Anne began writing a second version of her diary in May 1944, with the hope of publishing "a book entitled *Het Achterhuis* after the war. Whether I shall succeed or not, I cannot say, but my diary will be a great help" (61). If she had lived to accomplish this goal, she might hve chosen another way to express her thoughts. Yet having her words in diary form also bypasses several traditional artifices, such as reliance on reference, sacred writings, and contrived characters and dialogues that many utopian texts use to establish authority. Other utopian works, like Ernest Callenbach's *Ectopia* (1975), Eugene Zamiatin's *We* (1924), and George Orwells's *Nineteen Eighty-Four* (1949), include this form to add credibility and immediacy. But Anne's diary is more believable than fictional uses of the form. Even though her work, like all diaries, is a highly selective portrayal of reality—it contains only that part of the "truth" the writer perceives and selects for inclusion—the form speaks with the compelling voice of someone who has lived its message. It is a voice that, to many readers, will ring more convincingly than the voices of imaginary visitors to imaginary worlds. True, a diarist can come close to, but never succeed, at duplicating the "experience." But Anne's honest tone helps to overcome this problem. She acknowledged: "Although I tell you a lot, still, even so, you only know very little of our lives" (578). Furthermore, at least the first version of this diary—unlike Benjamin Franklin's or even Frederic Douglass's—seems more truthful because Anne wrote it for herself, not with the expectation it would be published and widely read.

Anne's religion and youth add credibility to the diary form. Since Anne was Jewish, this work is even more compelling as a firsthand account of a person who lived through the events, not as an outside observer, but as a victim. As a thirteen to fifteen year old, she's too naïve to be subtly manipulative, or at least the reader is less likely to assume manipulative intent. Anne writes with an innocence that allows the reader to identify with her. She hasn't yet learned to hide behind barriers; she's less afraid of exposing herself than many adults who have learned to censor their innermost thoughts, especially writers concerned with earning financial support from their audience. Her age also supports Ernst Bloch's theory of the Not-Yet-Conscious where he believed the universal utopian impulse resides and which is at its best in "youth, times which are on the point of changing, creative expression.... With puberty begins the mystery of women, the mystery of life, the mystery of knowledge .... If youth occurs in revolutionary times ... then it really does know what forward dreaming is all about" (117). Bloch also argues that utopia is more than forward dreaming, "not taken only as emotion, ... but more essentially as a directing act of a cognitive kind" (12). Indeed, Anne's diary not only lists her experiences, it offers a blueprint on how to live. When Pfeffer arrived on November 17, 1942, she presented him with typed "Secret Annexe Rules" which included, "Use of language: Speak softly at all times, by order! All civilized languages are permitted, therefore no German!" (312) Anne's humor—part of her coping arsenal—takes the sting (and boredom) out of the didactic nature inherent in many utopian works.

The diary reinforces her communication style. Anne doesn't preach; she illustrates. She creates a short story per entry. She presents vital images that ignite feelings and thoughts, creating blanks or "gaps," to use Wolfgang Iser's term, for the reader to fill. The diary form parallels her intent. Each "yours truly" gives the reader a pause to acknowledge feelings and formulate conclusions on each entry before proceeding to the next salutation. "Yours truly, Anne" forms a natural break, like ending a letter. Then "Dear Kitty" invites the reader back into the next communication. This stopping and starting also functions to mark time. Although Anne didn't realize this, the date at the top of each entry mimics the tick-tock of the time bomb the reader knows will ultimately explode her utopia. The date also underlines her subtle exhortation to live each day with joy and hope.

The diary form also adds even more immediacy than a straightforward first-person account in fiction or autobiography. As Kenneth M. Roemer asserts in his introduction to *America as Utopia*, "A literary utopia is ... a 'fiction' that encourages readers to experience vicariously a culture that represents a prescriptive, normative alternative to their own culture" (3). Anne pulls the reader into her culture each time she begins an entry for a vicarious experience that ends when she signs off in a manner that establishes her immediate presence. The "I" in a fictional narrative can too often blend into a third-person blur. In such a text, the reader may forget just who the narrator is and get lost in the events, descriptions, or other characters. Not here. Anne even signs her name differently—mostly it's a simple Anne, sometimes it's Anne Mary, Anne M. Frank or Anne Mary Frank—thus reminding the reader "This is me on this particular day." Given the overwhelming number of Holocaust victims, this constant repetition prevents the reader from viewing the number in a detached, alienated manner, from becoming numbed and overwhelmed by incomprehensibility. The reader must experience the horror of seeing Anne and, by implication, millions like her as suffering individuals.

Anne lives in her words. On April 4, 1944, she eerily acknowledged this possibility: "I want to go on living even after my death! And therefore I am grateful to God for giving me this gift, this possibility ... of writing, of expressing all that is in me" (587). The diary allows her to express this wish directly to readers who may shake their heads in utopian joy, glad she realized they would share in her immortality. Since the form makes it impossible for Anne to write about her own death, the text cannot refute this pretense.

When Anne and her family began another way of life, survival meant retreat. Faced with annihilation, the Franks entered a small space they would share with three, then four others. Instead of entering a bigger and better world, these eight hoped to survive by shrinking into almost nothingness. Their utopia wasn't a vast, expansive, visible model. Being seen by the Gestapo meant death. While typical late nineteenth- and early twentieth-century Utopian works, like Edward Bellamy's *Looking Backward* (1888) and Charolotte Perkins Gilman's *Herland* (1919) followed the prevailing assumption by presenting their ideal world on a society—or country-wide state, *The Diary of Anne Frank* used another approach to create the genre's requisite feeling of freedom. In doing so, this work may have pioneered a contemporary utopian approach to space. Anne Frank's work challenges

George Orwell's *Nineteen Eighty-Four*, where dystopia equals confinement to Room 101 and foreshadows smaller-scale modern utopias such as Marge Piercy's Mattapoisett in *Woman on the Edge of Time* (1976) and Ursula K. Le Guin's "Sur" (1982) and the worlds discussed by Robert Plank in his essay "The Modern Shrunken Utopia." Like Burris in *Walden Two* and the protagonists in many feminist utopias, Anne finds the ideal in small communities, interpersonal relationships, and inner growth. Again Levitas seems to be referring to Anne's diary when she writes, "contemporary utopias ... tend to withdraw into the interstices of a seemingly irredeemable actually existing society rather than confidently heralding its transformation" (158). Anne does this on two levels: she withdraws from Nazi-occupied Europe and then from the petty politics of family and strangers living in confined quarters into the utopian womb of her diary.

Since Anne Frank refused to retreat into a utopian fantasy more in keeping with More's good—but no—place, her work can be seen as a fitting illustrative companion text to several modern theorists besides Levitas. Forced into a real space, she made it good; thus supplying hope to post-Holocaust scholars like Marie Louise Berneri who could no longer assume civilization's steady march toward progress. Since the diary deals with Nazism—a seemingly universal evil—it serves as the battleground for an ongoing question in the field of utopian studies: "Is the good society more than a matter of personal preference?" (Levitas 183) *The Diary of Anne Frank* straddles both sides of other current quandaries: it is at once itself and its opposite. The work is both imaginary and historical—a distinction Berneri struggles with as she tries to define utopia (9); the theoretical and the practical (Bauman 14); the status quo and the alternative (Levitas 3) and the idea and the change (Levitas 75). The text is utopian in form and function—not only does the diary adhere to many utopian conventions, but it sets out a blueprint for how to create a utopian inner space instead of focusing on implementing the good society. Levitas's new definition of utopia supports this interpretation: "we learn a lot about the experience of living under any set of conditions by reflecting upon the desires which those conditions generate and yet leave unfulfilled. For that is the space which utopia occupies" (8).

This innovative way of redefining utopian space was not a literary exercise for Anne Frank. Forced into confinement to avoid unimaginable suffering and to escape the kind of existing society utopian socialists like Saint-Simon, Fourier and Owen would describe as "unjust, immoral and generally insupportable" (Levitas 39)—she could have retreated to madness or suicide. She did neither. Instead, she chose to enter a utopia that isn't an insane denial of reality, but the space between what is and what one hopes, a here and now made more tolerable by detailing what can be, a society "characterised by cooperation rather than antagonism" (Levitas 39) as the utopian socialists envisioned. Through her diary, she reinterprets her present and constructs a survival manual for overcoming a world gone mad—what Bauman called relativising the present: " ... by scanning the field of the possible in which the real occupies merely a tiny plot, utopias pave the way for a critical attitude and a critical activity which alone can transform the present predicament of man" (13). Utilizing many conventions of traditional utopian fictions, Anne Frank's diary details the imaginary world she created that pushed horrific reality into a tiny, and therefore, manageable plot.

Several of the utopian conventions that were particularly crucial to her imagined better world include: a journey to an alternative place, a prevailing attitude more hopeful than the reader's, a visitor and a guide who engage in a dialogue, a conversion narrative, a message the visitor returns with, foils, and an assured tone proclaiming that the alternate world is definitely superior to the reader's world. Gradually, as one gets into an effective utopian text, the reader escapes from a cruel, imperfect reality into a kinder, and more just, society. Anne Frank's works fulfills these criteria.

II

The openings of many well-known utopian texts, like Utopia, *Looking Backward*, *Herland* and *Walden Two*, are ground in familiar realities. Similarly, this diary begins during the least fearful and most comfortable time for both the writer and the post-Holocaust reader. Anne's first entries tell of her 13th birthday celebrations at home and at school before she goes into hiding. She writes about starting to date, and, perhaps, falling in love with, a young man she has recently met. All this chatty, normal teenager talk ends on July 8, 1942 when she says, "years seem to have passed between Sunday and now ... it is as if the whole world had turned upside down" (206).

Anne's journey may seem mundane compared to the time travel and strange voyages of other utopian travelers. Her family left their home to live in rooms located on the second floor, third floor, and attic of a warehouse owned by her father. But the journey Anne takes is spiritual as well as physical. She uses a common utopian device, traveling forward in time to a new world, to explain her feelings in the above excerpt. Her dated entries show that the Sunday she feels was years ago was really only three days before, but Anne has leapt into a utopia that she must believe promises life.

Further entries illustrate how sharply Anne differentiates between the utopia she has created and the nightmare surrounding it. Anne speaks of her "beautiful bathroom" and writes "although it sounds mad, I think it is the best place of all" (258); her "secret den" (300), of events in "our little passage" (301) and "our superpractical exquisite little 'Secret Annexe'" (311). Anne's language transforms these rooms into another world parallel to the real world outside. She speaks of "sitting cozily in the main office" (327) and asserts, it is "quiet and safe here" (332). She becomes uncomfortable leaving, even to go to a Christmas celebration in one of the warehouse offices. " ... (it made me shudder and wish I was safely upstairs again) ... " (321).

Anne takes a journey when she goes "upstairs again," a journey signifying more than simply ascending an ordinary flight of steps.

> I see the 8 of us with our "Secret Annexe" as if we were a little piece of blue heaven, surrounded by black, black rain clouds. The round, clearly defined spot where we stand is still safe but the clouds gather more and more closely about us.... We all look down below where people are fighting each other, we look above, where it is quiet and beautiful, and meanwhile we are cut off by the great dark mass, ... which stands before us as an impenetrable wall: it tries to crush us but cannot do so yet. (416)

She has turned the secret annex into her unreachable, sane, and happy nest, even though it's actually quite small, hot in the summer, smelly when circumstances force the inhabitants to use huge glass jars as chamber pots, and ultimately no safer for Anne than the reality she's left. Although Anne's "het achterhuis," like any imaginary heaven, cannot save her, her utopian attitude prevents "the great dark mass" from crushing her by keeping her spirit alive.

Of course, not all incidences of hiding away in confined areas constitute creating utopian spaces. American slave Harriet A. Jacobs hid for several years, not for survival, but to keep her children from being sold as plantation slaves. Her much smaller hiding space—nine feet long, seven feet wide and three feet at the highest—may explain Jacob's more negative attitude, but it is this martyred stance that prevents *Incidents in the Life of a Slave Girl* (1861) from being considered utopian. Told through the words of Linda Brent, the narrator she created, Jacobs wrote: "Dark thoughts passed through my mind as I lay there day after day. I tried to be thankful for my little cell, dismal as it was, and even to love it, as part of the price I had to pay for the redemption of my children" (123).

Hawthorne wrote in his allegory, "The Hall of Fantasy," that " ... even the actual becomes ideal ... in hope" (467). Anne armors herself with hope to carry her through irritating, everyday problems, on-going anti-German war events that fail to free her, and near discovery. Hope tells her not to question her ultimate survival and to prepare actively to re-enter post-Nazi Holland. While other utopian texts imaginatively solve the problems of poverty, over-work, or crime, this work shows how hope can (at least emotionally) detoxify a poisonous time and function "not merely as fictitious compensation for the discomforts of experienced reality, but a venturing beyond that reality" (Levitas 86).

> When the Frank family arrived at 263 Prisengracht, the living room and all the other rooms were chock full of rubbish, indescribably so.... We had to start clearing up immediately if we wished to sleep on decent beds that night. Mummy and Margot were not in a fit state to take part; they were tired and lay down on their unmade beds, they were wretched ... but the two "clearers-up" of the family Daddy and myself, wanted to start at once....
>
> We hadn't had a bit of anything warm the whole day but we didn't care, Mummy and Margot were too tired and keyed up to eat and Daddy and I were to busy. (215)

Anne is not one to be wretched over indescribably messed up rooms, or an indescribably messed up world. Interestingly, she uses the Dutch word "opruimers" (Dagboek 18), which has been translated into "clearers-up" instead of cleaners-up, to describe herself and her father as if recognizing her role as more of a remover of chaos than of dust and dirt.

Since Anne recognizes the gloom, her utopia isn't rooted in denial. On November 19, 1942, she wrote: "In the evenings when it's dark, I often see rows of good, innocent people accompanied by crying children ... bullied and knocked about until they almost drop. Nobody is spared, old people, children, babies, expectant mothers, the sick each and all join in the march of death" (316). Then the next day, she writes, "The news about the Jews had not really penetrated through to us until now" (317). Friedrich Pfeffer, who had just been invited to share their hiding place, gave them the latest information about the Jewish friends and acquaintances they had left behind.

Anne consciously chooses to triumph over the horror. "It won't do us any good or help those on the outside to go on being as gloomy as we are at the moment ... Must I keep thinking about those people whatever I am doing? Ought I then to cry the whole day long? No, that I can't do (317).

So Anne laughs. She laughs at her everyday discomforts: "We have a moth biscuit with syrup [the biscuit tin is kept in the wardrobe which is full of mothballs] and have fun"(245).

> One afternoon we couldn't go to the lavatory because there were visitors in the office; however, Peter had to pay an urgent call. So he didn't pull the plug. He put a notice up on the lavatory door to warn us, with "S.V.P. gas" on it. Of course he meant to put "Beware of gas"; but he thought the other looked more genteel. He hadn't got the faintest notion it meant "if you please." (336)

She laughs at her ineptitude: "I must cut Daddy's hair. Pim [her pet name for her father] maintains that he will never have another barber after the war, as I do the job so well. If only I didn't snip his ear so often!" (344). And after one of their cats used some wood shavings in the attic as a litter box and its urine dripped down into their barrel of potatoes: "The ceiling was dripping.... I was doubled up with laughter, it really was such a scream" (641).

Within the humor, Anne has shown us that her world isn't perfect, again heralding modern utopias that theorist Tom Moylan suggests "focus on the continuing presence of difference and imperfection within utopian society itself" (11). Anne's utopia is in keeping with Lyman Tower Sargent's point in his introduction to *British and American Utopian Literature, 1516-1985*: "It is important to realize that most utopias are not projected as perfect worlds but as much better ones" (xii).

Anne not only used humor in her diary to coat the real unpleasantness of hiding, she searched for and exaggerated the glimmers of hope in the war news of her day. She responds to Churchill's famous lines with overflowing joy, ignoring his equivocation. "This is not the end," Churchill said. "It is not even the beginning of the end. But it is perhaps the end of the beginning." After quoting these words in her diary, she writes, "Do you see the difference? There is certainly reason for optimism" (299).

On July 21, 1944, instead of bemoaning the failed attempted assassination of Hitler, she writes: " ... now things are going well at last. Yes, really, they are going well! Super news! An attempt has been made on Hitler's life and not even by Jewish communists or English capitalists this time, but by a proud German general, and what's more, he's a count, and still quite young" (695). Had Hitler been killed, Anne and her family might have survived. But Anne never contemplates how this failed assassination may result in her death or, at the very least, a longer time in hiding. Instead, she frames the event in an even more positive light as she continues in the same entry, "Perhaps the Divine Power tarried on purpose in getting him out of the way, because it would be much easier and more advantageous to the Allies if the impeccable Germans kill each other off" (695).

This approach parallels the approach of her co-religionist Karl Mannheim, who was exiled to England by the Nazis in 1933, when he stated, "Utopias [as opposed to ideologies] ... succeed through counteractivity in transforming the existing historical reality into one more in accord with their own conceptions" (195-6). Her work also exemplifies that of Bloch, a radical German-Jewish intellectual who was also exiled in the thirties, when he called for daydreams "not in the sense of merely contemplative reason which takes things as they are and as they stand, but of participating reason which takes them as they go, and also as they could go better" (4). While Anne Frank was not aware of Mannheim and Bloch's more global approaches to change, she nevertheless framed her world within their philosophies. One explanation for their common attitudes may be Judaism's emphasis on the here and now, as opposed to the utopian Christian heaven.

Jacobs illustrates this other worldly focus and resigned approach in the following excerpt:

> Sometimes I thought God was a compassionate Father, who would forgive my sins for the sake of my sufferings. At other times, it seemed to me that there was no justice or mercy in the divine garment. I asked why the curse of slavery was permitted to exist, and why I had been so persecuted and wronged from youth upward. These things took the shape of mystery, which is to this day not so clear to my soul as I trust it will be hereafter (123).

Unlike Jacobs, Anne remains rooted in her utopian present even when faced with near discovery. Although the inhabitants of the "secret annexe" are careful to be quiet when they know workers are about, they are afraid they were overheard and reported by burglars who had entered the warehouse the previous night. Anne writes "I prepared myself for the return of the police, then we'd have to say that we were in hiding; they would either be good Dutch people [the police], then we'd be saved, or N.S.B.ers [The Dutch national Socialist Movement], then we'd have to bribe them" (594)! Of course, this isn't what ultimately happens when they are discovered, but until then the utopian prism Anne holds up as she views real events keeps her from spiritual death.

On Friday, August 4, 1944, the outside world broke this prism. Harry Paape, under the auspices of the Netherlands State Institute for War Documentation, obtained oral and written accounts from those eyewitnesses that survived for his report on what happened that day. The following is a synopsis of his findings: When a German officer and several Dutch men in civilian clothes entered the warehouse, they were directed upstairs by a worker named Van Maaren, believed by some to be the informer. These men approached the bookcase that hid the entrance to the "secret annexe" with their guns drawn and demanded it be open, obviously knowing what they would find. According to Otto Frank, Anne's father, the Dutch officials appeared to belong to the German Sicherheitdienst (Security Service, or SD). While waiting for a truck that would transport the inhabitants to headquarters of the Amsterdam Bureau of the Commander of the Security Police and Security Service, the German, Karl Silberbauer, discovered Mr. Frank had been a German Reserve lieutenant during World War I.

"At once, Silberbauer's attitude changed," Frank told the Dutch detective that examined him after the war, "he even looked for a moment as if he was going to snap to attention in front of me" (22). Later, Silberbauer seemed ready to accept a bribe from a Dutch friend that had brought food and supplies to the "secrete annexe." But this strategy, that Anne had hoped would save them, proved futile. "I'm sorry but I can't do anything for you," Silberbauer told Miep Gies, "I'm not senior enough" (25).

Anne created a utopian space where she could hope; a place where she saw herself alive after the war. As Levitas explains, "utopia is the expression of desire and desire may outstrip hope while not necessarily outstripping possibility" (164), but in this case, Anne's desire may have outstripped possibility and not hope. Except for the very rare moments of introspection, Anne lives for the future she assumes will be hers. She maintains that the curtains she and her father put up the first day they arrived are "not to come down until we emerge from here" (217). She has decided to work hard at her studies, including French where she plans to "manage to pump in five irregular verbs per day," because she "doesn't want to be in the first form" when she's fourteen or fifteen (240). Later, she says, "We often discuss postwar problems, for example, how one out to address servants" (249). Several of her concerns and desires center on "after the war." "I'm afraid I shall use up all my brains too quickly, and I haven't got so very many. Then I shall not have any left for when the war is over" (330). "I can hardly wait for the day that I shall be able to comb through the public library" (589). When she and Peter get close, she doesn't worry if they will survive, instead she wonders how their relationship will progress: " ... I don't know what he will be like when he grows up, nor do I know whether we should love each other enough to marry" (554).

By assuming a better future—which in her case, is any future at all—Anne delineates a vast utopian space where she can look past the present, inspiring those who are faced with horrible circumstances beyond their control to do the same. Her attitude enlarges two cramped spaces: the physically small "Secret Annexe," and a depression-generated emotional cocoon that she refuses to enter. In conventional utopian terminology, she takes on the role of a guide. The visitor is Kitty; an imaginary audience she created to address in her diary. Anne makes Kitty her companion in retreat from the madness: "I don't want to set down a series of bald facts ... I want this diary to be my friend, and I shall call my friend Kitty" (177). She welcomes Kitty into her utopia with playful reassurance, telling her "it's more like being on vacation in a very peculiar boardinghouse" (216).

Anne continues to sugarcoat reality for Kitty by showing her how imagination can be a powerful coping mechanism. "When I get up in the morning, which is ... a very unpleasant process, I jump out of bed thinking to myself: 'You'll be back in a second'" (393). "If I have to eat something that I simply can't stand; I put my plate in front of me, pretend that it is something delicious, look at it as little as possible, and before I know where I am, it is gone"(393).

When the terror outside spills into Anne's world, she shields Kitty. On February 3, 1944, she reported overhearing a conversation among the adults that ended with the following: "... it's a fact that in Poland and Russia millions and millions of people have been murdered and gassed." Instead of pondering these facts, she reassures Kitty; and herself: "Kitty, I'll leave it at that, spare you further details. I myself keep very quiet and don't take any notice of the fuss and excitement" (481). After burglars have broken into the warehouse, the inhabitants of the "secret annexe" assume neighbors will call the police to investigate. When the police arrive, Anne hears them climbing up the stairs to their hiding place, rattling the swinging cupboard that disguises the entrance to "het achterhuis." Anne feared immediate capture: she wrote "this moment is indescribable" (593).

Contrasting Anne's approach with Jacobs's further elucidates the utopian intention of Anne's diary as opposed to Jacob's purpose in writing her after-the-fact narrative in diary form. "I have not exaggerated the wrongs inflicted by Slavery:" Jacobs wrote in her preface, "on the contrary, my descriptions fall far short of the facts.... I have not written my experiences ... to excite sympathy for my sufferings. But I do earnestly desire to arouse the women of the North to a realizing sense of the condition of two millions of women in the South, still in bondage, suffering what I suffered, and most of them far worse"(1).

Unlike Jacobs, and other inhabitants of the "secret annexe' who function as foils, Anne's purpose prevents her from dwelling on the worst. Her utopia functions the way Bloch describes a concrete utopia as "more centrally turned towards the world: of overtaking the natural course of events"(12). She sees the present and consciously alters it in her entries, thus supporting Raymond William's contention that "What makes something utopian is not just a quality of otherness, but the element of transformation, requiring continuity and connectedness to the present. And the transformation ... is a willed transformation, not one which comes about by technological change or the alteration of external circumstances" (quoted in Levitas 124). Anne couldn't affect her external circumstances, but by writing down her perceptions she willed the transformation of the Nazi-induced present into her own utopian space. Early on, she used her mother and sister to show Kitty what not to do, contrasting their collapsing with Anne's clearing up when the Frank family first went into hiding. In the following excerpt, she compares her mother's approach to melancholy with hers.

> Mummy[s] ... counsel when one feel melancholy is: "Think of all the misery in the world and be thankful that you are not sharing in it." My advise is: " ... think of all the beauty that's still left in and around you and be happy!"
>
> I don't see how Mummy's idea can be right, because then how are you supposed to behave if you go through the misery yourself? Then you are lost. On the contrary, I've found that there is always some beauty left, if only you look for it ... (519-20)

Anne says focus on the beauty to escape the misery. She concludes: "He who has courage and faith will never perish in misery!" (520)

Her thoughts went beyond facts to manufacture a resiliency to depression and defeat. The diary itself thus takes on another characteristic of a traditional utopia, the conversion narrative. Anne's conversion culminates with a poignant declaration of her firm faith in ideals "in spite of everything"—the overriding message for her audience of post-Holocaust readers. She sees how despondency destroys the soul and counterattacks it with a credo she sets down in the third from final entry in her diary, two-and-a-half weeks before the Gestapo was led to "het achterhuis."

"That's the difficulty in these times," Anne wrote on Saturday, July 15, 1944 after about two years and two weeks in hiding.

Ideals, dreams and cherished hopes rise within us, only to meet the horrible truth and be shattered. It's really a wonder that I haven't dropped all my ideals, because they seem so absurd and impossible to carry out. Yet I keep them, because in spite of everything I still believe that people are really good at heart.

I simply can't build up my hopes on a foundation consisting of confusion, misery, and death, I see the world gradually being turned into a wilderness, I hear the ever approaching thunder, which will destroy us too, I can feel the sufferings of millions and yet, if I look into the heavens, I think that it will all come right, that this cruelty too will end, and that peace and tranquility will return again. In the meantime, I must uphold my ideals, for perhaps the time will come when I shall be able to carry them out! (694)

III

Directly and succinctly, Anne explained why she delineated an imaginary better world when reality dictated otherwise, thus addressing Levitas's assertion that "sometimes utopia embodies more than an image of what the good life would be and becomes a claim about what it could and should be: the wish that things might be otherwise becomes a conviction that it does not have to be like this" (1). Anne's insistence on changing the present—if only in her diary—again underscores a perspective shared by other Jewish writers like Mannheim who wrote, "men, while thinking, are also acting" (295). By filtering the present through her words, Anne performs as one of Paul Tillich's "bearers of utopia ... those who are able to transform reality" (299) and delineates a utopia that does "transform reality in its own image" (Levitas 74). Anne's diary thus addresses a concern Levitas has with Mannheim. Levitas states "to identify an idea as a utopia ... we have to establish that the idea was instrumental in effecting the change, which in practice is very difficult to do even with the benefit of hindsight" (75). As pointed out in the introduction, Anne's work is both the idea and the change. As many of the above examples illustrate, it is precisely her ideas that changed her world.

Anne not only could, but had to write utopian literature as an affirmation of her "ideals, dreams, and cherished hopes." She had to fill the space opened up by Bloch—"the risen horizon that is rising even higher" (7)

—or as Levitas elucidates Block's Not-yet-Become—"the space that ... requires utopia in order that humanity may be able to imagine, will and effect the future" (101). As Tillich expressed it, "all utopias strive to negate the negative itself in human existence; it is the negative in existence which makes the idea of utopia necessary" (297). *The Diary of Anne Frank* blares a message of hope and direction amid the Holocaust-induced pessimistic view of humanity and as a tribute to the utopian force within the soul of a single human being. Anne exemplifies Bloch's positive conclusion to this first volume of *The Principle of Hope*: "Mankind and the world carry enough good future; no plan is itself good without this fundamental belief within it" (447).

IV

Perhaps there are over 15 million copies of Anne Frank's diary, a well-attended museum at the former "het achterhuis," and a recently published Dutch-language children's book (*Anne Frank* about her life before the Holocaust, because Anne offers more than Elie Wiesel's view of a Holocaust utopia: "In war years, another piece of bread is Utopia" (39). Wiesel wrote this after spending years in concentration camps while Anne Frank wrote her diary before she was sent to one. This may or may not explain why Anne can concentrate more on feeding and expanding the soul, not the body; the reader's soul as well as her own. Instead of assuming the impossibility of writing utopian literature during a time when a great deal of political, technological, scientific, and religious energy sought to empower evil, one could assume the opposite: such repression of good demands unrealistic hope and unreasonable courage. As her father, Otto Frank, wrote the introduction to *A Tribute to Anne Frank*, "However touching and sincere the expressions of sympathy I receive may be, I always reply that it is not enough to think of Anne with pity or admiration. Her diary should be a source of inspiration toward the realization of the ideals and hopes she expressed in it" (Steenmeyer 7). In the midst of horror, Anne Frank certainly made a utopian assumption by writing a survival manual for preserving ideals, thereby providing the hope we sometimes despair of finding. "the dream becomes a vision only when hope is invested in an agency capable of transformation. The political problem remains the search for that agency" (Levitas 200). *The Diary of Anne Frank* asserts that the agency capable of transformation is one of us at a time.

NOTES

*Acknowledgement—I would like to thank Professor Kenneth M. Roemer for his ongoing help in creating this article. His initial skepticism when I first presented the idea to him for my term paper pushed me toward more logical and complex justifications for my arguments. Once convinced, he provided me with unending support, encouragement and suggestions. I am deeply grateful.

" ... in addition to the six million Jewish men, women and children who were murdered at least an equal number of non-Jews were also killed, not in the heat of battle, not by military siege, aerial bombardment or the harsh conditions of modern war, but by deliberate, planned murder. These include Polish civilians killed after Poland's capitulation ...,the first, mostly non-Jewish victims at Auschwitz ..., the tens of thousands of victims of the Nazi euthanasia programme ... the non-Jews killed with Jews in the slave labour camps of the Sahara ..., the Serbs killed with Jews in April 1941 and January 1942 ..., the Czech villagers massacred at Lidice ..., the Poles expelled and murdered in the Zamosc province ..., the Gypsies deported to the death camps ..., the non-Jews killed with Jews in the reprisal action in Rome ..., Greeks and Italians taken hostage and drowned with Jews in the Aegean ..., the French villagers massacred at Oradour-sur-Glane ..., and the tens of thousands of Gypsies, Russian prisoners-of-war, Spanish republicans, Jehovah's Witnesses and homosexuals murdered at Mauthausen ... " (Gilbert 11).

"Secret Annexe" is put in quotation marks because it is not an exact translation of the Dutch expression "het achterhuis." As the editors of the English version of the diary published in 1952 explain in the frontispiece, this was done "to simplify the English text." It actually means "behind," or "in back of house"—"literally, the house behind."

REFERENCES

Bauman, Zygmunt. *Socialism: The Active Utopia*. Ed. T.B. Bottomore and M.J. Mulkay. Plymouth, Eng.: Clarke, Doble & Brendon, 1976.

Berneri, Marie Louse. *Journey Through Utopia*. London: Routledge & Kegan paul, 1050. NY: Books for Libraries Press, 1969.

Bloch, Ernst. *The Principle of Hope*. Trans. Neville Plaice, Stephen Plaice and Paul Knight. Vol. 1. Cambridge: MIT P, 1986.

Frank, Anne. *Dagboek Van Anne Frank: Het Achterhuis*. Amsterdam, The Netherlands: Contact, 1968.

Frank, Anne, *The Diary of Anne Frank: The Critical Edition*. Ed. David Barnouw and Gerrold van der Stroom. Trans. Arnold J. Pomerans and B.M. Mooyaart-Doubleday. NY: Doubleday, 1989.

Frontispiece. *Anne Frank: The Diary of a Young Girl* by Anne Frank. Trans. B.M. Mooyaart-Doubleday. NY: Pocket Book, 1973.

Gilbert, Martin. *The Macmillan Atlas of the Holocaust*. NY: Macmillan, 1982.

Hawthorne, Nathaniel. "Hall of Fantasy," *Selected Tales and Sketches*. Introd. Hyatte, H. Waggoner. 3rd. ed. NY: Holt, 12970. 461-473.

Iser, Wolfgang. *The Implied Reader: Patterns of Communication in Prose Fiction from Bunyan to Beckett*. Baltimore: Johns Hopkins UP, 1974.

Jacobs, Harriety A. *Incidents in the Life of a Slave Girl: Written by Herself*. Ed. L. Maria Child. Ed. Jean Fagan Yellin. Harvard UP, 1987.

Levitas, Ruth. *The Concept of Utopia*. Syracuse UP, 1990. Hemel Hempstead, Eng: Philip Allan 1990.

Mannheim, Karl. *Ideology and Utopia*. Trans. Louis Wirth and Edward Shils. NY: Harcourt, 1936.

Moylan,Tom. *Demand the Impossible*. NY: Metheun, 1986.

Plank, Robert. "The Modern Shrunken Utopia." *America as Utopia: Collected Essays*. Ed. Kenneth M. Roemer. NY: Burt Franklin, 1981. 206-230.

Roemer, Kenneth M., Ed. *Introduction. America as Utopia*. NY: Burt Franklin, 1981.3.

Sargent, Lyman Tower. *British and American Utopian Literature, 1516–1985*. NY: Garland, 1988.xii.

Steenmeyer, Anna G., ed., Frank, Otto and van Praag, Henri, collab. *A Tribute to Anne Frank*. NY: Doubleday, 1971.

Tillich, Paul. "Critique and Justification of Utopia." *Utopias and Utopian Thought*. Ed. Frank E. Manuel. Boston: Houghton, 1966.

[Wisel, Elie section from a group interview of numerous authors]. "Utopia." *Omni* (April 1988): 39.

LAWRENCE L. LANGER

The Literature of Auschwitz

In the beginning was the testimony. Any study of the literature of Auschwitz may start with judicial versions of the way it was, based on eyewitness accounts—but it can never end there. Readers of the proceedings of the so-called Auschwitz trial of former camp guards that ran for twenty months in Frankfurt (and which I attended for a few days in the summer of 1964) will discover not a narrative leading to insight and understanding, but a futile dispute between accusers and accused. The prisoners in the dock deny virtually everything: Mulka was not there when the prosecution says he was; Kaduk never shot anyone; Boger used his infamous torture instrument, the "Boger swing," only on rare occasions; Klehr was on leave during Christmas 1942, when he was charged with murdering inmates by injecting phenol into the heart. Guilt exists, but the agent is always someone else.

Little in this bizarre courtroom drama leads to a unified vision of the place we call Auschwitz. Scenes remain episodic and anecdotal; scenarios never coalesce; characters stay vague, as protagonists dissolve into helpless victims (through no failure of will, to be sure, but the tyranny of circumstance) while antagonists collapse into mistaken identities or innocent puppets maneuvered from afar. What awareness can emerge from an incident like the following, which casts its net of censure so widely that we strain to unsnarl the agents from the victims?

A group of prisoners in Auschwitz was excavating a ditch filled with

From *Admitting the Holocaust.* © 1995 by Lawrence L. Langer.

water. A witness testifies that some SS men forced them to leap into the
ditch:

> They had to jump into the water and swim. Then they ordered a
> prisoner named Isaac—he was called Isaac the Strong in the
> camp—to drown his comrades. Finally they also ordered him to
> kill his own father. In the act of drowning his father, Isaac went
> berserk and started to scream. So Stark [one of the SS guards on
> trial] shot Isaac in the water.

Faced with the accusation, Stark spurns his role: "I have nothing to say,
because I was not present at any of the incidents the witness described."[1]
Such painful testimony may carry the conviction of truth, despite Stark's
dissent, but by its very nature the judicial process does not allow it to do so
unchallenged. The defense promptly begins to discredit the witness with
witnesses of its own, whose evidence may indeed be false—the court is
dubious—but how can we ever know? At the moment when Isaac the Strong
became Isaac the Mad, he crossed a frontier separating the "normal world"
from the abnormal universe of Auschwitz, leaving us beyond the barrier
musing on the chance of ever entering into its reality ourselves.

The literature of Auschwitz exists to help us navigate that voyage. It is a
perilous journey but a crucial one, if we are ever to admit how little the idea
of justice helps us in our efforts to pierce the dark core of that death camp
experience. We must confront it on *its* terms, not ours, leaving behind
traditional casts of characters with their Isaacs the Strong, and the heroism
and tragedy implicit in such titles. In our search for the *meaning* of
Auschwitz, to our dismay, we meet often only its absence; what we have to
forgo to establish contact with such barren terrain is the theme that absorbs
most writers who venture into it.

Not all commentators, of course, agree that the terrain is so barren or
that we must forgo so much in order to wander there. The leading exponent
of the view that in spite of Auschwitz, life and suffering are unconditionally
meaningful, is Viktor Frankl, whose *Man's Search for Meaning* is still probably
the most widely read text on the subject. Frankl's strategy is to minimize the
atrocities he himself survived, and to stress the connections between pre- and
post-Auschwitz reality. Unintentionally confirming the wish of his
persecutors, he leaves his fellow victims anonymous, while naming and
quoting instead a long list of explorers of the human spiritual condition,
including Spinoza, Schopenhauer, Tolstoy, Dostoevsky, Rilke, Nietzsche,
and Thomas Mann. The reader is thus prompted to believe, for example,

that Tolstoy's Christian novel *Resurrection* or Dostoevsky's Christian declaration—"There is only one thing that I dread: not to be worthy of my sufferings"[2]—is somehow relevant to the Jewish victims of Auschwitz.

Frankl has managed to transform his ordeal in Auschwitz into a renewed encounter with the literary and philosophical giants who preceded its emergence, thus preserving the intellectual and spiritual traditions they championed and his own legacy as an heir to their minds. He uncovers truth by assertion, not analysis, as if the word were an eternally valid bulwark against the dehumanizing assaults of physical violence. Many witnesses in the courtroom at Frankfurt would have been bewildered by the scriptural finality of his proclamation that "if there is a meaning in life at all, then there must be a meaning in suffering."[3]

Frankl's language invites, indeed *requires* us to dismiss the petitions of despair before we confront them. Consider the testimony of Joseph Glück, who happened to be in the witness stand on one of the days that I was present in the courtroom. I remember the figure of a shrunken, elderly Jewish man who seemed crushed and exhausted by his memories, though he had not yet begun to recite them. He whispered hesitantly, seemingly intimidated by the large hall where the proceedings had been moved when the room in the Palace of Justice proved too small, by the ranks of the accused and their lawyers, and by the crowd of spectators.

He had been deported to Auschwitz from Klausenburg with 2800 other Jews, 400 of whom were chosen for work upon arrival. The rest were sent directly to the gas chambers, including his wife, two children, mother, sister with her two children, brother, mother-in-law, and sister-in-law. His situation is certainly not unique, but his statements stun the audience. Asked if he is the sole survivor, he replies "Yes": "For a moment the word hovers over the courtroom, irrevocable but uncertain to whom and where it should turn so that it might not only be heard but also comprehended. The old man sits motionless."[4] No one is foolish enough to ask him if there is meaning in his suffering, or whether he feels worthy of it. The judge shuffles the papers in front of him. Everyone there, including me, grapples with the question of how to translate his simple affirmative, a word haunting the air like a scrap of animated anguish, into a shareable experience. That instant remains vivid to me because it was one of the first times that I asked myself how a literature of Auschwitz, and of the Holocaust in general, might ever achieve such a goal.

This is the focus of our inquiry. From the multiple talents that have addressed themselves to this issue emerges a complex, at times contradictory vision of a way of existing that continues to elude precise definition. For example, against Viktor Frankl's insistence on the power of literature and philosophy to sustain the inner self during the camp ordeal, we have the contrary view of Jean Améry, a classic exposition of the futility of literary memory once it entered the precincts of Auschwitz. Because the mind in Auschwitz collided not merely with death, but with the kind of dying peculiar to an extermination camp, normal responses lost their value. The intellectual was left suddenly defenseless: "Death lay before him, and in him the spirit was still stirring; the latter confronted the former and tried—in vain, to say it straight off—to exemplify its dignity."[5] Frankl argues that Auschwitz challenged the individual to rise above his outward fate, furnishing him "with the chance of achieving something through his own suffering."[6] Améry insists that both fate and suffering disappeared from the vocabulary of Auschwitz, as did death itself, to be replaced by the single fear, shared by all, of *how* one would die: "Dying was omnipresent; death vanished from sight."[7]

Foreseeing the bleakness of a future without the heritage of his literary past, Frankl seems to have decided to treat Auschwitz as a temporary anomaly rather than a permanent rupture; his pledge to inner freedom and the life of the spirit flows from that choice. Entering the world of Auschwitz, as he reflected on it afterward, left Améry with a totally different vista of past *and* future:

> The first result was always the total collapse of the *esthetic* view of death. What I am saying is familiar [though less so, one suspects, than Améry believed]. The intellectual, and especially the intellectual of German education and culture, bears the esthetic view of death within him. It was his legacy from the distant past, at the very latest from the time of German romanticism. It can be more or less characterized by the names Novalis, Schopenhauer, Wagner, and Thomas Mann. For death in its literary, philosophic, or musical form there was no place in Auschwitz. No bridge led from death in Auschwitz to *Death in Venice*. Every poetic evocation of death became intolerable, whether it was Hesse's "Dear Brother Death" or that of Rilke, who said: "Oh Lord, give each his own death." The esthetic view of death had revealed itself to the intellectual as part of an esthetic *mode of life;* where the latter had been all but forgotten, the former was nothing but an elegant trifle. In the camp no Tristan music accompanied death, only the roaring of the SS and the Kapos.[8]

A major function of the literature of Auschwitz is to help us discard the moral, philosophical, and literary systems created by what Améry calls the "esthetic mode of life," systems defining character and action and the tragic sense itself. This becomes especially necessary when they bar the world of Auschwitz from our efforts to enter its realm.

How are we to understand Améry's avowal that in Auschwitz the intellect "nullified itself when at almost every step it ran into its un-crossable borders"? The results were devastating: "The axes of its traditional frames of reference then shattered. Beauty: that was an illusion. Knowledge: that turned out to be a game with ideas."[9] In the presence of this warning, we struggle to prevent our own discourse about Auschwitz from becoming merely a game with ideas. One way out of the dilemma is to accept the threatening possibility of how easily Auschwitz reduced earnest pleas like Rilke's "Oh Lord, give each his own death" to nothing but elegant trifles, utterly irrelevant to the modes of survival available in the camp. Our reluctant surrender of what Améry calls the "esthetic mode of life" is an admission of the powerful role it plays in shaping the conduct and belief of Western civilization and of how bereft we appear without its support, and of the social and economic "modes" that accompany it.

The arriver at Auschwitz entered a world of sensation, not mind: the roar of the SS and Kapos; the bursts of flame and smoke spiraling from chimneys; the rank smell of charred flesh. In a remarkable, little-known story called "Phantoms, My Companions," Auschwitz survivor Charlotte Delbo enacts this encounter, as her narrator journeys by boxcar toward Auschwitz, accompanied by leading characters of the French dramatic repertoire, from Molière to Giradoux. One by one, frightened by the uncertainties looming before them, they leap from the train, until when it arrives and the doors are thrown open, only Alceste, the Misanthrope, remains. He gazes wildly at the bleak, obscure landscape—and disappears, leaving the narrator to the world of corrosive sensation that the aesthetic mode of life had done nothing to prepare Alceste for. Denied the options of art, the narrator faces her doom alone.

Dialogue is the heart of drama; Molière's Misanthrope is disgusted by the social pretensions and hypocrisy that pass for talk among his peers. As Améry describes the content of dialogues in Auschwitz, however, we begin to glimpse how thoroughly camp reality disarmed traditional notions of the aesthetic mode of life, how useless an Alceste would be to counsel or rebuke in such a place: "Inmates carried on conversations about how long it probably takes for the gas in the gas chambers to do its job. One speculated on the painfulness of death by phenol injection. Were you to wish yourself a blow to the skull or a slow death through exhaustion in the infirmary?"[10] The literature of Auschwitz makes constant inroads on our assumptions not only about the aesthetic mode of life (which the quoted passage reduces to incoherence), but also about the actuality on which it is based. The universe of dying that was Auschwitz yearns for a language purified of the taint of normality.

Primo Levi, who more than anyone else wrote and rewrote the experience of Auschwitz in search of its significance for him and for us, evokes that instant when at war's end the world of the living faced in embarrassed silence the world of the surviving dead. He tries to analyze the internal content of that momentous meeting, as the first four Russian soldiers to enter Auschwitz gaze at Levi and his gaunt comrades:

> They did not greet us, nor did they smile; they seemed oppressed not only by compassion, but by a confused restraint, which sealed their lips and bound their eyes to the funereal scene. It was that shame we knew so well, the shame that drowned us after the selections, and every time we had to watch, or submit to, some outrage: the shame the Germans did not know, that the just man experiences at another man's crime; the feeling of guilt that such a crime should exist, that it should have been introduced irrevocably into the world of things that exist, and that his will for good should have proved too weak or null, and should not have availed in defence.[11]

Inversions cancel meaning here, and then challenge its rebirth in the desolate and arid moral soil of Auschwitz. Liberators "oppressed" by compassion; victims shamed by the crimes they witnessed, but did not commit; the innocent feeling guilty, the criminal unashamed; but most of all, the visible failure of good to carry out its historic mission of unmasking and overwhelming evil—such inversions discredit the traditional power of language and the meaning it is accustomed to serve.

More than any other commentator, Levi spent his life trying to explain the nature of the contamination that was Auschwitz. It represented a stain not just on individuals, but on time and history too. The Auschwitz trial was concerned with what was done, and by whom. The premise behind it was that identifying guilt and punishing crime would make a difference in a society based on order. But for Levi, the reach of the moral chaos that nurtured Auschwitz was so vast that justice could not begin to embrace it or define its limits. That was a task for the writer, as Levi shows:

So for us even the hour of liberty rang out grave and muffled, and filled our souls with joy and yet with a painful sense of pudency, so that we should have liked to wash our consciences and our memories clean from the foulness that lay upon them; and also with anguish because we felt that this should never happen, that now nothing could ever happen good and pure enough to rub out our past, and that the scars of the outrage would remain within us for ever, and in the memories of those who saw it, and in the places where it occurred, and in the stories that we should tell of it.[12]

Levi is honest enough to concede that moral fatigue at the hour of liberty may have been the initial source of this daunting vision. But when he wrote about it soon after war's end, he found the language to confirm its deep and permanent impact on our time:

Because, and this is the awful privilege of our generation and of my people, no one better than us has ever been able to grasp the incurable nature of the offence, that spreads like a contagion. It is foolish to think that human justice can eradicate it. It is an inexhaustible fount of evil; it breaks the body and the spirit of the submerged, it stifles them and renders them abject; it returns as ignominy upon the oppressors, it perpetuates itself as hatred among the survivors, and swarms around in a thousand ways against the very will of all, as a thirst for revenge, as a moral capitulation, as denial, as weariness, as renunciation.[13]

Some literature of Auschwitz, in a desperate retreat from charges like these about the infection spreading from the very existence of the place, seeks vindication in a countervision that would restore moral health to the victims, imposing shame and accusation on the culprits alone. It resists Levi's acute but paradoxical sense that shame and *self*-accusation, however unwarranted, nonetheless remained a burden for him and many of his fellow former prisoners throughout their lives—in the end, a burden that consumed and probably destroyed him.

The unendurable truths of Auschwitz that Levi expounded with such courage and distinction do not merge easily with traditional literary forms. Thirty years ago, Rolf Hochhuth's bold historical drama *The Deputy* burst on the literary scene in a scandal of controversy. Today it reads like a tame piece of theater indeed, though when I saw it in Vienna in 1964, Hochhuth's setting of the last act in Auschwitz itself seemed a dazzling and agonizing innovation. It testified to how little the imagination must have been prepared then for a literature of Auschwitz. Hochhuth himself paid tribute to this idea in some preliminary remarks in the printed text, revealing his conviction— common at the time, but less so, one hopes, today—that we "lack the imaginative faculties to be able to envision Auschwitz."[14] So much commentary currently exists on the camp (including this volume), that such an attitude now appears naïve and even antiquated. But it was a protective device, one thankfully discarded by artists greater than Hochhuth like Tadeusz Borowski and Charlotte Delbo.

In his efforts to realize Auschwitz on the stage, Hochhuth dismisses documentary naturalism as a stylistic principle, concluding that "no matter how closely we adhere to historical facts, the speech, scene, and events on the stage will be altogether surrealistic."[15] This is a perfectly legitimate point of view; Elie Wiesel describes his arrival at Auschwitz amid the flames of burning pits as a visionary nightmare. But when Hochhuth shifts from setting to character, he lapses into figures so conventional that he sacrifices any surrealistic effect achieved by the vague movements of the doomed toward the gas chambers in the dim recesses of the stage. The Priest and the Doctor are so clearly defined as adversaries in the contest between Good and Evil that they dwindle into allegory, a final fatal to *any* adequate representation of Auschwitz in art.

The confrontation between the Priest and the Doctor reflects, on a smaller scale, the epic encounters between Milton's Satan and God's angelic hosts, though Auschwitz has altered the theological balance. The Priest becomes a tragic martyr, improbably choosing to share the fate of the Jews, while the Doctor, the spirit of cynical negation, betrays his ancestry in Ivan Karamazov's devil, a less sinister but equally contemptuous literary prototype. His obvious real model is Josef Mengele, though Hochhuth is not interested in developing a reliable portrait of that notorious figure. He succumbs instead to the blandishments of literary precedents, offering a familiar metaphysical dispute between the ruthless nihilism of the Doctor and the compassion of the Priest, weakened by the failure of the pope and Catholic hierarchy to assert their spiritual force in opposition to the powers of destruction.

Sounding more like Dostoevsky's Grand Inquisitor than a character from a play about Auschwitz, the Doctor unwittingly reveals his literary origins:

The truth is, Auschwitz refutes
creator, creation, and the creature.

Life as an idea is dead.
This may well be the beginning
of a great new era,
a redemption from suffering.
From this point of view only one crime
remains: cursed be he who creates life.
I cremate life.[16]

The commonplace disguised as the profound may betray the limitations of the Doctor's intellect, since his voice falls far short of Ivan Karamazov's mighty indictment of God's world that still beguiles readers into accepting it as Dostoevsky's position too. The real point of *The Deputy* is to charge the Roman Catholic Church with a spiritual timidity that was partly responsible for enabling the historic designs of the Third Reich to end in the gas chambers of Auschwitz. But the verbal premises on which the structure of the play is built—good, evil, conscience, truth, spirit, love—do not carry us very far into the daily tensions and moral conflicts of life in Auschwitz itself, nor do they illuminate the natures of men like Mengele, whose elusive motives are hidden behind the taunting, caustic façade of the Doctor's single-minded voice.

A play that discards the metaphysics of Auschwitz as a theme and turns instead to what we might call its materiality is Peter Weiss's *The Investigation*, whose content derives almost wholly from testimony at the trial in Frankfurt. By blending and shaping statements from witnesses and the accused into a carefully organized pattern, Weiss creates from the futile courtroom dispute a fresh vision of the clash in Auschwitz between moral space and destructive place. Although naked testimony may lead the imagination only into confusion, silence, and despair, the form imposed on it by Weiss achieves the opposite effects. Guards and officers in the end indict themselves by their own relentless but transparently false denials of complicity, while the language of the victims finally sheds a terrifying light on the ordeals they succumbed to—or wretchedly survived.

Weiss's drama confirms the difficulty, not to say impossibility, of creating a literature of Auschwitz by relying purely on the powers of invention. In the cast of characters, he identifies each of the "accused" in his play by their real names, since it is these particular agents of mass murder we need to understand, not their dramatic prototypes. The witnesses, however, remain anonymous, spokesmen and spokeswomen for the vast numbers who are unable to speak for themselves (though a few of the witnesses represent the voices of former SS men not on trial who worked in various administrative capacities in the camp). The imagination is drawn into the landscape of Auschwitz by states of feeling inspired by the testimony, condensed evidence that slowly moves us from a sense of how things were to an encounter with what they implied.

Unlike Hochhuth, Weiss does not present Auschwitz as a harrowing inferno, alienating us through the awesomeness of the atrocities committed there. One of his witnesses insists:

> We must drop the lofty view
> that the camp world
> is incomprehensible to us
> We all knew the society
> that produced a government
> capable of creating such camps

Earlier, the same witness had insisted:

> When we talk of our experience nowadays
> with people who were never in a camp
> there is always something
> inconceivable to them about it
> And yet they are the same people
> who in the camp were prisoners and guards[17]

Weiss lowers the barriers of the unimaginable, however, not merely by the statements of his witnesses, but chiefly by the studied arrangement of the eleven multipart "songs" that constitute the scenes of his drama. Beginning with the "Song of the Platform" and the "Song of the Camp" and ending with the "Song of Cyklon B" (the chemical agent of extermination) and the "Song of the Fire Ovens" (the site of physical annihilation), Weiss gradually narrows the space separating the imagination from the camp, leading us from the ramp to the barrack, through various execution sites like the Black Wall (outside) and the cells of Block 11 (indoors), to the gas chambers and the body's final confined destination, the crematorium. The victim's shrinking fate is thus duplicated by the sequence of the testimonies, which in their quest for literal truth have made available through the shaping pen of the dramatist the imagined truth of Auschwitz too.

Unfortunately, the literature of Auschwitz can also be used for political purposes. One distressing enigma of Weiss's text is his refusal to identify the Jews as the primary victims of the murder machinery in the camp, though attentive readers could not possibly mistake his references to the 6 million "persecuted" or to those "killed for racial reasons." Because the events of Auschwitz are still anchored firmly in historical memory, mention of Mengele and Cyklon B and the crematorium are enough to remind us of the destruction of European Jewry. Weiss's universalizing tendency, however, may become more of a problem for future generations, for whom the allusive power of these brief labels will have lost their specific, not to say metaphorical, value. Fortunately, Weiss's play will not be the only source of Holocaust actuality for those generations, for whom the literature of Auschwitz will consist, as it does for us, of a multiplicity of voices and points of view to guide us through its dismal labyrinth.

The boundaries separating the historical moment from its imaginative portrayal may be instructively studied in Elie Wiesel's *Night*, still one of the most concisely powerful narratives of the Auschwitz experience. Although widely read as an autobiographical memoir, *Night* also continues to be classified and critically acclaimed as a novel, and not without reason. Because it is a written text, *Night* suffers the curbs and enjoys the privileges of art, from which courtroom testimony, or any oral account of the Auschwitz ordeal, is exempt. Art in its essence invites us to see life other than it literally was, since all art, even the most objective naturalism, requires selection and composition, thus altering the purity (or, in this instance, the impurity) of the original event. In one of its aspects, Wiesel's text is a study of fathers and sons in Auschwitz, with all inmates being the children of God the Father. This lifts the narrative, to its credit, to be sure, beyond the constraints of autobiography into the realm of imagined fiction; nothing is more "literary" or stylized in the story than the young boy's denunciation of God's world and implied renunciation of its Creator, the seeds of both of which are nurtured by passages in Dostoevsky and Camus, in addition to the conditions of Auschwitz itself.

The literature of Auschwitz is thus bound by its historical context in a way that most other literature is not. Within the above-mentioned constraints, it faces the challenge familiar to all serious writers; finding an appropriate tone and point of view, a suitable angle of vision, a valid and convincing center of consciousness through which to filter the trial of atrocity. Although extravagantly fictionalized historical material about the Holocaust (as in Leslie Epstein's *King of the Jews*) may alienate some readers, a subtly imagined center of consciousness, invented or not, can draw them against their will into the net of human abuse, where their own sense of normal reality struggles to escape from the lure.

One of the finest examples we have of such a strategy is Tadeusz

Borowski's collection *This Way for the Gas, Ladies and Gentlemen*, published in Poland in 1959, though many of its stories were written shortly after the war when Borowski was in his early twenties. Dismissing Hochhuth's premise that we lack the imaginative faculties to be able to envision Auschwitz (formulated, ironically, years *after* Borowski's suicide in 1951), Borowski chronicles the divorce between reader expectation and inmate behavior through a casual and understated first-person narrative style. His narrators disarm us with the simplicity of their opening gambits, feigning a disinterest that is slowly undone by subsequent events. He refuses to supply us with guidelines for the inhuman tour we are about to begin, teasing our curiosity with hints of disorder that gradually invade our lingering innocence.

"All of us walked around naked," begins one of his stories, leaving his reader to wonder whether the speaker is Adam in the Garden of Eden or the resident of a nudist colony. The narrative then eases us into the place we call Auschwitz: "The delousing is finally over, and the striped suits are back from the tanks of Cyclone B solution, an efficient killer of lice in clothing ... " The clinical clues are puzzling, but not yet sinister, until the sentence finishes: "and of men in gas chambers."[18] Generations from now, this passage may require footnoting; when Borowski wrote it, it needed only assent. What he forces us to assent to, however, violates every value that civilization presumes to cherish; Borowski's stories portray the systematic mutilation of such values in the Auschwitz he knew and experienced.

One test of a literature of Auschwitz is its candor in imitating the atmosphere of moral and physical mutilation that the Germans deliberately created in the camps. The notions of heroism and villainy so central to Frankl and Hochhuth in their visions of Auschwitz vanish from Borowski's literary horizon. Andrzej Wirth, a Polish commentator on Borowski's art, helps us to understand why; Borowski's scenario, he argues,

> has nothing to do with the classical conception based on the necessity of choice between two systems of value. The hero of Borowski's stories is a hero *deprived of all choice*. He finds himself in a situation without choice because every choice is base. The tragedy lies not in the necessity of choosing but in the impossibility of making a choice.[19]

When the goal of moral being is not virtue, but staying alive, then our sense of character loses its mooring in literature. Scripture, or philosophy, and succumbs to circumstance—the awful predicament that Borowski energizes in his Auschwitz stories.

In the culture of coping that defined existence in the deathcamp, the survivor depended for his life—at least for a brief time—on the death of someone else. If the tragic figure is one who through action or attitude rebels against his destiny, what are we to make of one of Borowski's narrators, who helps to drive victims from the cattle cars, unloads their belongings, watches them being led off to the gas chambers, feels rage at his involvement in their fate instead of pride at his mastery of his own, and finds in an attack of nausea little relief from an environment that dehumanizes everyone—murderer, victim, and survivor? Life gestures are contaminated by death or become death gestures themselves. The narrator spends his rage in impotent silence, bereft of meaningful choice: "The air is filled with ghastly cries, the earth trembles beneath me, I can feel sticky moisture on my eyelids. My throat is completely dry." Earlier he had broken his silence by explaining to some Greek inmates in what he called "crematorium Esperanto" the challenge that lay before the Canada Commando, in which they worked: "*Transport kommen, alle Krematorium, compris?*" In the global idiom of mass murder, words do not dignify and communication brings neither community nor communion. He is victim himself of what he calls the only permissible form of charity in Auschwitz, the camp law dictating that "people going to their death must be deceived to the very end."[20]

Among Borowski's most important contributions to the literature of Auschwitz are his portraits of what Levi would later name the "functionary-prisoners" in the camp, those squad leaders or Kapos or other inmates who through luck or manipulation joined the internal power hierarchy and thus entered the gray zone of its moral life, prolonging their own temporary survival amid the murder of others—before them, around them, often in their place. People staying alive, he suggests, must also be "self-deceived" about the origin of their survival, though the very consciousness of this fact lurks menacingly beneath the façade of indifference that usually dominates his narrator's voice. He is concerned with the state of mind bred by being among the "privileged," and the psychological price one pays to remain there.

But the internal power hierarchy in Auschwitz was neither exclusively male nor non-Jewish, though this is the prevailing rule in Borowski's fictional vision. Sara Nomberg-Przytyk's *Auschwitz: True Tales from a Grotesque Land*, in a series of interconnected stories, chronicles the odyssey of a Jewish woman who joins the ranks of female functionary prisoners before our eyes, learning through the process what one must discard of one's civilized moral and psychological baggage in order to gain and retain that status. Although she will be low down in the hierarchy, Nomberg-Przytyk's narrator is not blind to the gray zone she is soon to enter:

The SS men saw the splendor in which the camp functionaries lived, but all this took place with their silent approval. It was a devilish system in which the SS men and the functionaries were united by a chain of cruelty. The contrast between their splendor and our misery kept them constantly aware of what they stood to lose in the event that they failed to carry out the orders of the SS men. They used whatever methods were necessary to assure their own survival and their relatively comfortable way of life. If the voice of conscience chanced to awake in them, they would quiet it continuously with the same arguments: "We suffered so much in the first few years. We lived through those hard times. Now we are not going to die for the sake of some dirty *zugang* [new arrival]."[21]

Such a passage may tempt us to believe that selfishness and brutality were the vital conditions for staying alive in this milieu, but the narrator discovers that motives in Auschwitz are far more baffling, controlled not by some inner system of values, but by circumstances unrelated to one's will.

She remembers thinking, for example,

that in Auschwitz there was nothing more important than trying to help your fellow sufferers and yet, at the same time, how immoral it was to decide whose suffering should be alleviated and whose should continue unabated. Who had given us the right to condemn or to save another? In Auschwitz there was no fairness in the merciless struggle for survival. Those with scruples died isolated and abandoned. That was the new order of the concentration camp.[22]

This is what Wirth means when he suggests that in Borowski's Auschwitz all choices are base, including the decision to aid a fellow sufferer. If the literature of Auschwitz can help us to understand nothing more than this troubling but truthful paradox, it will have vindicated its vexing challenge to the imagination.

In October 1944, Nomberg-Przytyk's narrator is working as a clerk in the hospital barrack. One evening, while she and her comrades are discussing the difference between conscious and unconscious death, the other clerk in the infirmary interrupts with a story that freezes the momentum of their abstract debate. She tells of a group of 156 Polish girls from Krakow, who had been sent to the clinic, so they thought, for examination before being shipped to work in Germany. "They were talking loudly, laughing, never dreaming that they had been horribly deceived and that the *Leichenauto* [vehicle serving as a hearse] was coming for them in about an hour." Clearly they are "fellow sufferers" who, as the functionary prisoners know, are about to be killed by phenol injection. How does one define one's human role at a moment like this? "Perhaps I should shout it out to them," says the speaker, "'Calm down! Don't laugh. You are living corpses, and in a few hours nothing will be left of you but ashes!' Then what? Then we attendants would go to the gas chambers and the women would die anyway."[23] Suddenly the question "Is it better for a human being to know that he is about to die?" assumes dimensions of complexity that no prior system of belief allows us to simplify.

Nomberg-Przytyk shares Borowski's talent for sketching the rupture between Auschwitz reality and conjectures about it—the prisoners' and our own. "We didn't tell them the truth," the speaker says,

> not out of fear for our own lives, but because we truly did not know what would be the least painful way for the young women to die.... If we told them what was in store for them, then a struggle for life would ensue. In their attempt to run from death they would find only loneliness, because their friends, seeking to preserve their own lives, would refuse to help them.[24]

Difficult as it is for us to imagine, not to say concede, mutual support becomes an academic question when the issue is death by phenol injection. Courage and truth itself shrivel into privileged virtues reserved for those living beyond the ominous shadows of the gas chamber.

In this instance, the young women themselves eventually discover what is in store for them, and a terrible outcry erupts. They are surrounded and beaten, and then each "was dragged screaming, by two SS men, into the presence of Mengele," who presumably administers the fatal injection. Some of the remaining victims try to run away. "Then the dogs were set on them. Their deaths were completely different from the deaths of the first batch of women who went to their deaths unknowing. Who knows which death was more difficult, but the first group seemed to die more peacefully." This story, called "The Verdict," suspends judgment but goads the reader into the role of juror through its conclusion: "'I still don't know whether we should have told the women about the death that was waiting for them. What do you think?' None of us said anything."[25]

The reader is left speechless too, silenced by the sorrowful if contrary fates of victims *and* survivors. Is there such a notion as "complicity through the eyes," by which a witness is diminished simply because of what she has seen? When Nomberg-Przytyk's narrator is freed, she does not rejoice. "I felt comfortable, warm and clean," she admits. "But I was not happy. I did not know why. Again and again I repeated to myself the refrain: 'Be happy, you are free.' But this did not help I was sad. Sadness strangled me."[26] Her response will seem odd only to those who have not immersed themselves in the literature of Auschwitz, where they are forced to discover how closely woven, morally and emotionally, are the stories of those whom Primo Levi, in a striking image, has called "the drowned and the saved."

If the saved remain tainted in their memories by the misfortune of the drowned, this is one of the melancholy bequests of the camp experience. "It was a logical consequence of the system," wrote Levi: "an inhuman regime spreads and extends its inhumanity in all directions, also and especially downward; unless it meets with resistance and exceptionally strong characters, it corrupts its victims and its opponents as well."[27] A corollary "logical consequence" of Auschwitz, to be extracted by the diligent moralist, is unfortunately this: there was no rein on the shame, humiliation, and torment that the Germans could inflict on their prey, no check to their malice, brutality, lust for ruin; their talent for atrocity was unlimited. Goodness, on the contrary, was curbed among the victims at every turn, by fear, hunger, thirst, confusion, illness, and despair. The *will* to compassion may have remained intact, but its power to oppose the ungoverned ferocity of the camps faltered before the sterile cruelty inherent in the system.

Few writers in the tradition of Auschwitz convey this painful truth with the dense immediacy of Charlotte Delbo, whose trilogy *Auschwitz et après (Auschwitz and After)* explores the fragmenting of the self and the uncoupling of its milieu that were the most enduring legacies of the camp experience.[28] For Delbo, Auschwitz was simply a place of unnatural, premature dying; her art represents a resolute search for a prose and poetry equal to this dismal fact. In her vision, the self is inseparable from the cold, hunger, and exhaustion that slowly erode its substance, until the crust of dignity formerly enclosing a human being loses its protective value and decays. She insists that we join her in witnessing what remains, as she and her fellow prisoners peer from a barrack window:

> At first we are not sure what we see. It is difficult at first to distinguish them from the snow. The yard is full of them. Naked. Lying close to each other on the snow. White, a white that looks bluish against the snow. Their heads are shaven, their pubic hairs are straight and stiff. The corpses are frozen. White with brown

nails. Their upturned toes are truly ridiculous. Terrible, ridiculous.[29]

Is unaccommodated woman no more than this? Behind the logical consequences of Levi's Auschwitz, legitimate as they are, lies the physical assault on the body that mirrored its indelible nucleus.

Into the heart of this nucleus Delbo's incantatory prose lures us, groping toward images to match the abrupt reversals implicit in her theme:

> Standing, wrapped in a blanket, a child, a little boy. A tiny shaven head, a face in which the jaws and the brow ridge stand out. Barefoot, he jumps up and down without stopping, with a frenzied movement that makes one think of that of savages dancing. He wants to wave his arms too to keep warm. The blanket slips open. It is a woman. A skeleton of a woman. She is naked. One can see her ribs and hip bones. She pulls the blanket up on her shoulders and continues to dance. A mechanical dance. A dancing skeleton of a woman. Her feet are small, thin and bare in the snow. There are living, dancing skeletons.[30]

This is a true art of revelation, though not in the familiar sense. Unlike Frankl, Delbo has no qualms about exposing a culture built on mistaken identities, enticed by traditions of Enlightenment and Romanticism into forming idealized versions of the inviolable self. Auschwitz has disfigured those traditions, leading Delbo to focus on the violated human form and to ask how such fragmentation might be integrated into the ambitions of future generations.

The irony of such a quest, not to say question, does not escape Delbo herself. She follows her description of the living, dancing skeleton with an early example of what has become a postmodern fashion—a self-reflective admission of the artifice of art: "And now I am sitting in a café writing this story—for this is turning into a story."[31] Can a literature of Auschwitz *ever* span the chasm between what we were and what the camp's very existence has made us a part of? Throughout her narrative, Delbo pays tribute to the women friends who supported her at those moments when she felt unable to go on, as if one impulse of her story were to reaffirm the strength of human community despite the assault of Auschwitz on its spirit. But in the end, this support proves a wan comfort; she records the collapse of identity, the "failure" of character, the splintered unity, the merging of women with a mute, unfruitful earth.

The last vignette in *None of Us Will Return* (the first volume of *Auschwitz and After*) is called "Springtime," an ironic dirge to the season of renewal from whose solace Delbo and her friends seem endlessly barred:

> All these lumps of flesh which had lost the pinkness and the life of flesh were strewn about in the dusty dried mud, were completing the process of withering and decomposing in the sunlight. All this brownish, purplish, gray flesh blended in so well with the dusty soil that it required an effort to pick out the women there, to make out empty breasts amid this puckered skin that hung from women's chests.[32]

As Delbo the artist composes, her characters "decompose," and this is the challenge that a literature of Auschwitz will always have to face. The realities of the camp continue to contradict the premises of form and of language itself, resulting in a split that may in fact define the bond between the writer and this material, and our possible access to it.

In the second volume of her Auschwitz trilogy, *Une Connaissance inutile* (*A Useless Knowledge*), Delbo offers a distilled variant on this dilemma:

> I'm back from another world
> to this world
> that I didn't leave
> and I don't know
> which is real
> tell me have I come back
> from that other world?
> As for me
> I'm still there
> and I'm dying
> back there
> every day a bit more
> I die again
> the death of all those who died
> and I no longer know what's real
> in this world
> from the other world-back-there
> now
> I no longer know

when I'm dreaming
and when
I'm not dreaming.[33]

We have only to compare the returns of Odysseus and Aeneas from their "other world-back-there" with Delbo's to see how radically a demythologized literature of Auschwitz differs from traditional epic encounters with the realm of death. Odysseus carefully keeps the dead from profaning his living person, while Aeneas comes back from his visit to the underworld with a happy prophecy of a future civilization. Neither would understand Delbo's doom-laden line "I die again / the death of all those who died," a line that stretches the circle of its recruits to include its audience as well.

The experience of Auschwitz, like all of the Holocaust, cannot be left behind. Nor do we return from our encounter with its literature unblemished. Instead, like Delbo, Levi, and all the rest, we face the necessary burden of adjustment. When Delbo admits "I return / from beyond knowledge / now I need to unlearn / otherwise it's clear / I couldn't go on living," she intends not to slight her past, but to invite us to share with her the twin vision that a journey through Auschwitz has etched on our culture. We pay a price for learning how to imagine what happened; then we add to our debt by feigning that beyond those mounds of corpses and heaps of ashes a chaste future is still feasible: "because it would be too stupid / in the end," as Delbo agrees, "for so many to have died / and for you to live / without making something of your life." But she frames this with a more somber paradox, one that echoes hollowly through the Holocaust universe, leaving us little but a bleak query to kindle hope:

I've spoken with death
so
I know
how useless were so many things we learned
but I gained this knowledge at the price of suffering
so great
I wonder
if it was worth it.[34]

Notes

1. Bernd Naumann, *Auschwitz: A Report on the Proceedings Against Rober Karl Ludwig Mulka and Others Before the Court at Frankfurt*, trans. Jean Steinberg (London: Pall Mall Press, 1996), 146, 147.

2. Quoted in Viktor Frankl *Man's Search for Meaning*, rev, and updated ed. (New York: Pocket Books, 1984), p. 87.

3. Ibid., p. 88.

4. Naumann, *Auschwitz*, p. 217.

5. Jean Améry, *At the Mind's Limits: Contemplations by a Survivor on Auschwitz and Its Realities*, trans. Sidney Rosenfeld and Stella P. Rosenfeld (New York: Schocken, 1986). p. 16.

6. Frankl, *Man's Search for Meaning*, p. 89.

7. Améry, *At the Mind's Limits*, p. 17.

8. Ibid., pp. 16-17.

9. Ibid., p. 19.

10. Ibid., p. 17.

11. Primo Levi, *The Reawakening: A Liberated Prisoner's Long March Home Through East Europe*, trans. Stuart Woolf (Boston: Little, Brown, 1965), p. 12. Although the book appeared in Italy in 1963, Levi says he finished writing it in 1947.

12. Ibid., pp. 12-13.

13. Ibid., p. 13.

14. Rolf Hochhuth, *The Deputy*, trans. Richard Winston and Clara Winston (New York: Grove Press, 1964), p. 222.

15. Ibid., p. 223

16. Ibid., p. 249

17. Peter Weiss, *The Investigation*, trans. Jon Swan and Ulu Grosbard (New York: Atheneum, 1966), pp. 108, 107-108.

18. Tadeusz Borowski, "This Way for the Gas, Ladies and Gentlemen," in *This Way for the Gas, Ladies and Gentlemen*, trans. Barbara Vedder (New York: Viking, 1967), p. 29.

19. Andrzej Wirth, "A Discovery of Tragedy: The Incomplete Account of Tadeusz Borowski," trans. Adam Czerniawki, *Polish Review* 12 (Summer 1967): 45.

20. Ibid., pp. 41, 35, 37. In some of my comments on Borowski, I draw on passages from my *Versions of Survival: The Holocaust and the Human Spirit* (Albany: State University of New York Press, 1982),

21. Sara Nomberg-Przytyk, *Auschwitz: True Tales from a Grotesque Land*, trans. Roslyn Hirsch (Chapel Hill: University of North Carolina Press, 1985), pp. 20-21.

22. Ibid., pp. 45-46.

23. Ibid., p. 111.

24. Ibid., p. 112.

25. Ibid., p. 113.

26. Ibid., pp. 153-154.

27. Primo Levi, *The Drowned and the Saved*, trans. Raymond Rosenthal (New York: Summit, 1988), p. 112.

28. Only *None of Us Will Return* exists in an English Version. Rosette Lamont's translation of all three volumes will be published by Yale University Press in the spring of 1995. Her translation of *Days and Memory* (Marlboro, Vt.: Marlboro Press, 1990) is a separate volume, also partly concerned with Delbo's Auschwitz experience.

29. Charlotte Delbo, *None of Us Will Return*, trans, John Githens (New York: Grove Press, 1968), p. 20.

30. Ibid., p. 31.

31. Ibid.

32. Ibid., p. 122.

33. Charlotte Delbo, *Une Connaissance inutile* (Paris: Éditions de Minuit, 1970), pp. 183-184. [My translation]

34. Ibid., pp. 191, 190, 185.

MARK CORY

Comedic Distance
in Holocaust Literature

There is a moment in the screen version of Robert Shaw's *The Man in the Glass Booth* when the uniformed officer, played brilliantly by Maximillian Schell, is revealed not to be Lagerkommandant SS Col. Dorf but the survivor Arthur Goldman. The giveaway is his humor, his characteristically Jewish humor.

This is not a funny moment in Shaw's drama, but its effect as denouement depends upon our dawning realization that in fact the play has been laced with a great deal of humor, most of it sardonic and dark. In a work inspired by the Israeli abduction and trial of Adolf Eichmann in 1962, humor might seem incongruous or even insulting to victims of the Holocaust, but Shaw uses it effectively to build sympathy for his own victim-protagonist. Reflection yields still other examples of humor, a feature largely ignored in the huge critical literature on the Holocaust. The very different aspects of humor in these examples illustrate the complexity of the phenomenon. The adolescent impishness of Anne Frank's confessions to her diary have little in common with the bawdy jests of Rolf Hochhuth's characters in Act I of *The Deputy* and still less with the mocking laughter of his sinister Doctor. Peter Weiss's documentary drama on the Frankfurt Auschwitz trials, *The Investigation*, systematically employs humor as a way to characterize moral bankruptcy as in-jokes are traded among the accused at the expense of the surviving witnesses. By contrast, the careful avoidance of humor by these

From *Journal of American Culture* 18, no. 1 (Spring 1995). © 1995 by Ray B. Browne.

same witnesses signals the high seriousness of the moral issues at stake. In works written by actual Holocaust survivors, the most conspicuous comic elements tend towards gallows humor. In Simon Wiesenthal's novella *The Sunflower* the narrator reports an execution at which a village wag drapes each hanging corpse with the label "kosher meat." Later in the same work, the autobiographical protagonist jokes that he would rather just sleep until God comes back.

In his seminal work on humor and fear in Gothic literature, Paul Lewis suggests a taxonomy for the way humor can function in fearful circumstances: it can be used "to establish a temporary sense of normality," as a means of "coping with or minimizing fearful occurrences," by evil or benevolent forces "to assert and celebrate their superiority," by victims "in rising above their pain," and as a "sign of madness or demonic possession" (Lewis 112). Many examples of humor in Holocaust literature, including some of those cited here, function precisely in these same ways. Hochhuth's Doctor, based loosely on the infamous Dr. Mengele, is shown through his cruel and taunting sense of humor to be at least mad and perhaps possessed of incarnate evil. Anne Frank's spunky good humor "despite everything" helps her, and us as readers, rise above the deprivations of her life in the Secret Annexe. Wiesenthal's character Simon copes with his loss of faith by joking that God is on vacation. Laughter rises from the ranks of the accused in Weiss's *The Investigation* like an evil chorus as those on trial flaunt their perceived superiority. The initial comic appearance of Elie Wiesel's Moshé the Beadle in *Night* helps establish a sense of normality before the searing violations of the transports and camps introduce us to *l' univers concentrationnaire*.[1]

Some examples of humor in Holocaust literature take us beyond the functions of the comic in Gothic fiction, however, and call for an expanded taxonomy appropriate to an aesthetics of atrocity (Langer 22). One of these functions is to define the boundaries of our moral response to the events of the Holocaust.[2] This occurs paradoxically by the introduction of inappropriate, often savage humor in the depiction of negative characters, and then by the suppression of humor in those characters—whether victims or non-victims—with whom the author wants the reader to empathize. We empathize with Father Fontana in Hochhuth's *The Deputy*, with the Jewish victims and with the enigmatic SS officer Gerstein; our rejection of many of the other characters in the German military-industrial complex and the Catholic Church is conditioned by the tastelessness of their fascist jokes. An example is the banter of the character of Adolf Eichmann, as he remarks to Baron Rutta that Krupp's concern over the welfare of children born to

Russian forced laborers will disappear once a factory is set up in Auschwitz: "In Auschwitz nobody complains. And I've never heard (*he laughs knowingly;* RUTTA *joins him*) of any pregnancies in Auschwitz either" (43).

Another distinct function of humor in Holocaust literature is to mark the boundaries between different orders of reality. Lawrence Langer has shown how Jakov Lind successfully exploits lunatic characters to challenge the reader's perception of what is in fact possible in a supposedly rational world. Satire and the grotesque combine to break down our normal resistance to aberration and hence to prepare us for depictions of the Holocaust in which aberration was the norm.[3] In exactly complementary fashion, humor also serves to create a sense of verisimilitude in a fictional world whose contours defy comprehension, yet whose purpose collapses if the reader does not accept its historical reality. Viktor Frankl and David Rousset's independent observations on the surprising presence of humor in the camps[4] mean among other things that some examples, especially of gallows humor, function in part to contribute to this verisimilitude. Humor was a feature of camp and ghetto life, and so it appears in the literature depicting this experience. Wiesenthal's anecdotes serve this function, as does the instance in Elie Wiesel's *Night* when Elie's father reacts to the order to don the yellow star with "Oh well, what of it? You don't die of it" (20). Thus while it is true, as Lawrence Langer correctly and eloquently points out, that "to establish an order of reality in which the unimaginable becomes imaginatively acceptable exceeds the capacities of an art devoted entirely to verisimilitude"(43), Holocaust literature is obliged to forge a link to external reality in a way Gothic fiction is not. Humor helps.

Beyond marking moral boundaries and establishing nuances of credibility in incredible circumstances, the comic in Holocaust literature also functions as resistance, as protest. Although related to the use of humor by fictional victims in Gothic literature to rise above their pain, protest humor in Holocaust literature is more than comic anesthesia against political, moral and religious oppression. In his analysis of American Jewish and Afro American humor, Joseph Boskin has pointed out that minority cultures cope with the problem of subordination in part through a highly complex order of protest humor (55). A favorite device is the trickster motif, by which a member of a vulnerable group suffers but survives by outwitting his enemy. Hasek's good soldier Schweyk, Brecht's Azdak, Grass' Oskar Matzerath, Charlie Chaplin, and Buster Keaton have all enriched the tradition of wise fool and comic antihero in our century. As the trickster is manifested most commonly in the literature of the Holocaust, the "little man" appears as a boy who is launched on a nightmare journey through the reaches of hell.

Two works offer particularly clear examples of this motif, the recently released and highly controversial film *Europa, Europa* and Jerzy Kosinski's compelling and very disturbing *The Painted Bird*.

In the story of Salomon Perel's incredible survival, *Europa Europa* follows a German-Jewish teenager fleeing pogroms first to Poland then, after the invasion of Poland, further eastward into Soviet territory. What distinguishes this story from the parallel but unrelieved adventures of Jakob Littner as told by Wolfgang Koeppen in *Aufzeichungen aus einem Erdloch* is that the Perel teenager prospers. He is nurtured by a Soviet Communist youth league where he learns Russian, but by adroitly switching languages, shedding his newly-acquired Communist ideology and cunningly concealing his ethnic identity he later becomes the mascot of a German army unit when the Soviets are overrun. Although not a comedy per se, what raises the film above the tedium of the innocuous published memoir is the adroit interplay of light and dark moments achieved by director Agnieszka Holland. Audiences react with a rush of laughter when Perel as uniformed German mascot tries to rejoin his Soviet comrades by cover of night, only to be overtaken by a German surprise attack, which he then appears to be leading. For his heroism in this battlefield victory, which we know to have been an attempt to flee, he is rewarded by assignment to an elite academy for the Hitler youth, and in time by adoption and romance. The romance has its comic aspect, too, for although the chameleon can change his linguistic and ideological skins, he cannot change his foreskin. Painful though the attempt clearly is, it amuses by introducing into the desperate situation of the Holocaust some of the familiar anxieties of adolescence.

Kosinski's *The Painted Bird* probes an inconceivably hostile universe of persecution and cruelty through the eyes of an even younger witness. Both Perel's teenager, whom we meet on the eve of his Bar Mitzvah, and Kosinski's boy are torn out of a secure and happy environment and initiated into a bewildering world where they are threatened at every step. Like Perel, the boy survives his incredible series of misadventures by cunning adaptation, quick wits, and bizarre good luck. He survives his odyssey across eastern Europe, in and out of the grasp of superstitious peasants, of evil clerics, of Russian and German soldiers, despite always being "the other" and hence vulnerable. And yet he survives, and in surviving, triumphs. The comedy associated with his scrambling antics, with his initial naiveté, with his increasing cunning is the author's clever protest against the multiple afflictions of the Holocaust.

Not all the humor stemming from the trickster motif involves the young, however. In many ways the best known example is Jurek Becker's novel *Jacob the Liar*. As the little man whose white lies about the Soviet advance feed the hungry imaginations of his fellow ghetto dwellers starved for any hopeful sign, Jacob must become increasingly resourceful and inventive to avoid dashing the hopes his fictitious radio has raised. Over time, as the situation in the ghetto becomes more and more desperate, his stories must become increasingly detailed and encouraging. What started as a reflex leads Jacob to something approaching a struggle of heroic proportions (see Wetzel), but the comedic distance built into this struggle defeats the pathos Becker consciously sought to avoid. In part this distance is achieved through a depiction of little people coping with the predicaments of daily shtetl life in the tradition of Sholem Aleichem.[5] In part it is achieved through parody, as the ghetto children attempt their own acts of resistance (Brown 196-97). In the main, however, it is achieved through the nearly endless sequence of devices, each more clever and yet more desperate than its predecessor. These devices conceal the fact that no clandestine radio exists, to the end that all those who have come to rely upon Jacob's lies might survive for yet one more day.

Although, as these several examples show, humor has functioned in one way or another as a regular feature of Holocaust literature, Becker's *Jacob the Liar* remained to my knowledge unique for nearly two decades as *the* comic novel of the Holocaust. That exclusivity was challenged by the emergence in 1986 of the remarkable *Maus: A Survivor's Tale* by the American Art Spiegelman. The basic incongruity between humor and a subject as serious as the Holocaust is radically compounded by Spiegelman, who treats this same serious subject in a form which for most of us seems the exclusive domain of the infantile and the trivial: the comic book. The appearance of *Maus* and its companion volume *Maus* II in 1991 offers an unparalleled opportunity and unambiguous challenge to understanding the paradoxical relationship between atrocity and humor.

Not that the comic book, at least when spelled "comix," has much to do anymore with humor. The centuries-old tradition of witty graphic art that spawned the American comic strip gave way after the war to a different tradition when the newspaper funnies were paralleled by adventure series whose four-color superheroes—from Superman to GI Joe—substituted a black and white view of morality and justice for the "impish nonsense" (Mordden 90) of the originals.[6]

Art Spiegelman is more than conversant with these competing traditions in American popular culture. As instructor at the New York School of Visual Arts and co-editor (with his wife, Françoise Mouly) of the avant-garde RAW commix, Spiegelman is in the forefront of experimentation with what may be an emerging genre at the close of the 20th century: the graphic novel. He is also the son of Holocaust survivors. In *Maus*, he relates in words and cartoons the story of his Polish parents from pre-war bliss to the ghetto, to separation in Auschwitz and Dachau, to reunification and a troubled life in Rego Park, NYC. In conscious homage to the traditional funnies, he depicts the Jews as mice, the Nazis as cats, the Poles as pigs, the French as frogs, the Americans as dogs, and even the Swedes as reindeer. When the Polish Jews wish to pass as non-Jews, they don pig masks. When Spiegelman lets his own mask drop, his autobiographical character Artie is shown wearing a mouse mask.

The difference between these caricatures and the "funny animals" familiar through Disneyesque variations is as profound as the difference between the comic novel and traditional Holocaust literature. Graphically, Spiegelman's style is spare and suggestive, rather than fussy with three-dimensional detail. Dialog is conveyed with the traditional balloons when Vladek Spiegelman's story is acted out, but supplemented by narrative text when Artie's father is shown thinking or telling his story. Unlike Mickey and Donald, these animals inhabit an adult world. They smoke, they drink, they swear, and they kill and are killed.

Maus is unique in Holocaust literature to date. Despite its radical approach, it has received remarkably favorable critical reception in both Germany and the United States, where it has been called both "honest and brutal" and the "first masterpiece in comic-book history" (Mordden 91, 96).[7] It avoids trivializing its subject by focusing more on the formation of a consciousness of the past (in Artie) than on details of the past itself. This shift, to which I will return shortly, and the grittiness of Spiegelman's style, prevent *Maus* from falling into the category of "popular and pornographic indulgences" that Alvin Rosenfeld rightly claims only dull our political awareness and defeat our historical sense (104). The question remains whether as Holocaust comic novel *Maus* retains any humor, and if so, how that humor functions.

Writing for the *New York Times*, Lawrence Langer notes that "the animal characters create a distancing effect that allows us to follow the fable without being drowned in its grim, inhuman horrors" (15). The comedic distance achieved by the transformation of an autobiographical story into an animal fable is readily seen by comparing an earlier version of a portion of this story published in the pages of *Short Order Comix* in 1973, where the characters are not represented as animals and the effect is unrelieved.

Of course by invoking the cat and mouse paradigm, Spiegelman has been criticized for reducing a distinctly human evil to a hunter-prey phenomenon natural to the animal kingdom (Witek 112). Still, his use of the animal metaphor is at base nothing more than an extended coping mechanism, one entirely consistent with the conventional uses of humor reviewed earlier (Scheel 438). In fact, caricatures—some roughly analogous to Spiegelman's cartoons—account for some 20 percent of surviving Holocaust art.[8] Gallows humor of the sort mentioned earlier is also present in *Maus*, as when Art's mother and father are forced to hide in a cellar and Anja recoils in terror from the rats. Their hostess jokes, "Well—you're better off with the rats than with the Gestapo ... At least the rats won't kill you" (148), and of course we perceive yet another dimension to the joke at the thought of man-size mice being afraid of rats. Even the trickster motif surfaces, as Vladek develops a whole repertoire of cunning strategies for survival, from claiming to be a master of trades he actually knows little about, to "organizing" clothing and food to be bartered for improvements in his situation, to masking his appearance in order to pass as a non-Jew before his capture.

The principal comic effect in *Maus*, however, goes beyond any of the devices exploited by other authors thus far, and it is in this new comic dimension that Spiegelman's graphic novel merits our closest attention. For all its depiction of Polish ghetto life, of Mauschwitz, Birkenau, and Dachau, Spiegelman's *Maus* is only secondarily concerned with the Holocaust. Its primary concern is the imprint of that parental experience, the "death imprint" as it is called (Lifton and Berger 84), on the children of survivors. As such, this graphic novel joins the growing literature on the Holocaust written by or about the second generation of victims, works such as Susan F. Schaeffer's *Anya*, Saul Bellow's *Mr. Sammler's Planet*, Edgar Wallant's *The Pawnbroker*, and Jurek Becker's *Bronsteins Kinder*. Common to all such works is a complex syndrome of guilt at not measuring up to the strength, skill, and courage of one's survivor-parents, of a theological and existential quest for a meaningful relationship to the religion of those parents, and an aesthetic quest for the icons and images appropriate to the experience of second generation survivors.[9] The familial relationship is thus often highly ambivalent, filled with love-hate tensions. Fictional surviving fathers in particular are often portrayed as difficult, self-absorbed, demanding, cynical, and humorless—qualities easily conceded a survivor in the abstract but clearly problematic for his children. Jurek Becker chooses to leave Bronstein's bitter son little or no saving humor; in contrast, by making the prospect of having to move back home with his fussy father Art's real horror, Spiegelman makes it clear that Art's own survival depends very much on his sense of the comic (Mordden 92).

The uses of the comic in the father-son relationship are actually quite conventional. It is the larger context of those uses that lends them unusual power. Gallows humor takes on a new twist as Vladek tells his son how the doctor had to break his arm at birth to ease his passage down the birth canal, and how thereafter as a baby Artie's arm would twitch up in a caricature of the Nazi salute to an amused chorus of "Heil Hitler" from his parents. At that moment in the telling Vladek demonstrates the gesture, upsetting his carefully counted pills for the day: "Look now what you made me do!" he shouts at his son (*Maus* 30). Late in the second volume as Vladek relates his transport from Mauschwitz to Dachau he exclaims, "Here my troubles began" (*Maus II* 75). The significance is that the "troubles" really begin for Vladek with the suicide of his survivor-wife Anja in 1968 and his subsequent remarriage to another surviving Jew, Mala. Their post-war relationship is filled with such bickering that Mala eventually leaves Vladek as Volume II begins. Ever the trickster, Vladek feigns a heart attack to manipulate his son into returning his call and ultimately into staying with him for a while in his bungalow in the Catskills. On the page that leads up to that call we see by contrast the much more gentle humor between Art and Françoise as the artist makes it clear why he depicts his French wife as a mouse rather than a frog (she converted), but even this gentle humor issues from and seeks to deal with Art's profound estrangement from his father and his father's religion.

This survivor's tale ends with the death of Vladek Spiegelman from congestive heart failure in 1982. The final panel of a work that, taken together, occupied Art Spiegelman for 13 years, shows his parents' tombstone. In the penultimate panel the failing Vladek confuses Art with his older brother Richieu, who died in the camps and whose framed photograph haunts this remarkable comic novel of the effects of the Holocaust on survivors and their children. The tender irony in Vladek's final confusion is a measure of how humor in this important body of literature has evolved over the past 45 years. Humor in the ghettos and camps was a psychological response to danger and oppression; it functioned as both a coping mechanism and a means of resistance. As a literary device it has lent credibility to witness literature and functioned aesthetically to make the unfathomable accessible to the minds and emotions of the reading public. When its incongruity was exploited to the fullest, humor has served as a metaphor for evil, but in later works the trend has been if anything to use humor to soften the "cosmic significance" of the suffering depicted in this literature (Alter 26), to create, in Sarah Cohen's words, "an alternative to an ennobling death" (14). Finally, the incongruity of Art Spiegelman's comic vessel for the profoundly sad story of his parents' generation and the shadow those experiences cast over the lives of second generation survivors marks a turning point in the literature of atrocity. Writing for *Merkur*, Kurt Scheel has likened this achievement to Paul Celan's in his extraordinary poem, "Fugue of Death." Each has created a symbolic language for depicting the Holocaust which did not exist before: "Celan and Spiegelman should be mentioned in one breath because both poet and cartoonist have found languages adequate to their topic which previously did not exist" (Scheel 437).

NOTES

1. Original title of the important work by survivor David Rousset, now used as a metaphor for the incomprehensible world of the camps. Rousset, *The Other Kingdom*, trans. Ramon Guthrie (New York: Reynal, 1947).

2. See Paul Lewis in a second important article, "Joke and Anti-joke: Three Jews and a Blindfold," *Journal of Popular Culture* 21.1 (Summer 1987): 70.

3. See Langer 205-49.

4. See Rousset, *The Other Kindgom*, and Viktor Frankl, *Man's Search for Meaning* (New York: Simon, 1963), esp. 68f.

5. Russell E. Brown argues that "It was not Becker's purpose to give a dramatic picture of the terrible physical suffering of the ghetto ... but rather to create a comic novel of Jewish shtetl life in the Sholem Aleichem tradition" (208).

6. On the history of the comics see also Lawrence E. Mintz, "Humor and Popular Culture" *Handbook of Humor Research II Applied Studies*, ed. Paul McGhee and Jeffrey H. Goldstein (New York: Springer, 1983) 129-42; David Kunzle, *The History of the Comic Strip: The Nineteenth Century* (Berkeley: U of California P, 1990); M. Thomas Inge, *Comics as Culture* (Jackson and London: UP of Mississippi, 1990) and Joseph Witek, *Comic Books as History: The Narrative Art of Jack Jackson, Art Spiegelman, and Harvey Pekar* (Jackson, MS: UP of Mississippi, 1989).

7. See also the reviews by Lawrence Langer, "A Fable of the Holocaust," *NY Times Book Review* 3 November 1991: 1 and 35-36; Kurt Scheel, "Mauschwitz? Art Spiegelmans 'Geschichte eines Überlebenden,'" *Merkur* 43 (1989) 435-38; and Raymond Sokolov in *The Wall Street Journal* 13 November 1991: A 14. These are representative of the positive critical reception; also witness the nomination for National Book Critics Circle award for most distinguished book of biography-autobiography of 1991 and the Pulitzer Board Special Award for 1992 (see *Time* 20 April 1992: 37); note also the MOMA exhibit held in January of 1992 featuring Spiegelman's archives of his research and earlier versions from RAW (reviewed in the *New York Magazine* 13 January 1992: 65).

8. Sybil Milton, writing on the complex relationship between art and atrocity, lists caricatures as one of the half dozen distinct art forms issuing from the Holocaust. See Milton, "Art of the Holocaust: A summary," *Reflections of the Holocaust in Art and Literature*, ed. Randolph L. Braham (NY: Columbia UP, 1990) 147-52.

9. One of the several provocative issues posed by Alan Berger, "Ashes and Hope: The Holocaust in Second Generation American Literature" in Reflections 97-116. Specifically, Berger asks "What are the distinctive icons and images of the Holocaust employed in second generation writings?" (97).

WORKS CITED

Alter, Robert. "Jewish Humor and the Domestication of Myth." *Jewish Wry. Essays on Jewish Humor.* Ed. Sarah Blacher Cohen. Bloomington, IN: Indiana UP, 1987. 25-36.

Becker, Jurek. Jakob der Lugner. Berlin: Aufbau, 1969.____.Bronsteins Kinder. Frankfurt: Suhrkamp, 1986.

Bellow, Saul. Mr. Sammler's Planet. New York: Viking, 1970.

Berger, Alan L. "Ashes and Hope: The Holocaust in Second Generation American Literature." *Reflections of the Holocaust in Art and Literature.* Ed. Randolph L. Braham. Boulder: Columbia UP, 1990. 97-116.

Boskin, Joseph. "Beyong Kvetching and Jiving: The Thrust of Jewish and Black Folkhumor." *Jewish Wry. Essays on Jewish Humor.* Ed. Sarah Blacher Cohen. Bloomington, IN: Indiana UP, 1987. 53-79.

Brown, Russel E. "Jurek Becker's Holocaust Fiction: A Father and Son Survive." *Critique* 30 (1989): 193-209.

Celan, Paul. "Todesfuge." *Modern German Poetry*, 1910-1960: *An Anthology with Verse Translations.* Ed. and trans. Michael Hamburger and Christopher Middleton. New York: Grove, 1962.

Cohen, Sarah. Introduction. *Jewish Wry. Essays on Jewish Humor.* Bloomington, IN: Indiana UP, 1987. 1-15.

Europa, Europa. Agnieszka, Holland: Orion, 1991.

Frank, Anne. *The Diary of a Young Girl.* Trans. B.M. Mooyaart-Doubleday. New York: Doubleday, 1952. Trans. of *Het Achterhuis.* Amsterdam: Contact, 1949.

Hochhuth, Rolf. *The Deputy.* Trans. Richard and Clara Winston. New York: Grove: 1964. Trans. of *Derstellvertreter.* Reinbek: Rowohlt, 1963.

Koeppen, Wolfgang. *Jakob Littners Aufzeichungen auseinem Erdloch.* Munich: Klager, 1948. Frankfurt: Judischer Verlag, 1992.

Kosinsky, Jerzy. *The Painted Bird.* Boston: Houghton, 1963.

Langer, Lawrence. *The Holocaust and the Literary Imagination.* New Haven, CT: Yale UP, 1975.

Lewis, Paul. "Humor and Fear in the Gothic." *Comic Effects. Interdisciplinary Approaches to Humor in Literature.* Albany, NY: State U of New York P, 1989. 111-53.

Lifton, Robert Jay, and Alan L. Berger. "Holocaust Survivors and Children in *Anya* and *Mr. Samler's Planet.*" *Modern Language Studies* 16 (1986): 81-87.

Milton, Sybil. "Art of the Holocaust: A Summary." *Reflections of the Holocaust in Art and Literature.* Ed. Randolph L. Braham. Boulder: Columbia UP, 1990. 147-52.

Mordden, Ethan. "Kat and Maus." Rev. of *Maus. A Survivor's Tale,* by Art Spiegelman. *The New Yorker* 6 April 1992: 90-96.

Perel, Sally. *Ich war Hitlerjunge Salomon.* Berlin: Nicolai, 1992.

Rosenfeld, Alvin H. *Imagining Hitler.* Bloomington, IN: Indiana UP, 1985.

Schaeffer, Susan F. *Anya.* New York: Macmillan, 1974.

Scheel, Kurt. "Mauschwitz? Art Spiegelman's 'Geschichte eines Überlebenden.'" *Merkur* 43 (1989): 435-438.

Shaw, Robert. *The man in the Glass Booth.* New York: Harcourt, 1967.

Spiegelman, Art. *Maus. A Survivor's Tale.* New York: Pantheon, 1986.

———. *Maus II. And Here My Troubles Began.* New York: Pantheon, 1991.

———. "Prisoner on the Hell Planet." Short Order Comix #1 (1973).

Wallant, Edgar. *The Pawnbroker.* New York: Harcourt, 1961.

Weiss, Peter. *The Investigation.* English version by Jon Swan and Ulu Grosbard. New York: Antheneum, 1975. Version of *Die Ermittlung.* Frankfurt: Suhrkamp, 1965.

Wetzel, Heinz. "Holocaust and Literatur: Die Perspektive Jurek Beckers." *Colloquia Germanica* 21 (1988): 70-76.

Wiesel, Elie. *Night.* Trans. Stella Roadway. New York: Hill, 1960. Trans. of *La Nuit.* Paris: Les Editions De Minuit, 1958.

Wiesenthal, Simon. *The Sunflower.* Trans. H.A. Piehler. New York: Schoken, 1976. Trans. of *Die Sonnenblume.* Paris: Opera Mundi, 1969.

Witek, Joseph. *Comic Books as History: The Narrative Art of Jack Jackson, Art Spiegelman, and Harvey Pekar.* Jackson, MS: UP of Mississippi, 1989.

GEOFFREY H. HARTMAN

Public Memory
and its Discontents

I want to raise the issue of how to focus public memory on traumatic experiences like war, the Holocaust, or massive violations of human rights. You might think this is not an issue at all; that we are, in fact, too absorbed in such painful matters. I have often heard objections which say that the study of the Holocaust, in particular, is displacing among Jews a learning-tradition two thousand years old. There may be some truth to that charge; it is easy to become fascinated with cruelty and violence, with the mystery of such extreme inhumanity. But we cannot turn away from the world in which this happened; and the question of what impedes our focus is complicated by the very efficiency of modern media, their realism and representational scope.

The substantial effects of film and telecommunications are having their impact. An "information sickness," caused by the speed and quantity of what impinges on us, and abetted by machines we have invented that generate endless arrays, threatens to over personal memory. The individual, we complain, cannot "process" all this information, this incoming flak: public and personal experience are not being moved closer together but further apart. The arts, it used to be said, aspire to the condition of music; now the "total flow" of video seems to dominate. Can public memory still be called memory, when it is increasingly alienated from personal and active recall?

Among the symptoms of this malady of our age are philosophic discussions about the existence or nonexistence of a "post-humanist subject,"

From *The Longest Shadow: In the Aftermath of the Holocaust.* © 1996 by Geoffrey H. Hartman.

a conference on "The Uses of Oblivion," and the fear, openly expressed, that "our past will have no future in our future" (David Rieff). Even as our senses are routinely besieged, the imagination, traditionally defined as a power that restores a kind of presence to absent things, has its work taken away, and is in danger of imitating media sensationalism. It becomes, as Wallace Stevens said, a violence from within pressing against the violence from outside. In the midst of an unprecedented realism in fiction and the public media, there is reason to worry about a desensitizing trend, one that keeps raising the threshold at which we begin to respond.

How do we keep our sensitivity alive, when such vivid and painful events become our daily fare? How do we prevent denial or indifference from taking over? We have known for a long time that there is great suffering in the world, suffering impossible to justify. Such knowledge must have been with us at least since the Book of Job was written. But we also know from the time of Job's so-called friends to that of Holocaust negationists, that suffering is explained or rationalized against all odds.

Today we have entered a new period. Until recently, perhaps until news from Bosnia reached the screen, we clutched at the hope that had the indifferent masses in Germany or America known what was going on in the concentration camps, known with the same graphic detail communicated today by TV, surely the atrocities could not have continued. There would have been an outcry of the popular conscience and so much protest that the Holocaust would have had to stop.[1]

Yet right now we are learning a new truth about human indifference. As the media make us bystanders of every act of violence and violation, we realize that this indifference or lack of focus was not so incomprehensible after all. For we glimpse a terrible inertia in ourselves and can even find reasons for it. We register the fact that no event is reported without a spin, without an explanatory or talky context that buffers the raw images; and we realize that pictures on TV remain pictures, that a sort of antibody builds up in our response system and prevents total mental disturbance. Even while deploring and condemning the events, we experience what the poet John Keats called "the feel of not to feel it," as we continue with everyday life.

It is not my intent to add to our already considerable sense of guilt or powerlessness. My point is that the media place a demand on us which it is impossible to satisfy. Paradoxically enough, their extended eyes and ears, so important to informed action, also distance the reality of what is perceived. Terrible things, by continuing to be shown, begin to appear matter-of-fact, a natural rather than manmade catastrophe. Zygmunt Bauman has labeled this the "production of moral indifference."[2]

For our sensibility, however compassionate, is not superhuman: it is finite and easily exhausted. Sooner or later coldness sets in, whether we admit to it or not. We remain deeply engaged, however, because official morality does not cultivate that coldness. This is an important difference between our situation and that of Germans under the Nazi regime, so that viewer reaction splits schizophrenically into responding passionately to images of global misery and an exhausted self-distancing. Those images, for all their immediacy, become too often electronic phantoms.[3]

A desensitization of this kind (Robert Lifton calls it "psychic numbing") was already noticed by Wordsworth near the beginning of the Industrial Revolution. He complained in 1800 of a "degrading thirst after outrageous stimulation" which was blunting "the discriminating powers of the mind" and reducing it to "a state of almost savage torpor." People were losing their ability to be moved by ordinary sights and events, by "common life," because of "the great national events which are daily taking place, and the increasing accumulation of men in cities, where the uniformity of their occupations produces a craving for extraordinary incident which the rapid communication of intelligence hourly gratifies."[4] Wordsworth created, in response, a minimalist poetry, a "lyrical" ballad which reduced the narrative or romance interest to near zero, and urged the reader to "find a tale in everything."

Since Wordsworth's time psychic numbing has made considerable progress. The contemporary problem is not Bovaryism or Quixotism— seeing the real world (defensively) with an imagination steeped in romance— but looking at whatever is on the screen as if it were unreal, just an interesting construct or simulation. Actuality is distanced by a larger than life violence and retreats behind all those special effects. While Adorno discerns an "obscene merger of aesthetics and reality," it is not surprising that art historian Robert Rosenblum should defend what he calls Warhol's "deadpan" by claiming that it reflects a "state of moral and emotional anaesthesia which, like it or not, probably tells us more truth about the realities of the modern world than do the rhetorical passions of *Guernica*."[5]

But if the present has now less of a hold, if abstractness and psychic numbing have indeed infected us, how can we remain sensitive to the past, to its reality? Spielberg's *Schindler's List* won its acclaim in part by getting through to us, by lifting that anxiety—though not without deploying spectacular means.

Consider a related problem intensified by the media: whether we can trust appearances. Because our technical power of simulation has increased, but forgetfulness has not decreased—the speed with which events fall into "the dark backward and abysm of time" has, if anything, accelerated—the greatest danger to public memory is *official history*. Even the dead, as Walter Benjamin declared, are not safe from the victors, who consider public memory part of the spoils and do not hesitate to rewrite history ... or re-image it. Milan Kundera in the opening episode of *The Book of Laughter and Forgetting* recalls how a discredited Communist leader was airbrushed out of a famous historical photo—so readily is history falsified and public memory deceived.

You may have seen a movie that is set in Argentina under the military dictatorship. It could also have been set in Eastern Europe during the time of Soviet domination. Puenzo's film, *The Official Story*, tells a tragic and typical narrative of public deceit and personal discovery. It is the story of a mother who learns that her adopted child was stolen from a "disappeared" Argentinian woman. At first she does not suspect the truth, but a small doubt punctures the basic trust she has in the system: that doubt grows and grows, the search for the truth grows and grows, until—as also in Oedipus the King—a hidden past is revealed. But, tragically, her resolute pursuit of the truth breaks up the family and endangers the child.

What I have described comes close to being a universal kind of plot, as old as the historical record itself. What is the difference, then, between past and present? The contemporary difference can be summed up in a famous phrase of Emerson: "We suspect our instruments." The very means that expose untruth, the verbal or photographic or filmic evidence itself, is tainted by suspicion. All evidence is met by a demystifying discourse or charges of manipulation. The intelligent scrutiny to which we habitually submit appearances becomes a crisis of trust, a lack of confidence in what we are told or shown, *a fear that the world of appearances and the world of propaganda have merged through the power of the media*. To undo this spell and gain true knowledge would then be more tricky than in gnosticism, which distrusted nature and tried to gain a knowledge of the true god behind the god of nature.

What I have argued is that there is a link between epistemology and morality, between how we get to know what we know (through various, including electronic, media) and the moral life we aspire to lead. My account has been rather pessimistic: it implies that the gap between knowledge and ethical action has not grown less wide for us. The pressures to be politically correct, to say and do the right thing, have increased, but neither our thinking nor our actions have adjusted to the challenge so clearly stated by Terrence des

Pres, who said that, after the Holocaust, "a new shape of knowing invades the mind," one that opens our eyes—beyond the Holocaust—to the *global extent* of political misery.[6] In a democracy, moreover, and once we are in the electronic age, while there is more realism, there is also the liability that goes with that: a gnawing distrust of public policy and official memory. The free speech that is one of the foundations of truth in the democratic "marketplace of ideas" leads to a continual probing, testing, and even muckraking that has an unexpected effect on the integrity of the public life it was intended to assure.

Indeed, the more that official history is disputed by scholarship or media-journalism, the more an insidious and queasy feeling of unreality grows in us. What are we to do, for example, with all the speculations about Kennedy's assassination that parade as investigative journalism or docudrama? It is as if the political realm, and possibly all of public life, were inauthentic—a mask, a Machiavellian web of continuous deception.[7] This negative insight also undermines the gravity and uniqueness of lived, events, and encourages a deep skepticism about the world—or a relentless, compensatory belief in something fundamental and unfalsifiable, a something which often takes the form of nationalistic or religious fanaticism.

My aim in raising this issue of the relation of morality to knowledge in a democratic and electronic age is, frankly, moralistic. I seek to draw some conclusions, not only to describe as clearly as possible a contemporary dilemma. Terrence des Pres, again, states that dilemma with the precision of a proverb: "Thanks to the technological expansion of consciousness, we cannot not know the extent of political torment; and in truth it may be said that *what others suffer, we behold*."[8] The triumph of technology has created two classes which can coexist in the same person: those who suffer, and those who observe that suffering. This fact cannot be touted as moral progress, but there is one gain from it. Given our new eyes for the pain of others, and given that "we cannot not know," all monopolistic claims about suffering no longer make sense.

"What others suffer, we behold" is like a second fall from innocence, a second bite of the fatal apple. It removes all excuse by taking away our ignorance, without at the same time granting us the power to do something decisive. Often, therefore, we fall back on a religious feeling, as President Reagan did at Bitburg, though in his case it served the bottom line of NATO policy. At Bitburg, Mr. Reagan's reconciling memorial perspective equated fallen German soldiers, including Waffen SS, and the civilians they killed, many of them Jewish victims. This "dead" perspective shortcircuits reflection on a torment des Pres called political, because of its manmade rather than inevitable nature.

Even when the politics are not so obvious, skeptical contemporary thought sees them everywhere: in religion, in memory, in art. But that insight too has no activist or redemptive value. It simply confirms des Pres's hellish vision of universal political torment. When we ask, haunted like Tolstoy by such suffering, "What is to be done?" no course of action proposes itself as entirely credible. Rather, the ethical impasse breeds, I have suggested, desperate and manichean solutions, post-Tolstoy fundamentalisms, whether religious or political.[9]

A related reaction is cultural revolution and its instrument, the politicized memory. In flight from human and hermeneutic complexities, this kind of politics saturates everything with ideological content and claims redemptive power for a purified vision of the past. I have previously mentioned the role of official history, promoted by the apparatus of state. It manipulates memory like news.

Now it is true that a war is always going on to modify memory, and we all wage it in ourselves first: who does not remember moments of altering (or rationalizing or shading) experiences painful to self-esteem? When waged publically, however, such warfare leads to an institutionalized and bogus recollection, a churlish denial of the history of others (covering up, for instance, at Theresienstadt and Auschwitz, the Jewish identity of most of the victims), or an artificially inseminated perspective. A single authorized narrative then simplifies not just history but the only *active* communal memory we have, made of such traditional materials as legends, poetry, dances, songs, festivals, and recitations, the sum of which helps to define a "culture," when combined with various interpretive traditions.

Art as a performative medium—art not reduced to official meaning or information—has a chance to transmit *this* inheritance most fully. When art remains accessible it provides a counterforce to manufactured and monolithic memory. Despite its imaginative license, art is often more effective in "embodying" historically specific ideas than the history-writing on which it may draw. Scientific historical research, however essential it is for its negative virtues of rectifying error and denouncing falsification, has no positive resource to lessen grief, endow calamity with meaning, foster a vision of the world, or legitimate new groups.[10] But art remains in touch with or revives traditional materials that satisfy our need for community without repressing individualist performance.

We start indeed with a cultural inheritance, yet that cannot be fixed as immutably as doctrine is in theology. Memorial narratives asserting the identity of nation or group are usually *modern* constructs, a form of anti-memory limiting the subversive or heterogeneous facts. Invented to nationalize consensus by suggesting a uniform and heroic past ("O say, can you see ..."), they convert "great memories" into political theology. Cults and myths do not go away in modernity; on the contrary, revolution, national rebirth and the drive for political legitimation make blatant ideological use of paradigms from the past. So Marx objected in *The Eighteenth Brumaire* to the French Revolution's historical masquerade: its archaic revival of symbols from the Republican phase of the Roman Empire.[11] This tendency, taken to its extreme, views the culture of a community not as its "nonhereditary memory" but as a pristine essence to be repristinated, a foundation with biological or mystical force that determines history.

What is viable, then, in the notion of collective memory tends to be artistic rather than nationalistic; and unless we keep in mind this link between art and memory—recognized when the Greeks made Mnemosyne the mother of the Muses—national or ethnic politics will reduce culture to a tyrannous and frozen difference, a heroic narrative demanding consent.

A sense of the nation as vital to cultural memory arose in Romanticism. Throughout Europe, artists and scholars tried to free literature from the yoke of "foreign" classics by retrieving (and counterfeiting if necessary!) a native tradition. This literary nationalism was often a reconstruction, motivated by visionary nostalgia. "A people who lose their nationality create a legend to take its place," Edwin Muir wrote about Walter Scott's attempt to carry on a tradition that had lost its continuity. The ideal culture, according to Romantic historicism, was produced by the spirit embodied in a people, a spirit of the folk (*Volksgeist*) which expressed the true, distinctive voice of each nation among the nations.

Collectors and antiquarians hunted for old stories, songs, and ballads: relics of a past now disappearing too quickly, and to which popular or archaic strength was imputed. A lively interest arose for anything regional rather than cosmopolitan: the buzz words were "local attachment," "local romance," even "local superstition." Hence Wordsworth's "Hart-Leap Well," a self-consciously recreated ballad, typical of a return to stories represented as an emanation of particular places—places impressed on the collective memory and still part of the imaginative life of ordinary people.[12]

These legends about place stretch back to the Bible and seem to reflect traces of a popular memory. Being topocentric (subordinating time to place) they also lessen our anxiety that the ancient rapport between singer and audience, or artist and community, may have broken down. "We have no institutions," Alasdair MacIntyre declares, "through which shared stories can be told dramatically or otherwise to the entire political community, assembled together as an audience, no dramatists or other story tellers able to address such an audience.... Our audiences are privatized and dispersed, watching television in homes or motel rooms...." This panicky view shows how deep the nostalgia for a collective memory runs. Since it is indeed difficult to humanize modern urban spaces, to invest them with a historically charged sense of place, the picture arises of a storyless modern imagination moving from non-place to non-place, and even enjoying the anonymity of highways, airports, large hotels and shopping malls. It looks as if each sacred memory-place (*lieu de mémoire*) is emptied out to become what Marc Augé defines as a nowhere-place (*non-lieu*).[13] Yet the old myths die hard: Michael Kammen in *Mystic Chords of Memory* notices "the remarkable way in which local events can be conceptualized to conform to paradigms of religious tradition or to the totally secular needs of a modern state struggling for existence."

Before I discuss three recent literary ventures that respond to the challenge of reattaching imagination to the collective memory, or creating a communal story under modern conditions—conditions described in the introductory part of this chapter—let me add a few words to define contemporary public memory in its difference from the traditional *collective* memory.

Maurice Halbwachs, killed at Buchenwald, viewed the collective memory as a "living deposit" preserved outside academic or written history. "In general," he writes in his posthumous book, "history begins only at the point where tradition ends, at a moment where social memory is extinguished or decomposes.... [T]he need to write the history of a period, a society, even of an individual does not arise until they are already too far removed in the past" for us to find many living witnesses.[14]

Although these lines were probably composed in the 1930s, they already seem dated, for today we feel a need to record everything, even as the event is occurring; and the media not only make this possible but encourage it. It is this nervous effervescence that marks modern experience and the rise of public memory in distinction from collective memory. The loss or subsumption of the past in the present, a present with very little presence beyond the spotlight moment of its occurrence—which wearies itself out of the mind by its violence or is almost immediately displaced by another such moment, sound-bite, or instantly-fading image—this self-consuming present, both real and specious, vivid and always already a trace, is curiously like the collective memory in that it has, to quote the historian Yosef Yerushalmi, "not the historicity of the past but its eternal contemporaneity." (Yerushalmi offers the example that in Jewish liturgy the destruction of the First and Second Temples is conflated, as if it were the same *hurban*; and the Holocaust is often assimilated as the third *hurban*.) Of course, public memory is also utterly different: it strikes us as a bad simulacrum, one that, unlike the older type of communal or collective memory, has no stability or *durée*, only a jittery, mobile, perpetually changing yet permanently inscribed status.[15] Hence my opening question on what could focus public memory on the traumatic events it is busy recording.

Halbwachs's observation that we are motivated to write things down only when they are in danger of fading entirely can be made relevant to his own project: today the collective memory is in this danger. Doubly so: It is weakened because public memory, with its frantic and uncertain agency, is taking its place; and because a politicized collective memory, claiming a biological or mystical permanence, tries to usurp the living tie between generations.[16]

With this remark we return to literature. One reason literature remains important is that it counteracts the impersonality and instability of public memory, on the one hand, and on the other the determinism and fundamentalism of a collective memory based on identity politics.[17] Literature creates an institution of its own, more personal and focused than public memory yet less monologic than the memorializing fables common to ethnic or nationalist affirmation. At the same time, because today the tie between generations, the "living deposit" or "passé vécu," as Halbwachs calls it, is jeopardized, creative activity is often carried on under the negative sign of an *absent memory* (Ellen Fine) or *mémoire trouvée* (Henri Raczymow).[18] A missed encounter is evoked, through a strenuous, even cerebral exercise of the imagination, as if the link between memory and imagination had been lost.

I turn first to Toni Morrison's *Beloved*. Its epigraphs suggest not only a comparison between the political suffering of blacks and Jews but also that the pathos and the covenant have passed to the former. One epigraph is a dedication: "Sixty million and more." The second alludes through a New Testament quote to the concept of the Chosen People: "I will call them my people, which were not my people; and her beloved, which was not beloved" (Romans 9:25).

It is no exaggeration to call *Beloved* that people's *zakhor* ("Remember!"). Where in black history is there something comparable to a genealogy of "begats," or the millennia of myths, chronicles, scriptures, and scriptural interpretations that characterize the collective memory of the Jews? (Concerning the begats, Julius Lester reminds us, on the dedication page of *To Be a Slave*, that "The ancestry of any black American can be traced to a bill of sale and no further. In many instances even that cannot be done," and John Edgar Wideman prefaces *Damballah* with "A Begat Chart" and a "Family Tree.") African American memory remains to be recovered. But more important still, where is *the conviction of being loved that makes memory possible*? What kind of story could have been passed on, or who stayed alive long enough to remember a suffering that destroyed those who might have been tradents, a suffering that allowed no development of person, family or ethnic group? "Anyone Baby Suggs knew, let alone loved, who hadn't run off or been hanged, got rented out, loaned out, bought up, brought back, stored up, mortgaged, won, stolen or seized."

Between Baby Suggs, or Grandma Baby as she is also called, and Beloved, the little girl killed by her mother, there is no growth or normal history or significant genealogy. The child whose life was aborted at less than two years old, and who preternaturally reenters the mother's house as a young woman (now able to talk and carry on conversations of the most affectionate kind), is a ghost from folklore who expresses hauntingly the unlived life, a love that never could come to fulfillment except in this fantasy-form. Morrison's startling use of the *revenant*, the spirit-figure that returns in many a romantic ballad (a genre that itself needed "revival"), challenges us to a suspension of disbelief. Not so much, I would suggest, disbelief affecting the preternatural return of Beloved—for that partly pagan, partly Christian myth has "a foundation in humanity," as Wordsworth would have said—but disbelief concerning the atrocities suffered by African Americans, *that* ghost which we have not entirely faced.

African American history discloses, then, in a novel like Morrison's, a special difficulty concerning its "absent memory." The subject of that history, the black community, is so scattered by suffering, so "disremembered and unaccounted for," that the story to be passed on "is not a story to pass on," and Morrison can only represent it by a ghostly "devil-child," a fantasy-memory of the love or election this people has not known. In search of that reversal of fate, *Beloved* becomes a *Song of Songs*, the Shulammite's scripture.

My second example of absent memory is very different. The postmodern work of art, to which I now turn, cultivates that absence and does not seek to recover the very possibility of memory itself—of "rememory" as Morrison names it. Raymond Federman, for example, tries to do without resonant names and local romance in *To Whom It May Concern*, though he too, like Morrison, subverts an unfeeling realism. He uses gimmicks (as he admits) to fight "the imposture of realism, that ugly beast that stands at bay ready to leap in the moment you begin scribbling your fiction." He renounces realism even in a novel that recalls the great roundup and deportation of Jews from Paris in July 1942, and its impact on two children who escaped. His self-defeating venture takes courage from experiments, starting with Sterne and Diderot, which portray life as an infinite detour rather than a punctual drama or epiphany: as something less than heroic, composed of accidents, small gestures, and simple, even insignificant words. Thus the *non-lieu* gains a sort of authenticity. "The grim story of Sarah and her cousin should be told without any mention of time and place. It should happen on a timeless vacant stage without scenery. No names of places. No decor. Nothing. It simply happened, sometime and somewhere."

Federman is indebted to the New Novel that evolved in postwar France, and such films as *Last Year at Marienbad*. They depict memory as a mode of seduction—as a narrative of past encounter suggesting that the human condition is so empty or forgetful, so deprived of sacred space (*lieu de mémoire*) and therefore so needy, that it cannot be redeemed except by the construction and imposition of an imaginary history. This deliberate recourse to a perhaps fictional past returns us, of course, to the province of the collective memory, except that *Marienbad* seeks to erode the latter's historical and nationalist pretensions (the Versailles-like decor in the film is meant to be only that, a decor) in favor of the private, imaginative needs of one man and one woman. Federman, like Resnais or Robbe-Grillet, refuses to give his characters more memory than they have. The wound of an absence remains. In this he speaks for an entire postwar generation that lost parents or relatives, while they themselves missed the brunt of the war. "They suffered from not suffering enough," he writes of his escaped children.

My last example is a genre that in documentaries such as *Eyes on the Prize* or Lanzmann's *Shoah* or the witness-accounts in Yale's Video Archive for Holocaust Testimonies is also oriented toward an "absent memory." Personal testimony has long been a significant part of both religious and secular literature, and is usually considered a type of autobiography. Videotaped oral testimony, however, is partly a creation of modern technology and so has a chance of influencing that environment. As history it seeks to convey information, but as oral witness it is an act of remembrance. And as this spoken and more spontaneous mode, which can be recorded without being written down, it contributes to a group biography through highly individual yet convergent stories. The collective memory thus becomes a collected memory (James Young), at once a private and a public legacy, and through video itself counters video's dispersive flow.

Each testimony is potentially an act of rescue, as the Israeli poet, Haim Gouri, observed when covering the Eichmann trial: a rescue "from the danger of [survivors] being perceived as all alike, all shrouded in the same immense anonymity." Moreover, by recording an experience collectively endured, by allowing anyone in the community a voice—that is, not focusing on an elite—a vernacular and many voiced dimension is caught.[19] Memory collected this way is too plural and diverse to be politicized or sacralized. But I can characterize the genre of these testimonies best, and the Archive of Conscience they are building, by saying that they accept the *presence* of memory, however painful, rather than its absence.[20]

The amnesia that invades characters in postmodernist fiction (think of the difference between Beckett and Proust), creating a limbo in which the tape of memory starts and crashes, again and again—this amnesia may reflect a public memory that has become primarily space instead of place, anonymous and occupied by impersonal networks of information. As memory, then, it is purely virtual if not absent. In oral testimonies, however, a burdened recollection asserts itself and fashions a complex relation to the rupture between the positivism of historical experience and the symbolic stores of collective memory. Not only do memory's informative and performative (or ritual) functions try to unite again, but time present, in these testimonies, becomes more than a site of loss or nostalgic recuperation: more than the place which reveals that our capacity to experience has diminished, or that the past must be forgotten to be survived.[21]

Even if memory, as Rimbaud said of love, has always to be reinvented, this does not alter the truth that some kinds of memory are better than others. Though Plato suggested that writing would be harmful to recollection, it proved essential for transmitting thought, both in manuscript and print. Writing a thing down meant passing it on, for a communal or generational recipient. But who is the addressee of the new electronic writing, with its capacity for near-instantaneous reception and transmission? Every TV program is implicitly addressed "To Whom It May Concern," which begs the question of who must be concerned.

Videotaped oral history is an important compromise, because it comes

on the cusp between generations, addresses those still growing up, and at a
time when the collective memory is fading into the quasi-timeless,
panoramic simultaneity of public memory. From Abel Gance and Walter
Benjamin to Jean Baudrillard, this impact of technology on memory-
institutions such as art and history has been a subject of intense reflection. I
have emphasized the difficulty, moral as well as cognitive, of responding to
the images before our eyes in a critical or affective manner when the
audiovisual mode becomes ineluctable and bypasses or floods time-bound
channels of personal memory.[22]

I have also suggested that there is such a thing as memory-envy. It
shows itself in writers who seek to recover an image of their community's
past—a past deliberately destroyed by others or which was not allowed to
form itself into a heritage. Memory-envy also touches a generation that feels
belated: the "generation after" which did not participate directly in a great
event that determined their parents' and perhaps grandparents' lives.
Memory is lacking in both cases as a basis for the integrity of person or
group. At the level of the collective, moreover, memory-envy can take the
form of foundation narratives, myths of origin that fortify group identity.
Some of these decisive but also imposed identity-fictions must be labeled
false memories.

Increasingly, politicized and simplified aspects of the collective
memory take over from an actual artistic heritage. We still have the arts, and
literature in particular, to recall that each of us is a being made of many
beings, and that the heritage of the past is pluralistic and diverse. But as the
collective memory weakens, political religions (Eric Voegelin's name for
totalitarian regimes) falsify the complexity of the past and cultivate an official
story that seeks to reawaken ancient hatreds. This falsified memory, with its
foundation myths, or fundamentalist notions of national destiny and ethnic
purity, is the enemy. We cannot allow it to masquerade as history, as is
happening with the Pamyat movement in Russia, the attempt to rehabilitate
Tissot in Slovakia, and nationalistic nostalgia, whether in Bosnia or the
Middle East. The outbreak of unreal memory can be fought, but only if
younger bystanders, whether artists or scholars, bring testimony of their
own, ballads of their own, before our eyes. And only if, like the Caribbean
poet Derek Walcott, they accept the scarred rather than sacred, the
fragmented rather than holistic nature of what he names "epic memory,"
which has to be recomposed—performed—again and again. For oral
tradition, however monumental its aspiration, remains an art of assemblage.
To reconstruct "this shipwreck of fragments, these echoes, these shards of a
huge tribal vocabulary, these partially remembered customs" needs a special

love. "Nothing can be sole or whole / That has not been rent," Yeats's Crazy Jane tells the Bishop. "Break a vase," says Walcott, "and the love that reassembles the fragments is stronger than the love that took its symmetry for granted when it was whole."[23]

NOTES

1. The shock factor seemed greater during the Vietnam War, the Biafra famine, and even occasionally before that. In 1941, filmed Japanese atrocities in China, or, in the 1960s, pictures of southern brutality against blacks during the Civil Rights movement, caught the attention of the American public.

2. See Bauman, *Modernity and the Holocaust* (Ithaca: Cornell University Press, 1989). The context of his discussion is Nazi bureaucracy and Hannah Arendt's thesis on the banality of evil. Concerning immediate media coverage of the Bosnian conflict, Slavenka Drakulic asks in the *New Republic* (June 21, 1993): 12: "here they are, generations who have learned at school about concentration camps and factories of death; generations whose parents swear it could never happen again, at least not in Europe, precisely because of the living memory of the recent past. What, then, has all the documentation changed? And what is being changed now by what seems to be the conscious, precise bookkeeping of death?"

3. No wonder many in the younger generation, who are the most susceptible, are drawn to the unreality of fiction, to horror movies and other artificial plots, ever more crude, gothic, and violent: one can pretend that these, at least, are mere fantasy.

4. Preface to *Lyrical Ballads*. Compare Goethe's notation circa August 8, 1797, in his *Reise in die Schweitz* "Sehr merkwürdig ist mir aufgefallen, wie es eigentlich mit dem Publikum einer grossen Stadt beschaffen ist; es lebt in einem baestandigen *Tummel von Erwerben und Verzehren*." (It seems to me very peculiar and worthy of notice, the quality of public life in a great city; it is marked by a constant tumult of acquiring and consuming.) (Cf. Wordsworth's famous line, "Getting and spending, we lay waste our powers ... .") He goes on to mention, in particular, theater and the inclination of the reading public toward novels and newspapers as the major distractions. These early symptoms of a consumer culture show that, from the outset, sensations are among the commodities being produced and consumed.

5. " Warhol as Art History," in *New Art*, ed. A. Papadakis, et al. (New York: Rizzoli, 1991). Henri Lefebvre's theory of "everydayness" diagnoses a "generalized passivity" that accompanies the increasing uniformity of everyday life (itself a functionalist result of the industrial and electronic revolutions) and is often veiled by the surface of modernity. "News stories and the turbulent affectations of art, fashion and event veil without ever eradicating the everyday blahs. Images, the cinema and television divert the everyday by at times offering up to it its own spectacle, or sometimes the spectacle of the distinctly noneveryday, violence, death, catastrophe, the lives of kings and stars—those who we are led to believe defy everydayness." For Lefebvre, see *Yale French Studies* 73 (1987): 7–11. Or cf. Gianni Vattimo on what he characterizes as a "growing psychological dullness": "Technical reproduction seems

to work in exactly the opposite sense to *shock*. In the age of reproduction [the reference is to Walter Benjamin's essay of 1936 on that subject], both the great art of the past and new media products reproducible from their inception, such as cinema, tend to become common objects and consequently less and less well defined against the background of intensified communication." Gianni Vattimo, *The Transparent Society*, trans. David Webb (Baltimore: Johns Hopkins University Press, 1992), 47–48.

6. Des Pres, *Praises and Dispraises: Poetry and Politics, the 20th Century* (New York: Penguin, 1989), Prolog.

7. The result of this can also be comic: think of the energy some expend on seeking to prove that Shakespeare was really Francis Bacon or the Earl of Essex, or consider that even children's literature is beginning to exploit this revisionism, as in "The True Story of the Three Little Pigs" by Alexander T. Wolf.

8. *Praises and Dispraises*, Prolog (my emphasis). That which "we cannot not know" is "the real," according to Henry James.

9. Such as blaming the "white devil" or the Jew for the world's suffering, or the notion of an evil empire. One of the few treatises to take up the possibility of ethics in a technological age, Hans Jonas's *Das Prinzip Verantwortung* (Frankfurt a/M: Insel, 1979) argues that our sense of technological power has led to utopian expectations: that it is all too easy to conceive of action on the pattern of technical progress, and that we need, therefore, a new "modesty" as the basis of moral activism: "In view of the quasi-eschatological potential of our technical processes, ignorance about ultimate consequences becomes itself a ground for responsible hesitation—a second-best quality, should wisdom be lacking." In America, at the same time, televangelism spawns its own sublime simplicity: the sinful past can be overcome by turning to a savior figure. The sense of universal suffering conveyed (painfully) by the media is here relieved (painlessly) by the media.

10. Indeed, Jean-François Lyotard defines our "postmodern" condition as "incredulity toward metanarratives" produced by progress in the sciences. There is often a rupture, then, between the increasingly scientific history of the historians and the culture of the community, that is, collective practices structured by group memory. In Judaism this separation from communal ways of remembering becomes painfully clear after the Holocaust. The command *zakhor*, "remember!" that resounds throughout the Bible and Jewish tradition, used to refer to observances that stressed, in Yosef Yerushalmi's words, "not the historicity of the past, but its eternal contemporaneity." Today the same "remember!" documents in volume upon volume a genocide that has weakened Jewish continuity. A form of memorizing rather than remembrance, and information rather than performance oriented, it is very different from the liturgical memory, the collectively recited lamentations, petitions and hymns, or the scripture study, by which Jews as a community healed or at least integrated the catastrophes in their past. Amos Funkenstein reintroduces the notion of "historical consciousness" to show that the split between historical and liturgical memory is not, today or in earlier times, as absolute as Yerushalmi represents it: see "Collective Memory and Historical Consciousness," *History and Memory* 1 (1989) 5–27.

11. Two more contemporary examples. (1) East Germany's foundational cult, centered on the prewar Communist leader Thaelmann. Thaelmann may have been

brought to Buchenwald and executed there toward the end of the war. To magnify Buchenwald as the symbol of German resistance to fascism, the East German government identified the cell where he was killed, made it a cavernous shrine and used it to initiate young devotees of the youth movement. The Thaelmann cult excluded all perspectives on the Nazi era except that of heroic Communist revolt, and became a sterile and self-exculpatory "god-term" for East Germany, one that allowed its inhabitants to transfer guilt for fascism and war crimes exclusively to the citizens of the *other* (West) Germany. (2) The rebirth of Israel, as Saul Friedlander and Alan Mintz (among others) have shown, activated a "paradigm retrieval" which had long ago linked catastrophe and redemption. "The national historian," Funkenstein writes, "who in the nineteenth century enjoyed the status of a priest of culture, and whose work, even professional, was still read by a wide stratum of the educated public … even created some of [the symbols], some almost from nothing, such as the legend of Hermann, the victorious Cheruskian hero of early Roman-Germanic encounter." "Collective Memory," 21.

12. The stories often crystallize or cluster around proper names, especially place-names (Hart-Leap Well; Beth-El; Wessex; Balbec; Paris, Texas; Ole Kentucky; Chelm; Homewood). Some of these are fictional places; but such is the power of art that names outlive in our imagination referents they may never have had.

13. Pierre Nora, *Les lieux de mémoire: La Republique. La Nation* (1984–), and Marc Augé, *Non-Lieux: Introduction à une anthropologie de la surmodernité* (Paris: Seuil, 1992). The conception of *non-lieu* plays with the legal term by which courts refuse to receive a complaint or nullify its basis in law. Cf. Claude Lanzmann, "Le lieu et la parole," in *Les Cahiers du Cinema*, 37 (1985). He describes there how he develops a technique to overcome the "non-lieu de la mémoire." For MacIntyre, see *After Virtue: A Study in Moral Theory* (Notre Dame: Notre Dame University Press, 1984).

14. *La mémoire collective*, 2nd ed. (Paris: Presses Universitaires de France, 1968), 68–69. Halbwachs's "collective memory" is a broader concept than "communal memory": no memory, according to Halbwachs (in the wake of Durkheim and Marc Bloch), is purely individual but always depends, to be a memory, on an "affective community" (which need not be religious or ritual). Edward Shils in *Tradition* (Chicago: Chicago University Press, 1981) makes the case that there is a sense of the past which is inculcated early and which is important as a general "sensibility to past things" as well as for its specific contents.

15. "Commentators on American culture note that a sense of historicity is shifting away from singular stories that are forever true—away from story-lines that are hero-oriented and confrontational. There are fewer authentic moments of 'catastrophe time.' … "Don Handelman on "media events," in *Models and Mirrors: Toward an Anthropology of Public Events* (Cambridge: Cambridge University Press, 1990), 266ff.

16. Jacques Le Goff, in describing the work of Pierre Nora on memory-places, and a new history "which seeks to create a scientific history on the basis of collective memory," does not entirely confront this difference between public and collective memory in his rather optimistic assessment. "[T]he whole evolution of the contemporary world, under the impact of an *immediate history* for the most part

fabricated on the spot by the media, is headed toward the production of an increased number of collective memories, and history is written, much more than in earlier days, under the influence of these collective memories." *History and Memory*, trans. Steven Rendall and E. Claman (New York: Columbia University Press, 1993), 95.

17. Cf. the description of what J. Assmann names "das kulturelle Gedächtnis," which seeks a stability beyond the *saeculum* of oral history and the span of Halbwachs's collective memory. "Kollektives Gedächtnis und kulturelle Identität," in *Kultur und Gedächtnis*, ed. Jan Assmann and Tonio Hölscher (Frankfurt a/M: Suhrkamp, 1988). Funkenstein, "Collective Memory," sees the difference between a purely liturgical memory and a more dynamic, heuristic collective memory emerging in the historical consciousness. The latter, according to him, appears in the *hidushim* (new insights) of rabbinic (*halakhic*) law-finding, as well as in literature—but he does not provide us with a conceptualized understanding of the difference between "the liturgical incantations of a dynasty of tribal leaders" and "the poetry of Homer or the Book of Judges."

18. See Ellen S. Fine on post-Holocaust Jewish writers (especially the children of survivors) in "The Absent Memory," *Writing and the Holocaust*, ed. Berel Lang (New York: Holmes & Meier, 1988). Also Nadine Fresco, "Remembering the Unknown," *International Review of Psycho-Analysis*, 11 (1984): 417–27. For Henri Raczymow, see 95–96, above.

19. Videotape adds to that dimension by allowing the recording of "stylistic" and "prosodic" features, such as gestures, visually accented pauses, etc. As in photography generally, more detail previously thought of as incidental or accidental is included. This increases oral history's movement away from *histoire événementielle*.

20. Claude Lanzmann, in "Le lieu et la parole," *Cahiers du Cinema* (1985), goes so far as to say that his film seeks an "incarnation." "Le souvenir me fait horreur: le souvenir est faible. Le film est l'abolition de toute distance entre le passé et le présent" (374) (Recollection disgusts me: it is so weak. The film aims at the abolition of all distance between the past and the present).

21. I must leave aside, here, the more general issue of the revival, through history or art, of memory-places. For the sensibility, for example, that joins Wordsworth to Milton in understanding memory-place, see *Paradise Lost*, IX, 320–29. In terms of academic transmission the *lieu de mémoire* becomes a "topos"; but the boundary between discourse, on the one hand, and poetry and even living performance, on the other, is quite porous, as was shown by E. R. Curtius's magisterial book on the way the classical tradition reaches modern European literature, and by the famous research of Parry and Lord on the formulaic compositional methods of Yugoslav bards. For Halbwachs's interesting treatment of "Religious Space," see *La mémoire collective*, 145–46 and 160–65. Monuments too are *lieux de mémoire*, involving, like stories, real or legendary places.

22. For Hegel it would have needed the entire history of the world, together with an intellectual odyssey of millennia, before mind is mind, free of its *subservience* to sense-perception, and able to retrieve all its memory-stages in the activity of thought. Meanwhile (i.e., in everyday rather than visionary temporality) interesting makeshift solutions are found. I have mentioned Alexander Kluge; Claude Chabrol's recent

L'oeil de Vichy (1993) raises the spectator's consciousness of visual dependence by creating a film purely out of archival propaganda images, countered only by a dry historical commentary placing them in context. And Wilfried Schoeller has written: "Every museum, every monument, every memorial site recalling the Nazi era should reserve a moment of discretion, should leave something open and perhaps even claim the status of ruin or artifact, so that the imagination can still be active toward something in it."

23. Walcott, Nobel lecture, "The Antilles: Fragments of Epic Memory," in the *New Republic*, December 28, 1992: 27. However, in emphasizing the performative dimension we need to distinguish between an opportunistic recomposing of the collective memory, motivated by identity politics, and the creative-heuristic use of its traditions in art. Such notions as Schiller's "aesthetic education" may provide a beginning for theorizing that difference. The formalist's deinstrumentalizing emphasis on what is distinctively literary also responds to the need for a critical perspective.

LAWRENCE L. LANGER

Two Holocaust Voices:
Cynthia Ozick and Art Spiegelman

It is scarcely accidental that so few American writers have addressed the theme of the Holocaust with the direct and vivid imaginative command of their European counterparts. Ida Fink, Aharon Appelfeld, Charlotte Delbo, Tadeusz Borowski, and Primo Levi have created classic fictional and nonfictional works unequaled by all but a few of even the most accomplished authors in this country. Of course, Levi and the others had a unique advantage: they could depend on personal memory and experience to conjure up their tales because all of them had been involved as victims of the catastrophe themselves.

The same cannot be said of Cynthia Ozick and Art Spiegel-man, although as a child of survivors Spiegelman was able to base his narrative on the ordeal of his parents. Still, both he and Ozick had to face a challenge that their fellow writers from Europe were spared. They had to decide how to imagine this inaccessible event for themselves before they could expect readers to embrace their vision. Indeed, Spiegelman includes this very issue as a major source of tension in his *Maus* volumes. Whether writing biography and autobiography, as Spiegelman does or, as in Ozick's case, trusting pure invention, establishing an authentic voice and persuasive milieu for the uninformed memory of an American public was a critical problem they could not disregard.

From *Preempting the Holocaust.* © 1998 by Yale University Press.

The parallels between Ozick's Rosa stories and Spiegelman's *Maus* tales reveal some curious conjunctions. She writes about a mother who has lost her daughter, he about a father who has lost his son. Ozick does everything in her power to detach herself from her protagonist, suppressing the autobiographical impulse by creating a woman who, unlike her, is ashamed and disdainful of her Jewish heritage. Art Spiegelman, in contrast, cannot escape the net of personal family conflict. He is a character in his own narrative, weaving autobiography, biography, and history into a single text. Whereas Ozick harnesses the resources of style to brighten and complicate her fiction, Spiegelman reduces written lines to a minimum, using dialogue as an adjunct to the unique *visual* form he has created to draw readers into the actual world of his father's (and mother's) Holocaust past. Both Ozick and Spiegelman sympathize with the individuals whom they recreate, but they portray them with so many unappealing traits that the reader is both intrigued and repelled by their personalities. Ozick's Rosa and Spiegelman's Vladek continue to be haunted by their Holocaust past. But whereas Ozick carefully conceals her presence through her art, Spiegelman deconstructs his chronicle by constantly reminding us that his version of his parents' ordeal under the Germans is nothing more than that—a version. It is based on testimony rather than imagination, a painfully wrought rendition of reality, not to be confused with the unrecapturable truth.

Because Ozick's Rosa and Spiegelman's Vladek are innocent, victimized by atrocities not of their own making, we instinctively feel pity for them, though their creators are careful to burden them with enough distasteful features to repel readers even as they are attracted. Heroes and heroines belong to romantic legend, not Holocaust reality. Instead of being ennobled by the catastrophe they endured, Rosa and Vladek seem unable to escape its scarring legacy. Ozick and Spiegelman refuse to tell a story of the triumph of the human spirit, the vindication of suffering through transcendence. They know one pays a price for surviving Auschwitz and the other deathcamps; the debt may be suppressed, shifted to a lower level of consciousness, but never forgotten. Closure is impossible: Vladek's ailing heart and Rosa's ailing mind are constant signs that they must share the normal world they inhabit with the abnormal one they inherit.

Unlike Art Spiegelman, whose visual narrative invites us to engage his material on multiple levels, Ozick must rely on verbal ingenuity alone to convey the split milieu in which Rosa dwells. The virtuosity of her technique is dazzling. Language both trans-figures and disfigures reality, as contrary descriptions sketch in the competing tensions of her ordeal. In "The Shawl," the story recounting the murder of Rosa's child, Magda, nature is compelling: "the sunheat murmured of another life, of butterflies in summer." But the physical stench of the barracks is revolting: "excrement, thick turd-braids, and the slow stinking maroon waterfall that slunk down from the upper bunks, the stink mixed with a bitter fatty floating smoke that greased Rosa's skin."[1] If there is a branch of art called the poetry of atrocity, this line alone makes Ozick one of its practicing masters.

For Ozick, how we see hinges on how we say, and memory in turn relies on the language of recall to determine how one survives an anguish like Rosa's. The physical fact is that Magda wanders out of the barrack and is seized by an SS man, who hurls her tiny body against the electrified barbed wire. But the moment is imprinted on Rosa's mind by Ozick's stylized portrayal: "The whole of Magda traveled through loftiness. She looked like a butterfly, touching a silver vine." This view is both poetic and remote, since Rosa is not very close to the scene of the murder: "the speck of Magda," we are told, with words verging on the sinister, "was moving more and more into the smoky distance" (9). The opposition between butterfly and smoke will haunt Rosa into her contaminated future, as the fragile beauty of what might have been contends with the reality of what is inside a woman who has outlived her loss but not her pain.

Unlike Vladek Spiegelman, whose financial means allow him to enjoy some of the amenities of American middle-class life, Rosa remains a displaced person even more in the United States than in Europe. She is a fringe being, kept on the outskirts of society by her modest means as well as by what Ozick calls "the drudgery of reminiscence" (69). She violates the stereotype of the immigrant who sheds her burdensome past and finds success in her adopted land. For Ozick, this would have been a formula too easy, too glibly American, to pursue. In her Brooklyn store, where she sells cheap antiques, Rosa tries to tell her customers about the ghetto and the camp, but no one wants to hear. Her complaint is familiar among survivors: "Nobody knew anything" (66). When she moves to Miami, following the path of another kind of Jewish migration, little changes. There, nature pursues her with an ominous intensity: "The streets were a furnace, the sun an executioner" (14). She lives amid Jews, but not among them. Something is missing from her life—is not this the meaning of her "lost" underwear?—and nothing in the American landscape, not laundromats or cafeterias or her cheap hotel, can replace it. At least this is her stubborn conviction.

When Rosa tells the elderly Jew named Persky, a prewar Polish immigrant who tries to befriend her, that "my Warsaw is not your Warsaw," she reminds both him and us that the Holocaust is as misplaced in America as is Rosa herself. But she tells us more, and this is the crux of the tension dominating Ozick's Rosa stories. Rosa allies herself to a Polish professional and intellectual aristocracy rather than to a proud Jewish tradition, and in so doing she forfeits much of the sympathy she has gained from our knowledge of her camp ordeal. She speaks so disparagingly of Jews in the Warsaw ghetto—"we were furious because we had to be billeted with such a class, with these old Jew peasants worn out from their rituals and superstitions" (67)—that she is dangerously close to adopting the prejudice of her German persecutors. American readers are first shocked by her hostility to her own people, then driven to find a middle ground between sympathy and dislike for Ozick's disheveled and eccentric protagonist.

If one purpose of biographical narratives, whether fiction or nonfiction, is to integrate the character of their subjects, then both Ozick and Spiegelman are guilty of subverting this intention. Rosa and Vladek struggle to restore the shattered identities that their German oppressors were determined to efface, but mere chronology cannot erase the deep discontinuities of their lives. Although at the end of her story Rosa removes the shawl from her telephone and, accepting its message, allows the persistent Persky to come up to her room, Magda is not gone, only temporarily away. Rosa's injured maternity has not recovered from the scar etched on her memory by the murder of her daughter. She may give the human instinct another chance, but it cannot cancel the inhuman one that still lingers in the wings of her life's drama.

Unpleasant as she is in her speech and person, bleakly as her anti-Jewish sentiments continue to resound in our ears, the image of Rosa as a bereft mother rescues her from total censure. Vladek Spiegelman's chronic stinginess, his manipulation of his son's and wife's affections, and his outrageous bigotry against blacks make it plain that his camp ordeal—this is true for Rosa, too—has taught him little about generosity toward others. "Learning from experience" in the sense of moral education is a romantic and sentimental stereotype that both Ozick and Spiegelman seem determined to explode. Yet the harrowing narrative of what Vladek and Artie's mother, Anja, endured in ghetto and camps, in hiding and flight, the stories of the murder of family members, including Artie's own brother, can only rouse our sympathy and concern. Like Ozick, Spiegelman draws up two scenarios, forcing us to absorb both, allowing us to be comfortable with neither. Because they coexist in the internal lives of their protagonists, they coexist in ours, too, keeping in permanent tension the flow of chronological time and certain fixed moments of disaster from the past.

One of the recurrent refrains in Charlotte Delbo's Auschwitz memoir, *None of Us Will Return*, is "essayer de regarder, essayer pour voir"—"try to look, try to see." Spiegelman adopts this entreaty as the governing artistic principle of his work. I know of no other Holocaust account that uses it with such literal expertise. Spiegelman takes a familiar artifact of American popular culture, the comic strip, and elevates it to the level of serious literary biography. The visual style of *Maus* enables him to condense both time and space with an economy that is not possible in a prose narrative. On a single page he can move from the United States to Europe, from the city to the country, from Artie's home to his father's. He can alternate closeups with long shots, external with internal views of the same scene, forcing the reader to hold them in suspension while examining the chronicle from multiple perspectives. He can shift time as quickly as he maneuvers space, so that past and present are woven inseparably into one testimonial thread. By showing on the same page an image of Vladek telling his story to Artie, who is preserving his words on a tape recorder, and visual flashbacks recreating the episodes even as Vladek recalls them, Spiegelman can dramatize an ongoing debate between memory and truth. His technique raises a vital question, not only for readers of the *Maus* texts, but for anyone interested in the relation between fictional facts and factual fictions in Holocaust narrative: what changes are wrought by the imagination, even the imagination of the survivor, when his or her history becomes his or her story? What role does the intervention of time play in the effort to portray a past recaptured?

Vladek Spiegelman's testimony is ripe with accurate visual detail. We are not only invited but forced by the pictorial text to imagine features of the Holocaust that often elude even the most diligent reader. We get glimpses of underground bunkers, the inside of a boxcar, roundups, hangings, selections, death marches, the machinery of murder itself via architectural sketches of the gas chambers and crematoria of Auschwitz. The American reader is thus prompted to participate actively in the reconstruction of Holocaust reality emerging from Artie's prodding and his father's reminiscence. Just as Ozick's style tempts us to "see" by what is said, so for Spiegelman the design of a page controls the eye rather than the ear. Historical truth turns visible.

Perhaps the most celebrated example of this strategy at work is the first page of the chapter in *Maus II* called "Auschwitz (Time Flies)." In a succinct fusion of durational and chronological time, Spiegelman shows Artie sitting at his drawing board atop a mound of naked corpses vainly trying to organize the various crucial dates of his narrative and his life into a coherent sequence: the death of his father, the suicide of his mother, the impending birth of his daughter, the murder of Hungarian Jewry in Auschwitz, the enthusiastic critical reception of *Maus I*. Instead of feeling overjoyed by his achievements, however, Artie is depressed.

Why? Like this page, all Holocaust art, whether memoir, biography, or fiction, is built on a mountain of corpses, so that it can never be an act of celebration, a triumph of form over the chaos of experience. "A Survivor's Tale"—the subtitle of both parts of *Maus*—is never entirely that, since in the history of the Holocaust the fact of one person's staying alive cannot be isolated from the death of others less lucky. Indeed, in the Rosa stories and the *Maus* volumes, the impact of dead characters is as great as the role of the living: Rosa's daughter, Magda, Artie's brother, Richieu, his mother, Anja, whose suicide appears to complete the postponed dying she escaped in Auschwitz. Hence Vladek's self-reported ingenuity in manipulating others and devising schemes to keep himself and his wife alive, together with the general fidelity of his testimony, has its darker side.

The elder Spiegelman is not immune to this truth, though he prefers to speak of his more successful exploits. Near the end of *Maus II*, his dejected figure looms down the length of most of a page, photos of his wife's murdered family spread at his feet, while he tells his son of the fate of *his* side of the family: "So only my little brother, Pinek, came out from the war alive ... from the rest of my family, it's *nothing* left, not even a snapshot."[2] This includes his father, his three sisters with their six children, and three of his brothers. And of course, his own son Richieu.

Because not much of our literature has been erected on a mountain of corpses, or on the prospect of mass murder, American readers are obliged to adapt to an unfamiliar theme. Our greatest classics have been built around memorable names: Natty Bumppo, Hester Prynne, Captain Ahab, Huck Finn, Isabel Archer, Quentin Compson, Willy Loman. Insofar as they are loners, what Melville called Isolatoes, Rosa Lublin and Vladek Spiegelman share their tradition. But unlike their American predecessors, they are not memorable as individuals; they are creatures of an assault on the self that has no parallel in our history—except perhaps for the quite different crime of slavery, or the native American experience, on which Ozick and Spiegelman do not draw in their narratives.

The journey to and from Auschwitz and the other camps injects memory with a poison for which the American cultural landscape provides no antidote. Art Spiegelman confirms this in one of the subtlest touches of the *Maus* stories. Vladek spends one summer in a cottage in the region that used to be known as the Borscht Belt, where wealthy American Jews vacationed in fancy hotels, like the one Vladek sneaks into to play bingo without having to pay. Because the cost of utilities is included in the rent of his cottage, he leaves the flame on his gas burner permanently ignited, so that he won't have to waste matches each time he wants to cook something. We need no Hamlet bitterly crying "Thrift, thrift, Horatio!" to remind us of the sinister echo of this image, a fusion of gas chamber and crematorium that links Vladek inescapably to his dismal past. He may not be conscious of that connection himself, but it exerts its force over his mental life—and ours—nonetheless.

Indeed, how to connect a more or less normal present with a catastrophic past is the theme of both of the texts we have been examining. One role of Holocaust literature is to ease us into a position where we can imagine the struggle for those daily immersed in it. Because it was the story of his life as well as his craft, Art Spiegelman was in a unique position to illuminate that dilemma. He, too, inhabits two scenarios, as Artie the son of Holocaust survivors and Art the artist in quest of a visual narrative form for his experience. He is sensitive to the limitations of his task, admitting in several places the inadequacy of all efforts to reconstruct this atrocity; and to the flaws in his own motives, since he does not even like his father and in fact ignores and exploits his ill-health by smoking in his presence and pushing him to the point of exhaustion with his interviews. The testimony may provide material for Art as well as art, but it brings neither reconciliation nor peace.

I suspect that Ozick and Spiegelman never thought it would, or intended that it should. If one index of American culture is that it offers future opportunities to pacify a painful past, then these American Holocaust narratives challenge us to reshape and deepen that tradition. The opening image of *Maus II* is a photograph of the murdered Spiegelman son and brother, Richieu, to whom the volume is dedicated. But it is also dedicated to Spiegelman's own young daughter Nadja, whose name is not accompanied by a picture. What role will this member of a new generation play in the ongoing saga of her ravaged heritage? Will Nadja be more successful than her father in detaching her existence from the burden of a doomed ancestry?

If the beginning of *Maus II* invokes images of the dead Richieu and the living Nadja, the closing image remains equally ambivalent: the tombstone of Vladek and Anja Spiegelman, countersigned, as it were, by their surviving son, whose signature ends the text, followed by the dates of composition of the *Maus* volumes, 1978–1991. Thus both art and life have a chronology, a beginning and an end. But if the narratives by Ozick and Spiegelman, concerned as they are with an unprecedented event like the Holocaust, mean anything, it is that chronological time is insufficient to contain the impact of its atrocities on human memory and imagination. If life is to go on, we cannot confuse the dead with the living: but this is just what Vladek Spiegelman does in our last glimpse of him on the last page of the book, as he calls his living son by the name of his dead one. Rosa, too, writes letters to her murdered daughter as if she had a real existence beyond her death. Both Ozick's and Spiegelman's narratives are survivors' tales, but we are left wondering in the end who has survived with greater vitality—the living or the dead?

NOTES

1. Cynthia Ozick, *The Shawl: A Story and a Novella* (New York: Knopf, 1989), 8, 8–9.

2. Art Spiegelman, *Maus II, A Survivor's Tale: And Here My Troubles Began* (New York: Pantheon, 1991), 116.

JEFFREY M. PECK

The Holocaust
and Literary Studies

Although I am presenting the perspective of a literary critic, I must admit from the outset that my approach to the Holocaust is shaped by a number of other disciplinary and intellectual influences. My research and my institutional affiliation are interdisciplinary. I was trained in German and comparative literature and then became increasingly engaged with ethnographic and anthropological questions of national identity and minority discourses. My recent work—a book and a video documentary on survivors of the Holocaust, in this case Jews who escaped, lived in exile, and returned to both Germanies after World War II—was done in collaboration with an anthropologist.[1] In this framework, I am most interested in the problems of narrative, especially the interview as a genre that raises central questions about subjectivity, voice, position, and representation. Thus my comments are an interdisciplinary mixture of literary and cultural perspectives, albeit always with a fundamental interpretive bent grounded in literature and literary analysis. Literature plays a singular role as the most self-conscious and explicit portrayal of subjective experience of a horror that renders its own representation problematic.[2]

From its philological roots, literary criticism as the practice of describing, analyzing, and interpreting written texts has a long tradition, at least in Germany, in hermeneutics. As a philosophical procedure whose intention, most simply formulated, is to make the strange and the familiar

From *Lessons and Legacies III: Memory, Memorialization, and Denial*, ed. Peter Hayes. © 1999 by Northwestern University Press.

strange, the application of hermeneutical thinking to the Holocaust may seem at best contradictory. On the one hand, how can an event so catastrophic and horrible, "strange" only in the broadest metaphoric sense, be made familiar? And on the other hand, how can the gruesome images so familiar to us today continue to resonate? Theodor Adorno's now famous dictum that poetry is impossible after Auschwitz was but a harbinger of the trials of representation to come. It is precisely this issue of translating, explaining, and interpreting—all definitions of the Greek word *hermeneuin*, from which "hermeneutics" evolved—that seems to be the task of the literary critic when confronting the problem of writing about the Holocaust. I can only hope to remind us of some of the obvious problems.

The notion of text has been broadened by hermeneutical philosophers like Paul Ricoeur and anthropologists like Clifford Geertz[3] to make a place for actions, behaviors, and practices in culture to be interpreted like a text, turning, so to speak, texts and their contexts inside out. Nevertheless, this only adds a complicating dimension to the dilemma of capturing in words or images an event like the Holocaust, which at its core is unrepresentable yet demands of its victims and those spared its immediate terror a rendering of these experiences. On the one hand, the limitations of writing and the imagination of the literary writer and, on the other hand, the interpretive facility of the literary critic are manifestly taxed by the increased demands and responsibilities of writing on the Holocaust. Thus, writing about the Holocaust becomes the most extreme and vexing example of what all literary and ethnographic work is about—rendering experience comprehensible in a form that "makes sense" or "gives meaning," in the German sense of *Sinndeutung*.

Literature is usually thought of as the imaginative realm where the so-called realistic may mingle freely with the mythological, the symbolic, the metaphoric, or the allegorical. Many might think, and it has been said, that it is only in literature—in the sphere of the subjective and even emotional—that the Holocaust experience can be grasped. And there is, of course, a wide range of literature and literary criticism on the Holocaust.[4] However, I am more inclined to think that it is experimentation in structuring experience in different narrative forms, such as interviews, memoirs, and diaries, rather than just in thematics, that gives literary narrative its special status and draws us nearer to rendering the strange familiar.

Poststructuralist criticism has emphasized literature as only one of the many discursive fields composing culture. Nevertheless, this penchant to privilege the discursive and to recognize the "literary" or rhetorical quality of all narratives, even in the social sciences, underscores the importance of the literary text. Still, the identification of the literary aspect of storytelling and its fictional basis, compared to the documentary with its supposed claim on truth, raises thorny questions. Where is the boundary between fiction and reality in Holocaust testimony? Cannot the exclusive focus on the discursive nature of experience ignore, especially in the case of the Holocaust, AIDS, or atomic bomb victims, the materiality of experience, concretely rendered in the body?[5] While words are one of the few means at our disposal to literally represent experience—of course there are photographs, sculptures, and other artistic forms—how far can these signifying systems take us?

Elie Wiesel's novel *Night*, Rolf Hochhuth's play *The Deputy*, and Paul Celan's poem "Death Fugue" are all renderings of actual Holocaust experiences in a form called literary. They consciously and conscientiously rearrange, alter, or intensify a moment or feeling to touch our emotions as well as our intellect. But even in cases where "real" events are fictionalized as another tool in the struggle to represent the unrepresentable, such authors do not "fictionalize" in a traditional sense. While they may create characters, times, and locations that are not "real," they never veer too far from the Holocaust itself, which keeps its firm grip on verisimilitude. As if to ward off the evil spirits of those who would deny the Holocaust's very existence with fallacious claims and spurious overtones, using notions like "fictions" and "interpretations" as arguments, Holocaust writers recognize the need to temper their imaginations, even when presenting alternative scenarios. Nonetheless, imagination and fantasy fuel the literary spirit that provides readers with both documentary and emotional experience.

Literature portrays experience in a form that both distances and draws in the reader while offering insight into the emotions provoked by the Holocaust. Providing situations that might have been, rather than actually were, literature gives the author opportunities to rethink and re-evaluate actual events and feelings in a form that may allow him or her to work out existential or ethical dilemmas removed from the "real," protected from actual pain and suffering. For the reader, literature offers new or alternative avenues of entry into Holocaust experience. Art Spiegelman's *Maus: A Survivor's Tale* is a singular example. Its cartoon characters do not mock or trivialize, but rather intensify a range of feelings by replaying events and relations between victims and perpetrators as a literal cat-and-mouse game.

Yet, with the existential and ethical limitations imposed on us by the magnitude of the horror and our responsibility as critics to "do it justice," we face the limitations of words on the one side and emotions on the other. The latter are often too personal or painful to be shared or too individualistic to make sense to someone on the outside. As scholars we are consistently confronted with the gripping and unique firsthand testimony that defies translation. Literature can filter and temper such pathos and trauma. But this particular narrative form cannot accomplish the task alone. No one literary genre or verbal or artistic rendering is adequate. However, literature provides the necessary critical tools of interpretation, analysis, evaluation, and self-reflection, which can be applied to other Holocaust representations. While literature and its criticism are a way in, a combination of other critical practices is perhaps the way out of the conundrum of representing the Holocaust, which centers so much on remembering, reconstructing, and recording. Literature, history, and even memoirs perform these duties. Important work on monuments and memory enhance the discussion of meaning and interpretation. James Young's work in *The Texture of Memory: Holocaust Memorials and Monuments* and Jane Kramer's essay on the proposed Berlin Holocaust memorial, entitled "The Politics of Memory," are good examples.[6] To address issues of memory from another angle, video testimony of a survivor, psychoanalytic-literary approaches to testimony,[7] and a play like Peter Weiss's *The Investigation* provide complementary points of view.

All Holocaust scholars share responsibilities not only to a subject matter but also to human beings who suffered or perished simply because they were Jewish, communist, "Gypsy," Jehovah's Witness, or gay. Those who study or teach the Holocaust are condemned to always fall short of completeness. Nevertheless, by gathering texts and reading them in dialogue with one another, one can mitigate the inevitable problem of "partial truths," as the anthropologist James Clifford calls the ethnographic project of rendering foreign cultures.[8] For is it not precisely the "foreignness" of the Holocaust that makes its translatability so tenuous and the event itself even impossible to render comprehensible? Historian David Lowenthal, in his book entitled *The Past Is a Foreign Country*, reminds those of us struggling to interpret the Holocaust that the task at hand has both temporal and spatial dimensions.[9] The difficulty of bridging both of these gaps is compounded by the inexplicability of human malice and suffering. These tasks burden all scholars, no matter what their disciplines. They confront us with enormous responsibility to recognize our own personal and historical position toward such sensitive material and the ways it shapes what can only be serious and well-intentioned gestures toward objectivity.

In fact, achieving "objectivity" is possible neither by proclaiming neutrality toward a subject that demands individual human involvement, nor by a single work. Instead, a critically reflective, interdisciplinary perspective that takes advantage of various potential renderings (films, novels, plays, memoirs, diaries, autobiographies, documentaries, photographs, sculptures, paintings) and various critical approaches can get us closer to grasping Holocaust experience. It is precisely this frustrating incompleteness and partiality that can provide the opportunity for setting off texts and approaches next to and against one other. What the philosopher or historian cannot answer may well be complemented by the literary author or critic. The elusiveness of a complete grasp should not deter us from including the various versions of this experience rendered in the allegories of the novel, the voice of oral testimony or interview, or the supposedly more objective illustrations of a documentary film recording, for example, the liberation of a camp. Precisely at these points of juxtaposition, one gains critical perspective on the inability to capture "truth." However, when "read" together, these versions enable the one who was not there to at least approximate experience and approach what T. S. Eliot called an "objective correlative."

Holding up a mirror to nature, to use the metaphor of realism, always reveals its cracks, the position of the viewer, and the angle of the mirror. While these limiting conditions have to be taken into consideration, they do not undermine the validity of the attempt. As scholars, aware of our disciplinary imperatives, expectations, and methodologies, we must reflect in our work and with our students on the way that our particular disciplinary vision shapes our understanding of Holocaust experience and how the confrontation of various disciplinary positionings, discourses, and methods can improve our chances of grasping the ungraspable and representing the unrepresentable.

Engendered by literature and literary study, the critical task of interpretation provoked by the Holocaust is essentially a pedagogical experience.[10] Teaching the Holocaust puts the teacher and students into a singular constellation of intellectual and emotional relationships. While learning the facts and figures about death camps and gas chambers, students are also confronted with ethical questions of guilt and responsibility. Questions of perpetrator and victim resonate beyond the Nazi period when those issues are understood as interpretations of power, authority, free will, and obligation. In fact, how one understands the events leading up to the Holocaust and the Holocaust itself constitutes for the student a lesson in personal involvement, often with existential dimensions. There is no way to approach this very different kind of classroom experience. It requires both our openness and vigilance toward emotions, subjectivity, and personal engagement. Literature, I think, raises the challenge of facing the moral responsibility of understanding what this unique hermeneutical and human endeavor entails.

Notes

1. John Borneman and Jeffrey M. Peck, *Sojourners: The Return of German Jews and the Question of Identity* (Lincoln: University of Nebraska Press, 1995). The video documentary has the same title.

2. This problem of representation has been raised particularly in postmodernist criticism, especially in literature, history, and anthropology. For a more detailed discussion than I can provide here, see the essays in and especially the introduction to *Probing the Limits of Representation: Nazism and the "Final Solution,"* ed. Saul Friedlander (Cambridge, Mass.: Harvard University Press, 1992).

3. See, for example, Paul Ricoeur's "The Model of the Text: Meaningful Action Considered as a Text," in *Interpretive Science: A Reader,* ed. Paul Rabinow and William M. Sullivan (Berkeley: University of California Press, 1979), pp. 197–221. Almost any of Clifford Geertz's voluminous writings will steer the reader in this textualist direction, but see in particular his essays in *The Interpretation of Culture: Selected Essays* (New York: Basic Books, 1973) and *Local Knowledge: Further Essays in Interpretive Anthropology* (New York: Basic Books, 1983).

4. There are literally hundreds of titles on Holocaust literature. Some of the most prominent critics are Berel Lang, Lawrence Langer, Geoffrey Hartman, David Roskies, and Sidra Ezrahi.

5. On AIDS, see, for example, Sander Gilman, *Disease and Representation: Images of Illness from Madness to AIDS* (Ithaca: Cornell University Press, 1985). On atom bomb representations, see John Whittier Treat, *Writing Ground Zero: Japanese Literature and the Atomic Bomb* (Chicago: University of Chicago Press, 1995).

6. James Young, *The Texture of Memory: Holocaust Memorials and Monuments* (New Haven: Yale University Press, 1993), and Jane Kramer, *The Politics of Memory: Looking for Germany in the New Germany* (New York: Random House, 1996), pp. 254–93.

7. An excellent study is Shoshana Felman and Dori Laub, *Testimony: Crises of Witnessing in Literature, Psychoanalysis, and History* (New York and London: Routledge, 1992). The authors combine their expertise as literary critic and psychoanalyst to deal with "the relation between art and history, between art and memory, between speech and survival" (p. xiii).

8. James Clifford, "Introduction: Partial Truths," in his *Writing Culture: The Poetics and Politics of Ethnography* (Berkeley: University of California Press, 1986), pp. 1–26.

9. David Lowenthal, *The Past Is a Foreign Country* (New York: Cambridge University Press, 1985).

10. My understanding of this point was enriched by Irene Kacandes and a discussion she led on teaching the Holocaust at the 1996 Lessons and Legacies conference at Notre Dame University, South Bend, Indiana.

RITCHIE ROBERTSON

Rafael Seligmann's *Rubinsteins Versteigerung*: The German-Jewish Family Novel before and after the Holocaust

Rafael Seligmann is Germany's answer to Philip Roth.[1] His three novels *Rubinsteins Versteigerung* (1989), *Die jiddische Mamme* (1990), and *Der Musterjude* (1997) resemble *Portnoy's Complaint* and the Zuckerman novels in dramatizing male sexual anxieties and conflicts over Jewish identity. Of these, *Rubinsteins Versteigerung*, which provoked a scandal when published, stands out by its combination of savage humor, sentiment, and pain, and I will concentrate on it at the expense of the two other, lighter-weight novels. While *Rubinsteins Versteigerung* represents a no-holds-barred portrayal of a Jewish community in postwar Germany, anyone familiar with the long tradition of German-Jewish writing will notice how much the tensions that Seligmann depicts resemble those depicted in a series of novels and essays about the Jewish family in the age of assimilation. Besides elucidating what Seligmann as novelist and essayist has to say about the position of Jews in the Federal Republic, I want also to indicate these longer continuities.

Seligmann, surprisingly, is a Jew who left Israel and settled in Germany. He was born in Israel in 1947. His parents were emigrants from Germany. When he was ten they returned and settled in Munich. The Jewish community there consisted to a large extent (80 percent) of Displaced Persons who at the end of the war were either survivors of concentration camps or refugees from Eastern Europe. In addition, by 1959 some 9,000

From *The Germanic Review* 75, no. 3 (Summer 2000). © 2000 by the Helen Dwight Reid Educational Foundation.

Jews had returned to Germany from Israel or Latin America: Some were elderly people who could not adjust to their new homelands; their return was encouraged by the federal government as a sign of the country's democratization. The Munich Jewish community in which Seligmann was brought up was not large: Even by the mid-'80s it numbered only 3,900 people, and it was an elderly and conservative community.[2]

Seligmann is among those critics of German-Jewish relations in the Federal Republic—foremost among them Henryk M. Border—who argue that these relations were poisoned by dishonesty on both sides. Since the postwar Federal Republic showed insufficient concern to bring war criminals and Holocaust perpetrators to justice, nationalistic and anti-Semitic assumptions were allowed to survive; the official representatives of the Jewish community in Germany, the Zentralrat der Juden in Deutschland, founded in 1950, were so anxious to remain on good terms with the German state that they failed to defend Jewish interests against defamation and treated their Jewish critics with far more hostility than they did ex-Nazis. A survey undertaken by the sociologist Alphons Silbermann in the mid-'70s found that anti-Semitism was explicitly present in 15 to 20 percent of the West German population and latent in another 30 percent. These findings were rejected by representatives of the Zentralrat without adequate critical discussion. Silbermann describes this denial of anti-Semitism as a policy of appeasement and compares it to the stance taken by pre-1933 Jewish bodies such as the Central-Verein deutscher Staatsbürger jüdischen Glaubens (C.-V.), whose efforts to oppose anti-Semitism were hamstrung by a fear of taking a public stand as Jews and thus drawing attention to themselves.[3]

Yet there is ample published testimony by Jews living in the Federal Republic to the discomfort and unease they feel, even though they rarely experience open anti-Semitism. They know that the Germans around them may well be concealing anti-Semitism, may well be ex-Nazis or the children of Nazis. The petty intolerance and acceptance of authoritarianism that they see in everyday life remind them unpleasantly of the submissive mentality that helped to make the Holocaust possible. They feel unwilling or unable to identify with Germany. Like Broder, they may consider themselves "Paßdeutsche," holders of a German passport who cannot fulfill the racially based German criteria for full membership of the nation.[4] They may feel compelled to be constantly on their best behavior, like Artur Brauner:

> Ich versuche z.B. als Jude, soweit möglich, in vielen Fällen human
> bzw, humaner zu agieren als ein Nichtjude. Ich werde nie einen
> Kellner beschimpfen oder die Putzfrau verletzen, indem ich sie

im Befehlston zur Arbeit antreibe. Ich denke natürlich daran, daß schlechte aber auch gute Taten *eines* Juden erfahrungsgemäß auf das gesamte jüdische Volk abfärben.[5]

However appealing this may sound, it represents, too, a policy of appeasement, recalling the stance taken by Jews under the "emancipation contract" which required them to demonstrate their fitness for emancipation by adopting German standards of culture and behavior. One of the C.-V.'s leaders. Ludwig Hoiländer, said: "Die deutschen Juden sind Stiefkinder, und Stiefkinder müssen sich artig benehmen."[6] Yet such appeasement, as Broder has argued vigorously, is futile in the face of an anti-Semitism that is based on ingrained attitudes and not on empirical reactions to the actual behavior of Jews.[7]

While the repression of the Holocaust allows anti-Semitism to continue, the excessively high-minded discussion of the Holocaust creates another kind of dishonesty. Seligmann strongly opposes the conception of Jewish identity as determined by the Holocaust. He deplores those Jews who see themselves as victims. Such people collude with Germans, enabling the latter to express a shallow, perhaps insincere remorse, and in return receive a hollow Jewish identity as victims that makes up for the lack of real religious or cultural Jewishness in their lives. This collusion disguises the Germans' indifference to the real feelings of Jews and the Jews' resentment against the Germans:

> Wen kümmert's, wie die Juden in unserer Mitte leben? Welcher Judenfreund von eigenen Gnaden hat sich die Mühe gemacht festzustellen, daß kaum ein "jüdischer Mitbürger" in der Lage ist, seine Wut über den ganz normalen Wahnsinn deutscher Betroffenheitsheuchelei hinauszuschreien? Vielen Juden kommt die Einstufung als Opfer zupaß. Sie hilft ihnen, ihr Identitätsvakuum auszufüllen. Man hat sie als Juden verfolgt, also haben sie "dafür überlebt", daß sie Jude bleiben. Sie identifizieren sich als Holocaust- oder Postholocaust-Generation. Auf diese Weise erheben "moderne" Juden - ohne daß inhen dies bewußt wird - Adolf Hitler und die Seinen zum Schöpfer ihrer Identität.[8]

Seligmann goes on to criticize the spread of Holocaust museums, inspired by the foundation of Yad Vashem in 1953 and strongly encouraged by the opening of the Simon Wiesenthal Center in Los Angeles and the Holocaust Museum in Washington in 1993. Like other commentators, he is alarmed by the development of a Jewish identity based less on religion and tradition than on the Holocaust and hence on the consciousness of victimhood.[9] But while Jews in America and Israel have access to a Jewish culture independent of the Holocaust, Jews in Germany are constantly reminded of it by coming across the ruins of synagogues and Jewish cemeteries and by their awareness of the Nazi past. No wonder that they feel guilt at living in the land of the murderers and are obsessed by the Holocaust. Naturally they transmit this obsession to their children: "Entsprechend programmieren die Davongekommenen das Bewußtsein ihrer Kinder mit Holocaust-Neu-rosen, statt mit jüdischer Religiosität und Wissen. Jüdische Jugendliche in Deutschland sollen nach dem Willen ihrer Eltern nicht ihr Leben genießen. Sie haben vielmehr die Pflicht, durch ihr Judentum die Leiden der Eltern zu rechtfertigen."[10]

As a result, in Seligmann's opinion, Jews in Germany inhabit an invisible ghetto. They cannot mix easily with Germans, nor can they acknowledge their antipathy. On the German side, well-intentioned Germans are motivated by guilt and fear that make them idealize Jews and then feel aggrieved when Jews turn out to be only human: "Die Philosemiten begehren den moralisch unbefleckten Juden. Sie gieren danach, sich im Zerrbild seiner moralischen Reinheit in ihrer eigenen Schuld zu suhlen."[11] Other commentators have pinpointed the tendency to evade the implications of the Holocaust by converting penitence into monetary and hence quantifiable reparations.[12] Seligmann maintains that the Jews' unease is fostered by fear of renewed anti-Semitism. The Zentralrat encourages this fear not only by representing the Jews as victims and continually requesting pity for Jewish sufferings, but also when such leaders as the late Heinz Galinski and Ignatz Bubis go on the offensive by denouncing anti-Semisitsm. "Durch ständige Angstappelle werden die Juden an vergangenes und gegenwärtiges (Anti-Semitismus-) Leid erinnert. Man ermuntert sie, in ihrem vertrauten Angstghetto zu verharren."[13]

In talking about the emotional ghetto that Jews in Germany inhabit. Seligmann is reviving an image familiar from the turn of the century, when it was often argued that Jews in Germany and Austria had attained only a nominal and illusory assimilation and were really cut off from their Gentile fellow-citizens by the walls of an invisible ghetto. Silbermann even uses the phrase "das neue Ghetto" which is the title of the proto-Zionist play by Theodor Herzl, *Das neue Ghetto* (written in 1894 and first staged in 1898). The image of the "new ghetto" surrounding modern Jews was a common one in Herzl's generation. The French Jewish publicist Bernard Lazare applied the phrase to the hostile external force of anti-Semitism, but German and Austrian Jews applied it to the inner condition of the Jewish subculture.[14] Martin Buber says that Jews need to overcome "die Enge des Lebens und die Enge des Geistes, das äußere und das innere Ghetto."[15] Perhaps the harshest criticism of quasi-assimilated Jews came from Walther Rathenau. Judged by Rathenau's ideals of Prussian and military manhood, actual Berlin Jews looked and sounded deplorably unmilitary, ill-at-ease, unmannerly and overassertive. Instead of absorbing German standards of behavior, they remained voluntarily separate: "In engem Zusammenhang unter sich, in strenger Abgeschlossenheit nach außen: so leben sie in einem halb freiwilligen, unsichtbaren Ghetto, kein lebendes Glied des Volkes, sondern ein fremder Organismus in seinem Leibe."[16]

Thus Seligmann's understanding of German-Jewish life conforms to a long-established model. The problem he sees is still that of acculturation without assimilation. But the stakes are now higher. A century ago, Jews were isolated from a society that required them to prove their fitness for assimilation yet increasingly defined itself in racial terms as non-Jewish and hence unable to accept them. Now they still have to prove that they are "good Jews," virtuous victims, but the surrounding society frightens them by its genocidal history and is itself tormented by guilt towards those it has injured.

The new Jewish identity is not based on Jewish religion or culture. Many contemporary Jews in Germany were brought up without any interest in Jewish tradition. Their Jewish identity is one which the Gentile world imposes on them, or else, as with Jurek Becker, a biographical contingency that feels irrelevant.[17] Seligmann's hero is in a situation like that painfully described by Michel Lang:

Ich bin ein Schicksals-Jude. Aufgewachsen mit dem Bewußtsein und der Gewißheit, einer Volksgemeinschaft anzugehören, die seit 2000 Jahren unter einem ständigen Fluch zu leiden hat: dem Judenhaß. Und meine Eltern sorgten dafür, daß ich, von Kindesbeinen an, diese Tatsache als unveränderbar betrachetete. Diese "jüdische Angst" ist ein wesentlicher Faktor meiner Persönlichkeitsentwicklung geworden. Ich bin mittlerweile zu einem Paradestück jüdischen Daseins geworden. Mein Ich wird von diesem Jüdisch-Sein beherrscht, geleitet, motiviert. Es äußert sich in einer fast neurotischen Überempfindlichkeit gegenüber jedweder Unterdrückung und Intoleranz, einer beinahe masochistischen Lebensphilosophie, einer überpointierten Ich-Bezogenheit und einer gleichgültigen

Nonchalance allem gegenüber, was nichtjüdisch, eben gojisch ist.[18]

Hence some writers, like Broder, Silbermann, and Lang, have called for the lifting of taboos on the discussion of German-Jewish relations. Instead of professing a false high-mindedness, people should openly discuss the mutual antipathies that they feel. Seligmann shares this view. He urges honest dialogue as the recipe: "das *ehrliche* Gespräch."[19] Jews need to be accepted, and to accept themselves, not as victims or saints, but as ordinary people. And they need to be accepted as Germans. The false antithesis "Jews and Germans" ("Juden und Deutsche"), which provided the title of a well-intentioned "*Spiegel*-Spezial" in 1992, needs to be overcome. Seligmann declares that he regards himself as a German: "Ich fühle mich als Deutscher, gewiß als besserer Deutscher als etwa Herr Schönhuber und Konsorten," he said on TV in 1990, referring to the then prominent leader of the far-right Republican Party.[20] He demands that German Jews should accept their German identity: "Deutsch ist unsere Sprache und Kultur, wir haben deutsche Freunde und Lebenspartner, wir arbeiten und leben *hier*—in Israel machen wir nur Urlaub. Wir sind Deutsche, ob es uns oder anderen paßt oder nicht."[21] Innumerable such declarations could be collected from the era before Hitler.[22] Nowadays, however, by advertising his identity as a Jewish German, Seligmann has aroused embarrassment among well-intentioned non-Jews and hostility among Jews.

The underlying antipathies between Jewish and non-Jewish Germans have seldom found literary expression from the Jewish side. Seligmann has commented on the remarkable absence of hate or aggression from the work of Jewish authors in Germany. The reasons, he says, are fear and shame. Jews do have those feelings but are ashamed and afraid of expressing them. They do not wish to appear ill-natured: "What Jew wants to give the impression of a venom-spewing Shylock?"[23] He continues: "This complete abstinence from hate unmasks both Germans and Jews. Could the German critics really accept the idea that "their" Jews were better than those beyond their borders? That the German master race had come to be replaced by a Jewish master race that was morally pure, forgiving of everyone, loving everyone— even the murderers of their own families? Nobody, not even a German intellectual, could be so immeasurably naive."[24]

In some postwar German fiction we find a well-intentioned but patronizing portrayal of Jews, as Ruth Klüger has forcefully pointed out.[25] Thus Judith, in Andersch's *Sansibar oder der letzte Grund* (1957), is a "good" Jew who is also a passive near-victim, allowing good Germans to save her from the Holocaust. Such roseate portrayals of Jews and Germans avoid confronting the underlying tensions between them. Hence a virulent post-Holocaust anti-Semitism appeared in the late films of Fassbinder and in his play *Der Müll, die Stadt und der Tod*. Fassbinder's play includes the anonymous figure of "the rich Jew" who exploits Germans financially and German women, in particular, through his sexual potency; the film *In einem Jahr mit dreizehn Monden* (1978) features a Jewish Holocaust survivor who runs a brothel by the brutal techniques he learned in Auschwitz.[26] These works confirm Broder's statement: "Die Deutschen werden den Juden Auschwitz nie verzeihen."[27]

Until the late 1980s, according to Seligmann, "no German Jewish fiction was written about contemporary life in Germany."[28] Jurek Becker's *Bronsteins Kinder* (1986) was the first exception. In Becker's wake, Seligmann has revived that once flourishing genre, the Jewish family novel.[29] Around the turn of the century we find a number of novels and dramas that criticize the Jewish subculture by focusing on the family. The aporias of assimilation are represented by conflict within the family, usually between the generations, which are assimilated to different degrees. In Schnitzler's *Der Weg ins Freie* (1908) old Ehrenberg, a loyal Jew, is outraged by the hyper-acculturation of his foppish son Oskar, whom he sees emerging from a Catholic church. Adolf Dessauer's *Großstadtjuden* (1910) presents Viennese Jewish society as desperate to curry favor with Gentiles. Here the bookseller Josef Kastner has recently changed his name from Kohn to please his snobbish wife and son; the latter, like Schnitzler's Oskar Ehrenberg, is a Jewish anti-Semite who first affects Viennese dialect, then suddenly adopts a pseudo-aristocratic way of speaking. The search for a new Jewish identity is embodied in the ultimately fatal high-mindedness of Herzl's Jakob and in a whole range of Schnitzler characters. Therese Golowski has exchanged one form of marginality for another by becoming a militant socialist. Her brother Leo is a no less militant Zionist, and is thus trying to construct a new Jewish identity. Heinrich Bermann, a free-floating intellectual, rejects all those solutions yet is trapped in the futile, overingenious self-analysis that is represented as typically Jewish.

Seligmann had great difficulty in finding a publisher for his own first novel, *Rubinsteins Versteigerung*. Although Seligmann was already an established journalist, for four years the novel was rejected by publisher after publisher on the grounds that it had too much about sex, that the hero spoke horribly to his mother (as he certainly does), and that the book was anti-Semitic.[30] Underlying those objections, Seligmann plausibly surmises, was discomfort with a portrayal of Jews that did not idealize them. When

Rubinsteins Versteigerung was finally published, at the author's own expense,
the *Allgemeine jüdische Wochenzeitung* (the unofficial mouthpiece of the
Zentralrat der Juden in Deutschland) charged Seligmann with
"Nestbeschmutzung" and suggested that he was trying to curry favor with
non-Jewish readers by presenting Jews in a bad light. Later in the same
paper, Thomas Feibel, in an unenthusiastic survey of recent German-Jewish
fiction, described Seligmann's novel as a mere "Elaborat" and deplored its
attempt to be "kritisch, frech, witzig" as an effort to perpetuate stereotyped
"Jewish" qualities.[31] But would Feibel prefer Jewish writers to produce tame,
serious, conformist books? Certainly Henryk M. Broder would not. He
hailed Seligmann's novel in the following words:

> *Rubinsteins Versteigerung* ist das erste Buch eines deutsch-
> jüdischen Autors nach 1945, das den herrschenden Konsens—
> Nur nicht unangenehm auffallen! Die Anti-semiten würden sich
> freuen!—einfach ignoriert. Es nimmt auf die Angst der Juden vor
> Selbstenblößung ebensowenig Rücksicht wie auf die Bedürfnisse
> der Antisemiten nach Absolution. Deswegen kommt er der
> Wirklichkeit jüdischen Lebens in der Bundesrepublik weit näher
> als die vielen gutgemeinten Dokumentationen zu diesem
> Thema.[32]

The novel is set in the Munich Jewish community in 1959. According to
Seligmann, the invisible ghetto of postwar German Jewry is sustained by a
network of organizations that separate it from the non-Jewish environment:

> Deutschlands Nachkriegsjuden haben ein engmaschiges soziales
> Netz in ihr Ghetto gezogen. Von allem in den Großstädten
> Berlin, Frankfurt und München ist "man" von der Wiege his zum
> Grab fast autark. Es gibt jüdische Kindergärten, Schulen, Hoch-
> und Volkshochschulen, Restaurants, koschere Metzgereien,
> Sozialstellen, Altersheime, Jugend-, Kultur-, Gemeinde-, und
> sonstige Zentren. Vor allem aber, schließlich lebt man in
> Deutschland: Vereine, Vereine, Vereine.[33]

If Seligmann's account is accurate, then postwar Jewish life in Germany is
sustained by an associational structure just as it was in the nineteenth
century. David Sorkin has described how, in the age of emancipation,
German Jews acquired "Bildung" through a network of institutions that
inculcated German culture while isolating them from the wider German

society in a subculture of their own.[34] This "Vereinsmeierei" envelops Jonathan Rubinstein in *Rubinsteins Versteigerung*.

Jonathan is in part a mouthpiece for Seligmann's views: Jews are aliens in Germany; well-intentioned school lessons on the wickedness of anti-Semitism and the Holocaust merely create embarrassment, remind Jonathan that many of his classmates would have joined the Nazi Party or the SS given the chance, and don't prevent him from being asked questions like: "[Ob] die ganze Vergasung nicht ein jüdischer Schwindel ist, um Geld aus Deutschland zu holen?" He concludes by asking (like Broder): "Werden uns die Deutschen je ihr schlechtes Gewissen verzeihen?"[35]

However, the novel comes alive when portraying the tensions within the Jewish family and the larger (but not much larger) Jewish community. Rubinstein's family has a hothouse atmosphere combining intimacy with hostility: He calls his father "Fred" and his mother "Esel". Their love is unquestionable; it leads both to acts of generosity and to the most underhand acts of emotional blackmail. Jonathan experiences conflict especially with his mother. He denounces her and their fellow Jews for living in the "Nazi-Land" (12); she upbraids him for speaking to her in that way. Although this is recognizable as adolescent rage, it is intensified by Jonathan's age (he is twenty-one) and by guilt at living in Germany. Family conflict extends to a fistfight with his father as a result of tension stirred up by his mother, and Jonathan then feels that in striking his (smaller and weaker) father he has behaved like a Nazi. When his father has a heart attack, his mother blames him for alarming them by announcing that he will go to Israel and, according to Jonathan, uses the heart attack to pressure Jonathan into changing his mind. In this atmosphere of unremitting emotional pressure, children have no secrets from their parents, nor, ultimately, from anyone else in the community: because, according to Jonathan, they live "im Ghetto der Vorurteile unserer Eltern" (32).

The Jewish community seeks to perpetuate itself, not to integrate with the Germans. The worst thing that Jewish parents can imagine is a mixed marriage. Hence they arrange elaborate parties to promote friendships and marriages among Jewish children, with the result that boys like Jonathan are to marry wives who resemble their mothers and perpetuate the latter's dominance. He invites a Jewish girl home, his mother does not leave them alone, and he senses complicity between the girl and his mother. Outwardly, it might seem, the Jews could assimilate. Jonathan's father is fair-haired and blue-eyed. His friend Rachel Blum similarly looks stereotypically German, and hence all the more attractive. But he dreads the prospect of marrying her, for it would lock him into the same self-destructive confinement as his father's.

The life of the Jewish community is contrasted with its much richer past. Jonathan visits Ichenhausen, where his ancestors came from, a community which has been "judenrein" since 1942. He visits their graves, places a stone on his great-grandfather's grave, and utters the first sentence (all he can remember) of the Kaddish. In the Jewish past, he reflects, parents passed on Jewish traditions to their children, but now they transmit only their neuroses.

What alternative is there? Jonathan's fate is announced by the event that gives the novel its title, which occurs in his school classroom. A new woman teacher insists that she and the boys (it is an all-male class) must sit informally in a circle. Everybody wants the seat next to the teacher, Frau Taucher, but nobody dares sit there till Jonathan volunteers. Everyone envies his assurance. To maintain his dominant position among his classmates, he auctions his place and gets 100 Marks, whereupon a fellow pupil says: "Da schau her! Kaum reicht ihm eine deutsche Frau die Hand, schon versteigert sie der Rubinstein meistbietend. Jetzt verstehe ich, wie ihr zu eurem Geld kommt" (7). Rubinstein runs away in shame and locks himself in the toilet. From sheer lack of confidence, he has behaved like a stereotypical Jew as seen by anti-Semites: cheeky, horny, mercenary. Not only are Germans resolved to see him as a Jew, but his own behavior colludes with their hostility.

There are two possibilities of escape: to go to Israel and become an authentic Jew; or to marry a non-Jewish woman. The first of these is evoked by a visit from an Israeli General Almagor (meaning "fearless," we are told, in contrast to the timorous Rubinstein). Jonathan is shocked by his frank admission that the Israeli army uses napalm against tanks. Here Seligmann is using an experience of his own that told him that Israelis are not morally superior to other nations.[36] Rubinstein concludes that the Jews in Israel have in effect become Germans of the worst kind: "Das sind doch keine Juden mehr, das sind Preußen oder Maschinen oder was sonst auch immer" (85). He meets a friend who has returned from Israel, disillusioned by the militarism, the lack of culture, and the intolerance of criticism he has found there. Concluding that Jews need the diaspora, the friend prefers to be "der ewige Jude" (87). Jonathan, however, is still determined to go to Israel, for he cannot stand the emotional pressure of being a Jew in postwar Germany. His resolve is shaken when he meets a former KZ inmate, Herr Frankfurther, who, to Jonathan's surprise, refuses to hate the Germans: Not only is it wrong to hate a whole nation (as Jonathan does with his "Deutschenhaß"), but even murderers can deserve pity: "Wie konnte man Leute hassen, die nicht mehr waren als ein Häufchen Elend und Angst, sobald sie ihre Uniformen auszogen" (165–6). After this encounter Jonathan no longer feels able to separate himself from the Germans by hating them. The militarist Israeli, it seems, is simply a mirror-image of the bad German.

The second escape route looks more promising. For a while Jonathan goes out with a German girl called Susanne. However, his mother actively opposes their relationship. Jonathan is prepared to leave his mother for Susanne, since the relationships seem mutually incompatible. In constructing this dilemma, Seligmann acknowledges a familiar image of the possessive Jewish mother. Susanne, however, eventually reveals that her father was in the SS. She knows this fact will make their relationship impossible. She knows also that Jonathan would in any case submit to his mother. So they part, and the novel ends with Jonathan weeping uncontrollably on his bed.

Both Jonathan's escape routes have now been cut off. He is left with Germany, with his mother, and with the prospect of marrying a Jewish girl and ending up in the same kind of neurotic, overintense atmosphere as he inhabits now. The last line of the novel is: *"Ich bin ein deutscher Jude!"* (189; emphasis in original). That is his identity, and he cannot escape from it. It reads like a howl of pain, a hopeless admission of defeat. And yet, writing about his novel, Seligmann describes the experience of writing it as that of overcoming his own hatred of Germans and his sense of inferiority, and of finding "die seelische Kraft, mich zu meiner Identität zu bekennen: *'Ich bin ein deutscher Jude'"* [37] The conclusion may be read as ambivalent. At the moment, it is for Rubinstein an experience of loss and defeat; but if one can imagine the narrative of his life continuing after the end of the novel, the experience will turn out to be productive, the basis for a new stage in his life. Within the novel, though, his defeat seems unrelieved and bitter.

The fictional situation presented by Seligmann corresponds in many ways to that of young Jews in post-Holocaust Germany as described by the sociologist Lynn Rapaport. Here, too, we hear of Jews living in "an invisible ghetto," suspicious of Germans yet uncomfortable in their own closeness.[38] The Jewish community is so small and confining that one is constantly under surveillance. Sexual relations with fellow members of the Jewish community are inhibited by something like an incest taboo.[39] Parents disapprove of their children forming emotional relationships with Germans and actively destroy such relationships.[40] One woman learned that the father of a close German female friend had been in the SS and had been responsible for deporting Jews to Maidanek.[41] Seligmann's invention of Susanne's paternity is not merely a fictional cliché.

Although Seligmann's novel may well be a plausible report on life within the postwar Jewish community, it also fits into several well-known literary molds. Although Jonathan deplores the merely nominal continuity between the German-Jewish present and the past, Seligmann strengthens that continuity by establishing connections with the German-Jewish literary tradition. As a comic novel, *Rubinsteins Versteigerung* relies on many well established Jewish traditions. One of these is the tragicomic figure of the schlemiel. The schlemiel is the perpetual failure, unfortunate and unlucky. He is also the archetypal little man, in some ways a wise fool who sees through the illusions of the surrounding world. Of course the schlemiel as a comic figure does not have to be Jewish: Non-Jewish schlemiels include such characters as Paul Pennyfeather or Mike Doonesbury. Comedy helps all of us to accept our own awareness of failure and intimates to us that there is another set of standards than those of worldly success. But the literary history of the schlemiel is connected with emancipation. The failure articulated by the schlemiel figure is the failure to find a foothold in the non-Jewish world.[42] Nineteenth-century Yiddish literature has many famous schlemiels, such as Mendele Moykher Sforim's character Benjamin the Third, whose travels in search of the legendary river Sambatyon take him no further than the town near his shtetl, and Sholem Aleichem's characters Tevye the Dairyman and the *luftmensh* Menahem Mendl.[43] In German literature we have a noteworthy schlemiel, combining comedy with pathos, in Little Samson ("der kleine Simson"), a figure in Heine's novel *Aus den Memoiren des Herrn von Schnabelewopski* (1834). Little Samson is a devout reader of the Bible and a staunch believer in God, though God, as the narrator says, never seems to come to his aid. Samson fights a duel with an atheist in defense of God's existence. Mortally wounded, he has the story of his biblical namesake read out to him, and tries to emulate Samson's dying triumph over the Philistines:

> Bei dieser Stelle öffnete der kleine Simson seine Augen, geisterhaft weit, hob sich krampfhaft in die Höhe; ergriff, mit seinen dünnen Ärmchen, die beiden Säulen, die zu Füßen seines Bettes; rüttelte daran, während er zornig stammelte: Es sterbe meine Seele mit den Philistern. Aber die starken Bettsäulen blieben unbeweglich, ermattet und wehmütig lächelnd fiel der Kleine zurück auf seine Kissen, und aus seiner Wunde, deren Verband sich verschoben, quoll ein roter Blutstrom.[44]

Later in German-Jewish fiction we find a development of the schlemiel closer to Jonathan Rubinstein: the intellectual schlemiel who grasps in theory his situation between two communities but is unable to escape from it in practice. In Schnitzler's *Der Weg ins Freie* the self-tormenting Jewish intellectual Heinrich Bermann remains trapped in guilt and introspection while his Gentile friend Georg von Wergenthin overcomes his own sense of guilt and goes off to a new life in Germany. In the great comic novel by Sammy Gronemann, *Tohuwabohu* (1920), Heinz Lehnsen, the hero, ends up detached from his Berlin Jewish environment but unable either to enter Gentile life or to join the Jews whom he meets joyfully accepting their Jewishness as they travel to the First Zionist Congress. Jonathan is another of these intellectual schlemiels. As the author's mouthpiece, he analyzes his situation but is unable to escape from it either to Israel or into love with a non-Jewish woman, and ends up bitterly confronting his failure.

The weak Jewish schlemiel is contrasted with the strong, unworried Gentile. In postwar Jewish fiction he may also be contrasted with the strong Israeli. When Alexander Portnoy goes to Israel he finds himself impotent in the presence of Jewish men, and Jonathan Rubinstein encounters a morally unacceptable form of strength in General Almagor with his untroubled use of napalm. The schlemiel figure expresses another painful theme of German-Jewish literature, namely endangered masculinity. Jonathan is a virgin at twenty-one and ashamed of himself for it. His teacher partially seduces him; he blames himself for being so well-brought-up and self-controlled as not to take full advantage of the situation. He feels himself to be unmanly because Jewish, thinking that a German, by contrast, would have ignored her protests and raped her. Thus the Jew is more civilized, but feels his civilized behavior to be a form of weakness. Arranging an assignation with Rachel, he feels sure he will stop short of intercourse, "wie alle jüdischen Kastraten seit 2000 Jahren" (76), conveying his feeling that the diaspora Jew is unmanly. His insecurity is registered in his voice, a long-standing source of embarrassment in the literature of assimilation.[45] Threatened by Gentile men, he feels his voice is as squeaky as a budgerigar's; when nervous, he always "croaks" (5, 111).

A well-established stereotype defines the male Jew as "feminine" in relation to the German man, where femininity is understood as implying passivity, weakness, and cunning.[46] Otto Weininger notoriously describes Jews as feminine in his *Geschlecht und Charakter* (1903), and a less well-known essay by Otto Rank says that Jews are feminine in being uncreative: "They are, so to speak, women among the nations and must above all join themselves to the masculine life-source if they are to become 'productive.'"[47] Hence the early Zionists set great store by gymnastics and manual labor to produce a new generation of "Muskeljuden.'" [48]

One common response to this image of unmanliness was an attempt to identify with German militarism. Walther Rathenau suffered a painful disappointment when he was refused permission to serve in an elite guards regiment. The most extreme example is perhaps Ernst Lissauer, author of the bloodthirsty bestseller of August 1914, "Haßgesang gegen England," who is described by Stefan Zweig as a tubby little man, completely unmilitary in appearance.[49] Jonathan is offered the chance to identify with Israeli militarism in the person of General Almagor but rejects it.

Another response, often found in fiction, is to look for a Gentile woman as a sexual partner. This is the option preferred by Jonathan. It explains the sexual relationship between Alexander Portnoy and the Gentile woman he calls the Monkey; though her nickname indicates, as do Portnoy's extraordinary fantasies combining sex and food, that his upbringing has debarred him from adult sexuality, or rather, from a sexual relationship with someone whom he accepts as an adult. It is also the choice made by Christian Gumpel, alias the Marchese Christophoro di Gumpelino, in Heine's *Die Bäder von Lucca* (1829). Gumpelino is in love with the English aristocrat Julia Maxfield. Unfortunately, when she summons him to her bed, Gumpelino happens to be suffering from diarrhoea, for he is also a schlemiel. In a very interesting novel of the 1890s about failed assimilation, *Werther, der Jude* by Ludwig Jacobowski, the hero, Leo Wolff, seeks to free himself from Jewishness by immersing himself in the drinking and dueling rituals of German student life; he has a blonde German girlfriend, whom he treats with sadistic tyranny, getting her pregnant, callously ignoring her, and driving her to suicide. Like Jonathan Rubinstein, he is forced to realize that he is a Jew as defined by the outside world when news breaks not only of Helene's suicide but of his father's dishonest business dealings, and a newspaper comments: "Wieder ein neues Beispiel für die Korruption unserer Zustände durch die Juden! Die Alten betrügen den biederen, braven Michel, und die Jungen verführen seine Töchter!"[50]

Seligmann's presentation of endangered masculinity is naturally bound up with his portrayal of family life. In the nineteenth century the acculturation of German Jews coincided with their embourgeoisement and their adoption of the family as a small, inward-looking unit offering domestic warmth amid a dangerous world. Moreover, as traditional Jewish observance declined, "Jewish identity" was transferred from ritual to family life.[51] But such domestic inwardness can easily become oppressive and cloying, especially when it is made to carry an excessive emotional and symbolic weight. Hence in the early twentieth century we find both fictional and discursive analyses of the Jewish family that are quite as unsparing as Seligmann's. We do not know if the Bendemann family in Kafka's *Das Urteil* (written 1912) are Jews, but the family dynamics are unmistakable: the son is planning to escape into marriage, but his father first forces him by emotional blackmail to return to the role of the good and loving son; then he demolishes that role by appearing as a judge who passes sentence of death. And although in this story the mother is dead, her influence survives in the father, who keeps a corner of his room as a shrine devoted to her and claims that Georg's marriage plans are a violation of her memory. The good son is punished by drowning.

Among discursive analyses of the Jewish family, perhaps the most trenchant is by Anton Kuh in his study of Jewish self-hatred, *Juden und Deutsche* (1921). He argues that Jewish overintellectuality produces sexual unhappiness and spoils family life. His authority is Otto Gross, who maintained that the root of all evil is sexual violence, which has brought about the institution of marriage as the foundation of the authoritarian state, which projected itself as an authoritarian God. The Jews first did this, and their patriarchal order is embodied in the Jewish family, against which Kuh delivers a furious diatribe:

> Der Vater, Ur-Besitzer, schwingt die Erhaltungsfuchtel. Die Mutter, in ihrem Glück verkrüppelt, hegt die Kinder als Krüppel; die Töchter sind lebendig aufgebahrtes, wie Topfblumen betreutes Verkaufsgut; und die Söhne—lest es doch in ihren Schriften selbst, sofern sie sich, zwischen Tat und Bangnis zerklemmt, dem Worte verschrieben, wie sie die Glieder schütteln, um jenes verengende Wissen um die Menschenkleinheit in der Stube abzutun, wie sie, Schaum um den Mund, unterlaufenen Auges, an den Fesseln der Erinnerung zerren, und wie ihnen, deren kühnste Weltfahrt eine Trutzfahrt, [...] heute noch beim Rückgedenken "Träne auf-und niedersteigt".[52]

Kuh explains self-hatred as inability to break away from the patriarchal family: one thus remains adolescent, disguising one's lack of experience by a precocious intellectuality which becomes a substitute for experience.

A similar hothouse atmosphere is described by Arnold Zweig in his 1927 treatise on anti-Semitism and Jewish life, *Caliban*:

> Eine Art heftiger überreizender Innigkeit oder Brutpflege dringt ununterbrochen auf die Kinder ein, und je intensiver die Not des Lebenskampfes an den Eltern zehrt, desto leichter schlagen sie, und zwar als regelmäßige Gefühlshaltung, von heftigem Ärger

dem Kinde gegenüber in ebenso heftige Liebesbezeigung um, so
daß er schon, an den Eltern erlebt, ein Gefühl fortwährenden
Wechsels von Heiß und Kalt als Selbstverständlichkeit mit in sein
Leben einbaut.[53]

Compared to this intense atmosphere, the outside world seems cold,
especially if his Jewishness is met with hostility. Dividing the world into the
sheltering home and the hostile exterior, the Jew himself becomes a divided
personality. He acquires an inferiority complex vis-à-vis the outside world
that makes him try to satisfy its demands but may send him into neurosis or
madness: "Immer noch glaubt dieser Typ, körperlich weniger tauglich,
moralisch aber einer minderwertigen Rasse angehörig zu sein, und überdies
verpflichtet, immer wieder zu beweisen, daß er dem Gemeinwesen nicht
schädlich sei, sondern ein nützlicher Bürger, den man dulden müsse."[54]
These are also the pressures on Jonathan Rubinstein, except that, living in a
Germany that has replaced the ideal of assimilation with the memory of the
Holocaust, he feels no obligation to become a useful citizen.

What conclusion about German-Jewish relations does Seligmann's novel
suggest? Certainly, Seligmann has faced the problem of German-Jewish
relations by writing a brilliant comic novel about it. But he has not thereby
solved the problem. By a dialectical process, he has exposed new aspects of
it. For what kind of Jewish identity does *Rubinsteins Versteigerung* imply? Not
that of the martyr, certainly, but surely the identity of the Jew as victim, as
schlemiel, as reluctantly comic figure. Seligmann responds to stigma by the
process that Erving Goffman calls minstrelisation: He acts it out in public.[55]

The conclusion, "I'm a German Jew," may represent a personal victory
for Seligmann, and in the long run for Jonathan, but it does not promise any
reshaping of German-Jewish identity. On the other hand, the novel invites
our sympathy for an antihero, a troubled, unhappy, rather unpleasant young
man, and thus breaks down our naive tendency to divide people into virtuous
and vicious and to assume that Jews, because of their historic sufferings, must
be on the virtuous side of this division. It is not the experiences of the hero,
but the effects on the reader, that offer hope for a new, more honest approach
to relations between German Jews and German Gentiles.

NOTES

1. See Karen Remmler, "1980: The 'Third Generation' of Jewish-German
writers after the Shoah emerges in Germany and Austria," in Sander L. Gilman and

Jack Zipes, eds. *The Yale Companion to Jewish Writing and Thought in German Culture. 1096–1996* (New Haven: Yale University Press, 1997), 796–804 (797); Dieter Lamping, *Von Kafka zu Celan. Jüdischer Diskurs in der deutschen Literatur des 20. Jahrhunderts* (Göttingen: Vandenhoeck & Ruprecht, 1999), 160–1.

2. See Monika Richarz, "Jews in Today's Germanies," *Leo Baeck Institute Yearbook*, 30 (1985), 265–274.

3. Alphons Silbermann, "Jüdische Reaktionen auf eine Untersuchung über latenten Antisemitismus in der Bundesrepublik Deutschland," in Henryk M. Broder and Michel R. Lang, eds. *Fremd im eigenen Land. Juden in der Bundesrepublik* (Frankfurt: Fischer, 1979), 359–368.

4. Broder, "Warum ich lieber kein Jude wäre; und wenn schon unbedingt—dann lieber nicht in Deutschland," in Broder and Lang, eds. *Fremd im eigenen Land*, 82–102 (84).

5. Artur Brauner, "Es war nicht richtig, daß Juden wieder in Deutschland seßhaft geworden sind," in Broder and Lang, 76–81 (78).

6. Quoted in Kurt Blumenfeld, *Erlebte Judenfrage: Ein Vierteljahrhundert deutscher Zionismus* (Stuttgart: Deutsche Verlags-Anstalt, 1962), 51.

7. Henryk M. Broder, *Der ewige Antisemit. Über Sinn und Funktion eines beständigen Gefühls* (Frankfurt: Fischer, 1986).

8. Seligmann. "Ausbruch aus der Märtyrerrolle. Zur Definition des deutschen Judentums.' *Süddeutsche Zeitung*, 13 April 1993, 11.

9. Lionel Kochan, *The Jewish Renaissance and some of its discontents* (Manchester: Manchester University Press, 1992), 93–100; Michael Goldberg, *Why Should Jews Survive? Looking past the Holocaust toward a Jewish Future* (New York: Oxford University Press, 1995).

10. Seligmann, "Ausbruch aus der Märtyrerrolle," 11.

11. Seligmann, *Das deutsch-jüdische Verhältnis. Bestandsaufnahme und Perspektiven*, Schriftenreihe der Rudolf von Bennigsen-Stiftung (Hanover: Niedersachsen Verlag, 1994/95), 4.

12. Sigrid Weigel, "Shylocks Wiederkehr. Die Verwandlung von Schuld in Schulden oder: Zum symbolischen Tausch der Wiedergutmachung," *Zeitschrift für deutsche Philologie*, 114 (1995), Sonderheft, 3–22.

13. Seligmann, *Mit beschränkter Hoffnung, Juden, Deutsche, Israelis* (Munich: Knaur, 1993), 81.

14. Ernst Pawel, *The Labyrinth of Exile: A Life of Theodor Herzl* (London: Collins, 1990), 204–5.

15. Martin Buber, *Die jüdische Bewegung. Gesammelte Aufsätze und Ansprachen*, 2 vols. (Berlin: Jüdischer Verlag, 1920), 1, 91.

16. Rathenau ["Hartenau, W."], "Höre, Israel!," *Die Zukunft*, 18 (March 1897), 454–62 (454).

17. See Becker's contribution to *Mein Judentum*, ed. H. J. Schultz (Munich: dtv. 1986), 10–18.

18. Lang, "Fremd in einem fremden Land," in Broder and Lang, eds. *Fremd im eigenen Land*, 265–268 (266).

19. Seligmann, *Mit beschränkter Hoffnung*, 130.

20. Seligmann, *Mit beschränkter Hoffnung*, 166.

21. Seligmann, *Das deutsch-jüdische Verhältnis*, 17.

22. See Ritchie Robertson, The *"Jewish Question" in German Literature* (Oxford: Oxford University Press, 1999), esp. ch. 4.

23. Seligmann, "What keeps the Jews in Germany quiet?" in Sander L. Gilman and Karen Remmler, eds. *Reemerging Jewish Culture in Germany: Life and Literature since 1989* (New York: New York University Press, 1994), 173–83 (175).

24. Gilman and Remmler, 177–8.

25. Ruth Klüger, "Gibt es ein 'Judenproblem' in der deutschen Nachkriegsliteratur?," in *Katastrophen: Über deutsche Literatur* (Göttingen: Wallstein, 1994), 9–38.

26. See Janusz Bodek, *Die Fassbinder-Kontroversen, Entstehung und Wirkung eines literarischen Textes* (Frankfurt: Peter Lang, 1991).

27. Broder, *Der ewige Antisemit*, 125.

28. Seligmann, "What keeps the Jews in Germany quiet?." 174.

29. See Robertson, The *"Jewish Question" in German Literature*, 273–85.

30. Seligmann, *Mit beschränkter Hoffnung*, 153.

31. Thomas Feibel, "'Rachel, ich hab dich lieb'—'Ich dich auch, mein Jonny'. Die wenig begeisternde neue deutsch-jüdische Literatur anhand von drei Beispielen," *Allgemeine jüdische Wochenzeitung*, 2 August 1990, 5.

32. Broder, "Rubinsteins Beschwerden. Das witzige Roman-Debüt des Rafael Seligmann." *Die Zeit*, 11 August 1989, 41.

33. Seligmann, *Mit beschränkter Hoffnung*, 77.

34. David Sorkin, *The Transformation of German Jewry 1780–1840* (New York: Oxford University Press, 1987).

35. Seligmann, *Rubinsteins Versteigerung* (Munich: dtv. 1991), 16. Future quotations are identified by page number in the text.

36. Seligmann, *Mit beschränkter Hoffnung*, 151.

37. Seligmann, *Mit beschränkter Hoffnung*, 152.

38. See Lynn Rapaport, *Jews in Germany after the Holocaust: Memory, Identity, and German-Jewish Relations* (Cambridge: Cambridge University Press, 1997), 4, 189, 227.

39. Rapaport, 227–8.

40. Rapaport, 242.

41. Rapaport, 198–201.

42. See Sander L. Gilman, *Jewish Self-Hatred: Anti-Semitism and the Hidden Language of the Jew* (Baltimore: Johns Hopkins University Press, 1986), 107–38.

43. See Ruth R. Wisse, *The Schlemiel as Modern Hero* (Chicago: University of Chicago Press, 1971).

44. Heinrich Heine, *Sämtliche Schriften*, ed. Klaus Briegleb, 6 vols (Munich: Hanser, 1968–76), 1, 555–6.

45. Sander L. Gilman, *The Jew's Body* (New York and London: Routledge, 1991), ch. 1.

46. See Robertson, *The "Jewish Question" in German Literature*, 296–302.

47. Otto Rank, "The Essence of Judaism," in Dennis B. Klein, *Jewish Origins of the Psychoanalytic Movement* (Chicago: University of Chicago Press, 1985), 170–3 (171).

48. Max Nordau, "Muskeljudentum," in his *Zionistische Schriften*, 2nd edn. (Cologne and Leipzig: Jüdischer Verlag, 1909), 379–81.

49. Stefan Zweig, *Die Welt von Gestern* (Frankfurt: Fischer, 1970), 170.

50. Ludwig Jacobowski, *Werther, der Jude* (Berlin: Verlag Berlin-Wien, 1898), 351–2.

51. Marion A. Kaplan, *The Making of the Jewish Middle Class: Women, Family, and Identity in Imperial Germany* (New York: Oxford University Press, 1991), 10.

52. Anton Kuh, *Juden und Deutsche* (Berlin: Erich Reiss, 1921), 23–4.

53. Arnold Zweig, *Caliban oder Politik und Leidenschaft* (Potsdam: Kiepenheuer, 1927), 190.

54. Zweig, 187–8.

55. Erving Goffman, *Stigma: Notes on the Management of Spoiled Identity* (Harmondsworth: Penguin, 1968), 154.

AMY HUNGERFORD

Memorizing Memory

The question of whether those who did not experience the Holocaust become real survivors when they tell true stories about the Holocaust, the question I have argued *Maus* raises and then answers with its own version of the personified text, captured broad public attention in the scandal surrounding Binjamin Wilkomirski's memoir, *Fragments: Memories of a Wartime Childhood*. When the memoir was published in 1995, it was hailed as a powerfully moving account of the author's experiences as a child during the Holocaust, an account whose disjointed narrative and simple, almost abstract style was said not just to represent, but actually to demonstrate, the effects of trauma on its author. But at the time of its German publication there were already questions about the authenticity of Wilkomirski's story. The author's legal name turned out to be Bruno Dössekker, and his Swiss birth record indicated that he was born not in Riga, Latvia, as he had claimed in the memoir to have been, but in Biel, Switzerland, and that he could not have been as old as he had claimed he was during the war.

Because of these questions about his identity, Wilkomirski added an afterword to the book before publication, citing the birth record and explaining that it was simply part of the new identity "imposed" upon him by Swiss authorities after the war.[1] This confession seemed not to bother early readers of the memoir, who praised its seemingly artless and unsentimental representation of brutality. As André Aciman put it in a review for the *New*

From *The Holocaust of Texts: Genocide, Literature, and Personification*. © 2003 by The University of Chicago.

Republic, Wilkomirski's "aesthetic vision" was characterized by "incomplete or mistaken readings of reality, accompanied by rude, painful awakenings." [2] While this style could be attributed, he suggested, "to the writer's desire to describe the events of the Holocaust purely from a child's perspective," that would only mean that Wilkomirski had employed what Aciman called an "old" stylistic "trick." Instead, the reviewer argued, "the fragmentary nature of Binjamin's account is not so much a product of the grown man's style as it is a product of the young boy's experience" (31). It was this kind of claim—that the very "fragments" of Wilkomirski's narrative were the evidence of its truth—that led readers to accept it despite the doubts raised at the outset by Bruno Dössekker's birth record.

Most readers will know the end of this story: the book's publisher, having hired an independent historian to investigate the matter in 1998, decided that there was enough doubt about the truth of the memoir to justify taking it out of print. It was duly withdrawn from publication in the fall of 1999. Some continue to defend it, suggesting that to doubt its authenticity is not only to underestimate the thoroughness of the Swiss bureaucracy in covering up the traces of a child's original identity, but is also to perpetuate the brutalization the child Binjamin suffered at the hands of the Nazis.[3] But two extensively researched essays published in the summer of 1999—Elena Lappin's in *Granta* and Philip Gourevitch's in the *New Yorker*—and a later book-length study of the case by Blake Eskin, entitled *A Life in Pieces* (2002), seem to have convinced most readers that Wilkomirski, if not the calculating liar that Daniel Ganzfried (a Swiss writer and his earliest critic) describes, is at least a seriously and sadly deluded person who has invented for himself a terrible history.

Upon reflection, we might simply say that the story of Wilkomirski's memoir reveals how our desire for such memoirs of difficult lives has created an atmosphere conducive to fraud. In this chapter I demonstrate that there is, in fact, more to be said about the relation between the phenomenon of the false memoir and the common interest in trauma. For producing a fake is possible—and attractive to the would-be con artist—not only because the Holocaust memoir has become a form that has a certain cultural presence and worth, a worth evident in the various prizes and speaking tours that accompanied the general celebration of Wilkomirski's book.[4] Producing fakes is also possible simply because the Holocaust memoir *is* a form. As one reviewer of *Fragments* noted (even before the questions about Wilkomirski arose), "a peculiar set of conventions has come to cluster around depictions of the Holocaust.... the effect has been to turn the literature of genocide into a genre, with rules almost as constricting as those binding the Agatha Christie—style detective story."[5] This reviewer cites an "understandable and laudable" desire for representations of the Holocaust that are "consciously, even ostentatiously austere" as the origin of the genre as such (a fact underwritten, no doubt, by Adorno's famous assertion that to write poetry after Auschwitz is "barbaric"), but we might also note that the Holocaust memoir has become a genre—with all the conventionality that term implies—because trauma theorists in the academy have been working to elaborate, explain, and theorize about the things such memoirs have in common.

In saying this, I do not wish to argue, with regard to *Fragments*, that Wilkomirski read trauma theory and other memoirs in order to learn the conventions of the Holocaust memoir, his extensive personal archive of such books becoming, as Daniel Ganzfried has put it, a "laboratory" for creating his fraud.[6] While this may well be what happened (there are those, like his high school girlfriend, Annie Singer, who claim that Wilkomirski has always been a liar), there are other reasons why trauma theory would help explain the Wilkomirski story, help in a way that can account for the somewhat difficult fact that many people—some of whom are closely acquainted with the author—believe that he did not set out to produce a lie, that he fully and sincerely believes himself to be the child-survivor his memoir describes. The misery apparent to practically all who have seen him since the memoir was published certainly suggests that if he is lying, he is not doing it for the emotional pleasure inherent in his new identity.[7] If his book is a fraud, it may well be an unintended one, and it is this aspect of the Wilkomirski story, I will argue, that a close reading of trauma theory can illuminate.

Perhaps I should more accurately say that it is this aspect of the Wilkomirski story that can illuminate what we find upon a close reading of trauma theory, for there is nothing very new or interesting in saying that fakes require generic conventions—require, that is, a formal expectation that can then be met fraudulently. Indeed, my point will turn out to be more, and more complicated, than this. I will argue that in the process of becoming a form, the Holocaust memoir and the representation of trauma in general has been described by two of our most prominent theorists of trauma and literature—Shoshana Felman and Cathy Caruth—as embodying a certain relation between language and experience, a relation that ultimately asks us to understand *Fragments* not so much as a fraud, but as the epitome of the very assumptions that underlie trauma theory's analytic discourse. And further, I will show that these assumptions are not unique to trauma theory or to writing that specifically engages the Holocaust. These assumptions about language and experience are also integral to contemporaneous fictional understandings of the relation between memorization and memory, between what you know and who you are, between epistemology and ontology in an era dominated by the memory and the threat of genocide. This larger argument demonstrates why, after the Wilkomirski story has come to an end, the phenomenon of his memoir will continue to be worth thinking about.

A SURVIVOR OF WRITING

To understand how trauma theory could be useful to Wilkomirski apart from the narrative models it describes—apart, that is, from its value as a kind of formal handbook—it is worth noting some of the features of the memoir itself, features that echo and, indeed, rely upon some basic assumptions about the relation between language and experience that I will address later in the work of Felman and Caruth. The book opens with a lament for the loss of what Wilkomirski calls his "mother" and "father" "tongues." He first introduces himself as an orphan, that is, not by explaining that his parents were killed but by describing his loss of language. He is an orphan, in these opening sentences, because he has forgotten the Yiddish that his family spoke. "I have no mother tongue, nor a father tongue either," he writes; "the languages I learned later on were never mine, at bottom. They were only imitations of other people's speech" (3, 4). While one might object to the notion that any speech is anything but the "imitations of other people's speech"—surely the speech Wilkomirski claims to have lost was learned by imitation—what is more important here is to understand the belief that underlies this statement. In order for it to make sense, personal identity must be somehow the equivalent of language, and moreover, language must be imagined as a quasi-biological entity: it is not what you learn, what you "imitate," but what is yours "at bottom," the very source, like a parent, of your identity.

Indeed, the priority of language as parent over the actual figure of the parent in *Fragments* is underscored by a strange episode in the postmemoir life of Wilkomirski himself. On one occasion he decided to embrace, as his father, an Israeli survivor who had seen in him a resemblance to his first and (at that time) only son, thought to have been lost in the Holocaust. While Wilkomirski agreed to a blood test that, in the end, could not prove the relation, and while he later said that he was simply looking for a sort of stand-in father, his early enthusiasm for and evident desire to believe in the reunion can make one forget that *Fragments* gives a graphic account of his father's death (he was crushed by a truck) and, moreover, describes a large family in which Wilkomirski was the youngest of several brothers, which is to say, not his father's first and only son.[8] The episode makes it evident that for Wilkomirski the source of his identity was not, in a sense, an actual family. It was more importantly the ongoing discourse about that family which began in the memoir and continued to evolve even after the memoir was published. Standing at the airport in Tel Aviv during the reunion with his putative father, Wilkomirski thus spontaneously revised the text of *Fragments:* "I still see in my mind," he mused, "how my father was taken away in the direction of the gas chambers."[9] While his willingness to revise the memoir in light of new facts might suggest that he values some version of lived reality over the story he has told about himself, that he wants to correct what might be erroneous in his memoir, I would argue that the very fact of the story's constant evolution reveals its priority as the source of identity. Wilkomirski's narrative has become his life (as Elena Lappin put it, he "is his book"), and, by the looks of things, that narrative will continue to assimilate to itself all the new evidence that might appear about Wilkomirski's past and all experiences that will constitute his future.

It is the personal identity thus conceived and elaborated in his memoir that Wilkomirski appeals to in the afterword added at the request of his publisher when the first questions about his identity arose in 1994: "The document I hold in my hands ... gives the date of my birth as February 12, 1941," Wilkomirski writes, "but this date has nothing to do with either the history of this century or my personal history" (154). What makes the document false, according to this strangely vague statement, is not that it contradicts the facts of his birth, but rather, that it does not fit within two preexisting narratives, "the history of this century" and Wilkomirski's "personal history." There is a psychological interpretation that can be made here: we can see how Daniel Ganzfried, for example, might come to argue that Wilkomirski's desire for personal significance drove him to invent himself as a Holocaust survivor. The life he wants to call his own is one that matters to the history of the century, not the comfortable and insignificant life of an upper-crust Swiss son.[10] But there is also an assumption about language to be read in Wilkomirski's claim and, more specifically, an assumption about the relation between personal identity and "personal history." In this case, "personal history" can only be the memoir itself, for it is only in the memoir that evidence for Wilkomirski's claim about his identity exists. The belief required about language here has the same structure as the belief we see in the opening lines of the memoir, cited above: that personal identity inheres in language. In this version of the claim, it is not simply the kind of language one speaks that becomes the source of identity (the Yiddish mother tongue that makes you Jewish), but the narrative structure of one's language (its shape vis-à-vis the formal conventions of the survivor's memoir) that creates the personal identity that can then be appealed to over and against the competing "document" the author "holds in [his] hands."

One might object that ferreting out the fact that Wilkomirski thinks his story constitutes his personal identity does little more than demonstrate that Wilkomirski subscribes to a basically Freudian, and currently very common, version of the self, a self whose meaningfulness and identity across time is constructed through narratives that link together the discrete experiences of life into what we recognize as a story. Or, more interestingly, one might object that Wilkomirski is progressively rejecting an essentialist, biologically based notion of identity based on one's parentage. But to make either of these objections would be to mistake the order of priority at work here: the narrative comes first, the claim to experience—and to biology, which never ceases to matter even if it is subject to revisions—follows. Wilkomirski's friend Elitsur Bernstein (an Israeli therapist) makes this order apparent when he tells of receiving, by fax, the first part of what was to become the manuscript of *Fragments*. According to Bernstein, Wilkomirski had appended a question to the story he sent: "Could it have been so?"[11] Clearly, Wilkomirski's own beliefs about his "personal history" were produced, over time, by the production of the stories that then came to be called a memoir. And moreover, Wilkomirski is not alone in bearing this relation to his own narrative; his American readers were urged to replicate the relation themselves. "Beautifully written," proclaims the dust jacket of Carol Brown Janeway's English translation, "with an indelible impact that makes this a book that is not read but experienced." Philip Gourevitch, whose essay in the *New Yorker* called my attention to this blurb, suggests that what we are asked to experience here is not the memoir but the public "sensation" it had become. When we put the promotional claim next to Wilkomirski's implicit claims about language within the memoir and its afterword, and next to the account Elitsur Bernstein gives us of the memoir's origins, however, American readers are asked not so much to experience a media sensation as to replicate the relation to the narrative that its author instantiated. The public is invited to experience the Holocaust the same way Wilkomirski did: by reading his story.[12]

READING AND THE TRANSMISSION OF EXPERIENCE

Becoming a survivor by telling or reading a survivor story does not originate with Bruno Dössekker becoming Binjamin Wilkomirski, or with the readers of *Fragments* taking up the cover's invitation to "experience" the memoir. I have presented other examples of this structure in the previous chapter, specifically in *Maus* and in the psychotherapeutic practice of Dina Wardi. But perhaps the strongest precedent for such a transformation can be found in the very theory that tries to account for the way language and narrative works (or becomes fragmented) in texts like *Fragments*, that tries to account for why the story of trauma cannot in fact be read but must instead be experienced. This mode of transformation begins to appear in a peculiar parallel between Binjamin Wilkomirski's story of coming to discover his survivor identity and a story that Shoshana Felman tells about a graduate seminar she led at Yale. Wilkomirski, in interviews, has noted that he first began to understand what had happened to him when he studied the Holocaust in high school, seeing a film of the camps' liberation. It was only then, he claims, that he realized that the war was over, that he himself had been liberated; he only then began to understand what had happened to him. His high school girlfriend, Annie Singer, tells the story a different way, that when Wilkomirski was about eighteen he showed her "a picture book about the Holocaust" and at about the same time began to claim that he came from the Baltic states.[13]

   Whichever version of this story one believes, it is clear that studying the Holocaust in school was a pivotal point in the transformation of Bruno Dössekker into Binjamin Wilkomirski, and this fact echoes, in important respects, the account of a classroom experience that constitutes the subject of the first chapter of Shoshana Felman's *Testimony* (1992), a work whose juxtaposition of psychoanalysis and de Manian deconstruction has made it the theoretical model for those who seek to analyze the relation between traumatic experience and literature. Felman tells, in the opening chapter, of the experience of a class of Yale graduate students taking her "Literature and Testimony" seminar, a seminar whose syllabus included Dostoyevsky, Camus, Mallarmé, Freud, and Celan and concluded with a screening of two videotaped Holocaust testimonies from Yale's Fortunoff Archive. Felman describes how the class, after viewing the first of the two Holocaust testimonies, experienced a "crisis" in which the students were "entirely at a loss, disoriented and uprooted."[14] What the students needed, Felman concluded, was to be brought "back into significance" (48), and to accomplish this she prepared an "address to the class" that would "return" to the students "the importance and significance of their reactions" (49).

The significance that Felman decides to give to the students' reactions turns out to have much in common with the significance the young Bruno Dössekker gave to his own responses to the Holocaust history he encountered as a student: namely, that those responses indicated survivorship. "We have in this second screening session," Felman told her students, "the task of surviving the first session.... I will suggest that the significance of the event of your viewing of the first Holocaust videotape was, not unlike [Paul] Celan's own Holocaust experience, something akin to *a loss of language*" (49, 50; original emphasis; I might add, of course, that the "loss of language" is also not unlike Wilkomirski's response to trauma as he tells it in *Fragments*). Encouraging her students to explore their emotional responses to the tapes, Felman gave a final writing assignment that asked them to reflect on those responses in relation to the literature they had studied that semester. "The written work the class had finally submitted," she reports, "turned out to be an amazingly articulate, reflective and profound statement of the trauma they had gone through and of the significance of their assuming the position of the witness" (52). While Felman is not exactly claiming that her students became survivors of the Holocaust in the literal sense, in the sense that Wilkomirski makes that claim for himself, her analysis of this classroom experience nevertheless suggests that the experience of listening to Holocaust testimony produces symptoms of trauma equivalent to the traumatic symptoms produced by actually experiencing the Holocaust. Moreover, Felman suggests that the significance of the students' feelings was to be found in the significance we accord to survivors' feelings. The students could experience trauma by listening to testimony about trauma, Felman explains, because a "'life testimony' is not simply a testimony to a private life, but a point of conflation between text and life, a textual testimony which can *penetrate us like an actual life*" (2; original emphasis). The text is not only like a life, then, but it can become the actual experience of another life, an experience that then becomes ours.

I want to pause in the argument here to make clear that my contention is not that reading or viewing Holocaust testimony is not a moving experience. My own response to reading and viewing testimony attests to the fact that encountering the survivor's testimony must be understood as a lived experience that can have intense emotional effects on the person who has that experience. My point is not that watching—or reading, or hearing— survivor testimonies is not in its own way traumatic, but that it is so *in its own way*. It seems important, if only in the interest of accuracy, to distinguish this experience of trauma, if one wishes to call it that, from the trauma that the survivor herself has experienced and then represents in her testimony.[15] Geoffrey Hartman has written wisely about what he calls "secondary trauma," giving us a way of thinking about these emotional effects that avoids conflating the reader with the survivor. Hartman argues, and I think he is correct, that secondary trauma consists, finally, not so much in extreme feelings of sympathy and identification, but rather in numbing. Hartman suggests that in presenting testimony we must be careful to avoid both psychological numbing to the violence the survivor describes and false identification with the survivor through secondary trauma.[16]

Felman's account of the classroom experience, and the more general account that she and Dori Laub give of the relation between those who listen to Holocaust testimony and those who give that testimony, might seem to suggest that to transmit the traumatic experience one must have experienced the Holocaust, as is the case with Paul Celan or with the survivors to whose testimony the Yale students listened. Other chapters of *Testimony*—in particular, the essay on Claude Lanzmann and his film *Shoah*—revise that notion in what appears to be a significant way, implying that trauma can be transmitted not only by survivors but also by those who, like Lanzmann, show an intense concern with the subject despite the fact that they are not themselves survivors. This suggests that the one who transmits that trauma need not have had the experience of trauma. Such a revision highlights the centrality of sympathetic identifications to the process of transmission, a point evident also in Felman's descriptions of those who receive the transmission; all these cases suggest that to receive traumatic experience one must feel an identification with the victims of the Holocaust and willingly immerse oneself in the literature of testimony, as both Lanzmann and the Yale graduate students had done, and, indeed, as Bruno Dössekker had done in his own student days. Initially, then, the mechanism of identification Felman describes in these cases seems to require, on the theoretical level, a commitment to the importance of sentiment and desire in the production of that identification, over and above lived experience of the trauma represented.[17]

But Felman's analysis of Paul de Man's wartime journalism, also in *Testimony*, suggests otherwise, suggests, rather, that it is neither shared experience nor sympathy that enables the identification or makes transmission of trauma possible. Paul de Man never connected himself to the events of the war after it was over, and neither he nor his family were the victims of Nazi brutality. Unlike Celan and Lanzmann, de Man made no claim to a connection with the Nazis' victims, and as we know, de Man willingly wrote for a collaborationist newspaper in Belgium from 1941 to 1942, an activity that, when discovered after de Man's death, stirred anger among his friends and colleagues and a wave of critical articles in the press.[18] This controversy prompted Felman—a student of de Man's—to produce what reads as a defense of her former teacher, in an essay first published in *Critical Inquiry* in 1989, immediately after the wartime writings came to light, and later reprinted as a chapter in *Testimony*. But the essay's inclusion (unchanged) in the later book, and its relation to the other chapters, indicates that it is more than a defense of de Man; like the other chapters, it argues for a relation between writing and trauma like the one imagined in the analysis of the Yale seminar, a relation that allows trauma both to exist in and to be transmitted by writing or speech.

Felman builds her analysis of de Man's wartime writing around the "series of disasters [that] preceded, in de Man's life, the outbreak of the war" (124). When de Man was seventeen, "his brother Hendrik died in a bicycle accident at a railroad crossing; a year later his mother committed suicide on the anniversary of his brother's death. Consequently, Paul de Man's uncle, also named Hendrik, became a sort of adoptive father to his nephew" (124). "Young Paul," as Felman calls him in these sections of her essay, under the (presumed) sway of his charismatic, politically active, collaborating "adoptive father," starts writing for the collaborationist newspaper *Le Soir* once the Nazis gain control of Belgium. Felman constructs a speculative psychological portrait of a young man who, in response to personal traumas, makes unwise decisions out of emotional need. She writes that de Man might have collaborated because "Hendrik's claims [about the Flemish language] and his political focus as a leader seemed to offer his young nephew ... a renewed relation to the *mother tongue*, beyond the loss marked by the mother's suicide" (126; original emphasis).[19] Felman encourages her reader to feel sympathetic toward both Young Paul and Hendrik, suggesting that "what the young Paul must have found compelling" in the Nazi propaganda was the "ideology of *reconstruction* and *national salvation* ... [which] might have seemed to hold the promise of making up for personal and political disasters" (127; original emphasis). The story of de Man's collaboration, as we are given it here, is not a history of de Man's beliefs about fascist nationalism—as one might reasonably expect—but rather an account of the psychological and emotional context in which his collaboration took place.

Having thus set up de Man's biography and his decision to collaborate as a story of trauma and its aftermath, Felman reads his early writing career as another traumatic story. In what appears to be an effort to align de Man with the many Holocaust survivors who have taken their own lives, Felman reads a hiatus in his published writing, after he was fired from the publishing house where he had been working in addition to his freelance journalism, as a self-punishing suicide.[20] "Might both de Man's eleven-year-old silence and his radical departure [from Belgium] be viewed as substitutes for suicide?" Felman wonders (134–35), imagining de Man as analogous to Ishmael from *Moby-Dick*, who goes to sea as a substitute for suicide (de Man had published a Flemish translation of Melville's novel in 1945). And further, Felman wonders, might that "silence" be "suicide as the recognition that what has been done is absolutely irrevocable, which requires one in turn to do something irreversible about it?" (135). Felman goes on, then, to read de Man's lifelong silence about his wartime activities not as "an erasure of the past" but as a "quasi-suicidal, mute acknowledgment of a radical loss—or death—of truth, and therefore the acknowledgment of a radical loss—or death—or self" (135). The suicide Felman finds in de Man's publishing hiatus and the acknowledgement of "loss" and an "irrevocable" act (which seem very much like guilt here) she finds in his later silence together give de Man's life not only the suicide that structures one version of the survivor's life, but a kind of survivor's guilt as well.

The method of reading that Felman uses to argue for this suicide and for the meaningfulness of de Man's silence reveals more about Felman's assumptions regarding the relation between writing and persons than it reveals about de Man's view of his own activities. Recounting how de Man helped to arrange the publication of the French Resistance journal *Exercise du silence*, for example, she proceeds to read the journal's content as de Man's own reflections on his collaborative activities; it is worth quoting at some length in order to see not only what her reading does, but how that reading is done. Felman argues that "*Exercise du silence* had announced both literally and metaphorically the annihilation of the self, not only because the volume chose symbolically to open with a letter by Baudelaire announcing his own suicide ... but because the editorial introduction, entitled 'Exercise of Silence,' had included ... thoughts on the death of the self and its reduction to silence (thoughts that can uncannily be read as prophesying the silent violence of de Man's imminent departure)" (135). Despite the uncanny prophecy about de Man that Felman finds in this journal, the absence of de Man's name as the grammatical subject in certain key moments reveals the gap between the suicidal intention Felman assigns specifically to de Man and the actual content of the journal: "*Exercise du silence*," we are told, "announced ... the annihilation of the self"; "the volume" "chose ... to open with a letter by Baudelaire announcing his own suicide." The text stands in for de Man in such a way that any characteristic of the journal can also be read as a characteristic of de Man, despite the fact that his relation to the content of the journal was quite distant. Perhaps I should clarify that he was not the journal's editor, despite the weight Felman assigns to the content of the journal's editorial introduction. He simply helped arrange to have the journal published.[21]

Felman does acknowledge that she is speculating, that this interpretation is "conjecture," but even in the process of acknowledging this she insists on connections she has posited not only between de Man and the content of *Exercise du silence*, but also between de Man and other texts he might be said to be connected with, in particular, *Moby-Dick*, which he translated, and the writing of Walter Benjamin, which was important to the criticism he went on to produce during his long career in the United States. "My conjecture is," Felman writes, "that ... Benjamin's suicide might have resonated with the suicides that framed de Man's own life. Benjamin's aborted departure [from Europe during the war] might have evoked de Man's own radical departure and his violent annihilation—or erasure—of his Belgian self" (155). Felman concedes that this is "conjecture," but goes on to defend it with more of the same: "If the question remains open of whether de Man, like Ishmael, departed as a substitute for committing suicide, Benjamin commits suicide when he is in the process of departure and when he believes (mistakenly) this process to be disrupted" (155). In this instance, the conflation of de Man with Benjamin is offered as the grounding alternative to the "open" question of whether de Man was, in his emigration from Belgium, in fact performing Melville's Ishmael.

I am not the first to notice, or to question, the way Felman's essay thus represents de Man as a suicide, and moreover, as the equivalent of a Holocaust survivor. Kalí Tal, in *Worlds of Hurt* (1996), and Dominick LaCapra, in a 1992 essay published in *History and Memory*, mount parallel critiques of Felman's exoneration of de Man and her appropriations of survivor identity. LaCapra focuses on the equation Felman makes between de Man and Primo Levi and criticizes Felman for "filling in de Man's silences with views explicitly elaborated by others," a move he characterizes as "an extremely speculative form of contextualizing ascription."[22] Felman's whole effort to "elide" the difference between de Man and Levi constitutes, LaCapra argues, "an unfortunate lapse of judgment" (14) comparable to Ronald Reagan's infamous remarks at Bitburg.[23] He goes on to question both Felman and, in the second half of the essay, Derrida for using deconstructive readings to exculpate de Man. LaCapra argues that it is this use of deconstruction, not de Man's wartime activities, that poses a threat to the prestige of deconstruction as a theory.

Tal's critique, by contrast, centers on the way Felman's and her coauthor Dori Laub's ideas about testimony appropriate the experiences of survivors in order to elevate the psychoanalytic interpreter to a position of power. While Tal and LaCapra take issue with many of the same elements of Felman's essay that I have pointed to above (indeed, there seems to be a consensus about which passages cry out for interpretation), their purposes in mounting these critiques and their accounts of the essay's significance are quite different from what I wish to set out. In keeping with LaCapra's larger project—as we see it in *Representing the Holocaust* (1994)—he psychoanalyzes the relation between the scholar and her subject, suggesting that the dynamics of the transference best explain not only the kind of analysis Felman produces, but the kind of history that gets written about the Holocaust in general.[24] For Tal, Felman and Laub's work in *Testimony* is one instance of a more general phenomenon in which the survivor of trauma is "depoliticiz[ed]" and "medicaliz[ed]," thereby domesticating whatever social or political intervention she might wish to make.[25]

My point differs from both of these interpretations: I see Felman's reading of de Man not as an irresponsible use of deconstruction brought on by intense transferential forces, or as a manipulation with political consequences, but as the logical limit case of the trauma theory *Testimony* as a whole puts forward.[26] The "point of conflation between text and life," where writing or speech can come to embody and transmit the trauma of the "actual life" (2), not only allows those who sympathize with Holocaust survivors to draw their personal significance and their identity from the Holocaust, but also allows those—like de Man—who did not evince such sympathy, to have their significance, and indeed, a kind of moral status, drawn for them from the Holocaust.

The implications of this kind of transmission reach beyond Felman herself and her relation to de Man, for Felman's argument is only one version of a theoretical innovation we find in the 1990s, particularly in discourse about the Holocaust, that attempts to reimagine the relation between texts and persons in such a way that texts take on particular characteristics we ordinarily assign exclusively to persons. Other chapters in *Testimony* reveal, for instance, that while de Man can commit suicide by ceasing to write, those who bear witness to suffering reverse death. Felman claims that "the main role of the historian is, thus, less to narrate history than to *reverse the suicide*" (216; original emphasis),[27] suggesting, for example, that Simon Srebnik, a witness of the most extreme violence of the camps, comes back from the dead when he agrees to take part in Claude Lanzmann's film. Felman claims that "it is ... only now, in returning with Lanzmann to Chelmno [where Srebnik was held prisoner], that Srebnik in effect is returning from the dead (from his own deadness)" (258). Later, she repeats the assertion without its accompanying parenthetical. Simon Srebnik's return from the dead is no longer metaphoric and abstract but real, now capable of personifying yet another abstraction: "Srebnik's return from the dead personifies ... a historically performative and retroactive *return of witnessing* to the witnessless historical primal scene" (258; original emphasis).[28]

It becomes clear that Felman cannot—and does not wish to—contain the collapse of persons and representations by which de Man can commit suicide and Claude Lanzmann can raise the dead. Felman imagines, further, that language itself, in the abstract sense of all languages, is a Freudian subject who "splits" into German, French, English, Russian, and Hebrew in response to the trauma it—Language—experiences in the Holocaust (213). Whatever truth might lie behind her formulation—that the twentieth century included terrible and unprecedented events—and whatever stylistic tendency toward hyperbole might shape that formulation, I think it is worth taking her own language seriously. While Felman does not always imagine writing as itself a person in the way these final examples suggest, she does consistently imagine writing as the embodiment (rather than the representation) of the kind of experience—of "life"—that only persons can be said to have.

TRAUMA WITHOUT EXPERIENCE

In the two cases of holocaust discourse I have examined thus far, Binjamin Wilkomirski's false memoir and Shoshana Felman's *Testimony*, actual trauma—lived suffering—seems to be pertinent, even crucial, to the claims that traumatic memoir and trauma theory make about texts. No matter how far removed Yale graduate students may be from the actual violence of the Holocaust, that violence underwrites the substance of what they are said to experience, and I have shown how Felman points to the undeniable suffering in de Man's life—the death of his brother and the suicide of his mother—as the foundation of the story she will tell about the trace of trauma in his writings. And no matter how doubtful the facts behind Binjamin Wilkomirski's memoir have turned out to be, the violence described there is, for both Wilkomirski himself and his readers, the source of the story's power and its significance.

This concern with actual violence and the psychic pain it engenders seems consistent with ideas about Holocaust survivors that were prevalent from about the mid-1970s up through the early 1990s, a period defined by the Reagan-era resurgence of the Cold War. In this period, as I discussed in chapter 2, discourse about survivors tends to be more narrowly focused on what we might call literal survival—escaping from the camps with one's life—as epitomized by Terrance Des Pres's *The Survivor* (1976) and by Robert Jay Lifton and Eric Markusen's *The Genocidal Mentality* (1990).[29] But at the same time, Felman's work moves away from the emphasis on physical violence and literal survival that defines the Holocaust survivor for Des Pres or Lifton, focusing instead on the survivor's ability to "bear witness" to her own and others' suffering. In some respects, the turn away from biological life as the basis of survivorship turns back to the ground covered by Primo Levi in *Se Questo è un Uomo* (1958), who suggests that the survivor ceases to be a person in any significant sense while in the camps, precisely because of the minute and desperate measures to which the inmate is driven just to sustain the life of the body, measures that overtake any notion of civility or culture.[30] Levi's response is to tell the story of his oppression, to insist on producing meaning through representing those events. While Levi's work might thus appear to fall under Felman's category of "witness," Felman's commitment to deconstruction, which is to say the rejection of language as representational, already moves her away not just from Des Pres and Lifton, but also from Levi.

Indeed, the implications of that deconstructive shift from language as representation to language as performance—apparent in the idea that survivors can be produced on the basis of trauma that is experienced by being read—suggests that Felman's evident concern with the actual violence experienced in the Holocaust may be unnecessary to trauma theory at its most abstract level. This is indicated in part by the fact that trauma theory does not, as Levi does, treat the camps as the destruction of what makes persons significant as such, but instead imagines the existential crisis that structures the Holocaust experience as the very core of both culture and personhood—that is, as the very core of our common life. I am not referring here to the belief that the camps revealed something like the truth of human nature or the notion that they epitomize the cultural and moral bankruptcy of our century. Rather, trauma theory has suggested that the experience of trauma is what defines not only the survivor, but all persons.[31] The psychoanalyst Dori Laub argues in his own chapters of *Testimony*, for example, that "the survival experience, or the Holocaust experience, is a very condensed version of most of what life is all about," because "it contains a great many existential questions" (72). The implication, for Laub, is that "the Holocaust experience is an inexorable and, henceforth, an unavoidable confrontation with those questions" (72). In other words, the Holocaust is not unique but exemplary, and exemplary not so much of other genocides as of everyday life. The suggestion implicit in this notion of exemplarity, that the "Holocaust experience" is not confined to the events we have come to call the Holocaust, implies, further, that the experience of the Holocaust continues in the present. It is not the facts of the Holocaust—its history— that are "an inexorable and, henceforth, an unavoidable confrontation" with existential questions, but the experience itself.

While Laub thus suggests that the specific historical events of the Holocaust, which some experienced and the rest of us learn about, are in fact at the heart of everyone's continuing experience, Cathy Caruth pushes the point even further. For Caruth the traumatic nature of history does not begin with the Holocaust, to continue "henceforth," but rather, the structure of trauma characterizes all history and experience despite the fact that the notion of lived trauma is almost entirely absent from her analysis in *Unclaimed Experience* (1996).

It should be said, first of all, that Caruth, unlike Felman, is not writing about the Holocaust in *Unclaimed Experience*; she is interested instead in exploring trauma and its relation to history and literature in a more general sense. It should also be said that, while she does not specify a historical site of trauma as her subject, neither does Caruth move to the other extreme, claiming that all experience, and all history, is traumatic; indeed, she specifically disavows the notion that her work is "an attempt to identify experience with trauma." Caruth wants, rather, "to allow, within experience, for the very unexpected interruption of experience constituted by the traumatic accident."[32] By defining trauma and experience in this way, in relation to one another, Caruth thus suggests that she has avoided the mistake of "defining, and thus anticipating, the difference between experience and trauma" (115). While Caruth's effort to avoid both identifying experience with trauma and roping off the traumatic experience from experience itself, as something distinct, makes sense—"experience," after all, is simply what happens to us, and what happens to us includes both the traumatic and the nontraumatic—we need to look more closely at the other claim being made here, that to be able to categorize an experience is to be able to anticipate it, to be able to "anticipate the accident" (115). This, on the surface, looks implausible: just because we know what to call a train wreck does not mean we know when we might be in one or that when we are in fact in a train wreck we are any less surprised for being able to name it.[33]

But obviously Caruth does not mean precisely this. Rather, she seems to be suggesting that the accident is something that happens not just to people, but to language. To put it in the more general terms that Caruth develops in her reading of de Man, which makes up chapter 4 of *Unclaimed Experience*, experience and language are the same thing insofar as accidents of the sort she is describing as traumatic—epitomized, for Caruth, by Freud's account of the train wreck in *Beyond the Pleasure Principle*—include accidents within language. What Caruth calls the "impact" of the linguistic referent that de Man appears to deny in his theory becomes, on Caruth's reading, a moment of trauma that inheres in the very structure of language. Reference is thus a kind of accident for Caruth: not the sort of accident that de Man describes in "The Purloined Ribbon," where Rousseau's "Marion" accidentally refers (refers simply by chance) to an actual person, but an accident that is like "falling down" (74), like the "impact" of the falling body (7).[34] This abstract notion of falling, for Caruth, epitomizes the trauma inherent in language itself, the trauma that is explored and, indeed, concentrated, in the ambiguities and the indirectness of reference to be found in literary language, "a language that defies, even as it claims, our understanding" (5).

Caruth may well be right in her basic intuition that de Man's theories about language contain an unacknowledged pathos, in which one might read a kind of regret or loss associated with the mechanistic functioning of language and the concomitant evacuation of presence and meaning that de Man theorizes. But in finding this pathos and characterizing it as a fall (a characterization I do not find convincing, because it is never clear how falling can ever be more than an analogy for the functioning of language), Caruth simply replicates and amplifies the pathos without making its object—the failure of reference—any more plausible as an instance of trauma. By making trauma—that experience which cannot be fully understood or known because of its violence—inhere in the very structure of language as such and by asserting trauma's centrality to literary language in this way, Caruth in the end insulates her analysis from the more concrete notions of trauma that inform Felman's analysis. And she does so even as she, like Felman, argues that trauma is embodied, without mediation, in language.

We can see this most dramatically in Caruth's conception of history. History is not what we might think—it is not the violent events of the world; rather, history is the way psychoanalysis and literature imagine one's relation to the past. Caruth's examples of "history" thus include Freud's *Moses and Monotheism* (which he originally subtitled "an historical novel"), the film *Hiroshima Mon Amour*, and Jacques Lacan's reading of Freud's account of the dream of the burning child. These are histories by Caruth's account because of the way they imagine the stories of people who have survived a loss and whose lives are still structured around that loss. History is "the inextricability of the story of one's life from the story of a death" (8). While what we would ordinarily call history does come into Caruth's reading of Freud's *Moses and Monotheism* insofar as she reads the work in relation to Freud's precipitous departure from Austria to England in 1938, that traumatic departure is immediately subsumed into the text of *Moses and Monotheism* itself. The text becomes "the site of a trauma" that is "historically marked" (20). Rather than the text marking a trauma Freud experienced, here history "marks" the textual trauma. What is striking in Caruth's account, then, is the way actual history—the things that happen in the world—is either excluded from the discussion or reduced to a kind of trace, just as actual trauma—the railway accident itself as distinct from Freud's account of it—is also excluded.

I take this strange insulation in Caruth's analysis to result from the understanding of trauma to which she is committed, an understanding that makes trauma not only "like literature" in that it is a kind of "not knowing," but also "like psychoanalysis" because of the latter's interest in "the complex relation between knowing and not knowing" (3). What history, literature, and psychoanalysis all share for Caruth, because of this very insulation, is the ability to "transmit" trauma whenever they "transmit" (115, 106, and throughout) or "pass on" (71, 107, and throughout) what is not known. The literary language of these discourses, because it does not describe an accident but in some sense must be understood *as* an accident, allows trauma to be transferred from one person to another. This counts as an explanation, for example, of the transmission of trauma imagined in *Moses and Monotheism* (an explanation, it must be said, Freud himself does not produce, though he does suggest that transmission takes place).[35] If, Caruth reasons, the experience of trauma is "possession by the past that is not entirely one's own" then trauma is an "individual experience" that "exceeds itself," and as such, "the witnessing of trauma" may not occur in the individual who experienced it but rather in "future generations" (136).

The impact of this claim—that the experience of trauma can be cut free of the person to whom the trauma happens—saturates Caruth's study; it can be seen even on the level of style, in her peculiar use of gerunds such as "the witnessing," "a seeing," "a falling," "a forgetting," "a not-forgetting." While such nominalization of academic writing has occurred in part as a grammatical effect of the critical desire to stop referring back to authors as a way of understanding what we see in a text, in Caruth's case the implication would be more specific. Once what a subject does is detached from the subject—in these cases, detached from a person—the act of experiencing can become a thing in the world, like an object (and here we can begin to understand the book's title). Experience, like a lost glove, can be "claimed" or left "unclaimed." In other words, once "she forgets" becomes "a forgetting," the forgetting can belong to anyone, and indeed, can begin to have actions predicated upon it.[36] By cutting experience free from the subject of experience, Caruth allows trauma not only to be abstract in the extreme but also, by virtue of that abstraction, to be transmissible.

Ruth Leys has produced a thorough analysis and critique of this notion of transmissible trauma and the way it has played a role in the intellectual and institutional evolution of the psychoanalytic profession, linking it with the scientific work of Bessel van der Kolk and showing how Caruth's theories distort Freud's more complex (though admittedly ambiguous) understanding of trauma. And Leys has raised serious questions about the ethical implications of Caruth's notion of trauma, pointing out that even Nazi perpetrators can, under its rubric, be seen as victims.[37] While my argument is in some ways parallel—and certainly indebted—to Leys's work in this regard, my own extended reading of Caruth is meant to show how her work, and trauma theory more generally, produces not so much a certain understanding of trauma as a certain understanding of language. This is an understanding indebted to de Manian deconstruction but also departing from it at the very point where the autonomous literary language that de Man imagined is taken, by virtue of that very autonomy, to actually be the experience of persons.[38] Though I agree with Leys's ethical critique, which is akin to LaCapra's and Tal's critiques of Felman and my own implicit critique of Wilkomirski, I want to focus less on the ethical implications of trauma theory than on its position within a wider literary discourse about the destruction of persons in the second half of the twentieth century. For Caruth's understanding of trauma and language is neither new nor particular to the practices of deconstruction and psychoanalysis she explicitly engages. In the final section of this chapter I show how a certain fantasy about memorization that we find in Caruth—made possible by the deconstructive emphasis on the materiality of the signifier—is rehearsed in the two nuclear dystopias that I discussed (in other terms) in chapter 2, in Don DeLillo's novel of postnuclear culture, *Underworld* (1997), and finally, to return to where I began this chapter, in Binjamin Wilkomirski's false memoir of the Holocaust.

Memorizing Memory

Caruth's notion of transmissible trauma—trauma that can be passed unknowingly from one person to another—is perhaps best exemplified by a certain fantasy about memorization, and it is this fantasy that will connect her study to the novels I mention above. Caruth points out, as she concludes her reading of the film *Hiroshima Mon Amour*, that the Japanese actor in that film—Eiji Okada, who speaks perfect French throughout—in fact did not know a word of French. He memorized what could only be, to him, the sounds of French and delivered these sounds to the French woman in the film as if he were intending a meaning. It should not take much reflection to see why this happenstance is important to Caruth, for the story of Okada's memorization reproduces what she has been presenting as the characteristic—rather than exceptional—linguistic structure. Here the actor literally "performs" the words he speaks, appearing (though this could hardly be the case even if he did not know French) to produce them without knowing their meaning, telling his character's story of trauma—of his family being killed in the bombing of Hiroshima while he was away in the Army— without understanding that story even as he tells it.

For Caruth, this happenstance reveals not only the truth about language, but also a truth about the relation between cultural identity and language understood in these terms. She argues, for example, that a Japanese businessman, who in the film uses English phrases (which Caruth characterizes as being memorized from a guidebook[39]) in an effort to pick up the French woman in a bar, has willingly submitted himself to a culture not his own. In this particular case, he has submitted himself to the culture of English, the culture that was responsible for the destruction of Hiroshima; he thereby represents, according to Caruth, "a certain loss of self implicit in the speaking of another's language" (49). By contrast, Caruth suggests that the Japanese actor who memorizes without trying to learn, and who memorizes not English but French, maintains his cultural integrity while still connecting with the cultural other, his French lover. Unlike the speech of the businessman and of the fictional character Okada plays, whose "well-learnt French represents," according to Caruth, "the loss of the Japanese referent" (51), Okada's speech "cannot be considered in the same terms of loss and forgetting. Okada, in other words, does not represent, but rather voices his difference quite literally, and untranslatably" (51). Here, cultural integrity appears to entail the decision to speak—or, more accurately, to intend meaning—only in one's own language, the language, to use Wilkomirski's terms, that is not the "imitation of other people's speech" but one's "own, at bottom." The language of the other is preserved as incomprehensible by the operation of memorization as opposed to learning. But in a sense, we can see that memorized, incomprehensible language has become not the language of the other, but the language in which one is most oneself: on this model, language is not representation but ontology; not the vehicle for knowledge but the medium in which one "voices his difference quite literally," in which one simply is oneself.

Being oneself in this way in turn means being the subject of a trauma, since the meaninglessness of the actor's speech is aligned, for Caruth, with his character's story of having missed the destruction of Hiroshima and of his family and thus being unable to "*know*" (40; original emphasis) his own experience of trauma. If identity imagined in these terms preserves one's cultural integrity in the way Caruth argues, then cultural identity has the same structure as traumatic experience—cultural identity and trauma are incomprehensible experiences that get passed around. The valorized production of personal or cultural identity is thus not, as it is for a writer like Primo Levi, the commitment to telling the story of one's trauma, but is rather the commitment to actually passing on the experience of trauma without having the experience oneself. The way Caruth presents it, this looks like a vision of ultimate particularity—for both persons and experience— since particular experiences that constitute personal and cultural identity thus bear an unmediated or literal relation to language. And indeed, this is part of what Caruth is interested in showing us, since representation as such for her implies the replaceability of persons and experiences, and the potential universality of these things.[40] Caruth thus claims that Eiji Okada's "phonetic feat" made him particularly essential to bring back when *Hiroshima Mon Amour* had to be reshot because of technical problems and, further, that the film's own history in this way underscored the importance of particularity in the representation of trauma. But the traumatic structures Caruth has laid out actually mean that Okada's participation cannot be in any sense significant. For, apart from the certainly remarkable talent for memorizing sounds that he demonstrated, anyone could memorize the script, say the lines, and "transmit" the trauma. Far from preserving what Caruth presents—and values—as the unknowable particularity of the traumatic experience, this fantasy about memorization makes particularity meaningless and makes trauma available to anyone, not just without recourse to painful experience but without recourse to experience as such.

It is here, in the coincidence between memorization and the construction of identities centered on trauma, that trauma theory can be seen most clearly to take up questions characteristic of postwar novels that, in imagining American culture in the wake of a large-scale nuclear war, attempt in their own way to come to terms with the relation between literature and what we can—in the ordinary sense—call traumatic events. As I showed in chapter 2, Ray Bradbury's *Fahrenheit 451* and Walter M. Miller, Jr.'s *A Canticle for Leibowitz* both feature groups of people whose identities in the wake of nuclear war are a function of the books they memorize. In both of these novels, the memorized text is both mechanical and material—a set of words in a particular order, preserved and transmitted through what is described as a mostly mechanical action of the memorizer's mind or pen. Guy Montag finds that he has memorized Ecclesiastes despite his apparent inability to screen out the distraction of advertising jingles. His mind, as imagined by Bradbury, memorized of its own accord and without his knowledge, filtering out the jingles and preserving, photographically, the entire prophetic text. *A Canticle for Leibowitz* features memorizers and copyists who reproduce texts and diagrams whose basis in extinct scientific knowledge renders them even more remote from meaning than the words of Ecclesiastes seem to Montag. For *Canticle*'s memorizers, the text becomes an arrangement, as one copyist puts it, of "doohickii" and "thingumbob" (76). Miller pushes this conception of the text one step further in significance by imagining it not only as essentially material but also as sacred, and as such the embodiment of truth even when—or especially when—its content cannot be understood rationally.

We also see the structure of unintentional or nonrational memorization thematized in novels closer, historically speaking, to trauma theory than *Fahrenheit 451* and *Canticle*, particularly in Don DeLillo's work. In *Ratner's Star* (1976), for example, Ratner's rabbi confesses that he has resorted to memorizing the sacred writings instead of interpreting them, because he is not really capable of understanding what they mean. The image returns in *Libra* (1988), in a secularized version, when Lee Harvey Oswald memorizes the Marine Corps manual and the utterly arbitrary rules of the military prison where he serves time. But its appearance in *Underworld* (1997) makes explicit the relation between memorization and a postnuclear culture permeated with violence both intended and unintended. Here, we find one of the main protagonists, Nick Shay, memorizing the ideas in Catholic texts under the tutelage of his Jesuit mentor: when the priest asks whether Nick understands what is in the books he is reading, he replies that he understands "some of it.... What I don't understand, I memorize."[41] For Nick, memorizing ideas and even simply new vocabulary is, he thinks, "the only way in the world you can escape the things that made you" (543). In Nick's case, what "made" him was a difficult, impoverished urban childhood that, through a complicated set of circumstances, led him to kill a man—unintentionally—for which he was convicted of manslaughter. While it looks like "the things that made" Nick also made, in his brother Matt's case, a very different man, DeLillo is in fact imaging the two as alike in a crucial way; for Matt becomes a nuclear weapons engineer, epitomizing what it means for American culture as a whole—like Nick, who describes himself as a "country of one" (275)—to be made the unintentional agent of murder. The religious texts Nick memorizes appear to offer, for him and perhaps for DeLillo, the only alternative to the unintentionally criminal identities both Nick and his brother possess. The memorized texts preserve what appears, in *Underworld*, to be an unavoidable failure of agency and rationality in a postmodern world, while they substitute some other, and better, end result for the individual person whose agency is thus compromised. Memorizing for Nick—as for Bradbury's Guy Montag in *Fahrenheit 451*—takes what is not you, what you do not yourself intend or understand, and makes it you.

And this is precisely what I take Bruno Dössekker also to have done. He absorbed the accounts of camp life, the stories of extreme violence, the testimonies and histories and photographs, and they finally became him, finally made him Binjamin Wilkomirski. Despite the difference we understand between what we memorize (like the multiplication tables) and what we call our memories (to use Nick Shay's terms, our recollections of the "things that made" us), in the case of Bruno Dössekker memorizing and memory have become the same thing. Without setting out to memorize the map of Auschwitz, he nevertheless did, and in doing so, perhaps without intending to, he became a child survivor.

Having earlier set aside ethical questions of the kind that Ruth Leys, Dominick LaCapra and Kalí Tal raise about transmissible trauma, ethical questions that we cannot help but think about when we consider the case of Wilkomirski, I want to conclude by taking up those questions in a limited way. One of the most accomplished contemporary ethicists and theorists of personhood, Derek Parfit, provides a final example of the fantasy of transmitted experience and in doing so offers a response to such transmission that is diametrically opposed to the one implied in trauma theory.

Parfit is interested in what persons are and why what persons are might (or might not) matter. As he thinks through various propositions about what persons are in his *Reasons and Persons* (1984), he produces a version of the view of experience I have been describing in this chapter. We see this in one of the hypothetical examples he uses to tease out the logic of identity: the example of Jack and Jane's memory surgery. In the scenario Parfit imagines, Jack and Jane undergo surgery in which the memories of each are implanted into the other's brain. Parfit argues that after a while, Jane will not be able to tell which of her memories were the result of her experiences prior to the surgery and which were the result of Jack's experiences. Indeed, Parfit argues that, for all significant purposes, Jane will become the subject of Jack's experiences. The point is that since we can imagine Jane feeling that Jack's experiences bear the same relation to her sense of identity as her own, it would be incoherent to assert that identity lies in some singular entity that has experienced a certain set of things, that identity can be located within the subject of those experiences.

The example of Jack and Jane is just one scenario among several that Parfit uses to think through, and disprove, various ways of defining what persons are. The result of his analysis of existing theories leads him, finally, to what he calls the "Reductionist View." The Reductionist View states that "the existence of a person, during any period, just consists in the existence of his brain and body, and the thinking of his thoughts, and the doing of his deeds, and the occurrence of many other physical and mental events."[42] The ethical importance of the memory surgery example becomes clear when Parfit later describes the effects of believing the view of persons he arrived at, in part, through the idea of memory surgery. When one thinks of life as the Reductionist does, Parfit finds that "there is still a difference between my life and the lives of other people. But the difference is less." This, in turn, changes how Parfit thinks and feels about death: "After my death, there will be no one living who will be me. I can now redescribe this fact. Though there will later be many experiences, none of these experiences will be connected to my present experiences by chains of such direct connections as those involved in experience-memory, or in the carrying out of an earlier intention.... My death will break the more direct relations between my present experiences and future experiences, but it will not break various other relations" (281). What Parfit here calls "direct relations" are discussed in earlier parts of his argument as the narrative relations that we routinely generate to explain the events of our lives, narrative relations of the kind so evident in the example of Binjamin Wilkomirski. For Parfit this is not simply a linguistic activity, but also has to do with physical facts, such as the fact that the same brain perceives one event and then another, the same body does its deeds from one moment to the next. The Reductionist View suggests that these connections—both physical and narratological—are not morally significant even if they are emotionally compelling.

Without discounting the fact that our narratological sense of ourselves has a certain power (Parfit feels "better" about his own death, though we can still hear melancholy in this passage), he suggests that it is a kind of sentimentalism to believe that these narratological links between experiences are what matters in the world. What matters, rather, is that the sum total of experiences is predominantly good (Parfit clearly displays his utilitarian commitments here). For Parfit, unlike the trauma theorists and literary practitioners I have presented, seeing experiences as in some sense alienable from what we think of as the person (through the fantasy of memory surgery) leads to the devaluation of personal identity as such, let alone particular kinds of trauma-centered personal identity like the ones Wilkomirski and Felman construct or theorize. The "Reductionist," Parfit explains, "also claims that personal identity is not what matters," which is why a certain set of relations between experiences, produced by the narratives of an individual person, matters less to Parfit as he reflects upon his own death (275). In questioning the value of personal identity understood in terms of narratological links, he voids the cultural work trauma theory can be said to accomplish even while he shares its ambivalence about the tie between experiences and persons. The loose tie Parfit imagines, instead of conferring value on something like Wilkomirski's traumatic identity or the survivorship of Yale students, makes such identities morally irrelevant. It seems fair to ask, if Parfit reasons correctly (as I think he does) about what persons are, whether we should have any interest in imagining other people's experiences as our own.

NOTES

1. Binjamin Wilkomirski, afterword of *Fragments: Memories of a Wartime Childhood*, tr. Carol Brown Janeway (New York: Schocken, 1996). For their invaluable comments on an earlier version of this chapter, I would like to thank the members of the New York Americanists group, the editors at the *Yale Journal of Criticism*, and the members of the Holocaust Working Group at the Whitney Humanities Center, Yale University.

2. André Aciman, "Innocence and Experience" (a review of several books on the persecution of Jewish children), *New Republic* 218.3 (January 19, 1998): 30.

3. See, for example, Harvey Peskin, "Holocaust Denial: A Sequel," *Nation* 268.14 (April 19, 1999): 34–38. Peskin argues that the controversy may be causing other child survivors who could corroborate Wilkomirski's story to keep silent, because "to be disbelieved is to be hunted again" (38). This belief also played itself out in the way the press, especially in Europe, initially treated with great discretion the doubts about Wilkomirski's identity. Many reporters have been careful to insert into the story of those doubts a warning that Wilkomirski's errors might be used to

bolster the claims of Holocaust deniers who seek to discredit all testimonial evidence. The American coverage, by contrast, is rather more strident in tone.

4. Wilkomirski was awarded, for example, France's prestigious Prix de Memoire de la Shoah, and he was featured as a speaker during a fund-raising tour for the National Holocaust Memorial Museum in Washington, D.C.

5. Robert Hanks, "Where Naughty Children Get Murdered," review of *Fragments*, by Binjamin Wilkomirski, *Independent* (London), December 8, 1996, 31.

6. See Philip Gourevitch, "The Memory Thief," *New Yorker* 75.15 (June 14, 1999): 56.

7. His publisher recounts how Wilkomirski wept almost continuously through the book tour and fund-raising activities that followed *Fragments*'s publication and the prizes awarded to it, and this evident misery is cited by just about everyone who has written about or interviewed Wilkomirski, both before and after the questions about his identity intensified. Cited in Gourevitch, "Memory Thief," 51.

8. Wilkomirski has argued that he never actually claimed that he remembered the death of his father and the disappearance of his brothers, and indeed, these figures are identified hesitantly in the memoir: "maybe my father," "maybe my brothers." But this local hesitation is eclipsed by a narrative that goes on to assume, in myriad ways, that these were in fact memories of a father and brothers.

9. This account of Wilkomirski's comments comes from an article by Dan Perry, published in *Sueddeutsche Zeitung*, April 22, 1995; then cited (and translated by Martin Ostwald) in Aciman, "Innocence and Experience," 32. Aciman's essay, it should be pointed out, was written before the more damning discoveries about Wilkomirski, which came to light in Daniel Ganzfried's article later the same year.

10. Gourevitch, "Memory Thief," 65.

11. See Elena Lappin, "The Man with Two Heads," *Granta* 66 (Summer 1999): 43. Gourevitch gives a slightly different version of this episode, where Bernstein recounts what must have been his answer to Wilkomirski's question: "I told him it would be terrible if—"Bernstein recalls, "*if* those papers contained something that he had gone through" ("Memory Thief," 59; original emphasis).

12. It is interesting to note the claim that Blake Eskin makes about his own relation to the European past in the context of his discussion of Binjamin Wilkomirski. "I was born in America," he writes, "but Wilkomirski [the surname] represented who I was before I became an American. This heritage was unknown and perhaps unknowable, but seemed essential and was something I still carried with me" (*A Life in Pieces* [New York: Norton, 2002], 20). Eskin seems to be identifying himself not simply *with*, but *as* the relatives—by the name of Wilkomirski—whom his family had left in Riga when they emigrated to the United States in the early twentieth century. This is the only way to make sense of the claim that he "was" someone before he "became" an American at birth. The logic Eskin uses here is thus not substantially different from Binjamin's, though Eskin asserts what he clearly imagines as a more authentic claim to identity because he—unlike Bruno Dössekker—really is genetically related to the Wilkomirskis of Riga.

13. Gourevitch, "Memory Thief," 57.

14. Felman and Laub, *Testimony*, 47, 48; hereafter cited parenthetically.

15. On this point I am indebted to Johanna Bodenstab. Her comments on an early version of this essay, as well as her own work on survivor testimony from the Fortunoff Archive, have helped me to think through these issues.

16. Hartman, *Longest Shadow*, 152 ("secondary trauma"). Hartman suggests that, from the media's transmission of images of atrocity, "a 'secondary trauma' could arise" that would produce, finally, feelings of both fascination and indifference (152). The alternative is what Hartman calls "the testimony-encounter," the encounter with the survivor telling her story in a videotaped testimony. In such an encounter, "the narrative that emerges through the alliance of witness and interviewer does not present, however grim its contents, either a series of fixed images that assault the eyes or an impersonal historical digest. The narrative resembles that most natural and flexible of human communications, a story—a story, moreover, that, even if it describes a universe of death, is communicated by a living person who answers, recalls, thinks, cries, carries on. The hope is, then, that secondary trauma, insofar as it is linked to violent yet routinized images, will not injure either the witnesses recalling the events, or young adults and other long-distance viewers to whom extracts of the testimonies are shown" (154). He reflects that "it would be ironic and sad if all that education could achieve were to transmit a trauma to later generations in a secondary form" (154) and expresses reservations about "Laub's positive view of ... secondary trauma" in which the listener becomes " 'a participant and co-owner of the traumatic event' " (165, n. 10; second quotation is Laub, cited by Hartman).

17. Ruth Leys has pointed out, in response to an earlier version of this analysis, that identification on the Freudian model has little to do with choosing whom or what one identifies with, that identification is largely an unconscious and unwilled process. Leys is certainly right about Freud's version of identification (for a useful synopsis of Freud's ideas about identification, see J. LaPlanche and J.-B. Pontalis, "Identification," in *The Language of Psycho-analysis*, tr. Donald Nicholson-Smith [London: Hogarth, 1973; reprint, New York: Norton, 1974], 205–8); my analysis describes what I take to be the literary-critical use of the structure Freud describes. And so, while there may be unconscious reasons behind the Yale students' identification with the Holocaust survivors whose testimony they listen to, my concern here is not the facts of their psyches (which may or may not have accorded with the psychic states Felman imputes to them) but with Felman's representation of them. There are ways, of course, to read the kind of identifications that Felman describes in relation to her own psyche; indeed, this is what Dominick LaCapra has done (see my discussion below of his essay "The Personal, the Political, and the Textual"). But rather than trying, like LaCapra, to psychoanalyze the persons who are represented in and through her writing, I want to read the representation itself as a literary artifact, in order to show how the text works as such and how it fits into a history of late-twentieth-century literature.

18. For accounts of these discoveries and responses, see Alan B. Spitzer, *Historical Truth and Lies about the Past: Reflections on Dewey, Dreyfus, de Man, and Reagan* (Chapel Hill: University of North Carolina Press, 1996); Werner Hamacher, Neil Hertz, and Thomas Keenan, eds., *Responses: On Paul de Man's Wartime Journalism* (Lincoln: University of Nebraska Press, 1989); and Paul de Man, *Wartime Journalism,*

1939–1943, ed. Werner Hamacher, Neil Hertz, and Thomas Keenan (Lincoln: University of Nebraska Press, 1988).

19. We might note, once again, the similarity between Wilkomirski's account of himself at the opening of his memoir—his alienation from his "mother tongue"—and Felman's account of the traumatized person, in this case de Man.

20. Indeed, suicide has become part of the form of the authentic survivor story, a fact borne out in the Wilkomirski story. Wilkomirski's writing and his personal fragility have been compared with the writing and suicide of Primo Levi, and critics of Wilkomirski are sometimes warned by his supporters that their skepticism may cause Wilkomirski's suicide. Daniel Ganzfried suggests—perhaps outrageously—that some of those supporters would be secretly pleased if he did commit suicide, since that would become a kind of proof that he was telling the truth (Gourevitch, "Memory Thief," 65–66). Here, Felman provides de Man with a comparable suicide.

21. For a detailed account of de Man's precise relation to the publication of this journal, see "Paul de Man: A Chronology," in *Responses*, ed. Hamacher, Hertz, and Keenan, xviii (the entry for December 10, 1942).

22. Dominick LaCapra, "The Personal, the Political, and the Textual: Paul de Man as Object of Transference," *History and Memory* 4.1 (Spring/Summer 1992): 12.

23. In May 1985 President Reagan visited the military cemetery at Bitburg (in what was then West Germany), home to forty-nine graves of Waffen SS troopers, Hitler's elite guard. He and Chancellor Helmut Kohl laid a memorial wreath at the graves. As one might imagine, the incident outraged many in Germany and around the world.

24. In *Representing the Holocaust: History, Theory, Trauma* (Ithaca, N.Y.: Cornell University Press, 1994), LaCapra argues that the historian must "work through," in the Freudian sense of that phrase, the material he writes about and that doing so is particularly important for those writing Holocaust history because of the traumatic nature of the materials the historian must engage. LaCapra thus sees the psychoanalytic session—with its dynamics of transference and counter-transference—as the model for scholarly work.

25. Tal, *Worlds of Hurt*, 59.

26. It should be said, however, that LaCapra read the essay singly, not as part of *Testimony*, though I think it unlikely that his critique would be substantially different even if he had seen it in this context, or that, even if different, it would come to coincide with mine.

27. Her logic, in brief, runs as follows: The camps traumatized their survivors so deeply that some committed suicide; the suicide silenced their testimony to the trauma; the historian by his or her testimony to the trauma can restore what was lost in the suicide; therefore, the historian can reverse suicide.

28. Geoffrey Hartman has noted, and criticized, the way Lanzmann himself announces his film as bringing back the dead (*Longest Shadow*, 52). Felman seems to be following the filmmaker's lead in her analysis. Unfortunately—pointing up the risks of relying on such conflations—Srebnik is "killed" later by Polish villagers who give their (often ignorant) interpretations of the event that Srebnik describes among

them: "the Polish villagers are ... unaware of the precise ways in which they themselves are actually *enacting* both the Crucifixion and the Holocaust *in annihilating Srebnik*, in *killing once again the witness* whom they totally dispose of, and *forget*" (*Testimony*, 267; original emphasis). This "killing once again the witness" is, Felman tells us, a "second Holocaust." Felman thus turns effortlessly from Srebnik's resurrection to his murder.

29. See Des Pres, *The Survivor:* and Robert Jay Lifton and Eric Markusen, *The Genocidal Mentality: Nazi Holocaust and Nuclear Threat* (New York: Basic Books, 1990). Both of these studies, in their most general claims, argue that the significance of the Nazi genocide lies in its relation to the ongoing, and potentially more lethal, problem of nuclear war.

30. By contrast, Des Pres gives, as his best example of the "talent for life," a survivor's story about enjoying a bowl of soup in the camps; he argues that this ability to take pleasure simply in attending to the needs of the body is characteristic of those who survived and of the larger biological-cultural phenomenon he is describing. For an encapsulated version of Levi's opposite notion of the physical as the end of culture and personhood, we can look to the opening poem in *Survival in Auschwitz* (tr. Stuart Woolf [New York: Macmillan, 1961]; originally published as *If This Is a Man)*. It asks the reader, who returns home in the evening to "hot food and friendly faces" to

> Consider if this is a man
> Who works in the mud
> Who does not know peace
> Who fights for a scrap of bread
> Who dies because of a yes or a no.
> Consider if this is a woman,
> Without hair and without name
> With no more strength to remember,
> Her eyes empty and her womb cold
> Like a frog in winter. (8)

The implication, of course, is that this is not a man, not a woman, who lives this way. Levi thus suggests that what constitutes the person can be destroyed by such things as working in the mud, fighting for food, living only in the terrible present. For Des Pres, continuing simply to live—in the biological, literal sense—in the face of such things is precisely what marks the "talent for life" he finds central to personhood.

31. Walter Benn Michaels has argued (in " 'You Who Never Was There': Slavery and the New Historicism, Deconstruction and the Holocaust," *Narrative* 4.1 [January 1996]) that, by making it possible for people who could not experience the Holocaust historically to experience it through performative testimony, Felman allows Jewish identity to float free from race and religion to become entirely cultural (12–13). Though the "deconstructive performative" does indeed provide a technology that can connect the present person to a past she did not experience, it does not in *Testimony* enable the "complete triumph of the notion of culture," as Michaels suggests (13). Insofar as performative utterance performs trauma rather than performing the historical event we call the Holocaust, it strips race, religion, *and* culture from the notion of identity.

32. Cathy Caruth, *Unclaimed Experience: Trauma, Narrative, and History* (Baltimore: Johns Hopkins University Press, 1996), 115 n. 5 to the introduction; hereafter cited parenthetically.

33. As Freud and the psychoanalytic profession—and Caruth—conceive it, trauma is epitomized by the survivor of the accident who only later learns he almost died and who then becomes ill. Given this conception of the structure of trauma, one might argue that it is the ability to categorize the accident—in this case, as a near-death experience—that appears to bring on the symptoms of trauma. This is the sort of scenario that the film *Life Is Beautiful* leads one to imagine, in which categorizing a terrible experience as something else (in the film, as a children's game) prevents it from being experienced as trauma at all. Less fantastically, we might call to mind the way people become angry or upset at their parents' behavior toward them as children because, as adults, they understand—and can categorize—inappropriate behavior that, as children, they simply accepted as normal. These instances are simplistic, of course; most of us assume that Freud was accurate at least in the notion that we have what he called an unconscious, which registers things like our childhood experiences in a way that perhaps our conscious mind—the mind responsible for assigning experiences to categories—does not, opening the door for a conscious response to experiences after the fact. Here I want only to suggest that the mental action of categorizing appears not to preclude the experience of something as traumatic, but rather to enable it.

34. "De Man's critical theory of reference," Caruth explains, "ultimately becomes a narrative, and a narrative inextricably bound up with the problem of what it means to fall (which is, perhaps, de Man's own translation of the concept—of the experience—of trauma)" (*Unclaimed Experience*, 7).

35. See Ruth Leys's far more detailed account and critique of Caruth's use of *Moses and Monotheism* and implicit reliance on Lamarckianism, in chapter 8 of *Trauma: A Genealogy* (Chicago: University of Chicago Press, 2000), especially 285 and following.

36. Take, for instance, a sentence in the chapter "Literature and the Enactment of Memory": "It [the question of the difference between life and death] opens it [the woman's history] up, however, not by asking for a knowledge she owns and can thus simply state within her story, but by calling upon the movement of her not knowing within the very language of her telling" (37). Here, "not knowing" has something called "movement" within "her telling." It is not at all clear to me what it would mean for "not knowing" to move, but it is clear that such an ability is required in order for what is not known to be transmitted—that is, to move—from one person to another.

37. See Leys, *Trauma*, especially chapter 8.

38. Another way of describing this difference would be to say that both Caruth and Felman depart from de Man in taking his theories about language and extending them beyond the purview of the literary, into the realm of psychoanalysis. Where de Manian deconstruction is often accused of insulation from the historical, trauma theory's reading of de Man argues that rather than being divorced from history, de Man's ideas in fact give an account of the most significant and painful essence of history, its most infamous instances of violence, betrayal, and conflict. Trauma theory

is a departure from de Manian deconstruction, then, because it significantly extends the categories of object to which deconstruction applies.

39. Though Caruth mentions this as an instance of memorization more than once, it is clear that the businessman's attempts to speak English are distinct from Okada's memorization not only because the businessman memorizes English as opposed to French, but also because he memorizes phrases in order to use them as communication; he uses the language, that is, to intend meaning. By contrast, Okada, according to Caruth's account, memorizes only to perform, not to intend meaning.

40. This claim is worked out largely in Caruth's discussion of the French woman's story about her German lover. It is clear that in the film the French woman sees the act of telling the story of their love and his death as a betrayal, as a sign that the first love is replaceable by another love. Caruth, following Freud's analysis of mourning, generalizes this notion that representation is replacement, the turning of particular into universal; in its generalized formulation, the particular retains the pathos it gains as the object of mourning both in the film and in Freud's analysis (see chapter 2 of *Unclaimed Experience*, especially 27–33).

41. Don DeLillo, *Underworld* (New York: Scribner, 1997), 537. Hereafter cited parenthetically.

42. Derek Parfit, *Reasons and Persons*, corrected ed. (Oxford: Clarendon Press, 1987), 275.

Chronology

1921	On July 29, Adolf Hitler becomes the leader of the Nationalist Socialist 'Nazi' Party; James Joyce publishes *Ulysses*.
1923	*Time* magazine founded.
1924	Vladimir Lenin dies; the first Olympic Winter Games are held in Chamonix, France; J. Edgar Hoover is appointed director of FBI.
1925	Hitler publishes *Mein Kampf*; F. Scott Fitzgerald's *The Great Gatsby* and Virginia Woolf's *Mrs. Dalloway* are published.
1927	Charles Lindbergh becomes the first person to fly solo across the Atlantic; the first talking movie, *The Jazz Singer*, is released.
1928	Elie Weisel is born on September 30 in Sighet, Romania; penicillin is discovered.
1929	Anne Frank is born on June 12 in Frankfurt am Main, Germany; on October 29, the Stock Market on Wall Street crashes; William Faulkner's *The Sound and the Fury* and Ernest Hemingway's *A Farewell to Arms* are published.
1930	Germans elect members of the Nazi party, making them the second largest political party in Germany.
1932	Amelia Earhardt becomes the first woman to fly solo across the Atlantic; *Brave New World* by Aldous Huxley is published.

1933   Franklin Delano Roosevelt is sworn in as the 32nd U.S.
            President; Adolf Hitler is appointed Chancellor of
            Germany; on February 28, the Nazis set fire to the
            Richstag, one day later, Hitler is granted emergency
            powers; in addition to passing several laws restricting the
            rights of Jews, the Nazis open four concentration camps:
            Dachau, Buchenwald, Sachsenhausen, Ravensbrück (for
            women); Jerzy Kosinski is born on June 14; President
            Roosevelt establishes the New Deal program.

1934   German President von Hindenburg dies on August 2, and
            Hitler becomes Führer; Hitler receives a 90 percent 'Yes'
            vote from German citizens approving his new powers.

1935   September 15, the Nazis pass the Nuremberg Race Laws
            stripping all German Jews of their rights; Isaac Bashevis
            Singer publishes *Der Satan in Gorey* (*Satan in Goray*); Social
            Security is established in the U.S.

1936   The German Gestapo is placed above the law and Heinrich
            Himmler is appointed chief of the German Police; in an
            effort to gain favorable public opinion, the Germans
            temporarily refrain from actions against the Jews while the
            Olympic games are being held in Berlin; King Edward VIII
            abdicates the throne in England.

1937   Joseph Stalin begins his purge of Red Army generals; the
            Hindenberg Disaster occurs; Japan invades China.

1938   Nazi troops enter Austria and Hitler announces Anschluss
            (union) with Austria; on July 23, the Nazis order Jews over
            age 15 to apply for identity cards; in November,
            Kristallnacht, or "The Night of Broken Glass" occurs.

1939   September 1, Nazis invade Poland (Jewish pop. 3.35
            million, the largest in Europe); England and France declare
            war on Germany on Sept. 3; Soviet troops invade eastern
            Poland on Sept. 17 and the Nazis and Soviets subsequently
            divide up Poland; yellow stars are required to be worn by
            Polish Jews over age 10; John Steinbeck publishes *The
            Grapes of Wrath*.

1940   Nazis establish the Auschwitz concentration camp in
            Poland; on April 9, Germany invades Denmark (Jewish
            pop. 8,000) and Norway (Jewish pop. 2,000); on May 10,
            Germany invades France (Jewish pop. 350,000), Belgium
            (Jewish pop. 65,000), Holland (Jewish pop. 140,000), and
            Luxembourg (Jewish pop. 3,500); Paris falls on June 14,

and France signs an armistice with Hitler; The Battle of Britain takes place from July to October. In September, the Tripartite (Axis) Pact is signed by Germany, Italy and Japan. Hungary, Romania, and Slovakia become Nazi Allies in November, and the Warsaw Ghetto, containing over 400,000 Jews, is sealed off; John Steinbeck receives the Pulitzer Prize in fiction for *The Grapes of Wrath*.

1941   Nazis occupy Bulgaria (Jewish pop. 50,000), Yugoslavia (Jewish pop. 75,000), Greece (Jewish pop. 77,000), and invade the Soviet Union (Jewish pop. 3 million) on June 22; Bertolt Brecht's *Furcht und Elend des Dritten Reichs* (*Fear and Misery in the Third Reich*) is produced; in September, German Jews are ordered to wear yellow stars; on December 7, Japanese attack United States at Pearl Harbor; the next day the U.S. and Britain declare war on Japan.

On December 11, Hitler declares war on the United States; Roosevelt then declares war on Germany saying, "Never before has there been a greater challenge to life, liberty and civilization"; the U.S. enters the war in Europe and will concentrate nearly 90 percent of its military resources to defeat Hitler; Franklin Roosevelt and Winston Churchill sign the Atlantic Charter.

1942   Albert Camus publishes *L'Etranger* (*The Stranger*); Primo Levi receives a doctorate in chemistry from the University of Turin; in October, Himmler orders all Jews in concentration camps in Germany to be sent to Auschwitz and Majdanek; the deportations of Jews from Norway to Auschwitz begin; the internment of Japanese-Americans begins.

1943   On February 2, Germans surrender at Stalingrad in the first big defeat of Hitler's armies; in New York, American Jews hold a mass rally at Madison Square Garden to pressure the U.S. government into helping the Jews of Europe on March 1; in May, German and Italian troops in North Africa surrender to Allies; Nazis declare Berlin to be Judenfrei (cleansed of Jews); Allies land in Sicily in July; in November, the U.S. Congress holds hearings to address the State Department's inaction regarding European Jews, despite mounting reports of mass extermination.

1944   *Commentary*, a monthly magazine of Jewish cultural advancement, begins publication; on January 3, Soviet troops reach former Polish border; Elie Wiesel is deported to Auschwitz in March; on June 6, "D-Day," Allied forces land in Normandy; in August, Anne Frank and family are arrested by the Gestapo in Amsterdam, then sent to Auschwitz; Anne and her sister Margot are later sent to Bergen-Belsen; in October, Nazis seize control of the Hungarian puppet government, then resume deporting Jews, which had temporarily ceased due to international political pressure to stop Jewish persecutions; last use of gas chambers at Auschwitz.

1945   In January, Elie Wiesel's father dies in Buchenwald and Soviet Troops invade eastern Germany; on Jan 27, Soviet troops liberate Auschwitz. By this time, an estimated 2,000,000 persons, including 1,500,000 Jews, have been murdered there; Anne Frank dies of typhus at Bergen-Belsen in March, she was fifteen years old; in April, Soviet troops reach Berlin and the U.S. 7th Army liberates Dachau; Elie Wiesel is liberated from Buchenwald concentration camp; President Roosevelt dies and Harry S. Truman becomes the 33rd President of the United States; Hitler commits suicide in his Berlin bunker; in August, the United States drops the first atomic bombs on Hiroshima and Nagasaki, Japan, killing tens of thousands instantly; on September 2, Japan officially surrenders; the Nuremberg War Crimes Tribunal begins in November, with Nazi leaders put on trial for crimes against humanity; George Orwell publishes *Animal Farm.*

1946   Christopher Isherwood publishes *The Berlin Stories*; Winston Churchill gives "Iron Curtain" speech; Gertrude Stein dies; in October, The Nuremburg War Crimes Trials end; twelve defendants are sentenced to death by hanging, three to life imprisonment, four to lesser prison terms, and three acquitted.

1947   *The Diary of Anne Frank* is published—it was saved during the war by one of the family's helpers, Miep Gies; André Gide receives the Nobel Prize for Literature; the Marshall Plan is enacted.

1948   The state of Israel is formed; Ghandi is assassinated.

1949   George Orwell publishes *1984.*

1950   Ralph Bunche receives the Nobel Peace Prize for

	negotiating the 1949 armistice between Arab and Israeli states; the Korean War begins.
1948–1954	Sir Winston Churchill publishes *The Second World War*, in six volumes.
1951	J.D. Salinger's *Catcher in the Rye* is published.
1952	Princess Elizabeth is crowned Queen of England at age 25; Polio vaccine is created; Ralph Ellison's *Invisible Man* is published.
1953	Sir Winston Churchill receives the Nobel Prize for Literature; Joseph Stalin dies; Dwight Eisenhower takes office as the 34th U.S. President.
1954	In "Brown vs. Topeka Board of Education," segregation is outlawed in public schools.
1955	Albert Hackett and Frances Goodrich produce the drama *The Diary of Anne Frank*; Rosa Parks refuses to give up her seat on a Montgomery, Alabama bus, marking the beginning of the Civil Rights movement.
1956	Elie Wiesel publishes *Un Di Velt Hot Geshvign*.
1957	The Soviet Satellite *Sputnik* launches the space exploration age; Jack Kerouac's *On the Road* is published.
1958	Elie Wiesel's *Night* and Bernard Malamud's *The Magic Barrel* are published; NASA is created.
1959	Fidel Castro becomes dictator of Cuba.
1960	John F. Kennedy is elected President.
1961	The U.S. launches the failed Bay of Pigs invasion against Cuba; the Soviet Union sends the first astronaut into space; the Berlin Wall is built.
1962	The Cuban Missile Crisis places the U.S. and the Soviet Union on the brink of war.
1963	Martin Luther King, Jr. leads the Civil Rights march on Washington, where he gives his, "I Have a Dream" speech; President John F. Kennedy is assassinated on November 22; Lyndon Johnson becomes the 36th U.S. President.
1964	The Civil Rights Act is passed in the United States.
1966	Elie Wiesel's *Jews of Silence* is published; Mao Zedong launches the Cultural Revolution in China.
1967	Chaim Potok publishes *The Chosen*.
1968	Robert F. Kennedy and Martin Luther King, Jr. are

assassinated; the Tet Offensive begins in Vietnam; Richard Nixon is elected president.

1969   Neil Armstrong becomes the first man to land on the moon; Yasir Arafat becomes leader of the PLO.

1971   Cynthia Ozick publishes *The Pagan Rabbi, and Other Stories*; Jerzy Kosinski publishes *Being There*.

1972   Eleven Jewish athletes are killed by Palestinian terrorists at the Olympic Games in Munich.

1973   U.S. begins pulling out of Vietnam; Thomas Pynchon publishes *Gravity's Rainbow*.

1974   President Nixon resigns amid the Watergate Scandal; Vice President Ford takes office.

1975   Pol Pot becomes the dictator of Cambodia; Saigon falls to the communists.

1977   Jimmy Carter is sworn in as the 39th President.

1978   John Paul II becomes the Pope.

1979   William Styron publishes *Sophie's Choice*; Margaret Thatcher becomes the first woman Prime Minister of Great Britain; the Ayatollah Khomeini takes control of Iran and American hostages are taken there; Mother Teresa is awarded the Nobel Peace Prize.

1980   President Reagan takes office; the American hostages in Iran are released.

1982   Alice Walker's *The Color Purple* is published.

1984   Indira Ghandi is assassinated; *The Handmaid's Tale* by Margaret Atwood is published.

1986   Elie Wiesel is awarded the Nobel Peace Prize; the Challenger space shuttle explodes, killing all on board; Chernobyl nuclear disaster occurs.

1987   Primo Levi dies.

1988   Salman Rushdie's *The Satanic Verses* is published.

1989   The Berlin Wall falls, uniting East and West Germany; students are killed in China's Tiananmen Square; President George Bush takes office.

1990   Jerzy Kosinski dies; Nelson Mandela is freed from a South African jail; Lech Walesa becomes the first president of Poland.

1991   The Soviet Union Collapses; Operation Desert Storm commences with the invasion of Iraq.

1993	Bill Clinton is sworn in as the 42nd U.S President; Toni Morrison wins the Nobel Prize in Literature.
1994	Nelson Mandela is elected president of South Africa.
1995	The Alfred P. Murrah Federal Building in Oklahoma City is bombed, killing 168 people.
1998	NATO sends military forces into Serbia.
2000	George W. Bush wins the presidential election despite ballot controversy.
2001	September 11 terrorists attacks occur, destroying the World Trade Center and damaging the Pentagon, killing thousands and making it the worst terrorist attack ever on U.S. soil.

Contributors

HAROLD BLOOM is Sterling Professor of the Humanities at Yale University and Henry W. and Albert A. Berg Professor of English at the New York University Graduate School. He is the author of over 20 books, including *Shelley's Mythmaking* (1959), *The Visionary Company* (1961), *Blake's Apocalypse* (1963), *Yeats* (1970), *A Map of Misreading* (1975), *Kabbalah and Criticism* (1975), *Agon: Toward a Theory of Revisionism* (1982), *The American Religion* (1992), *The Western Canon* (1994), and *Omens of Millennium: The Gnosis of Angels, Dreams, and Resurrection* (1996). *The Anxiety of Influence* (1973) sets forth Professor Bloom's provocative theory of the literary relationships between the great writers and their predecessors. His most recent books include *Shakespeare: The Invention of the Human* (1998), a 1998 National Book Award finalist, *How to Read and Why* (2000), *Genius: A Mosaic of One Hundred Exemplary Creative Minds* (2002), and *Hamlet: Poem Unlimited* (2003). In 1999, Professor Bloom received the prestigious American Academy of Arts and Letters Gold Medal for Criticism, and in 2002 he received the Catalonia International Prize.

THOMAS A. IDINOPULOS is Professor of Comparative Religious Studies and Director of the Jewish Studies Program at Miami University, Oxford, Ohio. He is the consulting editor for the *Middle East Review* (New York) and has over 100 publications in various journals covering a wide array of religious and social topics. In 1990, Dr. Idinopulos' writings about the Holocaust were honored with his appointment as Educational Consultant to the center on Holocaust, Genocide, and Human Rights in Philadelphia.

ALVIN H. ROSENFELD is Director of the Robert A. and Sandra S. Borns Jewish Studies Program at Indiana University. He has written numerous books about Holocaust Literature, including, *The Americanization of the Holocaust*; *Confronting the Holocaust: The Impact of Elie Wiesel*; *Imagining Hitler*; *A Double Dying: Reflections on Holocaust Literature*; *Thinking About the Holocaust: After Half a Century* (Jewish Literature and Culture Series).

ROBERT SKLOOT is Associate Vice Chancellor at the University of Wisconsin-Madison. His research interests focus on contemporary drama, especially on the subjects of the Holocaust and genocide. He is the editor of *The Theatre of The Holocaust* and author of *The Darkness We Carry: The Drama of The Holocaust*.

JAMES E. YOUNG is Professor of English and Judaic Studies at the University of Massachusetts Amherst, and he is currently the Department Chair of the Judaic and Near Eastern Studies. His publications include *At Memory's Edge: After-images of the Holocaust in Contemporary Art and Architecture*, *The Texture of Memory* (winner of the National Jewish Book Award in 1994), and *Writing and Rewriting the Holocaust*, which won a Choice Outstanding Book Award for 1988.

JOSEPH SUNGOLOWSKY is Professor of French Literature and Jewish Studies at Queens College. His publications include two books *Alfred de Vigny et le dix-huitéme siécle* and *Beaumarchais*, several articles in scholarly journals such as *European Judaism*, and *Midstream*.

DEBORAH E. LIPSTADT is the Director of the Institute for Jewish Studies and Dorot Professor of Modern Jewish and Holocaust Studies at Emory University. Her most recent book, *Denying the Holocaust: The Growing Assault on Truth and Memory*, is the first full length study of the history of those who attempt to deny the Holocaust.

MICHAEL TAGER is the Chair for the Department of History, Philosophy, Political Science and Religion at Marietta College. He has published articles about Sam Shepherd and Joan Didion.

BARBARA CHIARELLO is Professor of multicultural American literature at the University of Texas at Arlington.

LAWRENCE L. LANGER is Professor Emeritus in English Literature at Simmons College. His publications include *The Holocaust and the Literary*

Imagination; Holocaust Testimonies: The Ruins of Memory; Art from the Ashes: A Holocaust Anthology; and *Preempting the Holocaust.*

MARK CORY is Professor of German at the University of Arkansas and the Chairperson for the Comparative Literature Department. His publications include over twenty journal articles and two books on contemporary German literature. He has served on two national editorial boards and for seventeen years served variously as associate dean and/or director of Humanities at Fulbright College.

GEOFFREY H. HARTMAN is Sterling Professor Emeritus of English and Comparative Literature at Yale University. Among his many publications are *The Unremarkable Wordsworth; The Longest Shadow: In the Aftermath of the Holocaust; The Fateful Question of Culture;* and *A Critic's Journey: Literary Reflections, 1958-1998.*

JEFFREY M. PECK is Professor of German at York University in Toronto. He recently completed a three-year term as Director of the Canadian Centre for German and European Studies at York and the University of Montreal. He has published in *German Studies, The German Quarterly,* and *German Studies Review.*

RITCHIE ROBERTSON is Professor of German Literature at St. John's College. His publications include books on Kafka and Heine and several articles, books chapters, and translations dealing with the work of Goethe, Nietzsche, Rilke, and Thomas Mann.

AMY HUNGERFORD is Assistant Professor of English at Yale University. Her primary area of interest is twentieth-century American literature, including fiction, poetry, literary criticism and literary theory. She has published articles on the relationship between Binjamin Wilkomirski's fake Holocaust memoir and trauma theory, and on Holocaust-centered identity in Art Spiegelman, Steven Spielberg, and the U. S. Holocaust Memorial Museum.

Bibliography

Aaron, Frieda W. *Bearing the Unbearable: Yiddish and Polish Poetry in the Ghettos and Concentration Camps*. Albany, NY: State University of New York, 1990.

Anatoli, A. *Babi Yar: A Document in the Form of Novel*. Cambridge, MA: Robert Bentley, 1979.

Appelfeld, Aharon. *Badenheim, Nineteen Thirty-Nine*. New York: Pocket Books, 1981.

Arendt, Hannah. "Letter to the Editor." *Midstream* 8, no. 3 (Sept. 1962): 85–87.

Baker, Leonard. *Days of Sorrow and Pain: Leo Baeck and the Berlin Jews*. New York: Oxford University Press, 1980.

Barnouw, David and Gerrold Van Der Stroom, Eds. *Diary of Anne Frank: the Critical Edition*. Translated by Arnold J. Pomerans and B.M. Mooyaart. Doubleday. New York: Doubleday, 1989.

Bauman, Zygmunt. *Modernity and the Holocaust*. Ithaca: Cornell University Press, 1989.

Begley, Louis. *Wartime Lies*. New York: David McKay, 1991.

Bettelheim, Bruno. "The Ignored Lesson of Anne Frank." *Harper's* v. 221, no. 1326 (November 1960): 45–50.

Bilik, Dorothy. *Immigrant-Survivors: Post-Holocaust Consciousness in Recent Jewish American Fiction*. Middletown, CT: Wesleyan University Press, 1981.

Bloom, Harold, Ed. Elie Wiesel's *Night*. Modern Critical Interpretations. Philadelphia: Chelsea House Publishers, 2001.

Boll, Heinrich. *Billiards at Half-Past Nine*. London: Wiedenfeld and Nicholson, 1961.

Borowski, Tadeausz. *This Way for the Gas, Ladies and Gentlemen*. New York: Viking Penguin, 1992.

Bosmajian, Hamida. *Holocaust*. New York: Routledge, 2002.

Breitman, Richard. *The Architect of Genocide: Himmler and the Final Solution*. New York: Alfred A. Knopf, 1991.

Brietman, Richard and Walter Lanqueur. *Breaking the Silence*. New York: Simon and Schuster, 1986.

Brenner, Rachel Feldhay. *Writing As Resistance: Four Women Confronting the Holocaust: Edith Stein, Simone Weil, Anne Frank, Etty Hillesum*. University Park, Pa.: Pennsylvania State University, 1997.

Bullock, Alan. *Hitler: A Study in Tyranny*. New York: Harper Collins, 1991.

Celan, Paul. *Collected Prose*. Manchester: Carcanet, 1986.

———. *Last Poems*. San Francisco: North Point, 1986.

———. *Paul Celan: Poems, A Bilingual Edition*. New York: Persea, 1980.

Cory, Mark. "Comedic Distance in Holocaust Literature." *Journal of American Culture*. 18, no. 1 (Spring 1995): 34–41.

De Silva, Cara. *In Memory's Kitchen: A Legacy From the Women of Terezin*. Northvale, N.J.: Aronson, 1996.

Delbo, Charlotte. *None of Us Will Survive*. Boston: Beacon Press, 1968.

Donat, Alexander. *The Holocaust Kingdom*. New York: Anti-Defamation League, 1963.

Doneson, Judith E. "The American History of Anne Frank's Diary." *Holocaust and Genocide Studies*. 2 no. 1 (1987): 149–160.

Edelheit, Abraham J and Hershel, Eds. *Bibliography on Holocaust Literature*. Boulder: Westview Press, 1986.

Eichengreen, Lucille. *From Ashes to Life: My Memories of the Holocaust*. With Harriet Hyman Chamberlain. San Francisco: Mercury House, 1994.

Eliach, Yaffa. *Hasidic Tales of the Holocaust*. New York: Vintage Books, 1988.

Epstein, Leslie. *King of the Jews*. New York: Coward, McCann & Geoghegan, 1979.

Ezrahi, Sidra D. *By Words Alone: The Holocaust in Literature*. Chicago: University of Chicago Press, 1980

———. "The Holocaust as a Jewish Tragedy 2: The Covenantal Context." *By Words Alone: The Holocaust in Literature*. Chicago: University of Chicago Press, 1980: 116–49.

———. "The Holocaust Mythologized." *By Words Alone: The Holocaust in Literature*. Chicago: University of Chicago Press, 1980: 149–76

Felstiner, Mary Lowenthal. *To Paint Her Life*. New York: HarperCollins, 1994.

———. "Charlotte Salomon's Inward-Turning Testimony." *Holocaust Remembrance: The Shapes of Memory*. ed. Geoffrey H. Hartman. Cambridge, MA: Blackwell Publishers, 1994: 104–16.

———. "Engendering an Autobiography in Art: Charlotte Salomon's 'Life or Theater?'" *Revealing Lives: Autobiography, Biography, and Gender*, Eds. Susan Groag Bell and Marilyn Yalom. Albany: State University of New York Press, 1990: 183–92.

———. "Taking her Life/History: the Autobiography of Charlotte Salomon." *Life/Lines: Theorizing Women's Autobiography*, Eds. Bella Brodzki and Celeste Schenk. Ithaca: Cornell University Press, 1988: 320–37.

Fine, Ellen S. "Women Writers and the Holocaust: Strategies for Survival." *Reflections of the Holocaust in Art and Literature*, Ed. Randolph L. Braham. New York: Columbia University Press and Boulder: Social Science Monographs, 1990: 79–98.

Fine, Ellen. *The Legacy of Night: The Literary Universe of Elie Wiesel*. Albany, NY: State University of New York Press, 1983.

Fink, Ida. *A Scrap of Time*. New York: Schochen, 1989.

Frank, Anne. *The Diary of Anne Frank: The Critical Edition*. New York: Doubleday and Company, 1989.

Frankl, Viktor. *Man's Search for Meaning: An Introduction to Logotherapy*. New York: Pocket Books, 1984.

Friedlander, Albert H. *Out of the Whirlwind: A Reader of Holocaust Literature*, comp. New York: Schocken Books, 1968.

Friedlander, Albert. *Out of the Whirlwind*. New York: Schocken, 1989.

Fuchs, Elinor, ed. *Plays of the Holocaust: An International Anthology*. New York: Theater Communications Group, 1987.

Gershon, Karen. *Selected Poems*. New York: Harcourt, Brace, Jovanovich, 1966.

Gillon, Adam. *Poems of the Ghetto: A Testament of Lost Men*. New York: Twayne, 1969.

Glatstein, Jacob, ed. *Anthology of Holocaust Literature*. New York: Macmillan, 1973.

Grotowski, Jerzy. *Towards a Poor Theater*. New York: Simon and Schuster, 1968.

Hecht, Anthony. *The Hard Hours: Poems*. New York: Atheneum, 1971.

Heinemann, Marlene E. *Gender and Destiny: Women Writers and the Holocaust*. Westport, CT: Greenwood Publishing Group, 1986.

Heinemann, Marlene E. *Gender and Destiny: Women Writers and the Holocaust*. Westport, CT: Greenwood Press, 1986.

Hersey, John. *The Wall*. New York: Knopf, 1950.

Herzig, Jacov Joshua. *The Wrecked Life*. Vantage Press, [c1963].

Heyen, William. *Erika: Poems of the Holocaust*. St. Louis, MO: Time Being Books, 1991.

Hilberg, Raul, et. al., eds. *The Warsaw Diary of Adam Czerniakow*. Lanham, MD: Madison Books, 1982.

Hillesum, Etty. *An Interrupted Life*. New York: Pocket Books, 1991.

Hinz, Berthold. *Art in the Third Reich*. New York: Pantheon, 1979.

Hochhuth, Rolf. *The Deputy*. New York: Grove Press, 1964.

Hungerford, Amy. "Memorizing Memory." *The Holocaust of Texts: Genocide, Literature and Personification*. Chicago, IL: The University of Chicago Press, 2003: 97–122.

Hyett, Barbara Helfgott. *In Evidence: Poems of the Liberation of Nazi Concentration Camps*. Pittsburgh: University of Pittsburgh Press, 1986.

Indinopulos, Thomas A. "The Holocaust in the Stories of Elie Wiesel." *Responses to Elie Wiesel*, Ed. Harry James Cargas. New York: Persea Books, 1978. 115–32.

Insdorf, Annette. *Indelible Shadows: Film and the Holocaust*. New York: Cambridge University Press, 1990.

Jackson, Livia E. Bitton. "Coming of Age." *Different Voices: Women and the Holocaust*, Eds. Carol Rittner and John K. Roth. New York: Paragon House, 1993: 73–83.

Keneally, Thomas. *Schindler's List*. New York: Simon and Schuster, 1992.

Kosinski, Jerzy. *The Painted Bird*. New York: Random House, 1993.

Kuznetsov, Anatoly. *Babi Yar*. New York: Farrar, Straus and Giroux, 1970.

Langer, Lawrence L. *Admitting the Holocaust: Collected Essays*. New York: Oxford University Press, 1995.

———. *The Age of Atrocity: Death in Modern Literature*. Boston: Beacon Press, 1978.

———. *The Holocaust and the Literary Imagination*. New Haven, CT: Yale University Press, 1975.

———. "The Literature of Auschwitz." *Admitting the Holocaust: Collected Essays*. New York: Oxford University Press, 1995: 89–107.

———. "Redefining Heroic Behavior: The Impromptu Self and the Holocaust Experience." *Lessons and Legacies*, Ed Peter Hayes. Evanston: Northwestern U. Press, 1991: 227–42.

———. "Two Holocaust Voices: Cynthia Ozick and Art Spiegelman." *Preempting the Holocaust*. New Haven, CT: Yale University Press, 1998: 121–31.

Laska, Vera, Ed. *Women in the Resistance and in the Holocaust: The Voices of Eyewitnesses*. Westport, CT: Greenwood Press, 1983.

Leak, Andrew and George Paizis, Eds. *The Holocaust and the Text: Speaking the Unspeakable*. New York: St. Martin's Press, 2000.

Lebow, Barbara. *A Shayna Maidel*. New York: New American Library, 1985.

Leitner, Isabella. *Fragments of Isabella: A Memoir of Auschwitz*. New York: Dell, 1983.

Levi, Primo. *Survival in Auschwitz*. New York: Macmillan, 1987.

Lipstadt, Deborah E. "The Holocaust." *The Shocken Guide to Jewish Books: Where to Start Reading about Jewish History, Literature, Culture and Religion*. Barry W. Holtz, Ed. New York: Schocken Books, 1992, 128–49.

Meed, Vladka. *On Both Sides of the Wall*. New York: Holocaust Publications, 1979.

Myers, D.G. "Responsible for Every Single Pain: Holocaust Literature and the Ethics of Interpretation." *Comparative Literature*, 51, no. 4 (Fall 1999): 265–85.

Miller, Arthur. *Broken Glass*. New York: Penguin Books, 1994.

Milosz, Czeslaw. *Selected Poems*. New York: Seabury Press, 1973.

Milton, Sibyl. "Women and the Holocaust: The Case of German and German-Jewish Women." *The Nazi Holocaust* 6, Part 2, "Victims of the Holocaust," Ed. by Michael R. Marrus. Westport, Connecticut: Meckler Corporation, 1989: 631–667.

Nir, Yehuda. *The Lost Childhood*. San Diego: Harcourt Publications, 1979.

Ozick, Cynthia. *The Shawl*. New York: Random House, 1990.

Patraka, Vivian M. "Shattered Cartographies: Fascism, the Holocaust, and Tropes about Representation." S*pectacular Suffering: Theatre, Fascism, and the Holocaust.* Bloomington, IL: Indiana University Press, 1999: 15–34.

Peck, Jeffrey M. "The Holocaust and Literary Studies." *Lessons and Legacies III: Memory, Memorization, and Denial,* Ed. Peter Hayes. Evanston, IL: Northwestern University Press, 1999: 45–50.

Pilinszky, Janos. "KZ Oratorio." In *Ocean at the Window: Hungarian Prose and Poetry since 1945.* Tezla, Albert. Minneapolis: University of Minnesota Press, 1981: 127–33.

———. *Crater: Poems, 1974–5.* London: Anvil, 1978.

Radnoti, Miklos. *Clouded Sky.* New York: Harper and Row, 1972.

Reznikoff, Charles. *Holocaust.* Los Angeles: Black Sparrow Press, 1975.

Ringelblum, Emmanuel. *Notes from the Warsaw Ghetto: The Journal of Emmanuel Ringelblum.* New York: Schocken, 1974.

Ringelheim, Joan Miriam. "Women and the Holocaust: A Reconsideration of Research." *Different Voices: Women and the Holocaust,* Eds. Carol Rittner and John K. Roth. New York: Paragon House, 1993. 373–418.

Rittner, Carol and John K. Roth, Eds. *Different Voices: Women and the Holocaust.* New York: Paragon House, 1993.

Robertson, Ritchie. "Rafael Seligman's *Rubinsteins Versteigerung*: The German-Jewish Family Novel before and after the Holocaust." *The Germanic Review.* 75, no. 3 (Summer 2000): 179–94.

Rosenfeld, Alvin H. *A Double Dying: Reflections on Holocaust Literature.* Bloomington, IN: Indiana University Press, 1980.

———. "Popularization and Memory: The Case of Anne Frank." *Lessons and Legacies.* Ed. Peter Hayes. Evanston: Northwestern U. Press, 1991: 227–242.

———. "The Problematics of Holocaust Literature." *Confronting the Holocaust: The Impact of Elie Wiesel.* Alvin H. Rosenfeld and Irving Greenberg, eds. Bloomington, IN: Indiana University Press, 1978: 1–30.

Roskies, David. *Against the Apocalypse: Responses to Catastrophe in Modern Jewish Culture.* Cambridge, MA: Harvard University, 1984.

Rovit, Rebecca and Alvin Goldfarb, Eds. *Theatrical Performance During the Holocaust: Texts, Documents, Memoirs.* Baltimore: Johns Hopkins University Press, 1999.

Sachs, Nelly. *O the Chimneys: Selected Poems; Including the Verse Play, Eli.* New York: Farrar, Straus and Giroux, 1967.

Salomon, Charlotte. *Charlotte: a Diary in Pictures*. Notes by Paul Tillich and Emil Straus. New York: Harcourt, Brace and World, 1963.

——. *Leven? of Theater? (Life or Theater?)*. Adapted and with an introduction by Judith C.E. Belinfante, Christine Fischer-Defoy, and Ad Petersen. Translated by Adrienne van Dorpen et al. Amsterdam: Joods Historisch Museum; Zwolle: Waanders Uitgevers, 1992.

——. *Charlotte: Life or Theater?: An Autobiographical Play by Charlotte Salomon*. Introduction by Judith Herzberg. Translated by Leila Vennewitz. New York: Viking Press; Maarssen, The Netherlands: G. Schwartz, 1981.

Schnabel, Ernst. *The Footsteps of Anne Frank*. Translated by Richard and Clara Winston. London: Longmans, Green and Co. 1958 (1959).

Schumacher, Claude, ed. *Staging the Holocaust: the Shoah in Drama and Performance*. New York: Cambridge University Press, 1998.

Schwartz-Bart, Andre. *The Last of the Just*. New York: Atheneum, 1961.

Semprun, Jorge. *The Long Voyage*. New York: Grove Press, 1964.

Sereny, Gitta. *Into that Darkness*. New York: Random House, 1983.

Skloot, Robert. "Tragedy and the Holocaust." *The Darkness We Carry: The Drama of the Holocaust*. Madison, Wisconsin: University of Wisconsin Press, 1988: 20–42.

Steenmeijer, Anna G. *A Tribute to Anne Frank*. In collaboration with Otto Frank, Henri van Pragg. Garden City, NY: Doubleday and Company, 1971.

Sungolowsky, Joseph. "Holocaust and Autobiography: Wiesel, Friedländer, Pisar." *Reflections of the Holocaust in Art and Literature*. Randolph L. Braham, Ed. New York: Columbia University Press, 1990. 131–43.

Szwajger, Adina B. *I Remember Nothing More: The Warsaw Children's Hospital and the Jewish Resistance*. New York: Simon and Schuster, 1992.

Tager, Michael. "Primo Levi and the Language of Witness." *Criticism*. 35, no. 2 (Spring 1993): 265–88.

Tory, Avraham. *Surviving the Holocaust: The Kovno Ghetto Diary*. Cambridge, MA: Harvard University Press, 1990.

Waaldijk, Berteke. "Reading Anne Frank as a Woman." *Women's Studies International Forum*. 16 no. 4 (July–Aug 1993): 327–35.

Weiss, Peter. *The Investigation: A Play*. New York: Atheneum, 1966.

Welt, Elly. *Berlin Wild: A Novel*. New York: Viking, 1986.

Whitman, Ruth. *The Testing of Hanna Senesh*. Detroit: Wayne State University Press, 1986.

Wiesel, Elie. *Night.* New York: Bantam, 1960.

——. *The Town Beyond the Wall.* New York: Schocken, 1982.

——. *Zalmen, Or the Madness of God.* New York: Random House, 1975.

Yoors, Jan. *Crossing: A Journal of Survival and Resistance in World War II.* New York: Simon and Schuster, 1971.

Young, James E. "Holocaust Documentary Fiction: Novelist as Eyewitness." *Writing and Rewriting the Holocaust: Narrative and the Consequences of Interpretation.* Bloomington, IL: Indiana University Press, 1988. 51–64.

——. *Writing and Rewriting the Holocaust: Narrative and the Consequences of Interpretation.* Bloomington, IL: Indiana University Press, 1988.

Acknowledgments

"The Holocaust in the Stories of Elie Wiesel" by Thomas Idinopulos. From *Responses to Elie Wiesel*. Copyright © 1978 by Persea Books. Reprinted by permission.

"The Problematics of Holocaust Literature" by Alvin H. Rosenfeld. From *Confronting the Holocaust: The Impact of Elie Weisel*. © 2003 by Indiana University Press. Reprinted by permission.

"Tragedy and the Holocaust" by Robert Skloot. From *The Darkness We Carry*. © 1988. Reprinted by permission of the University of Wisconsin Press.

"Holocaust Documentary Fiction: Novelist as as Eyewitness" by James E. Young. From *Writing and ReWriting the Holocaust: Narrative and the Consequences of Interpretation*. © 2003 by Indiana University Press. Reprinted by permission.

"Holocaust and Autobiography: Weisel, Frieländer, Pisar" by Joseph Sungolowsky. From *Reflections of the Holocaust in Art and Literature*, ed. Randolf L. Braham. © 1990 by Joseph Sungolowsky. Reprinted by permission.

"The Holocaust" by Deborah E. Lipstadt. From *The Schocken Guide to Jewish Books* by Barry W. Holtz. © 1992 by Schocken Books, a division of Random House, Inc. Used by permission of Schocken Books, a division of Random House.

"Primo Levi and the Languages of Witness" by Michael Tager. From *Criticism* 35:2, Spring 1993, with permission of Wayne State University Press.

"The Utopian Space of a Nightmare: The Diary of Anne Frank" by Barbara Chiarello.from *Utopian Studies* 5:1 (1994). © 1994 by the Society for Utopian Studies. Reprinted by permission.

"The Literature of Auschwitz" by Lawrence L. Langer. From *Admitting the Holocaust*. © 1995 by Lawrence L. Langer. Reprinted by permission of the author.

"Comedic Distance in Holocaust Literature" by Mark Cory. From *Journal of American Culture* 18:1. Spring 1995. © 1995 by Mark Cory. Reprinted with permission of the author.

"Public Memory and its Discontents" by Geoffrey H. Hartman. From *The Longest Shadow: In the Aftermath of the Holocaust*. © 1996 by Geoffrey H. Hartman. Reprinted with permission of the author.

"Two Holocaust Voices: Cynthia Ozick and Art Spiegelman by Lawrence L. Langer. From *Preempting the Holocaust*. Copyright © 1998 by Yale University Press. Reprinted by permission.

"The Holocaust and Literary Studies" by Jeffrey M. Peck. From *Lessons and Legacies III: Memory, Memorialization, and Denial*. Edited by Peter Hayes. Evanston: Northwestern University Press, 1999. © 1999 by Northwestern University Press. Reprinted by permission.

"Rafael Seligmann's Rubinsteins Versteigerung: The German–Jewish Family Novel before and after the Holocaust" by Ritchie Robertson. From *Germanic Review* 75: 3 (Summer 2000). Reprinted with permission of the Helen Dwight Reid Educational Foundation. Published by Heldref Publications, 1319 Eighteenth St., NW, Washington, DC 20036–1802. Copyright © 2000.

"Memorizing Memory" from *The Holocaust of Texts: Genocide, Literature, and Personification* by Amy Hungerford. © 2003 by The University of Chicago Press. Reprinted by permission.

Index

311